The Victorian Gothic

For Marie Mulvey-Roberts

The Victorian Gothic

An Edinburgh Companion

Edited by
Andrew Smith and William Hughes

EDINBURGH
University Press

© in this edition Edinburgh University Press, 2012
© in the individual contributions is retained by the authors

Transferred to digital print 2013

Edinburgh University Press Ltd
22 George Square, Edinburgh

www.euppublishing.com

Typeset in 10.5/13 pt Sabon
by Servis Filmsetting Ltd, Stockport, Cheshire, and
printed and bound in Great Britain by
CPI Group (UK) Ltd, Croydon, CR0 4YY

A CIP record for this book is available from the British Library

ISBN 978 0 7486 4249 6 (hardback)
ISBN 978 0 7486 5497 0 (webready PDF)
ISBN 978 0 7486 5499 4 (epub)
ISBN 978 0 7486 5498 7 (Amazon ebook)

The right of the contributors
to be identified as author of this work
has been asserted in accordance with
the Copyright, Designs and Patents Act 1988.

Contents

Acknowledgements

The authors would like to thank all those who have given their support both to this volume and to the two editors during the course of its commissioning and production. Thanks are due, first and foremost, to the individual contributors, and to Jackie Jones and Rebecca Mackenzie at Edinburgh University Press. The editors would also like to thank, at Bath Spa University, Colin Edwards, Tracy Brain, Elizabeth Wright, Catherine Robinson, John Newsinger, and Jo Dahn; and at the University of Glamorgan, Martin Willis and Alice Entwistle. We are also grateful to Anna Oxbury for her close copy-editing of the typescript.

This book has benefited, in all sorts of ways too numerous to describe, from our teaching of the Victorian Gothic over nearly two decades and so we owe a debt of thanks to our students.

Finally, thanks are due, as ever, to Gillian Wheeler and Joanne Benson for their love and support.

Introduction: Locating the Victorian Gothic

Andrew Smith and William Hughes

... its belt sparkled and glittered now in one part and now in another, and what was light one instant, at another time was dark, so the figure itself fluctuated in its distinctness: being now a thing with one arm, now with one leg, now with twenty legs, now a pair of legs without a head, now a head without a body: of which dissolving parts, no outline would be visible in the dense gloom wherein they melted away.

A Christmas Carol (Dickens, 1985: 68)

Here too was all the work by which man has been made repeated before my eyes. I saw the form waver from sex to sex, dividing itself from itself, and then again reunited. Then I saw the body descend to the beasts whence it ascended, and that which was on the heights go down to the depths, even to the abyss of all being. The principle of life, which makes organism, always remained, while the outward form changed.

The Great God Pan (Machen, 2006: 63)

Dickens's account of the manifestation of the ghost of Christmas past and Machen's description of the decomposition (and odd recompositions) of his fin-de-siècle femme fatale Helen Vaughan bear telling similarities and revealing differences. The sense of identity as potentially protean, unstable and incoherent suggests that these two models of the subject (which, given their dates of publication – 1843 and 1894 – are close to bookending the Victorian Gothic) capture an essential aspect of the Gothic form of the period: undecidability. Indeed this most Derridean of terms has played a key role in recent criticism on nineteenth-century Gothic. Julian Wolfreys explored the diversity of the Gothic in his preface to his co-edited collection *Victorian Gothic* (2000) where he argued that it was the function of the Gothic to evade the limits of form, so that

'The gothic becomes truly haunting in that it can never be pinned down as a single identity, while it returns through various apparitions and manifestations, seemingly everywhere' (Wolfreys, 2000: xv). Wolfreys was to elaborate these ideas in a more sustained Derridean-inspired reading in *Victorian Hauntings* (2002), where he argued that the critically commonplace view that the Gothic flourished between *The Castle of Otranto* (1764) and *Frankenstein* (1818), is belied by the Gothic's spectral return in the nineteenth century, in which it underpinned the ostensibly non-Gothic writings of Dickens, Eliot, Tennyson and Hardy. The Gothic thus transcends any formal aesthetic characteristics and in a claim which implicitly evokes the above images from Dickens and Machen, Wolfreys argues that 'the comprehension of the gothic is expanded through an understanding of the role gothic effects have to play in the constitution of modern, fragmented subjectivity' (Wolfreys, 2002: 13). The Gothic thus eludes its origins as it migrates into models of the self, ones which ultimately lead Wolfreys in a later essay on the Victorian Gothic to suggest that the very terms 'Victorian' and 'Gothic' constitute 'an agnostic embrace' in which they exist in perpetual 'desirous and destructive strife' (2006: 63). The Gothic, in other words, permeates Victorian culture in a complex way which evades any attempt to categorise it through the application of formal aesthetic criteria. This Gothic view of the Victorians is one that is also bound up with twentieth- and twenty-first-century perceptions of the Victorians.

Jarlath Killeen has termed the critical commonplace which connects the repressive hypothesis with the Victorians as the 'Dr Jekyll and Mr Hyde view' (Killeen, 2009: 9). It is a cliché which supports and perpetuates the perception that the Victorians were 'monsters of perversity who lived public lives of staid conformity but who came out of the closet nightly to perpetuate the most horrific versions of abuse' (2009: 8–9). The popular cliché thus supports a view of the Victorians as inherently Gothic, even though as Killeen acknowledges 'Victorian men and women were more likely to think of themselves as living in an age of civilised progress rather than Gothic barbarism' (2009: 4). How we historically view the Victorians inevitably shapes our modelling of the Victorian Gothic. However, critics have agreed that there are a number of themes, issues and aesthetic considerations which characterise the form.

First, it has been widely noted that sensation fiction from the 1850s onwards reworked a number of issues which were to be found in the earlier Gothic tradition. Alison Milbank has convincingly argued that the work of Dickens and Collins, for example, drew upon earlier female Gothic tropes (Milbank, 1992). Second, there are clearly very popular

Gothic texts by authors such as William Harrison Ainsworth, G. W. M. Reynolds and James Malcolm Rymer; and the Victorian period seems further to have represented something of a heyday for the ghost story, with significant contributions from Dickens, Gaskell and Oliphant, amongst many others. There has also been due critical acknowledgement that fin-de-siècle Gothic represents specific engagements with science, art and degeneration and so can be identified as a separate – because distinctive – expression of a late Victorian Gothic. There are also some clearly identifiable themes many of which, as we shall see, conceptually support the type of complexities identified by Wolfreys even whilst they seem to suggest the presence of potentially narrow preoccupations.

Alexandra Warwick in her 2007 essay on the 'Victorian Gothic' in *The Routledge Companion to Gothic* begins by acknowledging 'the problems inherent in periodising a form that escapes anything but the loosest definitions' (2007: 29), even if it recrudesces into the heart of a Victorian culture 'with its elaborate cult of death and mourning' (2007: 29). Warwick identifies two principal strands of the Victorian Gothic: the domestic and the urban. For Warwick, the work of the Brontës indicates a shift towards a domestic Gothic in which 'domestic spaces, and the state of marriage or family life that the spaces embody, are terrifyingly ambiguous' (2007: 30). Whilst it is Dickens who establishes the city as a new Gothic space by advancing 'a metropolitan sensibility that distinguishes a new Victorian Gothic' (Warwick, 2007: 30). The place of the city in the mid-Victorian Gothic has been explored at great length by Robert Mighall in his groundbreaking study of the city in the work of Dickens and Reynolds amongst others (Mighall, 1999) and he, like Warwick, notes the special place accorded to the fin-de-siècle Gothic, which Warwick sees as imbricated with other modes of writing such as science fiction and the detective story (Warwick, 2007: 34).

Warwick's emphasis on the gender considerations of an emerging domestic Gothic and Mighall's analysis of how discussions of Whig history shape the Victorian Gothic's fascination with the past have been given an important twist in Alison Milbank's account of Queen Victoria's representation in a number of Gothic texts from the period. Milbank notes that Ainsworth's *The Tower of London* (1853) and his *Windsor Castle* (1855), interrogate versions of Victoria which examine whether she emblematises a discredited past or else represents a figure of Whig progress that has transcended that past. If the former, then she resembles a Gothic heroine trapped by older forces which restrain her possible transformative energies; and, if the latter, then she embodies a different type of Gothic heroine, one who has been able to escape the forces of oppression. The question is whether she is victim or agent.

Milbank notes a similar view of Victoria in Reynolds's *The Mysteries of London* (1844–56) which is also unclear about her radical potential which can seemingly only occur under certain circumstances, so that 'Victoria can *become* a heroine only if she undoes the entrapment of others' (Milbank, 2002: 149). Ultimately:

> It is up to the reader to decide the future; whether to turn to Victoria as Gothic heroine and the people's friend, or decry her as a new Gothic tyrant and call for republican liberation from monarchical tyranny. (Milbank, 2002: 149)

The direction of history and debate about who controls it thus reflected familiar female Gothic plots which condition both the representation of Victoria and the domestic Gothic to be found in the Brontës and elsewhere.

Warwick's account of the Victorian Gothic closes with reference to Freud as 'the last of the great Victorian Gothic writers' (Warwick, 2007: 36), and Wolfreys emphasises the role of the 'uncanny' in any consideration of the Victorian Gothic (Wolfreys, 2002: 14–18; 2006: 71). Kelly Hurley also asserts the significance of the uncanny (Hurley, 2002: 198) in understanding the late Victorian Gothic. The uncanny provides one way of linking the domestic to the historical approach of Milbank and the aesthetic considerations identified by Wolfreys. The point of the domestic Gothic is that it represents a particular manifestation of the uncanny in which the 'home' now becomes, in Freud's terms, the site of troubled sexual secrets, so that far from guaranteeing safety, the domestic becomes the space through which trauma is generated (Freud, 1990: 339–47). This model can also be applied to the idea of history explored by Milbank in her account of the 'Gothicizing of Victoria' (Milbank, 2002: 147), in which 'the uncanny is that class of the frightening which leads back to what is known of old and long familiar' (Freud, 1990: 340). History repeats itself in the figure of Victoria who comes to represent continuity with a monarchy that was popularly regarded as dissolute. Killeen, following the dispersal of the Gothic into an ostensibly realist mode of the time mapped by Wolfreys, concludes that the Gothic considered in these aesthetic terms becomes assimilated when 'the Gothic and the realist cross-fertilise each other' (Killeen, 2009: 10). In his discussion of *Bleak House* (1853), Killeen implicitly registers this as a moment of the uncanny, when he claims that in his account of Chancery:

> Dickens constantly translates traditional Gothic tropes and props into modern realist terms, not to evacuate the Gothic or to strip it of its power,

but to introject it into the institutions and the situations pervasive throughout England. In this way the Gothic becomes more realistic, but the real also becomes more like a Gothic nightmare. (2009: 18–19)

This *Unheimlich* blurring of the real with the unreal points to the uncanny as being the key to understanding the instabilities within the Victorian Gothic.

The two epigraphs from Dickens and Machen which began this introduction might, however, suggest a flattening out of history, as if the fin-de-siècle Gothic of Machen inherits the Dickensian instabilities argued for by Killeen (and before him, by Wolfreys). However, these models of instability can be related to quite historically specific concerns. Dickens's tale of a haunted miser who lives in self-inflicted poverty and social isolation, symbolically engages with the idea of economic uncertainty that characterised the period (which was known as 'the hungry forties', due to its ongoing recession). In that regard the instabilities of the ghost echo the fluctuations of an unpredictable economy – Dickens's solution to which is to put Scrooge (and his money) back into social and economic circulation.[1] For Kelly Hurley, the type of fluctuations recorded in *The Great God Pan* are of a different order. For her 'Such a Gothic body – admixed, fluctuating, abominable – can best be called an *abuman* body' (Hurley, 2002: 190), and this is a key characteristic of the fin-de-siècle Gothic with its bodily morphing characters: vampires, doubles and Machen's femme fatale. The scientific ambience of such a Gothic is also closely related to these transformations as exemplified in *The Great God Pan* by the opening experiment of Dr Raymond which seems to conjure Helen Vaughan into being (seemingly as the child of Pan and Raymond's patient, Mary), and in the account of her bodily transformations recorded by a Dr Robert Matheson in a chapter tellingly titled 'Fragments'. Indeed, the fin-de-siècle Gothic operated under quite different pressures from its mid-Victorian counterpart, and how the late nineteenth-century Gothic engaged with and explored theories of degeneration has proved a fertile area of critical enquiry. And yet, there is still something about the uncanny which persists, as if it, too, morphs in its transition from the mid to the late Victorian.

Alison Milbank has noted that the type of afterlife envisaged within spiritualist beliefs reworked Emmanuel Swedenborg's affirmation of a precise and very human-looking 'heaven' in which it 'had been utterly naturalized and spatialized into a primary reality and a city of which the earthly world was a suburb. Making the transcendent material thus rendered the actual world spectral' (Milbank, 2002: 160). This is a view which, as Milbank notes, corresponds with Marx's understanding of how a world of material objects is ghosted by the labour which has produced them. Such a move parallels Killeen's suggestion that in Dickens's writings the real becomes unreal as the Gothic makes its claims on reality. Milbank also asserts this link by arguing for its presence not just in Dickens but also in the 'realist techniques' employed by Gaskell, Riddell, Oliphant, Le Fanu and Collins (Milbank, 2002: 161). For Milbank this represents an emerging spiritualisation of the everyday (she cites Collins's 'A Terribly Strange Bed' (1852), Eliot's 'The Lifted Veil' (1859) and Le Fanu's 'Green Tea' (1869), as examples). She notes of such texts:

> All this realist craft is expended in making the supernatural concrete and eliding it with the natural, which thereby acquires materiality. Thus, while many authors have stressed a 'naturalized supernatural' in this period, it is crucial to realize that it had an exact counterpart in a 'supernaturalized natural', which means that we are talking here about *anything but* secularization. (Milbank, 2002: 161)

The uncanny is thus articulated much earlier in the Victorian Gothic than is usually acknowledged and whilst the fin-de-siècle Gothic might seem to be a clear expression of that with its pervasive use of the doppelganger, nevertheless there is a complex language of morphology at work within it which develops these earlier Gothic elisions. These images of psychic and social instability can also be widened to include the Imperial Gothic, with its complex explorations of the relationship between self and other in which the potentially problematic figure of Queen Victoria and her links to the past and to empire are subject to some critique via the figure of Ayesha in Haggard's *She* (1887).

Reality is thus subject to uncanny returns in the nineteenth century, as it both informs the Gothic and is assimilated within it – an image of consumption that is forcibly captured in *Dracula* (1897) in the image of the vampire as both an abnormal, Gothic predator, and as a distorted reflection of the barely concealed desires of the vampire hunters. Locating the Victorian Gothic is thus indeed a problematic, slippery, process, although one which this volume aims to go some way towards pinning down.

It is important to acknowledge the diverse ways in which the Victorian Gothic was manifested. To that end there are contributions to this volume which explore its presence on the stage, in poetry, and in specific textual formations such as the ghost story. There are also contributions which examine the contexts in which we can locate the Victorian Gothic, including the cultures of science, medicine, and the social, theological and psychological concerns about death and dying which seemed to haunt the Victorians. How the Gothic can be explored in terms of gender and read through the critical prism of Queer Studies is also examined, as well as the Imperial contexts and the influence of mainland European Gothic writings on a British tradition. The Gothic's relationship to realism is explored as are the Gothic's appearance in pulp fiction and in sensation fiction. A discrete chapter addresses the Gothic at the fin de siècle. This book thus provides a comprehensive account of the Victorian Gothic and the critical issues which are involved in its exploration.

Martin Willis, in 'Victorian Realism and the Gothic: Objects of Terror Transformed', explores the various ways in which leading Victorian novelists employed the Gothic as part of their realist narrative projects. Beginning with a consideration of recent critical calls for the Gothic mode to be defined more astutely when it is found in combination with other genres, Willis shows how contemporary criticism has done a great deal to uncover the importance of the Gothic throughout the Victorian period but has never formulated a critical practice that allows for its specific roles to be addressed in sufficient detail. Making a start on doing just that, Willis argues that the Gothic's emergence in Victorian realist fiction requires particular attention to its role as an interrogator of realism's own limitations. Drawing examples from canonical Victorian fiction by Emily Brontë, Charles Dickens, Benjamin Disraeli, and George Eliot, Willis shows how several of the keynotes of realist narrative – secrecy, alienation, and monstrosity – were delivered via the Gothic; often by the introduction of Gothic objects or by setting scenes within explicitly Gothic spaces. Realist writers drew on the Gothic in such circumstances, Willis concludes, because that mode offered the opportunity to illuminate invisible relations between characters, and between things, that realism could not do without breaking the generic boundaries of the real. The Gothic, therefore, did not only intervene to highlight realism's limits but also to support the very project of Victorian realist fiction.

In 'Sensation Fiction: A Peep Behind the Veil' Laurence Talairach-Vielmas traces the evolution of the codes of the Gothic genre from the seminal sensation novels of the 1860s (Wilkie Collins's *The Woman in White* (1860*)*, *No Name* (1862), *Armadale* (1866) and Mary Elizabeth Braddon's *Lady Audley's Secret* (1861–2)) to later novels, such as Collins's *The Law and the Lady* (1875) and *Heart and Science* (1883). The way in which sensational novels revised the Gothic is examined through a study of the novels' excessive codification of the body, which often turn characters into spectral or liminal figures hovering between the realm of the living and the dead. As a result, she argues, the spectrality of the modern body which sensation novels foreground brings about tension in the texts: sensation novels constantly contrast texts and painted surfaces with hidden depths, obsessionally leading their readers into churchyards in order to find clues as if to resurrect the dead. Indeed, the genre's contrast between buried secrets which must be dug up and images of seamless surfaces constantly prevents closure. Thus, as the detectives attempt to decipher letters on tombstones or to read body parts to exhume the past and reconstruct the truth, their excavating activities revise Gothic images of verticality and trope modern fears related to research into the history of the earth and the place of humanity in that history.

Jarlath Killeen in 'Victorian Gothic Pulp Fiction' focuses on scenes of violence and torture in James Malcolm Rymer's *Varney the Vampire* (1845–7) and George Reynolds's *Wagner the Werewolf* (1846–7). This chapter examines the treatment of extreme violence upon the body in 'pulp' literature and argues that such violence should be seen as central to understanding Victorian culture. Although punishment for criminality was increasingly privatised through the nineteenth century, particularly with the end of public execution (1868), and there were a number of campaigns to mitigate or eradicate public forms of cruelty and suffering, the desire to experience and witness bloody punishment in narrative form remained high. Killeen argues that the representation of extreme violence to the body in Victorian pulp can in part be seen as a shift in versions of cultural hatred. Whereas previously, images of violence to the body concentrated on the destruction of enemies of the state (especially Catholics, as reflected in the popularity of Foxe's *Book of Martyrs*), during the nineteenth century this violence came to be directed towards a less focused and more diffused constituency that could ultimately include anyone.

Diane Long Hoeveler in 'Victorian Gothic Drama' chronologically examines the early, middle and late dramatic works that have been classified as 'Gothic' by theatre historians. The early period, 1820–50, focuses on those plays that were largely dramatic or melodramatic adaptations of popular and canonical Gothic novels, such as James Planché's *The Vampire, or, The Bride of the Isles* (1820); William T. Moncrieff's *The Spectre Bridegroom, or a ghost in spite of himself* (1821); and Richard B. Peake's *Presumption, or the Fate of Frankenstein* (1823). These works were revived and held their popularity through the middle of the nineteenth century, gradually giving way to a middle period of Victorian Gothic, 1850–80, during which time melodramas like Dion Boucicault's *The Corsican Brothers* (1852), an adaptation of Dumas' novel of the same name, were extremely popular. Finally, the essay examines late Victorian Gothic dramas (1880–1910), like those produced by Bram Stoker and Henry Irving at the Lyceum theatre: Henry Merivale's *Ravenswood* (1890), an adaptation of Scott's *Bride of Lammermoor*; *Faust*; and *The Flying Dutchman*. Hoeveler also examines the techniques used in the theatre and provides a critical examination of how various theatrical genres shaped the stage Gothic of the period.

Opening with the unscrewing of a Highgate coffin, Caroline Franklin and Michael Franklin's 'Victorian Gothic Poetry: The Corpse's [a] Text' considers the Gothic light thrown upon the production of Elizabeth Siddal's body, its textualization and death-in-life representation in Dante Gabriel's Rossetti's poems and paintings, re-mirrored in the virtual-corpse reflections of some of Siddal's own influential oneiric texts. Rossetti's retrieval of his wife's corpse's text, the fair-copy of 'Jenny', is refracted in Pound's elision of Lizzie with 'poor Jenny's case'/ text/body/casket. The year of Siddal's death – 1862 – is linked firstly with the publication of her sister-in-law's 'After Death', a text proceeding from a body inscribed by rejection; and secondly with the likely date of the binding of Emily Dickinson's Fascicle 16 and the various corpse-texts that issue from her personae's 'granite lips'. Dickinson famously asked Thomas Higginson: 'Are you too deeply occupied to say if my Verse is alive? [...] Should you think it breathed – and had you the leisure to tell me, I should feel quick gratitude' (Johnson and Ward, 1986: 260). Arguing that nothing is so fully alive as her corpses, the authors suggest these posthumous speakers breathe an 'arch and original Breath' into the 'body of lovely Death'. What exactly 'crash Paul' meant in 1 Corinthians 15 is also approached via the neglected poetry of Elizabeth Stuart Phelps, whose consolatory postbellum Gothic was simultaneously intensified and compromised by the dread inability of the resurrected corpse to communicate with the living loved.

Nick Freeman, in 'The Victorian Ghost Story', provides an overview of the development of the ghost story. This reveals its emergence from the somewhat formulaic plotlines of first-generation Gothic and folkloric traditions. Freeman outlines the history of the ghost story from 1820 to 1914, noting its major practitioners and the means by which it could be bluntly shocking (as in E. Nesbit's 'Man-Size in Marble' (1893)), highly sophisticated (as in the work of Vernon Lee and Henry James), and even parodic (in the stories of Oscar Wilde, Jerome K. Jerome and others). He also explores the key role women writers played in the development and popularisation of the ghost story. Examples include Elizabeth Gaskell, Charlotte Riddell, Amelia Edwards, Margaret Oliphant, Vernon Lee, and E. Nesbit. Finally Freeman illustrates how the ghost story was a key ingredient of the Victorian literary world, one that adapted to and successfully incorporated cultural and technological change from the railway (Dickens's 'No. 1 Branch Line: The Signalman' (1866)) to the recording device of Richard Marsh's 'The Adventure of the Phonograph' (1898).

Avril Horner suggests that the current tendency to see Victorian Gothic as thoroughly 'domesticated' can result in a neglect of interchanges between European and British authors during the nineteenth century. It was not for nothing that images of the Bastille and the French Revolution haunted many Gothic fictions well into the nineteenth century. In her essay 'Victorian Gothic and National Identity: Cross-Channel "Mysteries"', Horner argues that we can discern an implicit post-Revolutionary dialogue about social inequality across Eugène Sue's *The Mysteries of Paris* (1842–3), G. W. M. Reynolds's *The Mysteries of London* (1844–8) (both best-sellers in their time) and Dickens's *A Tale of Two Cities* (1859) – the last not usually seen within the 'Mysteries' tradition. Horner suggests that Dickens's use of the word 'mysteries' and his evocation of the uncanny in *A Tale of Two Cities* (not least in creating Sydney Carton as Charles Darnay's double) signals a deliberate continuation of what was, in effect, a cross-Channel dialogue concerning the evolution of democracy in nineteenth-century society. She concludes that the Gothic – in the form of the uncanny and the abject – was brilliantly appropriated by Sue, Reynolds and Dickens in order to interrogate the social and political realities of their time.

In 'The Victorian Gothic and Gender', Carol Margaret Davison takes issue with the ongoing and frequently unsupported claims – particularly by feminist critics – that the Gothic has been over-intellectualised. To the contrary, she argues, substantial textual evidence exists in a notably broad cross-section of literary works that it served as a popular aesthetic/discourse/mode during the Victorian era, and one that was consciously deployed by writers to interrogate socially dictated and institutionally entrenched attitudes and laws relating to gender roles, identities and relations. Davison examines how, to what ends, and with what implications, works of Victorian Gothic contested and/or consolidated the boundaries of gendered 'masculine' and 'feminine' identities. The chapter ranges from a consideration of the Brontës, to an account of sensation fiction and a concluding argument about the Imperial contexts of Gothic and gender during the period.

Ardel Thomas, in 'Queer Victorian Gothic', examines queer Gothic within familial, medical and legal institutions and systems of power. Utilising a broad definition of 'queer' which encompasses its nineteenth and early to mid-twentieth century historical contexts as well as the theoretically complex and politically charged late twentieth- and early twenty-first-century renditions and reclamations of the term, Thomas explores how Queer Theory within the Gothic enables multiple, potentially polyvalent readings relating to gender, sexuality, race, class and familial structures beyond heteronormative (and often bourgeois) social constructs. Writers explored in this chapter include Wilkie Collins, Elizabeth Gaskell, J. Sheridan Le Fanu, Richard Marsh and Florence Marryat

In 'Victorian Gothic Death', Andrew Smith begins with an overview of death in the Romantic Gothic, arguing that *Frankenstein* (1818, 1831) represents a break with earlier, Radcliffean, fears of death by replacing them with a new emphasis on psychology, the body and images of creativity. These issues underpin later representations of death. George Eliot's 'The Lifted Veil' (1859), for example, explores the relationship between art and death through images of mind-reading and prevision. Creativity and death are thus conditioned by an argument about Art and immortality which can be usefully contextualised to the discussion of the mind in Herbert Mayo's work on mesmerism, published in 1850, which also has relevance for a reading of Poe's representation of death and dying. Later images of death in the works of H. Rider Haggard and Bram Stoker are explored in relation to F. W. H. Myers's *Human Personality and its Survival of Bodily Death* (1903), where a scientifically modelled version of the afterlife provides a helpful context for locating images of the afterlife in the fin-de-siècle Gothic.

Kelly Hurley in 'Science and the Gothic' explores Victorian psychology and the Gothic, and more particularly, the Gothic's representation of criminal hypnosis in the 1880s and 1890s following a debate that emerged within experimental psychology as to whether or not a hypnotized subject could be made to act in violation of his or her basic moral character. Both experimental psychology and the Gothic explored the possibility of hypnotists gaining complete control over their subjects: implanting criminal suggestions, forcing uncharacteristic behaviours, and even eliciting sexual desire or love from the unwilling victim. Both types of discourse described human beings losing their integrity and becoming uncanny to themselves and others as they are evacuated of subjectivity and set in motion like automatons. She examines such scenarios in the work of Marsh, Stoker and Hocking, amongst others, concluding with a discussion of the Gothic's formal struggles to incorporate the new paradigms of human identity provided by criminal hypnosis into its traditional representative armory, focusing on Arthur Conan Doyle's 'John Barrington Cowles' (1886) and Dick Donovan's 'The Woman with the "Oily Eyes"' (1899) .

In 'Victorian Medicine and the Gothic' William Hughes acknowledges the importance of both the mind and the body in Victorian Gothic. The chapter opens with a consideration of how medicine functions as a rhetorical practice, the legal implications of medical casework being acknowledged in particular by way of the structure of Le Fanu's *In a Glass Darkly* (1872) and his 'Green Tea' (1871), and Dickens's *A Christmas Carol* (1843). Hughes then considers how the intellectual and rational functions of the mind may be compromised by the mundane consumption of both innocuous substances such as foodstuffs and beverages, and through the recreational or experimental ingestion of drugs and intoxicants. The reciprocal relationship between the alimentary system and the circulation of the blood is explored by way of a reading of William B. Carpenter's *Principles of Mental Physiology*, a medical work published in 1874, and the Victorian theories of mental health exposed in that work are considered in conjunction with Bram Stoker's *Dracula* (1897) and Robert Louis Stevenson's *The Strange Case of Dr Jekyll and Mr Hyde* (1886). This latter work is also central to the chapter's reading of how addiction and debilitation are configured as aspects of personal responsibility and moral management in the Victorian period. Hughes concludes with a short consideration of the doctor as unethical experimenter, attention being paid in particular to Wilkie Collins's *Heart and Science* (1883) and Arthur Machen's *The Great God Pan* (1894).

Patrick Brantlinger in 'Imperial Gothic' argues that a suspicion that domestic realism in the novel had run its course underlies the rebirth of 'romance' in the last third of the nineteenth century. As in Robert Louis Stevenson's *Dr Jekyll and Mr Hyde*, 'romance' could refer to 'Gothic' narratives of uncanny or supernatural occurrences in domestic settings, but it could also refer to adventures in the faraway places of the British Empire and even beyond its frontiers – as in the countless tales for young male readers published from the 1830s well into the 1900s including, for example, Stevenson's *Treasure Island* (1883) and *Kidnapped* (1886). From roughly the 1870s on, supernatural, Gothic elements were frequently combined with adventure tales, for example in H. Rider Haggard's *King Solomon's Mines* (1886), *She* (1887), and his many other 'romances'. 'Imperial Gothic' refers to the use of Gothic conventions in adventure romances that take their protagonists to unfamiliar, faraway places, but also to romances in which characters, creatures or uncanny objects from those places appear in Britain, disturbing domestic peace and harmony, as in Bram Stoker's *Dracula*. Brantlinger also outlines the work of writers who utilised Gothic conventions in some or all of their fiction and who also touched upon issues relating to Britain's empire, its current power and glory, and its potential demise including – besides Stevenson, Haggard and Stoker – Joseph Conrad, Arthur Conan Doyle, and H. G. Wells.

In 'Fin-de-siècle Gothic' Victoria Margree and Bryony Randall address a paradox at the heart of fin-de-siècle Gothic fiction: the gendered definition of both the canonical works, and of the crucial, timely issues raised within these. The authors note that beyond the now-canonical works of male writers such as Robert Louis Stevenson, Bram Stoker, Oscar Wilde, Henry James and H. G. Wells, much Gothic output of the period was female-authored. Until recently, this work has been neglected or ignored and by arguing for the importance of this neglected resource, Margree and Randall demonstrate how the literature of the period also reveals desires and anxieties of a specifically feminine kind. What might be monstrous to the male literary imagination, may represent a figure of emancipation for women writers. The chapter is structured around three recurrent fin-de-siècle figures: the vampire, the man of science and the ghost. Due consideration is also thus given to how female writers such as E. Nesbit, Margaret Oliphant and Charlotte Riddell complicate the critical picture of the fin-de-siècle Gothic.

All of the chapters have been specially commissioned for this volume and the various contexts which they discuss provide an innovative way in which to address, and account for, the textual, cultural and intellectual diversity that constitutes the Victorian Gothic.

Note

1. This is an argument developed in depth in Smith (2010).

References

Dickens, Charles (1985). *A Christmas Carol* in *The Christmas Books* [1843], vol. 1, ed. and introduction Michael Slater. Harmondsworth: Penguin, pp. 45–134.

Freud, Sigmund (1990). 'The Uncanny' [1919] in *Art and Literature: Jensen's 'Gradiva', Leonardo Da Vinci and Other Works*, vol. 14 in the Penguin Freud Library, ed. Albert Dickson. Harmondsworth: Penguin, pp. 335–76.

Hurley, Kelly (2002). 'British Gothic Fiction, 1885–1930' in *The Cambridge Companion to Gothic Fiction*, ed. Jerrold E. Hogle. Cambridge: Cambridge University Press, pp. 189–207.

Johnson, Thomas H. and Theodora Ward (eds) (1986). *The Letters of Emily Dickinson*. Cambridge, MA: Harvard University Press.

Killeen, Jarlath (2009). *Gothic Literature 1825–1914*. Cardiff: University of Wales Press.

Machen, Arthur (2006). *The Great God Pan* in *The Great God Pan and The Hill of Dreams*. New York: Dover, pp. 9–66.

Mighall, Robert (1999). *A Geography of Victorian Gothic Fiction: Mapping History's Nightmares*. Oxford: Oxford University Press.

Milbank, Alison (1992). *Daughters of the House: Modes of Gothic in Victorian Fiction*. Basingstoke: Macmillan.

——(2002). 'The Victorian Gothic in English Novels and Stories, 1830–1880' in *The Cambridge Companion to Gothic Fiction*, ed. Jerrold E. Hogle. Cambridge: Cambridge University Press, pp. 145–65.

Smith, Andrew (2010). *The Ghost Story 1840–1920: A Cultural History*. Manchester: Manchester University Press.

Warwick, Alexandra (2007). 'Victorian Gothic' in *The Routledge Companion to Gothic*, ed. Catherine Spooner and Emma McEvoy. London and New York: Routledge, pp. 29–37.

Wolfreys, Julian (2000). 'Preface' to *Victorian Gothic: Literary and Cultural Manifestations in the Nineteenth Century*, ed. Ruth Robbins and Julian Wolfreys. Basingstoke: Palgrave, pp. xi–xx.

——(2002). *Victorian Hauntings: Spectrality, Gothic, the Uncanny and Literature*. Basingstoke: Palgrave.

——(2006). 'Victorian Gothic' in *Teaching the Gothic*, ed. Anna Powell and Andrew Smith. Basingstoke: Palgrave, pp. 62–77.

Chapter 1

Victorian Realism and the Gothic: Objects of Terror Transformed

Martin Willis

In 1860 George Eliot, already among the most significant of realist writers, found herself turning aside from her work on what would become *Romola* (1862–3) to focus instead on a smaller novel, *Silas Marner* (1861). As David Carroll notes, *Silas Marner* 'thrust itself' (Carroll, 1996: viii) rather unannounced into Eliot's consciousness. This would have been a familiar interjection for Eliot; a year earlier her Gothic short story 'The Lifted Veil' had intervened when she was at work on *The Mill on the Floss*. *Silas Marner* was not to be a further adventure in the Gothic: rather it was another considerable achievement in realism. Yet, when Silas Marner is introduced to the reader upon his arrival in the rural village of Raveloe, it is the language of late eighteenth-century Gothic that Eliot employs to depict his status in that community. Marner is described as one of those 'wandering men' (Eliot, 1996: 5) who, like Maturin's Melmoth, is unknown and unexplainable. He is 'alien-looking', carries a 'mysterious burden' and appears to belong to the race of 'certain pallid, undersized men' (Eliot, 1996: 5) who are characterised specifically by their difference, their suspicious nature and their skills which approach to magic or witchcraft. By describing Marner in this way, Eliot also anticipates Rossetti's 'Goblin Market' (1862), which was published the following year but had been composed earlier.

Eliot's use of the Gothic here is self-consciously intertextual and purposeful. As the narrative voice makes clear, if not actually explicit, the Gothic mode is being employed playfully and for several purposes. It highlights Marner's originality, certainly, but it also serves to delineate the narrator from the villagers of Raveloe upon whom the novel will focus. It is the villagers who place Marner within a Gothic tradition, but it is the narrator alone who recognises this and can comment on the meanings and effects of their doing so. The Gothic produces, therefore, a space between characters and an additional space between character and narrator that will be exploited as the novel progresses. Eliot's use of the Gothic, then, illuminates how that mode may be put to use as part of an interrogative realist project; the kind of ethnographic and philosophical realism at which Eliot so excelled.

As this brief example shows, it is possible to ask generative questions of the role of the Gothic in Victorian realism. However, Gothic criticism has largely not done so, preferring instead to undertake multiple projects of identification and colonization: first finding the Gothic in numerous works of fiction more usually characterised as belonging to other modes or genres, and then claiming these as newly discovered examples of Gothic's tremendous reach and significance. From this perspective Dickens becomes almost exclusively a writer of popular Gothic (Houston, 2005; Robbins and Wolfreys, 2000) and even Marx's *Capital* (1867) is transformed into a work of Gothic political economy that leads to the extraordinarily reductive conclusion that 'Marxism has depended on Gothic referents to make its point' (Shapiro, 2008: 2). While work of Gothic aggrandisement was common enough in the 1990s, it was given greater impetus in the first volume of the journal *Gothic Studies* by Jerrold E. Hogle, who called on scholars to 'focus on how cultural productions that do not seem "Gothic" on the face of them actually are' (1999: 8). While understandably enthusiastic about the potential for studies in the Gothic, Hogle's desire to find and privilege the Gothic in places where it is actually subordinated is not entirely useful.

Indeed it was not long before other leading critics of the Gothic were sounding a more cautionary note. Andrew Smith, for example, in a review article in 2002 argued that the Gothic required greater attention to its own defining features, and particularly 'a re-examination in order to explain *why* the Gothic is manifest in apparently non-Gothic forms' (Smith, 2002: 79; my italics). Indeed, for Smith, Gothic was in danger of becoming 'so flexible that everything, potentially, becomes a kind of Gothic mood piece' (2002: 79). More recently, Alexandra Warwick has concluded that Gothic appears to be everywhere because it has been substituted with both meaning and text so that 'everything becomes possibly identifiable as Gothic, because what is there that is not meaning or text, criticism or literature?' (Warwick, 2007: 8). This, Warwick argues, renders it 'useless as an interpretative framework, simply because it is so large as to be meaningless' (2007: 8). To be able to return to the particularities of the Gothic – to make it once again meaningful – Warwick urges us to ask of any text or cultural artefact, 'what are the conditions of its gothicity?' (2007: 10). Both Smith and Warwick stress the importance of asking why, and in what ways, the Gothic might work within other textual modes, rather than asking what might be claimed as Gothic. Their focus is therefore on Gothic epistemologies not ontologies.

This chapter will investigate the Gothic within Victorian realism on the basis of this key principle: that it is not *where* the Gothic might be found that is important, but *why* it is found there, what it is employed to do, and under what conditions it achieves this. If we begin to uncover at least a few of the different epistemologies of realism where the Gothic has an influence this will allow us to develop a much deeper understanding of the generic relationships between realism and the Gothic. At the very least it should mean we can go further than simply pointing, say, at Dickens's work and exclaiming that he is being Gothic here, look, and there. This is important, for even when the Gothic is explored with critical suppleness in other genres it is often done by importing Gothic meaning into a text rather than discovering that text's own natural resources. Gary Farnell neatly exemplifies this practice in a recent article when he argues that a specific character in one of Angela Carter's short fictions 'embodies a generative hole in the Real that marks the starting point for the order of symbolic exchange by which we might make sense of [the text's meanings]' (Farnell, 2009: 119).[1] What this actually means is that the hole torn in the realist text by the discovery of the Gothic allows Gothic meanings to pour in, and the critic to make exclusive use of them in analysis. By illuminating the Gothic mode from realism's perspective we may, then, come to know more about what realist writers believe the Gothic mode offers outside of its own generic boundaries and traditional meanings.

To do so we need also to reconsider some of the principles of Victorian realism. Perhaps because of the significance and success of interdisciplinary study, genres of literature such as realism are now readily accepted as continually evolving and open to inter-penetration from other forms and modes. David Amigoni, in a recent critical guide to Victorian literature, stresses the importance of recognising that realist fiction is a 'great exercise in sympathetic assimilation and critical appropriation' (2011: 69). In fact, Amigoni (speaking of Eliot's *Middlemarch* (1871–2)) goes further, arguing that part of the reason realist fiction 'feels like reality' is because 'it has assimilated so many of the available languages and genres of Victorian writing' (2011: 69). For Tom Lloyd, realism's power comes from astute authorial handling of these many languages and genres, so that 'desire for meaning and the recognition of life's multiplicity and potential incoherence' can be maintained in 'radical interplay' (1997: 14). Looking back further through the critical history of realism, George Levine, one of its finest commentators, also understood the genre to be 'polymorphous' in its serious efforts to portray real experience (1981:

11). For Levine, realist writers were always conscious of 'the difference between truth and the appearance of truth' and understood that this necessitated 'several layers of mediation' that drew on other genres for its expression. Ultimately, Levine argues, realism sits in 'complicated relation to all those literary forms in which it confusedly manifests itself' (1981: 12). These critical views show how realism might be read as a cross-bred genre, taking characteristics from other forms and genres. However an alternative, and more extreme, view is available. It might be argued that realism is less a jumble of inherited characteristics and more the ultimate expression of sophistication and complexity where all other genres are manipulated and transformed into the single generic category of the real. To find the Gothic in such a genre is impossible, for even when it is identified it is only as further evidence of realism itself.

Although this is how realism is often presented – as a single royal genre – there is a significant body of critical work that suggests that certain modes or themes of writing, evoked often by the Gothic, are of great importance to the further understanding of realist fiction. Caroline Levine, for example, regards suspense and the keeping of secrets as one of realism's exemplary strategies. It is used, she argues, to invite speculation and curiosity, the essential desire to know that drives reading. (2003: 2–3). For Alison Byerly, realism's essential characteristic is otherness; like suspense, it is epistemologically opaque. By representing otherness, Victorian realists aimed to avoid the problem of finding there was 'a spectrum of experience [that was] impossible to describe' (Byerly, 1997: 5). Otherness was able to 'render the ambiguity of perception' (1997: 5) that the more fixed real world could not. Both Lloyd and George Levine find secrecy and alienation in realism's engagement with, and estrangement from, monstrosity. The monstrous is, in Lloyd's phrase, the 'verbal antitrope' (1997: 16) in realist fiction; it is sublimated yet leaves traces that emerge as aporia in the textual surface, creating powerful anxieties for character and reader alike. Levine, too, suggests that there is an impulse in realism 'to affirm the referentiality of language' (1981: 57) and that in doing this the genre exposes itself not only to the rewards wrought by art but also to the potential it has 'to turn monstrous' (1981: 57).

Realism's invocation of the Gothic mode – through its key tropes of secrecy, alienation and monstrosity – is central to the creation of meaning, and indeed to supporting its complex epistemology that figures the real as the multiple convergences of natural and unnatural, ordinary and extraordinary. In practice, realist fiction introduces the Gothic mode through a variety of Gothic objects – which may be characters, but are also physical sites and immaterial spectres. Such objects are introduced self-consciously by realist writers because they can, as Elaine Freedgood has argued, 'mean something that reality by itself cannot' (2006: 9). Freedgood's reading of the things of realism is helpful because her work reminds us that to read objects is not simply to read the text's surface, but to see moments of splitting which reveal the novel's unconscious and its divisions (2006: 3).

Charles Dickens's *Great Expectations* (1860–1) provides a fine early example of this use of Gothic objects. They are found not, though, in the introductory scene where Pip encounters Magwitch in the graveyard, or later at the Battery, as some critics (for example, Mighall, 2008) suggest, but instead in the early chapters of the novel when Pip is summoned to Satis House, the home of Miss Havisham. The Gothic mood in Pip's meetings with Magwitch is certainly apparent around the edges of Dickens's language but this is undercut by what would now be recognised as exemplary Dickensian humour. So, while the early morning on which Pip sets out to take Magwitch his food and file is suspenseful, leading Pip to comment that 'the mist was heavier yet when I got out upon the marshes, so that instead of my running at everything, everything seemed to run at me', he is soon admitting his guilt to an ox who wears a cravat and has 'something of a clerical air' (Dickens, 1996b: 17). There may be something of the Gothic humour that Victor Sage has identified here (Sage, 1994), but it is of a different order from the monstrous alienating force of Miss Havisham and her manor house.

Pip's arrival at Satis House banishes humour altogether (Mr Pumblechook is denied entry), allowing Dickens to concentrate the Gothic in the place and its inhabitants. This is set up with the common tropes of entrapment and decay that typify Gothic architectures: Satis House is gated and 'rustily barred', its courtyard has grass 'growing in every crevice' and its brewhouse is silent and unproductive (Dickens, 1996b: 55–6). Once inside, Pip finds that 'the passages were all dark' and Miss Havisham's dressing room, although pretty, is unnaturally lit (1996b: 56–7). It is, though, Miss Havisham herself whom Dickens constructs as the central Gothic object of this already Gothicised space:

> I saw that everything within my view which ought to be white, had been white long ago, and had lost its lustre, and was faded and yellow. I saw that the bride within the bridal dress had withered like the dress, and like the flowers, and had no brightness left but the brightness of her sunken eyes. I saw that the dress had been put upon the rounded figure of a young woman, and that the figure upon which it now hung loose, had shrunk to skin and bone. Once I had been taken to see some ghastly waxwork at the Fair, representing I know not what impossible personage lying in state. Once, I had been taken to one of our old marsh churches to see a skeleton in the ashes of a

rich dress, that had been dug out of a vault under the church pavement. Now, waxwork and skeleton seemed to have dark eyes that moved and looked at me. (1996b: 57–8)

This is one of the most powerfully Gothic moments in the novel (and indeed in any of Dickens's novels) that both 'others' and makes monstrous Miss Havisham. She is the Other, clearly, to both her younger self so enthusiastic about her imminent marriage, and to all brides on their wedding day. She is made monstrous by the associations with a waxwork and skeleton that suggest she is, simultaneously, a living corpse, an aberrant copy of humanity, and an automaton given supernatural life.

Yet what is perhaps most striking here is Dickens's (and Pip's) repetition first of 'I saw that' and later 'Once I had been taken'. What the Gothic does here is to create a temporal connection between things previously discrete; between Pip's present observations and his previous visual experiences of waxwork shows and skeletal remains. This concludes with the very present-tense, 'Now', where these Gothic objects formerly witnessed now coalesce into the object of Miss Havisham and in doing so gain the power to look back at Pip. The Gothicity of this moment, then, allows Dickens to draw a connection between Pip's history and his present position, and additionally it should hint at a connection between the encounter with the monstrous Magwitch and his present introduction to Miss Havisham. This connection is given depth and texture only a few moments later, when Pip describes yet another Gothic scene – his vision of Miss Havisham's corpse hanging from a beam in Satis House's Brewery:

> I saw a figure hanging there by the neck. A figure all in yellow white, with but one shoe to the feet; and it hung so, that I could see that the faded trimmings of the dress were like earthy paper, and that the face was Miss Havisham's, with a movement going over the whole countenance as if she were trying to call out to me. In the terror of seeing the figure, and in the terror of being certain that it had not been there a moment before, I at first ran from it, and then ran towards it. And my terror was greatest of all, when I found no figure there. (1996b: 64)

Here the comparison with Pip's encounter with Magwitch is striking, if rather aslant. The reader is invited to recall, via Miss Havisham's shoeless foot, the limping figure of Magwitch as Pip finds him in the Battery. More potently, the hanging of Miss Havisham recalls Magwitch's own reference to 'that there gallows' (1996b: 18) which might indicate his own future fate. And indeed Pip's movement here in the Brewery replicates his running from Magwitch on the night of their first encounter, and then his running to him the following morning.

The Gothic nature of Pip's vision allows Dickens to highlight connections that are, in the novel's present, entirely unseen. The Gothicity of Miss Havisham's spectral presence enables a form of magical thinking that allows for interconnections that seem unreal but which, as Dickens will show, can exist within the real world. The Gothic drives realism in this instance, and it does so by placing characters in alignments that appear paranormal. Pip's Gothic encounters with Miss Havisham (real and ghostly) illuminate the unlikely and still phantasmagorical links with Magwitch. Yet these encounters also reveal how Dickens wishes the reader to realise that Pip's position is as marginal as that of his key interlocutors. Like Miss Havisham and Magwitch, Pip too is a prisoner of social circumstance and will become marginalised through his inheritance. It is by his use of the Gothic mode that Dickens first makes this apparent.

It is for the same reason that Dickens employs the Gothic in *Bleak House* (1853) to depict Tom-All-Alone's as a place not only on the margins but also at the centre of London society. This slum, so closely associated with Chancery, is a dark space of 'tumbling tenements' that 'contain, by night, a swarm of misery' (Dickens, 1996a: 256). It is these streets of unsanitary housing that have

> bred a crowd of foul existence that crawls in and out of gaps in walls and boards; and coils itself to sleep, in maggot numbers, where the rain drips in; and comes and goes, fetching and carrying fever, and sowing more evil in its every footprint. (1996a: 256–7)

Dickens's supernatural animation of disease, which is given consciousness enough to sow evil, is allowable here in a Gothic space that is itself personified (as 'Tom'). In these initial Gothic descriptions Tom-All-Alone's appears entirely marginalised, even though Dickens invites the reader to wonder 'what connexion can there be' (1996a: 256) between it and the other spaces of the novel.

Yet the Gothic mode itself provides a link between Tom-All-Alone's and, at the other end of the class spectrum, the aristocratic seat of Chesney Wold. For Chesney Wold's paved terrace, the Ghost's Walk, is also inscribed as a Gothic space; a place of spectral presence that through specific objects is aligned with Tom-All-Alone's. Dickens's narrator first introduces the Ghost's Walk in foul weather: 'The rain is ever falling, drip, drip, drip, by day and night, upon the broad flagged pavement, The Ghost's Walk' (1996a: 103). Following a lengthy caesura, Dickens returns to his theme through Mrs Rouncewell's warning of the Ghost's Walk's spectral figure, who paces the pavement unseen:

> If the tread is an echo, it is an echo that is only heard after dark, and is often unheard for a long while together. But it comes back, from time to time; and so sure as there is sickness or death in the family, it will be heard then. (1996a: 113–14)

Here lies the answer to Dickens's query about connections. The later drips of rain in Tom-All-Alone's are arguably intended to remind the reader of the Ghost's Walk, and indeed to reconstitute the 'tread' of the ghost in the footprints of infection. In effect, Dickens employs the Gothic to marginalise these two sites but also to relay the spectral quality of their connectedness and thereby bring them towards the centre of the narrative.

This tactic of using the Gothic to uncover invisible relations that seem to stand outside the realm of realism is found also in fictions by other realist writers. Benjamin Disraeli's *Sybil, or the Two Nations* (1845) reveals this both in its use and also its elision of the Gothic mode in the description of two key sites, the village of Marney and Marney Abbey. Disraeli depicts the village of Marney as a rural Tom-All-Alone's: a place of pestilential disease and poverty. Indeed the descriptive vocabulary foreshadows Dickens's later vision. Marney is 'rotten', 'unfit' and 'decomposing into disease' (Disraeli, 1985: 80). The 'wretched tenements' are surrounded by 'foul pits' which are 'spreading into stagnant pools, while a concentrated solution of every species of dissolving filth was allowed to soak through and thoroughly impregnate the walls and ground adjoining' (1985: 80). While Disraeli closes on the Gothic at one point in describing typhus as hunting for its 'next prey' (1985: 81), the view taken here of Marney village is closer to the discourses of those medical reports, such as Edwin Chadwick's (1842), that sought to describe the conditions of sanitation in the poorer classes of Britain's housing stock. What might easily have become Gothic is maintained as a particularly vivid realism, and would certainly have been interpreted by contemporary readers as aligned with medico-sociological language.

Marney Abbey, however, is decidedly Gothic. For the visiting aristocrat, Egremont, the Abbey is associated with:

> his first and freshest fancies; every footstep was as familiar to him as it could have been to one of the old monks; yet never without emotion could he behold these unrivalled remains. (Disraeli, 1985: 86)

The emotional intensity of Egremont's observations and the connections between the Abbey's past and its present are reinforced in Disraeli's lengthy ensuing description:

Over a space of not less than ten acres might still be observed the fragments of the great Abbey: these were, towards their limit, in general moss-grown and mouldering memorials that told where once rose the offices and spread the terraced gardens of the old proprietors ... But it was in the centre of this tract of ruins, occupying a space of not less than two acres that, with a strength that had defied time, and with a beauty that had at last turned away the wrath of man, still rose if not in perfect, yet admirable, form and state, one of the noblest achievements of Christian art, – the Abbey church. The summer vault was now its only roof, and all that remained of its gorgeous windows was the vastness of their arched symmetry ... The body of the church was in many parts overgrown with brambles and in all covered with a rank vegetation ... This desecration of a spot, once sacred, still beautiful and solemn, jarred on the feelings of Egremont. (1985: 87–8)

The Abbey's sublimity, its qualities as picturesque ruin, and its association with a lost religious tradition keenly felt by Egremont, is modish in its Gothicity. Yet this very self-conscious use of the form immediately prefigures Egremont's vital encounter with Walter Gerard and Stephen Morley, whom he discovers almost as part of his perusal of the Abbey's Gothic spaces, 'standing beside a tomb' (1985: 89). Indeed, Gerard is described in the same architectural and temporal terms as the Abbey's impressive ruins. Egremont notes first that he is 'of lofty stature' but also that 'his complexion might in youth have been ruddy, but time and time's attendants, thought and passion, had paled it; his chestnut hair, faded, but not grey, still clustered over a noble brow' (1985: 89). Time, as well as disenfranchisement (as we later learn), has made Gerard the personification of the Abbey's ruins, and additionally situates him in the Gothic mode that Disraeli employs to describe those ruins.

It is, then, the Gothic that subtly illuminates the connections within the novel that the reader is not yet aware of at the level of the realist plot. Shortly, Disraeli will uncover Gerard's claim to actual nobility and later the connections between Gerard and Egremont will deepen as Egremont becomes involved (in the persona of Franklin) in the political activities that these two strangers lead. Of course, the connections run deeper than this; they run towards the marriage of Egremont to Gerard's daughter, Sybil. At the moment of meeting at Marney Abbey, it is the Gothic mode that allows these still invisible links between disparate, perhaps even oppositional characters, to be drawn in a manner that places them outside the realism of the world Disraeli describes through plot and structure.

In fact more might be said of Egremont's response to the Gothic scene he encounters. His distaste for the Abbey's descent into the Gothic is suggestive of a reactionary politics that would have ancient tradition restituted at the expense of radical political action (that action being, in this instance, the Tudor dissolution of the monasteries – but the reader should be aware that this might refer also to the Chartism Disraeli later introduces). Obversely, however, Egremont also appears to recognise that it is the Gothic nature of the Abbey that gives it its power and beauty; radical political action might be said to lead ultimately to a grander and more beautiful structure that draws its power from having been changed. These, of course, are the key questions Disraeli asks in discussing possible solutions to the problems of the 'two nations' he views as existing side by side in 1840s Britain. The Gothic mode, then, also enables the author to introduce the psychological and social tensions that exist for Egremont, and that will continue to trouble his relationship with Gerard and Morley. Although clearly it is the Gothic that delivers this political prophecy, this does not make it any less a part of the realism of the novel. As Margaret E. Mitchell has shown, a number of critics 'have argued that realism itself is fundamentally concerned with justice and humanity' (2003: 183). Citing Lukács, Mitchell argues that realism is predominantly a moral form engaged in a struggle against the movements of contemporary thought (2003: 183). Certainly, this is Disraeli's apparent aim in *Sybil*, and it begins to emerge only at the point in the novel where the Gothic mode draws together the key actors in his drama. For Disraeli then, as for Dickens, the Gothic was not a moment out from realism but one of its central components, able to say something important about the world outside the restrictions that language places on the real.

Writing only a year or so after Disraeli, Emily Brontë employed the Gothic more extensively in *Wuthering Heights* (1847). Her sense of its power both to reveal hidden associations and suggest something of the centrality and marginality of specific characters is as apparent as in the works of Dickens and Disraeli. One of the scenes most commented on by critics is the moment early in the novel when the narrator, Lockwood, is visited by Cathy's ghost, who appears at the window of his bedroom. Scholarship has drawn attention to this as an exemplar of Brontë's interest in spatial boundaries (Nestor, 2003: xxvi), and Pauline Nestor, in particular, reads the appearance of Cathy's ghost as one of the ways in which Brontë 'challenges not only the limits of life, but those of reality' (2003: xxix). Whatever focus critical commentaries have taken, all agree that the scene symbolises Brontë's broader analysis of the position of women: Lockwood's violence against the spectre of Cathy and his subsequent piling of books against the window are active metaphors for both female oppression and women's limited access to systems of education. Such analysis is sharp, and undoubtedly revealing of the aims of the novel. However, Brontë's use of the Gothic at this point suggests that more complex relationships are under investigation.

The episode is in its entirety too long to excerpt easily, but the Gothic mode is introduced not with the arrival of Cathy's ghost but rather with Lockwood's recognition that the strange rapping in his dream is not supernatural in origin but only 'the branch of a fir-tree that . . . rattled its dry cones against the panes! [of his window]' (Brontë, 2003: 24). This is the delayed terror finally subsumed by natural explanation employed often in late eighteenth-century Gothic and characteristic particularly of Ann Radcliffe. Lockwood, however, is not content with this ordinary conclusion, and in a decidedly strange move, proceeds by 'knocking my knuckles through the glass, and stretching an arm out to seize the importunate branch' (2003: 25). At this point Brontë turns terror into the horror of Lockwood's recognition that a spectre *is* actually haunting him, when he finds that his 'fingers closed on the fingers of a little, ice-cold hand!' (2003: 25). As Cathy's ghost sobs and pleads to be let in, Lockwood turns to violence, slicing open the ghost's wrist on the broken window pane. As Cathy again wails 'Let me in!' Lockwood replies, 'Let *me* go, if you want me to let you in!' (2003: 25). Taking advantage of a momentary lull in their fight at the window Lockwood then 'hurriedly piled the books up in a pyramid against it' (2003: 25). Taking succour from this success, he then shouts 'I'll never let you in, not if you beg for twenty years!' to which Cathy answers, 'It's twenty years . . . twenty years, I've been a waif for twenty years!' (2003: 25).

As was the case with Pip's Gothic encounter with Miss Havisham, what is most interesting here is the number of Brontë's linguistic repetitions and reversals; repetitions of 'fingers' and 'twenty years', reversals of touch and grip, and of who should let go or be let in. What is stressed in the language of the Gothic is not their opposition but how much Lockwood is *like* Cathy's ghost, and how he acts just as she acts. The question that the Gothic mode invites the reader to ask is not only what does Lockwood's violent assault *mean*, but also what is it that connects him to Cathy's ghost?

The Gothicity of this section of *Wuthering Heights* reveals that their connection resides in their similarly doubled alienation, one form of which the reader is witnessing or has witnessed and one form of which remains to be discovered. Lockwood, as the opening section of his narrative has made clear, is recently removed from 'the stir of society' (Brontë, 2003: 3), and is unremittingly ignorant of the affairs and character of rural life. He is, therefore, caught in a social limbo, although not one that appears to trouble him. Cathy's ghost, likewise, is caught in that space between life and death, but has been unable (for twenty years, it seems) to find her entrance back into the life of the Heights, or to Heathcliff. We do not yet realise, of course, that Cathy's alienation from both Heathcliff and the Heights began much earlier in her life, at the hands of her own family and of the Lintons. In an uncanny parallel, Lockwood is about to be cast out of the Heights by Heathcliff, who orders him out of the house and the yard, with a final dismissive 'away with you!' (2003: 28).

The Gothic therefore illuminates the alienation that readers already know, but also hints at further forms of alienation that readers do not yet know; connections that are still to be discovered as the plot advances are at this point suggested by the symmetry between Cathy and Lockwood during their Gothic encounter. Yet, the Gothic mode suggests something further, too. It highlights Lockwood's violence towards Cathy, despite their sympathetic alignment. In doing so, it symbolises Lockwood's monstrous moral character, and gives evidence of his future narrative violence against Cathy's ghost, whom he will not, in his mediation of Nelly Dean's story, allow back in. This, of course, is the importance of the symbol of the stacked pyramid of the books: not only a sign of women's educational deficit but also of Lockwood's power as narrator.

It was in the use of the Gothic mode to illustrate the spaces between character and narrator that this essay began, with a brief discussion of *Silas Marner*, and it is with *Silas Marner* that this chapter will close. In that novel, the Gothicity of Marner's arrival at Raveloe tells the reader of the secrets he carries with him, and how they have marked his character. The Gothic also tells us of the alienation he is likely to feel in Raveloe, where a number of villagers are ready to believe the tales of terror told of wandering men. That is, Eliot uses the Gothic mode to show the reader those who align the Gothic with the real, and see no difference between them. Marner is clearly a Gothic object, both in narrative terms and for those other characters who witness his arrival. Yet for Eliot's narrator those other characters are also objects of the Gothic. They are not identified through the Gothic mode, but are instead shown to be bringing the Gothic to bear on others. The narrator is sympathetic to this, noting by way of explanation that 'the world outside their own direct experience was a region of vagueness and mystery' (Eliot, 1996: 5).

Nevertheless the narrator's commentary on their employment of Gothic tropes to try to understand Marner further underscores the hierarchy apparent in the novel's opening pages; from Marner the Gothic object; through Raveloe's citizens as users of the Gothic; to the narrator's commentary on the Gothic mode in its totality. What Eliot is able to make explicit in her fiction like no other realist writer is first of all that the Gothic mode is part of real experience, and therefore essential for realism. Additionally, however, Eliot in this example reveals how using the Gothic does not turn realist fiction into Gothic writing. Rather, it is the reverse. Realism assimilates the Gothic mode and makes it part of a larger realist project. If evidence is required to refute Hogle's claim that non-Gothic forms are actually Gothic, we should look no further than *Silas Marner*'s narrator, who views the Gothic mode from an omniscient space far above it, a space that is realism.

Note

1. Farnell's interesting essay deals with psychoanalytic readings of the 'thing' as a new methodology for Gothic study. The short fiction he addresses in the quotation used above is Angela Carter's 'The Lady of the House of Love' (1979).

References

Amigoni, David (2011). *Victorian Literature*. Edinburgh: Edinburgh University Press.

Brontë, Emily (2003). *Wuthering Heights* [1847]. London: Penguin.

Byerly, Alison (1997). *Realism, Representation, and the Arts in Nineteenth-Century Literature*. Cambridge: Cambridge University Press.

Carroll, David (1996). 'Introduction' to George Eliot, *Silas Marner*, ed. David Carroll. London: Penguin, pp. vii–xxv.

Chadwick, Edwin (1984). *Report on the Sanitary Conditions of the Labouring Population* [1842]. Edinburgh: Edinburgh University Press.

Dickens, Charles (1996a). *Bleak House* [1853]. London: Penguin.

——(1996b). *Great Expectations* [1861]. London: Penguin.

Disraeli, Benjamin (1985). *Sybil, or the Two Nations* [1845]. London: Penguin.

Eliot, George (1996). *Silas Marner* [1861]. London: Penguin.

Farnell, Gary (2009). 'The Gothic and the Thing', *Gothic Studies*, 11/1, 113–23.

Freedgood, Elaine (2006). *The Ideas in Things: Fugitive Meaning in the Victorian Novel*. Chicago: University of Chicago Press.

Hogle, Jerrold E. (1999). 'Introduction: Gothic Studies Past, Present and Future', *Gothic Studies*, 1/1, 1–9.

Houston, Gail Turley (2005). *From Dickens to Dracula: Gothic, Economics and Victorian Fiction*. Cambridge: Cambridge University Press.

Levine, Caroline (2003). *The Serious Pleasure of Suspense: Victorian Realism and Narrative Doubt*. Charlottesville: University of Virginia Press.

Levine, George (1981). *The Realistic Imagination: English Fiction from Frankenstein to Lady Chatterley*. Chicago: University of Chicago Press.

Lloyd, Tom (1997). *Crises of Realism: Representing Experience in the British Novel, 1816–1910*. Lewisburg: Bucknell University Press.

Mighall, Robert (2008). 'Dickens and the Gothic' in *A Companion to Charles Dickens*, ed. David Paroissien. Oxford: Blackwell, pp. 81–96.

Mitchell, Margaret E. (2003). 'Preface to Special Issue on Victorian Realism:

"The Mirror is Doubtless Defective"', *Literature Interpretation Theory*, 14, 179–84.

Nestor, Pauline (2003). 'Introduction' to Emily Brontë, *Wuthering Heights*, ed. Pauline Nestor. London: Penguin, pp. xv–xxxv.

Robbins, Ruth, and Julian Wolfreys (eds) (2000). *Victorian Gothic: Literary and Cultural Manifestations in the Nineteenth Century*. Basingstoke: Palgrave.

Sage, Victor (1994). 'Gothic Laughter: Farce and Horror in Five Texts' in *Gothic Origins and Innovations*, ed. Allan Lloyd Smith and Victor Sage. Amsterdam: Rodopi, pp. 190–203.

Shapiro, Stephen (2008). 'Introduction: Material Gothic', *Gothic Studies*, 10/1, 2–3.

Smith, Andrew (2002). 'Rethinking the Gothic: What Do We Mean?', *Gothic Studies*, 4/1, 79–85.

Warwick, Alexandra (2007). 'Feeling Gothicky?', *Gothic Studies*, 9/1, 5–15.

Chapter 2

Sensation Fiction: A Peep Behind the Veil

Laurence Talairach-Vielmas

Not now, for the first time, has the collective British novel-reader sat up of night's reading how the wicked but fascinating lady has married a baronet of ancient family during the lifetime of an absent but obscurer husband – how, when this latter becomes obtrusive, she buried him in a convenient well, and thus happily disposes of an unpleasant and disagreeable persecution. Not now, for the first time, has the collective British play-goer endured heat and hustling, and crush and struggle to see a plunge (without a splash) into mimetic waters, and gallant rescue from drowning; or the prevention of a Deed of Blood in a lonely quarry, happily accomplished by the agency of a bending sapling. Such devices were popular years and years ago, and the dramatic 'sensation', more or less modified, will always be in favour. (Anon, 1863: 517)

As this reviewer makes explicit, the Victorian sensation novel – here epitomised by Mary Elizabeth Braddon's best-seller *Lady Audley's Secret* (1861–2) – is heavily indebted to earlier plots, finding its inspiration in late eighteenth-century Gothic narratives. The well, the waters or the lonely quarry as crime sites are highly symbolic, underlining the importance of depths in Gothic novels and their enduring presence. The search for the secret in sensation novels was, indeed, much modelled on that in its Gothic predecessors. Bodies and texts recording the crimes of the past are buried, dug up and read. However, as this chapter contends, the sensational narratives' obsessional quest for the truth must be contextualised and looked at through the prism of emerging new theories which radically transformed the view of the earth and its origins. As sensational detectives try to lift the veil over the mysteries of the past, the novels increasingly align the investigation of the criminals' bodies with explorations of and recent theorisations on nature.

Gloomy Churchyards, Deep Wells, Lonely Quarries

In Tim Fywell's 1997 BBC production of *The Woman in White*, Walter Hartright, the drawing master, spends his time haunting churchyards with his easel, believing that the woman in white will appear so that he may discover her secret. Fywell's choice of having the artist practise in a churchyard is telling. The whole adaptation features paintings and reproductions, climaxing when one of the canvasses reproducing *Beata Beatrix* (1872) reminds Marian Halcombe of Dante Gabriel Rossetti's exhumation of Elizabeth Siddal's body (on this episode, see Chapter 5 in this volume). Although anachronistic, the detail nonetheless leads the detective to the truth: Walter and Marian exhume a lock of hair and a diary revealing Anne's (sexual) secret (her marriage to Sir Percival Glyde) from Laura's father's grave. Fywell's production is a very good illustration of the way in which sensation novels reworked the Gothic, resurrecting the past through plays between surfaces (be they texts or paintings) and depths. Reading the text or decoding the picture thus leads to more earthly depths containing human remains that serve to identify their owner and rewrite the story. The search for the secret appears, therefore, as a journey aimed to investigate the depths of the body or/and those of the earth.

In most sensation novels forged letters and registers – just like biased medical verdicts and warped legal evidence – construct and erase identity, fashioning individuals according to the terms of artificial codes, and turning life and death into figures of speech. In *The Woman in White* (1860) the ghostly Anne Catherick dies and is interred under the name of her half-sister Laura Glyde, while the latter is metaphorically buried alive in the asylum: the switch of identities is written into the lettering on a tombstone or the label on a shirt. More significantly still, sensation fiction capitalised on the artificiality of the modern world and the rise of consumer culture, enticing women to play parts and conceal themselves beneath layers of make-up and fashionable clothes. The most sensational villainesses are undoubtedly Mary Elizabeth Braddon's eponymous heroine in *Lady Audley's Secret*, or Lydia Gwilt in Wilkie Collins's *Armadale* (1864), both playing upon their appearance to deny the passing of time and seduce men, and both closely related to the celebrated Madame Rachel who professed to make women look young again with mouth wash, creams, soaps, hair washes, elixirs or ointments, though at an extortionate price.[1] As sensational illustrations of the widespread objectification of the female body throughout the nineteenth century and of the constitution of the self as a 'commodity spectacle' (Richards, 1990: 196), Braddon's and Collins's villainesses highlight how in sensation novels this excessive codification of the body turned characters into spectral or liminal figures hovering between the realm of the living and that of the dead – their bodies becoming mere cyphers which only an elite class of professionals is able to read.

Indeed, the spectral in sensation novels recurrently functions as a sign of artificiality, signalling the characters' lack of corporeality, even for highly sensuous villainesses like Lydia Gwilt, or for characters like Magdalen Vanstone in *No Name* (1864), who has used artificial aids and cosmetics to pass for Miss Garth, and is mistaken for a ghost by Mrs Wragge. The significance of sensation writers' definition of the body as a page easily erased and rewritten – as a coded manuscript – explains why sensation writers' Gothic revisions often suggest that the crimes of the past must be dug up to resurrect the truth. The truth lies beyond the smooth surface of the skin – or of the earth – a buried manuscript waiting to be discovered and deciphered. For Robert Mighall, the development of criminological discourse in the second half of the nineteenth century 'helped to demarcate a new territory for Gothic representation, with the body providing a site for ancestral return' (1999: 153). In Victorian Gothic the body replaces the old manuscript buried in a chest, concealing secret narratives in its unfathomable depths. As a consequence, the contrast between smooth appearances, painted surfaces and unfathomable depths leads the detectives to investigate sites where the material body may be found – churchyards, deadhouses, dust-heaps, laboratories. Secrecy and the body go hand in hand, and the more sensation novels highlight the elusiveness or artificiality of human identity, the more hair-raising Gothic loci appear as the ultimate place where fragments of the truth can be recollected and reunited and the story rewritten.

Collins's woman in white is found time and again cleaning the surface of Laura's mother's tombstone, the churchyard becoming a meeting point for the characters hoping to discover her secret and the place where Laura is found by Hartright after her supposed death as if she had just walked out of her own grave. In *Lady Audley's Secret*, Robert Audley starts his investigation with the tombstone at Ventnor where Helen Talboys is said to be buried, and later dreams that the tombstone is gone. As words lie on tombstones, the detectives must discover the secret narrative that tells the real story of the body, as in *The Moonstone* (1868), where both a buried manuscript and the body of a suicidal maid guide Franklin Blake to the truth, inviting him to probe the quicksand shivering with pleasure. Likewise, in *The Law and the Lady* (1875), the investigation leads the heroine to disinter 'from their foul tomb' (Collins, 1992: 396) the remains of Sarah Macallan's manuscript which could clear her husband of murder. Buried under the household refuse, the letter is scattered into fragments which must be reconstructed, and the dust-heap becomes a symbolic burial mound, as if hosting the dismembered pieces of the woman's skeleton. The sensational revision of the Gothic manuscript buried in dung, merging textual fragments and bodily remains, is another striking instance of buried narratives, texts invisible to the naked eye or illegible to non-professionals which relate the story of the body and which the investigations help to recover.

Collins's *Jezebel's Daughter* (1880), where Mrs Wagner, locked up in a deadhouse, narrowly escapes live burial due to a medical misreading of the signs of death is another clear example which suggests that the truth is never skin deep. The novel epitomises how sensation narratives metaphorise the secret concealed beneath the skin (the characters are insane or/and undead) through the darkness and mystery permeating such Gothic sites. This parallel between what lies in the unfathomable depths of the grave, the earth, the quicksand, the dust-heap or the deadhouse and beyond the skin can be linked to other sensational discoveries or revelations of the time, connected to the power of science to rewrite the history of the earth and its origins.[2] As a matter of fact, while *The Woman in White* was serialised in *All the Year Round* between November 1859 and August 1860, reviews and discussions of Charles Darwin's *On the Origin of Species by Means of Natural Selection, or the Preservation of Favoured Races in the Struggle for Life* was published, making the two books appear as the two sensations that influenced the content of the journal, which was launched in late November 1859. An article entitled 'Natural Selection' published in July 1860 followed an instalment of *The Woman in White*, showing Walter Hartright on his way to Knowlesbury, in search of Sir Percival Glyde's secret: 'Smoothly and fairly as appearances looked in the vestry, there was something wrong beneath them' (Collins, 1860: 293). The readers of Collins's text, eagerly awaiting the next installment, were promised even more sensations by the review of Darwin's book which followed, arguing that 'Astronomical and geological innovations render possible the acceptance of doctrines that would have made people's hair stand on end three centuries ago' (Anon., 1860: 293). The similarities between the novel and Darwin's thesis are strengthened, as Darwin's quest is also presented as a search for the truth: ' "What *is* Truth?" Mr. Darwin believes he knows, or is on the way to know' (Anon., 1860: 294). His theory, the reviewer contends, depends on 'the question of the interpretation to be given to certain appearances and occurrences; it is a matter of circumstantial evidence' (Anon., 1860: 294). As Darwin's theory suggested, the earth buried archival material that could be dug up and read:

To the earth, man instinctively turns for the archives of the past – to the earth – the great Keeper of the dead – the Preserver of extinct forms and vanished dynasties. (Anon., 1859: 26)

Thus, the search for buried texts in sensation novels aligns the quest for the secret with a search for origins – an attempt at uniting what lies in the grave to a name, an identity, a history, as typified by Collins's and Braddon's first seminal sensation novels. The secret must be exhumed, as the version of *Lady Audley's Secret* which appeared in the *Sixpenny Magazine* from January to December 1862 suggested. The jarring contrast between Robert Audley's innocent-looking aunt and Lady Audley's sensual Pre-Raphaelite portrait haunts the detective at night. The canvas is torn to reveal sensational abysses, as Robert Audley's nightmare depicts Lady Audley as a living representation of death, a liminal figure hovering between the realm of the living and that of the dead, and the villainess tripping out of a grave:

> In another dream he saw the grave of Helen Talboys open, and while he waited, with a cold horror lifting up his hair, to see the dead woman arise and stand before him with her still, charnel-house drapery clinging about her frigid limbs, his uncle's wife tripped gaily out of the open grave, dressed in the crimson velvet robes in which the artist had painted her, and with her ringlets flashing like red gold in the unearthly light that shone about her. (Braddon, 1862: 65)

Elisabeth Bronfen's study of female bodies 'not safely interred beneath the earth' underlines how the female corpse unsettles semiotic meaning and disseminates ambiguity through the narratives (1992: 291). Here, the female spectre is no trope of live burial as in many a Gothic novel, but the living dead creature who prevents both the closure of the grave and the story, suggesting precisely that the truth lies in the depths of the grave. Revealingly, Braddon's horror narrative is not simply concerned with discovering the rotting corpse of Lady Audley's first husband who lies at the bottom of a well and confounding the murderess. Rather, the spiral of crimes and secrets which the narrative gradually unravels takes us down into the depths of the woman's degenerate physiology, down to the core of the heroine's rotten nature concealed beneath the artificial mask of beauty and velvet dresses which orchestrate her masquerade.[3] Throughout the novel, the detective frequently associates the female protagonist with underground worlds where regression prevails – metamorphosing the picturesque verticality of the Gothic setting into unfathomable watery sites: Audley Court's deep well gives way to darker depths where water reflects the mermaid-like seductress's criminality.

Thus, by revamping Gothic images of verticality, the detectives' 'excavating' activities convincingly trope modern fears directly linked to research into the history of the earth and the place of man in that history. As we will see, as later sensation novels gradually replaced the churchyard with more modern sites, such as the laboratory, the narratives still highlight man's desperate attempt at connecting the body to a history. However, this time, through medical experimentation, the bodies of the Gothic heroines, villains and villainesses are examined so as to be connected to a greater chain of being. The buried manuscript is the story of humanity that Promethean scientists try to recover. In fact, the method of detection in sensational narratives, as Lawrence Frank or Ronald Thomas have argued (Frank, 2009; Thomas, 1999: 55), reveals detective fiction's debt to comparative anatomy and the rise of such new scientific disciplines which reconstructed reality from elements or clues which could not be directly apprehended – partially invisible data – climaxing in Darwin's theory of natural selection (Ginsburg, 1992: 103). Interestingly, the founder of comparative anatomy, Georges Cuvier (1769–1832), was not only found in literary texts, influencing detectives such as Poe's Dupin, but was also invoked by legal scholars 'to justify the elevation of circumstantial evidence over direct testimony in the reform of criminal law' (Thomas, 1999: 55). In most sensation novels, the investigations rely upon circumstantial evidence – using smears, stains or letters as proofs – showing how such methods were becoming 'the model for the discovery of truth in forensic science' (Thomas, 1999: 55).

Beneath the Skin, Beyond the Veil: In Search of Origins

The sensation novels which followed Collins's *The Woman in White* and Braddon's rewriting of Collins's plot in *Lady Audley's Secret* stressed even more the genre's interest in forbidden or inaccessible depths. Questioning the artificiality of identity as well as constructions of the self, many of them increasingly used the medical field and medical discoveries to image secret depths. Like the archives of the earth that keep the dead, the archives of the self reveal to the professional's eyes sensational secrets. Heroines' and villainesses' minds are made up of disorderly scattered fragments, the layers of the brain sometimes seeming to have been effaced by the passing of time – or by sustained anxiety and emotional shocks – although remaining buried in the depths of the mind, like haunting thoughts likely to visit the upper layers of consciousness when excited. From Laura Fairlie in *The Woman in*

White to Carmina in *Heart and Science* (1883), cases of psychic shocks or double consciousness brand Collins's plots throughout his career. However, the investigations of sensational characters' minds, be they heroines, villains or villainesses, reveal older buried manuscripts – the story of human evolution and potential degeneration. In Collins's *The Haunted Hotel* (1878), even if the original palace is effaced through renovation and the corpse disintegrated (but for the head), the repressed memory of the crime returns unconsciously through automatic writing, Countess Narona telling the truth through writing a play relating the murder. From the beginning, Countess Narona, as a modern revision of the cursed character of traditional Gothic narratives, is subjected to a medicalised reading that revamps the Gothic tale of cursed legacy into a medical exploration of brain disease and associates her with characteristics said to typify animals and savages – and so criminals, as Victorian criminologists and late Victorian anthropologists researching racial 'types' argued. Likewise, Collins's and Braddon's epileptic suspected criminals (this time male) in *Poor Miss Finch* (1872) and *Thou Art the Man* (1894) provide other instances of memory lapses related to crimes, as in Braddon's *The Fatal Three* (1888). Interestingly, in *Thou Art the Man*, the suspected criminal's African past aligns him with the superstitious and bedevilled Dark Continent, his mind becoming a territory to be explored, a terrain where geography and psychology merge, and where the buried manuscript of the crime – the suspected murderer's degenerate nature – is linked to the history of man's evolution.

As the example of Braddon's *Thou Art the Man* makes explicit, late Victorian Gothic increasingly used mental physiology to revamp Gothic depths, swapping gloomy churchyards for morbid brains concealing crimes buried under layers of matter. This clearly demonstrates the connections that sensation novels made between the narrative's exploration of the body's secrets and those of the earth. A case in point might be Collins's *Heart and Science*, as the novel examines the place of the human in nature, whether through positioning 'man' on an evolutionary scale and aligning the human with other species or by pointing to humanity's insignificance in the earth's history and its potential extinction. While in the first decades of the nineteenth century geology had evidenced the insignificance of humanity on time's scale, evolutionary biology, which had been inspired by geology, pointed to the insignificance of humans on the evolutionary scale (Beer, 2000: 14–16). By combining references to research in geology, palaeontology and evolutionary biology through two scientists involved in the natural sciences, on the one hand, and in mental physiology, on the other, Collins revises the

Gothic romance through subjecting the defenceless heroine to the blade of a vivisector eager to pry into the secrets of nature.

The orphan Carmina, a wealthy heiress, becomes subject to the legal authority of her aunt, Mrs Gallilee, on her father's death. Secretly engaged to her guardian's son, the surgeon Ovid Vere, Carmina is forced into seclusion by her mercenary and debt-ridden aunt who seeks to prevent her niece's marriage in order to inherit her fortune. Collins's narrative obviously echoes the old Radcliffean Gothic romance of female victimisation, as the pure and innocent Carmina appears increasingly nervous and hysterical. She becomes the prisoner of her aunt, the aptly named Mrs Gallilee, who has a passion for science, and whose overt cruelty Carmina must silently and patiently endure. The heroine seeks to escape her aunt's cruelty and join her lover Ovid in Quebec. But when her letter to Ovid is intercepted and Mrs Gallilee falsely accuses her ward of being the illegitimate child of an adulteress, the combined shock of the discovery and the accusation turn Carmina's nervous anxiety to 'partial catalepsy' (Collins, 1994: 255). Carmina's romantic sensitivity is transformed into brain disease, and Carmina then becomes the helpless patient of Dr Benjulia, a vivisector investigating the mysteries of the human brain.

Collins's novel brings to light the link between the disciplines which aimed to reconstruct the past from fragmentary evidence and the rise of evolutionary biology, belonging to what Virginia Zimmerman terms 'the literature of excavation' (2008: 3). Indeed, the choice of catalepsy as a plot device to play on memory points to excavating activities directly inspired by geology and palaeontology: sinking lower and lower into unconscious levels of function, as if regressing to a previous stage of human development, cataleptic patients looked dead-alive, and often even risked live burial. Metaphorically speaking, the curing of the medical patient was therefore akin to resurrecting or digging out the truth from the depths of their unconscious. Moreover, allusions to geological research permeate the narrative. At the end of *Heart and Science*, Mrs Gallilee's 'At Home to Science' welcomes 'three superhuman men, who had each a peep behind the veil of creation, and discovered the mystery of life' (Collins, 1994: 348). In one corner, a philosopher argues that 'The sun's life . . . begins with a nebulous infancy and a gaseous childhood' (1994: 348). As the reference to the birth of the sun suggests, *Heart and Science* undoubtedly alludes to the nebular hypothesis of astronomer Pierre Simon Laplace (1749–1827), also developed by John Pringle Nichol (1804–59), professor of astronomy at the university of Glasgow.[4] Not only was Laplace's theory a kind of precursor of evolutionary theories, but, as Lawrence Frank argues, Laplace's hypothesis was also appropriated and developed by British writers, among whom were Robert Chambers (1802–71), who published the *Chambers and Edinburgh Journal*, and John Tyndall (1820–93), who promoted Darwinian evolution. Collins was known to have the ten volumes of Chambers's *Encyclopaedia* in his library, and his friendship with Dickens, who refers to Laplace's hypothesis in *Bleak House* (1852–3), for instance, makes his knowledge of the nebular theory very likely (Baker, 2002: 88). Furthermore, at the end of *Heart and Science*, once Benjulia has freed all the 'creatures' he experimented on, the vivisector is seen, his head 'turned to the stars', held spellbound by 'the bright wintry heaven' (Collins, 1994: 343–4). The mesmerising sight of heaven is situated at the moment when the scientist is struggling with his own conscience and wondering about the existence of God just before he commits suicide: 'Do you believe in God? ... I wonder whether she is right ... It does not matter: I shall soon know' (1994: 341). The conflation of the stars with the scientist's calling into question the existence of God encapsulates the narrative's probing of the origin of life – and thus of the birth of stars and solar systems leading to the beginning of life itself – and is another potential allusion to the nebular hypothesis. In addition, the image of the veil is also used to map out the search for the heroine's origins. Collins had already linked veiled women to secrecy in *Armadale*. But in *Heart and Science* the veil, hinting at origins, is both metaphorical[5] and literal. The 'horrid stain' (1994: 215) which smears Carmina's mother's memory (just as it smears Benjulia's walking stick further on in the novel) is that she is suspected of having had an affair with one of Benjulia's fellow-students in Rome, whilst hiding behind a veil. Though Benjulia had no peep behind the veil, Carmina is accused of being the illegitimate daughter of the veiled woman, the knowledge of which triggers her catalepsy, subjecting her to the gaze of the scientists. Thus, the novel sets side by side two scientists ultimately both attempting to lift the veil on the origins of the earth and of life, and both experimenting on a weak young woman whose origins are unclear.

The novel's focus on vivisection and the value of life, whether human or animal, through the work of Dr Benjulia, works in tandem with Mrs Gallilee's dabbling in science and her interest in physics, astronomy, geology or palaeontology: the character, who knows 'on the best authority, that the world had created itself' (1994: 300), illustrates the new understanding of the earth and of the human's place in the evolution of the globe. Just like the vivisectionist, who aligns 'man' with the other animals on the evolutionary scale and points to 'the insignificance of man' (1994: 102), Gallilee's research into geology or astronomy foregrounds the decentralisation of humanity in the world's ecology: the human acts like the other animals, is no longer at the heart of the system and may even destroy other creatures. Raising the spectre of people's mortality and potential extinction, the two scientists' fields of research inevitably tend to reduce humanity to matter. Mrs Gallilee, whose 'religious convictions began and ended with the inorganic matter of of [*sic*] the earth' (1994: 45), has a 'protoplastic point of view' (1994: 114) very similar to Dr Benjulia's. In fact, if natural historians, astronomers and geologists believed that living creatures originated from atoms of inorganic matter in perpetual motion that were gradually 'transformed into the living cell that became the basis of animate nature' (Frank, 2009: 75), mental physiologists probed consciousness as a protoplasmic mass of matter whose mechanisms could be understood. Hence, through its two villains, the novel questions the view of the universe as merely born out of matter, comparing it with research in mental physiology and the view of humans' consciousness in purely naturalistic terms that parallel it with that of animals.

In medical schools the rise of evolutionary science led physiologists 'to pry into the secrets of Nature' (Collins, 1994: 70); in Collins's novel spies literally intrude upon Carmina's private interviews with Ovid, who himself betrays their secret engagement to his mother, thus triggering Carmina's torments. As her privacy is physically violated (people enter her bedroom, her letters are opened and read, her luggage found), Carmina gradually sinks into a form of morbid sensitivity which the local doctor's tonic cannot touch. Little by little her nervous system begins to exhibit hysterical symptoms, while her body comes to shake and shiver at the slightest sound. Carmina's weak will gradually revamps the Gothic plot, as the image of the fragile and passive heroine becomes enmeshed within the language of physiology.

As suggested, the physiological secrets that may be revealed through (medical) dissection go hand in hand with nature's secrets, both the medical and the natural history fields showing heartless scientists in search of the origins of life. Mrs Gallilee studies the theory of creation and the mechanisms of life, her research resonating with evolutionary theory as she is familiar with zoophyte fossils (1994: 35) and knows everything about 'Geographical Botany' and 'coprolites . . . the fossilized ingestions of extinct reptiles' (1994: 83–5). Mrs Gallilee's interest in coprolites is not just meant to deride the scientist, as has frequently been argued. Of course, the idea of studying fossilised faeces was probably intended as a humorous vignette. But arguably Collins's resort to such a palaeontological vignette aims to strengthen the link between the two mad scientists of the novel. The palaeontological motif conjures up images of excavation activities and scientists' search for the history of life. Moreover, the violence that coprolites revealed by displaying dino-saurs' cannibalistic dietary habits defined the coprolite as an epitome of predation. Thus, Collins's use of coprolites foregrounds palaeonto-logical research, its discoveries and its implications: as palaeontological discoveries revealed the predatory relationships of monstrous extinct creatures, the ecosystems that the scientists reconstructed pointed to the issue of the 'survival of the fittest', gradually paving the way for the development of evolutionary biology. The violence at stake, illus-trated by Mrs Gallilee's success in 'dissecting the nervous system of a bee' (1994: 35) and her passion for dissecting flowers, or Benjulia, the 'dissector of living creatures' (1994: 176), successfully modernises the Gothic plot, hinting at quarries and other earthly depths as images of utter violence. The depths of the body which Benjulia seeks to probe and the depths of the earth host the same buried manuscript, revealing the extent to which, in Robert M. Young's terms, the study of the mind 'had become a biological science' as scientists applied 'the categories of science to the interpretation of man's place in nature' (Young, 1990: 7).

Benjulia is at the last stages of his research when the Gothic plot reaches its climax. Carmina hovers between the animate and the inanimate, rigid and dumb, insensible to touch, and sometimes drift-ing into 'partial unconsciousness' (Collins, 1994: 280), resembling her Radcliffean foresisters' climactic passionate convulsions, in a medical representation of the *Scheintod* or death trance. Framed by medical dis-course, her 'death-struck look' and 'simulated paralysis' (Collins, 1994: 269, 313) reflect the deathlike spells then seen as characteristic of certain hysterical disorders – for example, the 'lucid hysterical lethargy' distin-guished by the French neurologist Gilles de la Tourette (1857–1904). In such cases the patient's pulse rate fell, the heartbeat became inaudible, and the patient grew pale, still and cold, often remaining in that state for several days and facing the risk of live burial (Bondeson, 2002: 251). As a result, Carmina's hypersensitivity, her visionary excitability – as for example when irrationally and superstitiously fearful of her aunt or Benjulia – reconstruct her as a case of double consciousness that calls for a medicalised reading. Carmina then becomes the ideal case study for Benjulia, who allows the incompetent practitioner Mr Null to deal with the patient so that he will be able to witness the evolution of the disease from bad to worse. Benjulia's study of the patient draws upon the methods of comparative anatomy, ultimately confusing Carmina with one of Benjulia's animals: 'she was to take her place, along with the other animals, in his note-book of experiments' (Collins, 1994: 290).

Of course, the immorality associated with dissection and vivisection leads Collins to use another manuscript to recover Carmina's entombed past and stop digging too deeply into the body. The deceased physiologist's manuscript Carmina's lover inherits and which rescues the heroine furthers the narrative's play upon layers of knowledge which must be reconstructed, since the story of this stranger, just like his manuscript, is embedded in one of Ovid's letters to Carmina. In contrast to Benjulia's perverse dissection, Ovid prescribes chemicals for Carmina to help recollect the fragmented pieces of her brain, and the novel seemingly puts an end to its scientists' quests for the origins of life. Or does it, really? As suggested, the novel closes on Mrs Gallilee as a happy woman, entertaining scientists who have discovered the mystery of life. This final example testifies to the changes that marked the sensation novel from its appearance in the early 1860s to the last decades of the nineteenth century, as evolutionary theory had been popularised and increasingly accepted in scientific circles, and as the earth and its mysteries concealed in its bowels had partly revealed the narrative of humanity's history on earth. No longer simply buried in churchyards, human remains were more and more exhibited in medical museums, proudly sitting on the shelves of medical practitioners' offices, as in *Armadale* where a collection of medical cases can be found in Dr Hawbury's house and shapeless dead creatures float in yellow liquid in Dr LeDoux's sanatorium. Exhumed and immortalised in glass jars, these fragments of humanity were part of of a new manuscript that scientists were daily completing. The thrilling stories that sensation novelists offered to their readers from 1859 onwards thus revisit the history of human evolution, and use the Gothic to rewrite the materiality of the human body at a time when identity could be bought behind the counter and when false teeth and hair blurred the boundaries between the human and the artificial.

Notes

1. Rachel's career started shortly after 1859, when she was stricken with fever and had to shave off her locks. One of the doctors of King's College Hospital gave her a lotion to make her hair grow again rapidly and furnished her as well with the recipe. This particular product helped her commercial career on New Bond Street where she opened a shop in the 1860s. Her first attempt as an enameller was undercapitalised and sent her to Whitecross Street Prison for debt. But she was again in business in 1862 and had become very successful by 1863, as her shop front and pamphlet 'Beautiful for Ever' attracted gullible female customers. Yet the effects of her miraculous rejuvenators (mere mixtures of carbonate of lead, starch, Fuller's earth, hydrochloric acid and distilled water) and baths of bran and water did not last. She was tried at the Old Bailey in 1867 for swindling a client, undertaking to make her young again in order for her to charm a nobleman (Anon., 1894: 322–4; Altick, 1991: 540–5).

2. Charles Dickens's *Our Mutual Friend* (1864) goes further than Collins in *The Law and the Lady* by emphasising the parallels between prodding into dust-mounds and palaeontologists' excavating activities.

3. In *Lady Audley's Secret*, body parts play a key role in the investigation: a lock of hair makes Robert realise that the woman buried in Ventnor church-yard is not George's wife, George's letter describing the features of his pretty wife and Lady Audley's 'hand', that is, her handwriting, incriminate the heroine.

4. Laplace's nebular hypothesis posited that galaxies had originated from a diffused cloud of heated gases; the stars and solar systems were formed by the diminishing of the temperature and the condensation of such gases over vast periods of time. Our sun was thus created by such centres of cooling gas, while the orbiting planets were formed by 'the condensed remnants of rings of vapour thrown off by centrifugal force from the cooling, rotating sun' (Frank, 2009: 32–3). Laplace had been influenced by William Herschel's (1738–1822) observation of a luminous nebula of heated gases within the constellation of Orion – which could thus herald the formation of other stars and solar systems. Nichol developed Laplace's hypothesis, as expounded in the latter's *Exposition du système du monde* (1796), and used the metaphor of the veil to dramatise the mystery of the origin of the world: 'a time may come, when the veil can be drawn aside' (Nichol, 1839: 196).

5. The metaphor of the veil, which serves the philosopher to trope the mysteries of life at the end of the novel, was frequent in science writings. Science was deemed able to unveil the mysteries of the universe and to reveal its hidden order (Gibson, 1958: 60–8; Gliserman, 1974–5: 432).

References

Anon. (1859). 'Subterranean Switzerland', *All the Year Round*, 2 (5 November), 25–32.

——(1860). 'Natural selection', *All the Year Round*, 3/63 (7 July), 293–9.

——(1863). 'Not a New Sensation', *All the Year Round*, 9 (25 July), 517–20.

——(1894). 'Madame Rachel', *Notes and Queries*, 8/6, 322–4.

Altick, Richard (1991). *The Presence of the Present: Topics of the Day in the Victorian Novel*. Athens, OH: Ohio State University Press.

Baker, William (2002). *Wilkie Collins's Library: A Reconstruction*. Westport, CT and London: Greenwood Press.

Beer, Gillian (2000). *Darwin's Plots: Evolutionary Narrative in Darwin, George Eliot and Nineteenth-Century Fiction*. Cambridge: Cambridge University Press.

Bondeson, Jan (2002). *Buried Alive: The Terrifying History of Our Most Primal Fear*. New York: Norton.

Braddon, Mary Elizabeth (1862). *Lady Audley's Secret, Sixpenny Magazine*, vol. 3.

Bronfen, Elisabeth (1992). *Over Her Dead Body: Death, Femininity and the Aesthetic*. Manchester: Manchester University Press.

Collins, Wilkie (1994). *Heart and Science* [1883]. Stroud: Alan Sutton.

——(1992) *The Law and the Lady* [1875]. Oxford: Oxford University Press.

——(1860) *The Woman in White. All the Year Round* 3/63 (7 July), 293.

Frank, Lawrence (2009). *Victorian Detective Fiction and the Nature of Evidence: The Scientific Investigations of Poe, Dickens, and Doyle*. London: Palgrave Macmillan.

Gibson, Wilker (1958). 'Behind the Veil: A Distinction Between Poetic and Scientific Language in Tennyson, Lyell, and Darwin', *Victorian Studies*, 11, 60–8.

Ginsburg, Carlo (1992). *Clues, Myth, and the Historical Method*. Baltimore: Johns Hopkins University Press.

Gliserman, Susan (1974–5). 'Early Science Writers and Tennyson's *In Memoriam*: A Study in Cultural Exchange', *Victorian Studies*, 18, 277–308; 437–59.

Mighall, Robert (1999). *A Geography of Victorian Gothic Fiction: Mapping History's Nightmares*. Oxford: Oxford University Press.

Nichol, John Pringle (1839). *Views of the Architecture of the Heavens: In a Series of Letters to a Lady*. 3rd edn. Edinburgh: William Tait.

Richards, Thomas (1990). *The Commodity Culture of Victorian England: Advertising and Spectacle, 1851–1914*. London: Verso.

Thomas, Ronald R. (1999). *Detective Fiction and the Rise of Forensic Science*. Cambridge: Cambridge University Press.

Young, Robert M. (1990). *Mind, Brain, and Adaptation in the Nineteenth Century: Cerebral Localization and its Biological Context from Gall to Ferrier*. New York and Oxford: Oxford University Press.

Zimmerman, Virginia (2008). *Excavating Victorians*. Albany: State University of New York Press.

Chapter 3

Victorian Gothic Pulp Fiction
Jarlath Killeen

Public executions in the nineteenth century were gruesome and dirty affairs – though also apparently great fun (for a good study, see Gatrell, 1994). The condemned were marched from prison to the gallows through streets thronged with jeering, cheering spectators who gorged on food sold by the wandering street sellers and entertained themselves by throwing a large variety of disgusting missiles at both the prisoners and those guarding them: dead cats were a favourite, but the entrails of slaughtered animals, dung and other excreta, dead fish and vegetable refuse were common projectiles as well. By the time the prisoners actually arrived at the gallows they were covered with the debris of urban life, stank to high heaven and were often bleeding from injuries inflicted by thrown objects. Prior to one execution in 1810, the public almost stormed the pillory where four men were waiting to be executed and continued to pelt the prisoners with a huge variety of objects: 'mud, dead cats, rotten eggs, potatoes, and buckets filled with blood, offal, and dung' (quoted in White, 2006: 405). So smelly did such scenes get that one commentator, G. J. Holyoake, claimed that the crowd attending an execution in Glasgow in 1853 resembled 'an avalanche of ordure' (quoted in Gatrell, 1994: 60).

The actual hanging itself was enjoyably gory as well. A. S. Taylor's *The Principles and Practice of Medical Jurisprudence* (1894) described the:

> lividity and swelling of the face, especially of the ears and lips . . . the eyelids swollen, and of a blueish colour, projecting forwards, and sometimes partially forced out of their cavities . . . a bloody froth or froth mucus . . . escaping from the lips and nostrils . . . urine and faeces are sometimes involuntarily expelled at the moment of death. (quoted in Gatrell, 1994: 46)

It generally took a while for the prisoner to die, and she or he would often convulse and spasm for a long time with the crowd yelling and applauding each agonising twitch. After the execution of James Greenacre in 1837 (for the murder of Hannah Brown), the *Morning Chronicle* of 7 May complained that: 'as the body hung quivering in mortal agonies, the eyes of the assembled thousands were riveted upon the swaying corpse with a kind of satisfaction. . . . The crowd seemed as if they never could satisfy themselves with gazing at the hanging murderer' (Anon., 1837: 2). Of course, the indignities of the executed did not end upon death, nor did the enjoyment of the crowd. After the execution of William Corder, convicted of the murder of his lover, Maria Marten in 1827 (the famous 'Red Barn' case), the eight thousand strong crowd were treated to a display of the dead man's naked body at the town's Shire Hall. The corpse was later subjected to galvanic experiments, and Corder's pickled scalp was exhibited by an Oxford Street leather seller (Flanders, 2011: 53–5).

Charles Dickens was especially disgusted by the scenes he witnessed at the execution in November 1849 of Maria and Frederick George Manning who had been convicted of the murder of Maria's lover Patrick O'Connor. Dickens was so appalled by the spectacle that he wrote a letter to the *Times* condemning the entire day's amusement, noting particularly the pleasure the thirty thousand strong crowd had enjoyed:

> I believe that a sight so inconceivably awful as the wickedness and levity of the immense crowd collected at that execution this morning could be imagined by no man, and could be presented in no heathen land under the sun. The horrors of the gibbet and of the crime which brought the wretched murderers to it faded in my mind before the atrocious bearing, looks, and language of the assembled spectators. When I came upon the scene at midnight, the shrillness of the cries and howls that were raised from time to time, denoting that they came from a concourse of boys and girls already assembled in the best places, made my blood run cold. As the night went on, screeching, and laughing, and yelling in strong chorus of parodies on negro melodies . . . were added to these. When the day dawned, thieves, low prostitutes, ruffians, and vagabonds of every kind, flocked on to the ground, with every variety of offensive and foul behaviour. Fightings, faintings, whistlings, imitations of *Punch*, brutal jokes, tumultuous demonstrations of indecent delight when swooning women were dragged out of the crowd by the police, with their dresses disordered, gave a new zest to the general entertainment. (Dickens, 1981: 12–13)

In other words, a good time was being had by all, except the moral minority. In 1866 the Revd S. G. Osborne, a Dorsetshire rector, complained that public executions attracted 'a crowd notoriously composed of those who are the very scum of mankind', and whose behaviour was so filthy as to 'pollute the very air' (quoted in McGowen, 1994: 267; for more on crowd behaviour in this period, see Laqueur, 1989a).

Victorian executions were rather tame affairs in comparison to the executions of previous centuries. Michel Foucault's *Discipline and Punish* (1975), famously opens with a description of the public execution of Robert-Francois Damiens the regicide on 2 March 1757. Damiens was sentenced to have:

> the flesh ... torn from his breasts, arms, thighs, and calves with red-hot pincers, his right hand, holding the knife with which he committed the said [regicide], burnt with sulphur, and, on those places where the flesh will be torn away, poured molten lead, boiling oil, burning resin, wax and sulphur melted together and then his body drawn and quartered by four horses and his limbs and body consumed by fire, reduced to ashes and his ashes thrown to the winds. (Foucault, 1977: 3)

Such public scenes of extraordinary violence and gore were slowly phased out of public life in the course of the nineteenth century. Increasingly, conventional histories tell us, the Victorians became less interested in seeing real violence on their streets and legislation was passed to banish such bloodshed from public view (see Halttunen, 1995). This 'humanitarian' discomfort with cruelty emerged from the eighteenth century's cult of sensibility and the growth of Romanticism. Sensibility emphasised the need to awaken to a considerate concern for the sufferings of others, for which cult the 'man of feeling' became a kind of poster boy. The 'man of feeling' could be driven to tears at the sight of the pain of others and he despised all kinds of cruelty and torture. Compassion became a sensitivity fashionable to maintain, while any enjoyment of brutality was considered a badge of barbarism and savagery (for these changes see, among many others, Thomas, 1984; Barker-Benfield, 1992). Campaigns to banish displays of pain from public life succeeded. In 1835 bear-baiting, bull-baiting and the baiting of wild animals were banned. There were numerous reforms in the treatment of the insane, with new methods of 'moral management' replacing what came to be seen as barbaric practices. Flogging in the navy came under scrutiny as an inhuman practice. Even corporal punishment of children was looked on with disfavour by some of the new sentimentalists. And, of course, the public punishment and execution of criminals was brought to an end in 1868 (see Andrew, 1980; Bending, 2000: chs. 4, 5 and 6; French, 1975; Ignatieff, 1978; Laqueur, 1989b; Malcolmson, 1973; McGowen, 1994; Plumb, 1975; Ritvo, 1987; Scull, 1981; Spierenburg, 1984; Thomas, 1984; Wiener, 1990: ch. 3).

Fascination with violence and gore had not gone away, of course. Traditional accounts emphasise that instead of public displays the masses had to resort to private consumption of violent literature to get their bloody fill, but especially the versions of pulp fiction found in publications such as the *Terrific Register* (1825) (a collection of gruesome stories of 'true crimes'), the *Newgate Calendar* (eighteenth-century criminal biographies), the 'Newgate novels' (especially *Paul Clifford* (1830) and *Eugene Aram* (1832) by Edward Bulwer-Lytton, and *Rookwood* (1834) and *Jack Sheppard* (1839) by William Harrison Ainsworth which had criminal protagonists and which were accused, essentially, of glamorising crime), Penny Bloods and Penny Dreadfuls. Penny Bloods – a name first used as a term of attack – were cheap (one-penny) serials sold primarily to an audience locked out of the novel market because of price and were mostly published in the early half of the nineteenth century, chiefly on historical and criminal subjects. They were written in staccato style, with short sentences and single-sentence paragraphs, and were extraordinarily repetitious. Penny Dreadfuls emerged out of the Bloods, but were aimed specifically at a juvenile audience and were mostly published in the second half of the century. Together, they constitute an extraordinarily large body of work, a body of which it is impossible to gain critical mastery (these genres are still relatively neglected, but see: Anglo, 1977; Drotner, 1988; Hollingsworth, 1963; James, 1974; Springhall, 1999). One crucial ingredient of a great deal of this pulp fiction is a focus on violence, torture, blood and gore which has tended to be read as a kind of imaginative replacement for the public spectacles of violence coming under attack and finally outlawed in the same period. As Karen Halttunen argues: 'Historically, just as the spectacle of punishment was coming under humanitarian attack, an imaginative literature appeared . . . the social theater of public punishment gave way to a solitary fantasy theater, which staged private, interior scenarios of cruelty; legitimate spectatorship was replaced by furtive voyeurism' (1995: 334).

This argument seems plausible, and it was certainly felt that the same people who attended public executions, and enjoyed urban blood sports, were also the readers of penny fiction. John Hibbert MP claimed in 1864 that the kind of people who attended public executions were 'generally speaking, not the most intelligent and reflecting, but, on the contrary . . . of the classes most hardened, and who could witness executions without being in the least moved or deterred by them' (quoted in McGowen, 1994: 268–9). And this was exactly the readership the penny fiction aimed at attracting. Likewise, if, for Henry Rich MP, the crowds at executions were drawn there 'by a certain fascination or attraction for scenes of blood and strong excitement' (quoted in McGowen, 1994: 269), this was to be precisely the charge laid at the door of pulp fiction readers who were accused of a blatant immorality in having such bad taste.

For Foucault, the shift from public spectacle to private reading, the new humanitarianism which banished cruelty from public spaces, is ideologically suspicious. The supposedly sympathetic treatment of the insane, for example, and the humanitarian treatment of criminals, moved treatment inside and away from the public eye, but this did not genuinely make it any less violent. Instead of the previously straightforward manner in which the bodies of criminals were broken in public, the mind of the criminal was now shaped and made docile by the implementation of psychological regimes of control which disciplined the soul. Foucault appears to celebrate the spectacle involved in public execution and punishment – no matter how bloody and violent – because there is in it a sense of potential state subversion. He suggests that:

> If the crowd gathered round the scaffold, it was not simply to witness the sufferings of a condemned man or to excite the anger of the executioner: it was also to hear someone who had nothing left to lose curse the judges, laws, power, religion. Death-by-torture allowed the condemned man this momentary saturnalia, where nothing was prohibited or punishable. (1977: 60)

Public execution confers a kind of greatness on the criminal who is to suffer in such an extraordinary manner, and allows the crowd to simultaneously condemn and yet also celebrate this figure who has transgressed the boundaries of normative behaviour. In their own 'disgusting' actions around the gallows, the crowd breeches the niceties of state control and, together, both the act of criminality and the celebrations at the punishment manifest how humans challenge public control. Public fun at executions is thus a kind of threat to the state (for an alternative reading of the penitentiary reforms, see Spierenburg, 1984). The shift to reading about blood rather than witnessing it directly tames the subversive potential in public execution.

The Penny Bloods and Dreadfuls come under the broad genre of 'Gothic', and Gothic has always been interested in torture, bodily violence and gore. According to Darryl Jones, the genre emerged in the eighteenth century partly to articulate English nationalist hatred towards foreigners: hating others is one of the primary reasons that horror exists (2002: ch. 1). This hatred was directed towards literal 'others': the French, the Italians, the Scottish, the Welsh, the Irish and Catholics. Gothic expressed and appeased a legitimate hatred towards 'otherness' and bodies carrying otherness. To penetrate and destroy the Catholic body, or to depict foreign 'others' attempting to penetrate the Protestant self, in texts like *The Monk* (1796) or *Melmoth the Wanderer* (1820), was to attempt to isolate and eliminate the terrifying monstrosity that threatened the integrity of the self: Gothic was a means of self-protection in an era of danger from war and invasion. This literature certainly supports Elaine Scarry's argument that torture is a complex system which exists not in order to elicit dangerous secrets from enemies but to project an image of power for a regime that finds itself under threat (Scarry, 1987: 28). But it also functions to demonstrate the horrific alterity of the torturer when he is practising torture on the body of the good self. Torture and representations of torture confirm the power of one group by denying the voice, the agency, ultimately the civilization of the other side through conversion of an individual's pain. Again, we cannot overplay this as altogether innovative in terms of Gothic. Martyrologies, and especially John Foxe's *Book of Martyrs* (1563), revelled in describing acts of horrific brutality carried out by Catholics against innocent Protestants, and had some really good illustrations thrown in as well. Scenes of torture were the *raison d'être* of Foxe's text, one encountered by practically every person in Britain. If anything, the Gothic novel toned down the kinds of torture you could encounter in your visits to church. In monstering the Catholic and foreign other, a stable British identity – and a stable cosmopolitan identity – could be constructed, and in enacting a kind of scapegoating violence upon that other body, a national catharsis could be achieved.

The difference between this early body horror and that found in the nineteenth-century penny press is that whereas public and private spectacles involving bodily disintegration and desubjectivity had been directed previously at 'others' – however we may figure those others – in the Victorian period such attacks on subjectivity became more expansive and embraced everyone; rather than articulating a hatred of others, the penny press articulates a hatred of everybody (including the reading self). In witnessing representational acts of torture and violence on a weekly basis in the penny press, an extraordinary violence directed everywhere and nowhere, at everyone and no one, the readers could imagine that they too were being taken to pieces, that they too were human dirt and debris, and that human subjectivity itself was being done away with in fantastical and terrifying ways.

A bourgeois attempt to control and channel the dangerous and disgusting pleasures of the working classes is, *pace* Foucault, not really the best explanation for the explosion in nineteenth-century body horror, and there is a less intellectually exhilarating reason why desubjectivity and dismemberment became so widely consumed in the nineteenth century. For one thing, there appeared to be an all-out assault on the integrity of the human subject in the growing disciplines of geology, biology, archaeology and anthropology, and as nineteenth-century citizens came to grips with the immeasurability of 'deep time', and the relative insignificance of individual human life, many turned to certain genres to provide a kind of consolation for the apparent loss of human significance (for the existential shock inflicted by 'deep time', see Buckley, 1966; for Victorian autobiography, see Buckley, 1984). And if intellectual assaults on previous notions of human integrity and individual subjectivity help to partly explain why the literate classes of Victorian England should have turned to the penny press to supply a virtual slaughterhouse of representational examples of such desubjectified bodies, the working classes, crowded into the rather less intellectually stimulated and salubrious quarters of city life, had to encounter such desubjectification every day of their lives. London, for example, was a city in which the slums had grown exponentially throughout the century, and where what Roy Porter calls 'catastrophic overcrowding' was simply a fact of life. Porter cites the 1841 census which recorded that in Goodge Place, off Tottenham Court Road, 485 people occupied a mere 27 houses, a kind of overcrowding that seemed to simply increase as the century progressed (quoted in Porter, 2000: 324). In Andrew Mearns's famous *Bitter Cry of Outcast London* (1883), he describes attempting to penetrate one slum:

> To get to them you have to penetrate courts reeking with poisonous and malodorous gases arising from accumulations of sewage and refuse scattered in all directions and often flowing beneath your feet; courts, many of them which the sun never penetrates, which are never visited by a breath of fresh air, and which rarely know the virtues of a drop of cleansing water . . .You have to grope your way along dark and filthy passages swarming with vermin. Then, if you are not driven back by the intolerable stench, you may gain admittance to the dens . . . (Mearns, 1970: 58)

Of course, life for medieval man was hardly a picnic, but there were never so many of them in the one place at the same time, and never so many who required reading materials to satisfy cultural hunger. It is difficult to imagine how human dignity was maintained in these places, although, as the sociologist Louis Wirth outlines, the development of an 'urban personality' which reduces humans to functional cogs, appears to be one way of coping in such an environment. As Wirth explains:

> the multiplication of persons in a state of interaction under conditions which make their contact as full personalities impossible produces that segmentalization of human relationships . . . the reserve, the indifference, and the *blasé* outlook which urbanites manifest in their relationships may thus be regarded as devices for immunizing themselves against the personal claims and expectations of others. (Wirth, 1938: 19–20; see also Simmel, 1950: 409–24)

In 1851 the Ecclesiological Society recorded that after death, working-class families often had to keep a corpse in shared living quarters for many days before the burial, often with the carcass liquefying and become putrescent before their eyes (Gatrell, 1994: 76). Existential unease combined with appalling living conditions make for a potent brew, which might partly explain a mass consumption of fiction in which the squalid self is central. The violence to the body in Victorian pulp, and the wallowing in gore and disgust found in the street theatre of public violence, can be read as attempts to come to terms with the ever-increasing sense of desubjectivity and depersonalisation experienced by large numbers of people in the Victorian cities on a daily basis.

The centrality of violence to these pulp fictions can scarcely be exaggerated. Whereas in the traditional Gothic novel, scenes of torture and gore were payoffs of sorts, in that a long novel would contain relatively few and usually occluded (though satisfying all the same) moments of violent extremity, in the Bloods and the Dreadfuls, the plots (where they had one – the commentator James Greenwood was particularly contemptuous of the lack of actual storyline), were merely vehicles to get the reader from one scene of gore, violence and torture to the next: 'There is no such thing as 'plot' in this sort of literature. Such an arrangement would only embarrass the publisher, whose sole and single aim is to go on supplying his public' (1874: 160–1). Torture as plot device is appropriated by the Dreadfuls from the Gothic, but while torture is ideologically driven in John Foxe's work as a way of monstering Catholics, there is no 'other' who is monstered in the penny press. It is difficult to imagine the Dreadfuls as connected ideologically. As a genre pulp is literally dissolute, out of the control of individual authors or publishers. The sheer number of Bloods and Dreadfuls is difficult to estimate, but there were about one hundred publishers of penny fiction which Judith Flanders reckons is ten times the number publishing respectable fiction (2011: 58). The various authors themselves held very different ideological positions or (most usually) none at all in that pulps were written by those who just wanted to make a quick buck. Gore and torture are provided by them all, not because they are ideologically committed to the Protestant cause, but because that is what the genre demanded of them. They were not about (or only incidentally about) hating others, and more interested in hating everyone – everyone was grist for the gore mill, anyone could be next for the chop.

In Penny Dreadfuls such violence is not incidental or simply a means of driving the plot. The plot is, instead, structured around the moments of intense violence. Even in Dreadfuls where these scenes are relatively short or take up a relatively small amount of textual space, blood is essentially the reason why they exist in the first place. As the publisher Edward Lloyd emphasised to one of his woodcut illustrators, 'there must be more blood, much more blood!' (Sala, 1895: 175). Kaplan is essentially correct when she argues that 'telling stories about trauma . . . [may] permit a kind of empathetic "sharing" that moves us forward, if only by inches' (2005: 37), and in nineteenth-century pulp, what needs to be 'worked through' is a collective loss of subjectivity, and an entropic attraction to this loss of subjectivity.

In specific instances, this does not immediately seem to be the case. One of the most prolific writers of Victorian pulp, G. W. M. Reynolds, in many ways simply continued the kinds of chauvinistic nationalist bias found in early Gothic, using the form as a means of attacking his political opponents but also opponents of the state. Given his republican, atheist, revolutionary sympathies this meant that his targets were broad and everyone from Queen Victoria to petty bureaucrats in the Ottoman Empire was bombarded with hysterically aimed verbal assaults. His *Wagner, the Wehr-Wolf* (1846–7) is in part an attack on Christianity itself, though mostly the Catholic expression of it, as a diabolically prejudiced, torturing, ignorant force in the world. The novel is set in the sixteenth century, and involves Wagner, a man in his nineties when the story opens, who is persuaded by Faust to accept monthly transformation into a wolf in exchange for a return to youth and an expanded intellect. Wagner falls fatally in love with an extraordinarily beautiful yet sociopathic Florentine, Nisida, whose pathological pride in her family name and deranged desire to revenge the murder of her mother by her father, leads her to kill, maim and imprison anyone she considers a threat. Many scenes take place in those crucibles of early Gothic fantasy, the dungeons of a convent and the torture rooms of the Inquisition, and so continue that venerable tradition of representing Catholics as sex-repressing torturers.

The interesting point about these scenes is that whereas the ideological force behind them is still evident, the inflicted violence exceeds what is necessary to make the political point. For example, towards the end of the book one of the minor characters, Giulia, Countess of Arestino, is being racked by the Inquisition, mainly because she has been carrying on an affair with the feckless though handsome Manuel d'Orsini:

> . . . agonising – oh! most agonising were the female shrieks and rending screams which emanated from the lips of the tortured victim . . .
>
> The white and polished arms were stretched out, in a position fearfully painful, beyond the victim's head: and the wrists were fastened to a steel bar by means of a thin cord, which cut through flesh, muscle, and nerve to the very bone!

The ankles were attached in a similar manner to a bar at the lower end of the rack – and thus from the female's hands and feet thick clots of gore fell on the stone pavement. But even the blood flowed not so fast from her lacerated limbs as streamed the big drops of agony from her distorted countenance. (Reynolds, 2006: 394–5)

The shift here is away from the ideological reasons behind the torture and to the torture itself, and the aesthetic reduction of a character to clots of gore and blood, looks of agony. Giulia is rendered into a body here, her character stripped away, replaced by a mass of pain and bodily fluid. The problem with this torture scene in *Wagner* becomes all too clear: it is not simply excessive, it is beyond any kind of ideological point that could possibly be made. And given that Reynolds is one of the most explicitly ideological of all the Dreadful writers, this is what is most surprising. Of course, the werewolf transformation central to the plot re-enacts the central drama of the torture scene over and over again, because in the horrific change from man to beast, Wagner too is desubjectified and made animalistic. The description of the morphosis emphasises the dehumanisation of a character we have come to care about as Wagner's 'handsome' features:

elongate into one of savage and brute-like shape – the rich garment that he wears becomes a rough, shaggy, and wiry skin – his body loses its human contours – his arms and limbs take another form; and, with a frantic howl of misery . . . the wretch starts wildly away – no longer a man, but a monstrous wolf. (2006: 63)

Varney the Vampire; or, The Feast of Blood (1845–7) was published in 109 parts and was almost certainly written by James Malcolm Rymer (though there may be interpolations from other writers hired by the publisher, Edward Lloyd), one of the most prolific hack writers of the century. It concerns the adventures of Sir Francis Varney, as he attempts to satisfy his desire for blood, and is a surprisingly sympathetic portrait of a genuinely tortured individual who becomes so tired of his life that at the end he throws himself into Mount Vesuvius.

The incidents of violence in this 'novel' are plentiful and – when the apparent 'plot' is abandoned half-way through – become much more numerous. In chapter 48 of the interminable series, for example, the villagers rush a local inn in which they believe Varney to be resident, take control of the corpse of a recent guest who had died, and propose driving a stake through its body:

This was a terrific proposition; and even those who felt most strongly upon the subject, and had their fears most awakened, shrank from carrying it into effect. Others, again, applauded it, although they determined, in their own minds, to keep far enough off from the execution of the job . . .

We cannot, for we revolt from the office, describe particularly the dreadful outrage which was committed upon the corpse; suffice it that two or three, maddened by drink, and incited by others, plunged the hedge-stake through the body, and there left it, a sickening and a horrible spectacle to any one who might cast his eyes upon it.

Some asserted, that at that moment an audible groan came from the dead man, and that this arose from the extinguishment of that remnant of life which remained in him . . .

Others, again, were quite ready to swear, that at the moment the stake was used, there was a visible convulsion of all the limbs, and that the countenance, before so placid and calm, became immediately distorted, as if with agony.

But we have done with these horrible surmises; the dreadful deed has been committed, and wild, ungovernable superstition has had, for a time, its sway over the ignorant and debased. (Rymer, 2008: 222)

Some critics have been rather taken in by the narrator's position in this section. For Troy Boone, for example, the lesson of this scene is obvious: it tries to get its readers to realise that though violence may be fascinating, they should rather emulate the narrator than the mob and find themselves 'sickened' by it. In this scene specifically, the narrator 'raises the reader's interest in violence in order to undermine fascination with it and to direct the reader's interest towards other possibilities' (Boone, 2005: 57, 53). *Varney* is, in this reading, a text which constantly returns to extreme images of violence to simultaneously acknowledge our fascination with such things only to effectively warn us against such an obsession (by making us repulsed by it).

This argument is certainly very attractive, but comes against the problem that the incident takes place in chapter 48, and that we have to get to chapter 236 before reaching the end of all this violence. Far from being redirected away from violence, the readers are encouraged to come back for more and more – and it was not Rymer's decision to cut his serial short at 236 chapters; his publisher, Edward Lloyd, simply got tired of it. Although it sometimes inveighs against violence and superstition, against attacks on the body, *Varney* is really just another excuse for indulging in such attacks. Rather than a genuine warning against tales of violence and repellent murder, *Varney* is another of those tales (and for that reason found itself condemned by the gatekeepers of high culture). Warning against violence is just another excuse to present yet another violent scene.

Indeed, *Varney* could be accused of using such warnings as ideological screens to distract from the nihilism of the violence it does depict.

This, of course, is not really a reason to condemn it, though its false representation of itself as something other than a catalogue of violent deeds is highly suspicious. While *Varney* rhetorically seeks to critique a dependence on violence by its readership, it actively promotes it by always promising that the best and more violent incidents are still to come. *Varney* becomes more violent as the serial progresses, not so that readers becomes so overloaded with scenes of violence that they eventually become repelled, but because an increase of violence meant an increase in sales. When a reader becomes jaded by the violent scenes it is because Rymer has run out of novel ways to present such violence, not because it is the violence itself that becomes tiresome.

Moreover, in *Varney*, the violence can go anywhere. In Chapter 80, for example, an apparently random figure bumbles into the area where Varney is terrorising the Bannerworth family, and immediately finds himself suspected of being a vampire. He pleads with the crowd, 'I am no vampyre . . . I am new to these parts . . . I have done you no wrong. Hear me, – I know nothing of these people of whom you speak.' He is attacked and tries to run, but is struck down and while he pleads for his life, he is ignored: 'The man attempted to get up, but, in doing so, he received a heavy blow from a hedge-stake, wielded by the Herculean arm of a peasant. The sound of the blow was heard by those immediately around, and the man fell dead' (2008: 318–19). Violence here is random rather than directed – the potential existence of vampires is merely an excuse to see another body being pummelled. The notion that the desire for violence is confined to the working classes and the peasantry is not, however, really entertained by the 'novel'. After all, Sir Francis Varney, despite his sympathetic depiction, rather enjoys his own acts of violence, and often creeps up on his victims slowly (like the narrative itself) as if to prolong the suffering: 'The intruder gazed at the young girl for some moments, and clasped his hands with trembling eagerness, and a ghastly smile played upon his features, while a fearful fire shot from the eyes of one who thus disturbed the slumbers of the living' (2008: 499). He describes his blood drinking as 'midnight orgies', explicitly connecting his acts of violence and exploitation with sexual pleasure (2008: 627).

Reading nineteenth-century pulp fiction raises serious questions about human subjectivity and agency, and directs the reader back to the social and intellectual conditions in which this material was produced. The extraordinary number of Bloods and Dreadfuls, and the mind-boggling obsession with gore and violence in them, warns against too easy a reading of the Victorian as an increasingly 'humanitarian' age, and tells a great deal about the kind of dehumanisation suffered by vast numbers of people in the towns and cities who sought out a reflection and interrogation of this daily squalor in the reading material they purchased.

References

Andrew, Donna T. (1980). 'The Code of Honour and its Critics: The Opposition to Duelling in England, 1700–1850', *Social History*, 5, 409–34.

Anglo, Michael (1977). *Penny Dreadfuls and Other Victorian Horrors*. London: Jupiter Books.

Anon. (1837). 'The Execution of Greenacre', *Morning Chronicle*, no. 21,053.

——(1858). 'The Byways of Literature: Reading for the Millions', *Blackwood's Magazine*, 84, 200–16.

Barker-Benfield, G. J. (1992). *The Culture of Sensibility: Sex and Society in Eighteenth-Century Britain*. Chicago: University of Chicago Press.

Bending, Lucy (2000). *The Representation of Bodily Pain in Late Nineteenth-century English Culture*. Oxford: Clarendon Press.

Boone, Troy (2005). *Youth of Darkest England: Working-Class Children at the Heart of Victorian Empire*. New York and London: Routledge.

Buckley, Jerome H. (1966). *The Triumph of Time: A Study of the Victorian Concepts of Time, History, Progress, and Decadence*. Cambridge, MA: Harvard University Press.

——(1984). *The Turning Key: Autobiography and the Subjective Impulse since 1800*. Cambridge, MA: Harvard University Press.

Dickens, Charles (1981). *The Pilgrim Edition of the Letters of Charles Dickens*, vol. 5: *1847–49*, ed. Graham Storey and K. J. Fielding. Oxford: Oxford University Press.

Drotner, Kirsten (1988). *English Children and Their Magazines, 1751–1945*. New Haven, CT: Yale University Press.

Flanders, Judith (2011). *The Invention of Murder*. London: HarperCollins.

Foucault, Michel (1977). *Discipline and Punish: The Birth of the Prison*, trans. Alan Sheridan. Harmondsworth: Penguin.

French, Richard D. (1975). *Antivivisection and Medical Science in Victorian Society*. Princeton: Princeton University Press.

Gatrell, V. A. C (1994). *The Hanging Tree: Execution and the English People, 1770–1868*. Oxford: Oxford University Press.

Greenwood, James (1874). *The Wilds of London*. London: Chatto and Windus.

Halttunen, Karen (1995). 'Humanitarianism and the Pornography of Pain in Anglo-American Culture', *The American Historical Review*, 100/2, 303–34.

Hollingsworth, Keith (1963). *The Newgate Novel, 1830–1847: Bulwer, Ainsworth, Dickens, and Thackeray*. Detroit: Wayne State University Press.

Ignatieff, Michael (1978). *A Just Measure of Pain: The Penitentiary and the Industrial Revolution, 1750–1850*. Basingstoke: Macmillan.

James, Louis (1974). *Fiction for the Working Man, 1830–50: A Study of the Literature Produced for the Working Classes in Early Victorian Urban England*. Harmondsworth: Penguin.

Jones, Darryl (2002). *Horror: A Thematic History in Fiction and Film*. London: Arnold.

Kaplan, E. Ann (2005). *Trauma Culture: The Politics of Terror and Loss in Media and Literature*. New Brunswick, NJ: Rutgers University Press.

Laqueur, Thomas W. (1989a). 'Crowds, Carnival and the State in English Executions, 1604–1868', in *The First Modern Society: Essays in Honour of Lawrence Stone*, ed. A. E. Beier, David Cannadine, and James S. Rosenheim. Cambridge: Cambridge University Press, pp. 305–56.

——(1989b). 'Bodies, Details, and the Humanitarian Narrative', in *The New Cultural History*, ed. Lynn Hunt. Berkeley: University of California Press, pp. 176–204.

Malcolmson, Robert W. (1973). *Popular Recreations in English Society 1700–1850*. London: Cambridge University Press.

McGowen, Randall (1994). 'Civilizing Punishment: The End of the Public Execution in England', *Journal of British Studies*, 33, 257–82.

Mearns, Andrew (1970). *The Bitter Cry of Outcast London*. Leicester: Leicester University Press.

Plumb, J. H. (1975). 'The New World of Children in Eighteenth Century England', *Past and Present*, 67, 64–95.

Porter, Roy (2000). *London: A Social History*. Harmondsworth: Penguin.

Reynolds, George W. M. (2006). *Wagner the Werewolf* [1846–7], ed. and intro. by Dick Collins. London: Wordsworth.

Ritvo, Harriet (1987). *The Animal Estate: The English and Other Creatures in the Victorian Age*. Cambridge, MA: Harvard University Press.

Rymer, James Malcolm (2008). *Varney the Vampire* [1845–7], introduction and notes by Curt Herr. Crestline, CA: Zittaw Press.

Sala, George Augustus (1895). *The Life and Adventures of George Augustus Sala, Written by Himself*, vol. 1. New York: Charles Scribner's Sons.

Scarry, Elaine (1987). *The Body in Pain: The Making and Unmaking of the World*. Oxford: Oxford University Press.

Scull, Andrew (ed.) (1981). *Madhouses, Mad-Doctors, and Madmen: The Social History of Psychiatry in the Victorian Era*. London: Athlone.

Simmel, Georg (1950). 'Metropolis and Mental Life' [1903] in *The Sociology of Georg Simmel*, trans. Kurt Wolff. Glencoe, IL: The Free Press, pp. 409–24.

Spierenburg, Pieter (1984). *The Spectacle of Suffering: Executions and the Evolution of Repression; From a Preindustrial Metropolis to the European Experience*. Cambridge: Cambridge University Press.

Springhall, John (1999). *Youth, Popular Culture and Moral Panics: Penny Gaffs to Gangsta Rap, 1830–1996*. New York: St Martin's Press.

Thomas, Keith (1984). *Man and the Natural World: A History of the Modern Sensibility*. Harmondsworth: Penguin.

White, Jerry (2006). *London in the Nineteenth Century: 'A Human Awful Wonder of God'*. London: Jonathan Cape.

Wiener, Martin J. (1990). *Reconstructing the Criminal: Culture, Law, and Policy in England, 1830–1914*. Cambridge: Cambridge University Press.

Wirth, Louis (1938). 'Urbanism as a Way of Life', *The American Journal of Sociology*, 44, 1, 1–24.

Chapter 4

Victorian Gothic Drama
Diane Long Hoeveler

Victorian Gothic drama can most fruitfully be examined by recognising that it was not a 'pure' genre, but rather a hybridised form that made use of a number of formulaic 'Gothic devices', such as the foreboding or premonitory dream, the uncanny double, the confusion between the real and the fantastic, the devilish villain with quasi-supernatural powers, and the use of cathedrals or exotic locales as settings. Contemporary theoretical writings on the drama of this period are relatively sparse and limited to the overviews written by Archer, Filon, Scott, and James. Critics today tend to claim that the drama of this period was concerned with exploring thematic concerns like changing gender roles, marriage and class issues, nationalistic anxieties about invasion and empire, and xenophobia (Booth, 1965; Hadley, 1995: Taylor, 1989).

Victorian Gothic Drama can also be approached by dividing it into early, middle and late periods. The early period, 1820–50, is characterised by revivals of even earlier Gothic dramas, like Matthew Lewis's *The Castle Spectre* (1797) or Thomas Holcroft's *A Tale of Mystery* (1801), but more importantly by new plays that were melodramatic adaptations of popular Gothic poems, stories or novels, most notably James Planché's *The Vampire: or, The Bride of the Isles* (1820), Richard B. Peake's *Presumption, or the Fate of Frankenstein* (1823), and Edward Fitzball's *Esmeralda; or The Deformed of Notre Dame* (1834). The first two early plays were consistently revived and held their popularity through the middle of the nineteenth century, indeed Dion Boucicault would write another version of *The Vampire* in 1852, featuring Alan Ruby, a Restoration vampire who is finally dispatched by Dr Rees, a student of the supernatural, with a charmed bullet (Murray, 2004: 189). And Fitzball in 1855 would write the English libretto for a four-act opera by Edward Loder, *Raymond and Agnes*, itself an earlier melodramatic adaptation of one of the inset tales within Lewis's novel *The Monk* (1796). The multiple adaptations of *Frankenstein* and *Dracula* (1897) would spawn in mutated form the later film franchises that became so prominent within the horror film genre. The third work listed above was the first of literally dozens of dramatic and filmic adaptations of Victor Hugo's novel *Notre-Dame de Paris*. Gradually, however, Victorian Gothic drama gave way to a middle period, 1850–80, during which time technical innovations like the 'vampire trap' or 'Pepper's Ghost' became popular in melodramas like Dion Boucicault's *The Corsican Brothers* (1852), an adaptation of Dumas' novel of the same name, and John Pepper's adaptation of Charles Dickens's novella 'The Haunted Man, and the Ghost's Bargain' (1862). Finally, in late Victorian Gothic dramas (1870–1910), a rise and prominence of 'star vehicles' occurs, such as those produced by Bram Stoker and starring Henry Irving at the Lyceum theatre: Leopold Lewis's *The Bells* (1871); W. G. Wills and Percy FitzGerald's *Vanderdecken* (1878), an adaptation of Wagner's *The Flying Dutchman*; W. G. Wills's adaptation of Goethe's *Faust* (1885); and Henry Merivale's *Ravenswood* (1890), an adaptation of Scott's *Bride of Lammermoor*.

A brief understanding of theatre's clientele may help to explain some of the editorial decisions made in adapting plays for the English stage and patrons. Stuart explains that the nature of the rough and vulgar audiences led to the need for a recessed stage area (1994: 91). Thus, instead of a thrust or forestage, the proscenium style of stage gained popularity during the early 1800s (Stuart, 1994: 91), hence the use of tableaux (Meisel, 1983). To offer an idea of what the typical audience was like at this time, Stuart also offers some statistics: London was undergoing an influx of poor and lower-class individuals and members of the middle class were moving out (1994: 5); one in five people signed their marriage license with an 'X', so considering that many poor could not afford marriage and many illiterate people could not write their own names, we can conclude that there was a fairly high illiteracy rate (1994: 5); by 1840 London had a population of 1.5 million people with 80,000 prostitutes (one in nine women) and '30,000 "professional" beggars' (1994: 5).

As far as formalistic elements are concerned: Victorian drama used four dominant modes under which the Gothic wrote its dramatic script: the *Tableau*, a portrait-like, freeze-frame with moments that could be taken for still pictures (Stuart, 1994: 80); the *Melodrama*, or the use of music, stock characters and action (Booth, 1981; McFarland, 1987: 25). Other characteristics of the melodrama are its simplicity of themes, unambiguous plot, the triumph of virtue – like providence or deus ex machina – and the use of spectacle. The *Burletta*, a combination of the 'operatic mode' with the 'burlesque tradition in literature', produced a comedic opera that deals 'in a ludicrous way' with a myth or historical tale (Dircks, 1976: 69). Dircks cites *The Vampire* as a 'typical example' of a burletta, accommodating its audience with a 'simple plot, light music, and spirited performance' and 'careful and specific instructions in the dramatic text' (1976: 75; 70; 74–5). Finally, the *Extravaganza*: 'a genre which most effectively theatricalized the growing Victorian fascination with art and literature of fantasy' and was: 'directed especially at a middle-class audience and tended to reflect its standards, concerns, and mores . . . [for example] establishing and enforcing rules of conduct . . . within the increasingly complex social hierarchy' (Fletcher, 1987: 10–11). Fletcher further argues that 'perhaps more than any other single feature, the portrayal of male characters by women illustrates the obsessive concern with sexual definition which pervades the extravaganza', while the subject is light and fanciful and the atmosphere is of extreme importance (1987: 31).

Early Victorian Gothic Drama

John William Polidori's novella *The Vampyre* (1819) was written in 1816 while he was living in Switzerland with Lord Byron, functioning as his travelling companion and personal physician. Polidori appears to have been influenced by the short and unfinished ghost story written by Byron, *A Fragment* (1819), as well as Goethe's 'Die Braut von Korinth' (1797), Robert Southey's *Thalaba the Destroyer* (1801) and John Herman Merivale's *The Dead Men of Pest* (1802), all of them featuring fictional vampires who are noticeably different from the aristocratic and human Lord Ruthven of Polidori's tale. Originally pirated and published under the name of Byron, the novella went through five editions in its first year (Macdonald, 1991: 190) and was praised by Goethe as Byron's masterpiece (Butler, 1956: 55). Polidori had to threaten legal action to have his authorship acknowledged, and even then he was paid only £30 by Henry Colburn, the publisher (Stiles, Finger and Bulevich, 2010: 798). The story of a seductive vampire who preys on the blood of beautiful virgins made its way quickly to the stage and during the nineteenth century there were approximately thirty-five different versions on British, French and American stages, most of them indebted to Polidori's novella as their source (Stuart, 1994: 3). James Robinson Planché, author of 72 original plays and 104 adaptations/translations, adapted Polidori's novella for an August 1820 London adaptation, *The Vampire; or, The Bride of the Isles*. This is the best-known and longest-running version on the British stage, although it is also indebted to the French melodramatic adaptation of the novella, *Le Vampyre: mélodrama en trios actes* (June 1820) by Charles Nodier, Pierre Carmouche and Achille de Jouffroy (Stuart, 1994: 41). Sleep-walking, hypnotic trances, foreboding dreams and visions, and optical illusions figure prominently in Planché's version and suggest that the supernatural has begun to be figured within the Gothic as a biological force that science will eventually be able to explain and control. On a lighter note, the play was moved to Scotland for its setting because the theatre troupe happened to have a set of kilts left over from an earlier production of *Macbeth*.

The drama opens as the heroine, Lady Margaret, has a foreboding dream that warns her not to marry the hypnotic Lord Ruthven, but she is powerless to resist his gaze: 'I could not even turn mine eyes from this apparition' (Planché, 1986: 53). McFarland addresses many of the changes made by Planché: the name changes (and costuming) are intended to reflect the Scottish locale, and he adds a comic buffoon, McSwill, to 'supply the broad comedy that Planché's audience demanded' (McFarland, 1987: 30). Nine songs were added so that, according to the Act of 1737 which had limited 'legitimate' drama to the approved theatres at Drury Lane and Covent Garden, the play would qualify as a 'musical' (McFarland, 1987: 30, 29). This licensing act was in effect until the Theatre Regulation Act of 1843 which then did require melodramas and burlettas to obtain a license before performance. Planché's vampire, in contrast to the ones in his sources, receives a human lineage – traced to a tyrant – which makes him 'a heinous sinner rather than a non-human, blood-sucking monster' and establishes some sympathy for him (McFarland, 1987: 30–1). Interestingly, this also makes him a supporter of the aristocracy through the sacrifice of the working-class Effie so that Margaret could be 'spared' (McFarland, 1987: 31). Class becomes an issue again with the creation of the working-class Robert as the hero. This difference is 'a change that no doubt was calculated to appeal to the proletarian audience' (McFarland, 1987: 32). The violence occurs offstage, as Ruthven carries Effie offstage for her demise and he himself is also shot offstage. Also, the ending reaffirms one of the melodrama's most cherished tenets: that providence will come to the rescue and provide a happy ending with solid closure and survival of the family unit.

Many theatre historians have addressed the play's ending by discussing one of Planché's many contributions to the theatre: the 'vampire trap'. The vampire trap consisted of two doors made of India-rubber on springs and built into the stage with a blanket tied securely underneath them (Emmett, 1980: 78–9). A 'slide' is used to allow actors to walk on the doors and is then pulled at a signal from the prompter (Emmett,

1980: 79). In trapping the stage in this manner the actor may disappear from the audience's unhindered view instantly while landing safely elsewhere. In *The Vampire* the 'vamp trap' allowed Lord Ruthven to seem to disappear into the walls of the stage. This most Gothic aspect of the drama, suggesting the immateriality of the material, confirmed for the audience the continued existence of the spiritual or transcendent realms in the midst of increasingly realistic dramatic fare.

Mary Shelley's novel *Frankenstein, or the Modern Prometheus* (1818) is, along with Bram Stoker's *Dracula*, one of the seminal Gothic texts of the British tradition. It too was quickly adapted for the stage, first by Richard B. Peake as *Presumption, or the Fate of Frankenstein* (1823), a play that was thought by many to be impious, so much so that it was picketed and leaflets were distributed against its performance (Cox, 1992: 386). Despite all of the negative publicity, the play was a success, with the *Theatrical Observer* (1 August 1823) claiming that: 'The moral here is striking. It points out that man cannot pursue objects beyond his obviously prescribed powers, without incurring the penalty of shame and regret at his audacious folly' (Cox, 1992: 387). In this version, the creature is nameless, but listed in the Larpent version as 'the demon' (Cox, 1992: 387), while Forry has noted that in this adaptation the creature is 'Calibinized' (Forry, 1990: 22), perhaps revealing the extent to which Shakespeare's works were still part of cultural parlance. In this version, Victor has been driven to impious experiments because he has been separated from his true love, Agatha De Lacey. Elizabeth is now the sister of Victor and Clerval is engaged to marry her; Fritz, a servant to Victor, is introduced, along with his wife Madame Ninon, and 'gypsies' and 'villagers' also appear in order to explore class issues. Clerval and Elizabeth sing of their love for each other, while Victor darkly acknowledges his belief in the devil, who he is sure is motivating him to pursue his strange and dangerous scientific experiments: 'It's the Devil – for I'm sure *he's* at the bottom of it, and that makes me so nervous' (quoted in Cox, 1992: 392). Through a series of complications, Agatha finds herself suddenly confronted by the Demon, who at first causes her to fall into a river, and then rescues her just as Victor appears and shoots the Demon in order to free Agatha from his arms (Act 2). This melodramatic adaptation of the novel retains the Gothic trope of the identificatory locket, but as there is no Justine in this version, the locket is worn by Agatha and never given to William, although William is snatched by the Demon and never seen again. The most Gothic scene of the drama occurs in the last act, when the stage directions make it clear that the Demon creeps into Agatha's room and strangles her: 'In a large glass – Agatha appears on her knees with a veil over her head. – The Demon with his hand on her throat – she falls – the Demon disappears – after tearing a locket from Agatha's neck' (Cox, 1992: 423). The fact that this dream-like scene is 'reflected in the glass' to audience members recalls the earlier history of Gothic drama, its tendency to obscure onstage the most violent and Gothic moments of any play, just as gauze had been used earlier to introduce the ghosts in James Boaden's *Fountainville Forest* (1794), an adaptation of Ann Radcliffe's *Romance of the Forest* (1791).

Victor Hugo's very popular novel *Notre-Dame de Paris* (1831) was similarly adapted fairly quickly for the British stage following its translation into English in 1833. There were three nineteenth-century English stage adaptations, two by Edward Fitzball (1834; 1836), and one by Andrew Halliday (1871), all of them giving Hugo's novel a happy ending while erasing its republican politics and social criticism (Szwydky, 2010: 469). Fitzball was in fact so prolific that during his 35–year career, he wrote 170 dramas, most of them melodramas. The one that is most consistently Gothic, however, is Fitzball's first attempt at adapting Hugo's novel, *Esmeralda*, in which the heroine lives, Quasimodo dies, and Phoebus arrives at the last minute with a pardon for Esmeralda from the king. The drama was popular enough to be included in *Miller's Modern Acting Drama: Consisting of the Most Popular Pieces Produced at the London Theatres* (vol. 3; 1834), and it was revived at the Adelphi in 1840 (Szwydky, 2010: 472). The scene that was most famous in all adaptations was the climactic event of the novel, Quasimodo's call for 'Sanctuary!' as he descends the cathedral's walls in an effort to save the condemned Esmeralda. Fitzball stages Quasimodo's rescue of Esmeralda from the axe in a particularly sensational moment as he delivers this speech:

> Forbear this hellish rite! She is innocent and shall not die. Men-at-arms, move one step towards me – the strength of worlds is in this determined hand – this uplifted axe shall strike him dead that follows Esmeralda to the shrine. Comfort, Esmeralda! To the sanctuary – to the sanctuary! 'Tis the refuge of the guilty – shall be of the innocent. The sanctuary! (Fitzball, 1834: Act 2, 3)

Fleeing into the cathedral, Esmeralda is locked inside a tomb by Frollo, the villain, until she is freed by the efforts of Quasimodo, who reveals the secret to unlocking the tomb by pressing the hand of a statue. As Szwydky notes, this scene is particularly reminiscent of Matthew Lewis's subterranean convent rescue scene in *The Monk* (Szwydky, 2010: 485).

Middle Victorian Gothic Drama

The English Opera House, where Planché's drama premiered in 1820, burned to the ground in 1830, but was rebuilt as the Lyceum, the scene of Bram Stoker's own career as a producer of Gothic-inflected dramas. Critics have argued that the structure and themes of Stoker's novel need to be placed within the context of the theatre in which he spent his adult life (Richards, 1995: 145). Belford claims that '*Dracula* is all about Irving as the vampire and Ellen Terry as the unattainable good woman' (1996: 106), while Moss compares Dracula's absence of a mirror reflection to the theatrical trick commonly known as 'Pepper's ghost' (1999: 128). In 1862, inventor Henry Dircks developed what he called the Dircksian Phantasmagoria, a technique used to make what looked like a ghost appear onstage. He tried unsuccessfully to sell his idea to theatres, but the method, as he developed it, would require theatres to be completely rebuilt just to support the effect. Later in the same year, Dircks set up a booth at the Royal Polytechnic to display the invention, where it was seen by John Pepper, who realised that the method could be modified to make it easy to incorporate into existing theatres. Pepper first showed the effect during his own adaptation of a scene from Charles Dickens's Christmas novella turned melodrama, *The Haunted Man, and the Ghost's Bargain* (1862), to great success. Though he tried many times to give credit to Dircks, the title 'Pepper's ghost' became permanent. According to Helen Groth, Pepper's 'Ghost' first succeeded as a theatrical device when it was combined as an optical illusion with Dickens's uncanny tale of a man named Redlaw, compelled somewhat like Scrooge to confront the consequences of his past deeds. It is at this moment, when Redlaw's spectral double appears to grant his wish that his memory be erased, that the device of the Pepper's ghost is used. His wish is accompanied by a curse that condemns all those who come in contact with him to the same fate:

> Confronted with the brutal consequences of his desire, Redlaw ultimately repents, and his punitive ghost lifts the curse. Dickens's insistence on the civilizing power of memory, its ability to suppress the chaos of individual desire and to foster social responsibility, nicely complemented Pepper's own didactic use of illusion to promote rational responses to seemingly inexplicable supernatural events. (Groth, 2007: 43)

In addition to the popularity of Pepper's Ghost, the 'vampire trap' made a return to the London stage, most famously in Charles Kean's 1852 production of *The Corsican Brothers* at the Princess's Theatre. Now labelled the 'gliding' or 'Corsican Trap', the device produced what Yzereef calls 'one of the most thrilling supernatural scenes in the mid-century Victorian theatre' (1992: 4). As he notes, Act 1 ends with the ghost of Louis dei Franchi appearing before his brother Fabien in a visionary tableau that reveals how he was murdered by the villain Château-Renaud. In order to stage this effect, Kean had to use a double to play one of the identical twin brothers on the stage and he had to employ three different scene painters to design the various visionary tableaux, one of which has the ghost of Louis dei Franchi pointing to the vision of his own death, while his mother and brother stand transfixed in front of the scene (Yzereef, 1992: 6). Kean also had to revive the 'Corsican Trap' so that, while playing the role of Fabien, he could remain on stage writing a letter to his brother while another actor, portraying the murdered Louis, rose slowly through the stage floor on the trap and enacted the murder scene that had occurred some days earlier in France. Anxious about a pain he feels in his side, Fabien writes to his brother, inquiring about his situation, and he receives the supernatural news he most dreads:

> He folds the letter, seals it, during which Louis dei Franchi has gradually appeared rising through the floor, in his shirt sleeves, with blood upon his breast; and as Fabien is about to place his seal upon the wax Louis touches him on the shoulder. Fabien then looks up and exclaims, 'My brother! Dead!' (Boucicault, 1996: 105)

The pain that Fabien had felt earlier is in exactly the same place that his brother had been stabbed:

> I felt a sudden pang, as if a sword had pierced my chest. I looked round and saw no one. I laid my hand upon the place, there was no would. My heart felt crushed, and the name of my brother leapt unbidden to my lips. I looked at my watch; it was ten minutes after nine. (Boucicault, 1996: 104)

The playscript goes on to detail this most Gothic scene in the drama:

> Louis waves his arm towards the wall, and disappears; at the same time the back of the scene opens and discloses a glade in the Forest of Fontainebleau. On one side is a young man wiping blood from his sword with a pocket handkerchief. Two seconds are near him. On the other side, Louis extended on the ground, supported by his two seconds and a surgeon. Act drop slowly descends. Tableau. (Boucicault, 1996: 105)

The clocks in Fabien's house all stop at ten minutes after nine, the hour when he learns his brother has been killed. George Henry Lewes found the scene to be 'more real and terrible than anything I remember', while

Queen Victoria was also impressed, and recorded in her diary that the scene 'was beautifully grouped and quite touching. The whole, lit by blue light and dimmed with gauze, had an unearthly effect, and was most impressive and creepy' (quoted in Yzereef, 1992: 13). Bram Stoker was also strongly influenced by this production, reviving it in the 1880s as a vehicle for Henry Irving. Stoker observed that its power derived from the uncanniness of the twin brothers seeing themselves, one living and one dead, at the same time:

> Another feature [of *The Corsican Brothers*] was the 'double'. In a play where one actor plays two parts there is usually at least one time when the two have to be seen together. For this a double has to be provided. In *The Corsican Brothers*, where one of the two SEES THE OTHER SEEING HIS BROTHER, more than one double was required. (Stoker, 1906: 170; his emphasis)

As Kendrick has noted, the Corsican trap: 'is an extreme example of the lengths to which stagecraft was pushed by the desire for horrid effects . . . [T]echnicians had to make ghosts rise, demons appear, wounds drip blood, ghastly fires burn – all with the most rudimentary equipment' (Kendrick, 1991: 126).

Late Victorian Gothic Drama

Henry Irving's name is, along with that of Bram Stoker, associated with the success of the Lyceum Theatre. In fact, the theatre was guaranteed its success with the first performance of Irving as the guilt-stricken murderer Mathias in *The Bells* (25 November 1871), a role that 'catapulted him to stardom' (Belford, 1996: 48). Irving was the first actor to be knighted and, although he was scorned by George Bernard Shaw for his aversion to the modern 'problem' plays of Ibsen, Irving continued to be popular and successful, mainly because of the power of his alternating performances of 'Victorian melodramas with reputable Shakespearean productions' (Hughes, 2009: 12). Irving's first great success was in Leopold Lewis's *The Bells*, adapted from *Le Juif Polonaise* (*The Polish Jew*) by Emile Erckmann and Alexandre Chatrain, and he continued to perform in the lead until shortly before his death in 1905. Like the Dickens novella and the even earlier Gothic melodrama, Thomas Holcroft's *A Tale of Mystery*, *The Bells* is predicated on the idea that evil deeds from the past have the power to return and 'haunt' the protagonist until restitution is accomplished. In the case of *The Bells*, the past returns in the form of a haunting vision of the itinerant Polish Jew who had been murdered and robbed by Mathias fifteen years earlier.

And again, the 'Corsican trap' was used to bring this ominous vision up out of the stage floor in order to float in front of Mathias's haunted eyes. At the conclusion of Act 1, Mathias hears the bells:

> 'What is this jangling in my ears? What is tonight? Ah, it is the very night – the very hour! [Clock strikes ten.] I feel a darkness coming over me. [Stage darkens.] . . . Shall I call for help? No, no, Mathias. Have courage! The Jew is dead!' But just as he is reassuring himself, 'the back of the scene rises and sinks', revealing in tableau: 'the JEW is discovered seated in a sledge . . . the horse carrying Bells; the JEW's face is turned away; the snow is falling fast; the scene is seen through a gauze; lime light . . . vision of a MAN dressed in a brown blouse and hood over his head, carrying an axe, stands in an attitude of following the sledge; when the picture is fully disclosed the Bells cease . . . [He] starts violently upon seeing the vision before him; at the same time the JEW in the sledge suddenly turns his face, which is ashy pale, and fixes his eyes sternly upon him; MATHIAS utters a prolonged cry of terror, and falls senseless.' (quoted in Kendrick, 1991: 159–60)

During the fifteen years that Mathias has prospered and grown rich on the murdered Jew's money, he has also raised a daughter who is on the verge of marrying the handsome Christian, and wedding plans are underway when the horrific haunting from the past recurs to Mathias's appalled eyes and ears. The ringing of the bells on the Jew's sled are heard by Mathias throughout Acts 2 and 3 until he goes completely mad and imagines a trial scene, where he is led before a judge and the entire courtroom to be hypnotised in order to enact the murder scene before their eyes. He dies from the shock of reliving and confessing to his earlier crime in front of the entire community. At the play's conclusion the wedding guests find the dead Mathias in his bedroom, in bloodstained brown clothes, to the ringing of the Jew's bells. In ways that are similar to *The Corsican Brothers*, *The Bells* tries to depict the interconnection between the material and immaterial worlds, while the internal, psychic world is portrayed in two ghostly, hallucinatory tableaux. According to the leading contemporary critic, Clement Scott, the performance of Irving in this final scene was mesmerising: 'the young actor had held his audience fast as in a vice, and, most wonderful of all, in a scene probably the most risky and exhausting in the long catalogue of the modern drama' (Scott, 1899, vol. 2: 49).

Fitzball had earlier adapted the legend of a doomed ship forced to sail for ever as punishment for a crime as *The Flying Dutchman, or the Phantom Ship: a Nautical Drama, in three acts* (1826), a highly Gothicised melodrama for the Adelphi, and Richard Wagner's opera (1843) had revived the theme to great success throughout Europe, so much so that the Lyceum attempted its own version, *Vanderdecken,* in June of 1878, with Irving in the main role of the demonic immortal. The play was not a creative or financial success; however, it does reveal the interest that Stoker and Irving had in staging material with a supernatural theme. In this adaptation of the *Flying Dutchman* legend, Vanderdecken is compelled to sail the seas for ever in a phantom ship with blood-red sails and a ghostly crew. Much like the Wandering Jew, Coleridge's Ancient Mariner, or Maturin's Melmoth, this man is forced to wander for ever for some crime, but he has been given a way out through a pact with the devil: he will be free if he can find a woman who will truly love him and offer herself up in sacrifice for his soul. Every seven years he is allowed to depart the ship and seek this bride, and Irving's adaptation explores Vanderdecken's pursuit of a beautiful Norwegian named Thekla, who ultimately renounces her mortal fiancé for the mysterious and demonic stranger.

Irving's greatest success as an actor came in his performance as Mephistopheles in an adaptation of Goethe's *Faust* (1808; 1828). Stoker is believed to have been instrumental in encouraging Irving to perform in Wills's adaptation of this work (Murray, 2004: 181), which turned out to be the greatest financial success that the Lyceum ever had. As Murray has noted, Wills's version of the Faust story contains elements that would recur later in Stoker's *Dracula*, like a demonic villain, horrific dreams, the shape-shifting of human to animal and mysterious lights (Murray, 2004: 182), but much of this is stock Gothic paraphernalia and had long been in use in any number of Gothic texts. The Lyceum's production takes place in Nuremberg around 1550, with Mephistopheles tempting the ambitious Faust to sell his soul in exchange for eternal youth and the love of the beautiful young virgin Margaret. A magic potion puts Margaret to sleep so that Faust can sexually possess her, but the act kills Margaret's mother (much like the climactic scene in Lewis's novel *The Monk*). Margaret gives birth to a baby which she then kills, and she refuses the escape from justice that Faust offers her, preferring to pay for her sins. While her soul is saved, Faust is damned, carried away by the triumphant Mephistopheles (again, the similarities to the conclusion of *The Monk* are obvious). This play was the first to use electric flashes in a fight scene on stage, but Henry James was not impressed with the technology and George Moore referred to it as 'the fricassee of Faust, garnished with hags, imps, and blue flame' (quoted in Murray, 2004: 183).

Irving's 1890 production of the melodrama *Ravenswood* focused on the theme of forced and destructive marriage and seems to be influenced, according to Wynne, not simply by Walter Scott's novel, but also by the Gothic and doomed marriages depicted in Charles Maturin's *Melmoth the Wanderer* (1820) and J. Sheridan Le Fanu's 'Schalken the Painter' (1839), and the marriage of the actress Genevieve Ward to a Russian aristocrat forced by order of the Czar himself. Stoker's later novel *The Lady of the Shroud* (1909) appears to be an imaginative retelling of Ward's marital melodrama, complete with a 'bride-to-be emerging from a burial crypt for a midnight wedding to a man who fears that she may be a vampire' (Wynne, 2006: 251). Set in Scotland amid property disputes between rival clans, *Ravenswood* compares Lucy's father to a vampire in his stealing of Edgar's estate, while also providing in Edgar's suicidal ride into quicksand the fulfilment of a legend: 'when the last Lord of Ravenswood to Ravenswood shall ride, to woo a dead maiden to be his bride, he shall stable his steed i' the Kelpie's flow, and his name shall be lost for evermo' (quoted in Wynne, 2006: 255).

Stoker wrote *Dracula* while continuing to serve as Irving's manager at the Lyceum, and certainly, as numerous critics have observed, the composition of *Dracula* reveals numerous traces of Stoker's knowledge of various theatre productions. During Stoker's lifetime, however, only one stage performance, basically a crudely staged reading of the novel, occurred on 18 May 1897, a 'copyright performance, put on purely to protect the plot and dialogue from piracy' (Ludlam, 1962: 109). Billed as *Dracula or The Un-Dead*, the play lasted more than four hours, and had five acts with a total of forty-seven scenes read by a cast of fifteen. The prologue itself had nine scenes and was set in Transylvania. When Stoker asked Irving what he thought of the performance, Irving replied: 'Dreadful!' (Ludlam, 1962: 114). This copyright performance allowed Stoker's widow to sue successfully against the German expressionist film adaptation *Nosferatu*, produced by F. W. Murnau in 1922. The play was finally adapted with her approval by Hamilton Deane, an Irish actor in Irving's travelling theatre company, who wrote a stage version that was first performed in June 1924 at the Grand Theatre, Derby. After a successful run in the provinces, the play opened in London at the Little Theatre on 14 February 1927. Deane's adaptation began immediately in Jonathan Harker's Hampstead house rather than in Transylvania, with the two additional scenes set in Harker's study and then in Mina's boudoir. In the epilogue, Dracula is hunted until he is found in a coffin at Carfax, and then staked by Van Helsing. Deane played the role of Van Helsing and hired Raymond Huntley to take the part of Dracula, introducing on stage for the first time the famous black cape that would be Dracula's signature for his filmic appearances. Panned by London critics as a 'hack' work, and 'the world's worst' play, *Dracula* was an immediate success with the public, with so many audience members fainting that Deane decided to hire a nurse to stand in the aisles, adding to the play's notoriety (Ludlam, 1962: 157–62). Victorian Gothic drama concludes, then, with the successful stage production of *Dracula*, the immediate predecessor to the vampire theme in films, which at this date includes more than 170 different versions.

Victorian Gothic drama is an interesting hybrid – part melodrama, part morality play, part proto-technical spectacle. As a literary genre, it straddles two important periods in the history of the dramatic form – the earlier era, with its heavy use of the supernatural in such classic Gothic dramas as *The Castle Spectre* – and the later period that saw the development of the twentieth-century horror film genre with its steady proliferation of *Frankenstein* and *Dracula* adaptations. Victorian Gothic dramas continued to investigate religious and spiritual issues, a topic that has long been one of the most important in this genre. *Vanderdecken* and *Faust* employ the supernatural, but increasingly these plays moved beyond their source materials, which were largely based on a medieval worldview, or perhaps their failures as vehicles suggests that their audiences had moved beyond such a cosmology. *The Corsican Brothers*, arguably the most successful of the high Victorian Gothics, invoked the supernatural and spiritual realms, but in this work the supernatural is invoked as a type of 'natural supernaturalism', a scientifically inflected, self-consciously referenced supernaturalism that could be neatly stylised in the use of the 'Corsican Trap'. *Presumption* privileged the devil's continued literal existence, while *The Bells* worked to internalise the conscience of a guilt-stricken sinner, suggesting an increased privatisation of the religious impulse. With its melodramatic focus on the fetishised and virginal female under assault by a demonic male figure, the Victorian Gothic drama not only recalls the assaults on Angela (*The Castle Spectre*) or Esmeralda, but it also looks forward to one of the horror film's most cherished tropes: 'the final girl' (Clover, 1992), who comes through innumerable attacks to survive the film while sexually compromised women are sacrificed to a sadistic male libidinal gaze. There is no question that contemporary viewers of the horror film, whether sadistically (Mulvey, 1992) or masochistically (Clover, 1992) aligned, owe a visual and cultural debt to the many advances and experiments made by the Victorian Gothic drama.

References

Archer, William (1882). *English Dramatists of Today*. London: Sampson.

Belford, Barbara (1996). *Bram Stoker: A Biography of the Author of Dracula*. New York: Knopf.

Booth, Michael (1965). *English Melodrama*. London: Herbert Jenkins.

——(1981). *Victorian Spectacular Theatre 1850–1910*. Boston, MA: Routledge.
Boucicault, Dion (1996). *The Corsican Brothers: A Dramatic Romance in Three Acts* [1852], ed. George Taylor. Oxford: Oxford University Press, pp. 87–125.
Butler, E. M. (1956). *Byron and Goethe: Analysis of a Passion*. London: Bowes and Bowes.
Clover, Carol (1992). *Men, Women, and Chainsaws: Gender in the Modern Horror Film*. Princeton: Princeton University Press.
Cox, Jeffrey (ed.) (1992). *Seven Gothic Dramas 1789–1825*. Athens: Ohio University Press.
Dircks, P. T. (1976). 'James Robinson Planché and the English Burletta Tradition', *Theatre Survey*, 17, 68–81.
Emmet, Alfred (1980). 'The Vampire Trap', *Theatre Notebook: A Journal of the History and Technique of the British Theatre*, 34, 128–9.
Filon, Augustin (1897). *The English Stage: Being an Account of the Victorian Drama*, trans. Frederic Whyte. London: Milne.
Fitzball, Edward (1834). *Esmeralda: or, The Deformed of Notre Dame: A Drama in Three Acts*. London: Lacy.
Fletcher, Kathy (1987). 'Planché, Vestris, and the Transvestite Role: Sexuality and Gender in Victorian Popular Theatre', *Nineteenth Century Theatre* 15, 9–33.
Forry, Steven Earl (1990. *Hideous Progenies: Dramatizations of 'Frankenstein' from Mary Shelley to the Present*. Philadelphia: University of Pennsylvania Press.
Groth, Helen (2007). 'Reading Victorian Illusions: Dickens's *The Haunted Man* and Dr. Pepper's "Ghost"', *Victorian Studies*, 50, 43–65.
Hadley, Elaine (1995). *Melodramatic Tactics: Theatricalized Dissent in the English Marketplace, 1800–1885*. Stanford: Stanford University Press.
Harse, Katie (2001). 'Melodrama Hath Charms: Planché's Theatrical Domestication of Polidori's "The Vampyre"', *Journal of Dracula Studies*, 3, 3–7.
Hughes, William (2009). *Bram Stoker: Dracula*. New York: Palgrave.
James, Henry (1948). *The Scenic Art: Notes on Acting and Drama, 1872–1901*. New Brunswick, NJ: Rutgers University Press.
Kendrick, Walter (1991). *The Thrill of Fear: 250 Years of Scary Entertainment*. New York: Grove.
Ludlam, Harry (1962). *A Biography of Dracula: The Life Story of Bram Stoker*. London: Foulsham.
Macdonald, David Lorne (1991). *Poor Polidori: A Critical Biography of the Author of 'The Vampyre'*. Toronto: University of Toronto Press.
McFarland, Ronald E. (1987). 'The Vampire on Stage: A Study in Adaptations', *Comparative Drama*, 21, 19–33.
Meisel, Martin (1983). *Realizations: Narrative, Pictorial, and Theatrical Arts in Nineteenth-Century England*. Princeton: Princeton University Press.
Moody, Jane (2000). *Illegitimate Theatre in London, 1770–1840*. Cambridge: Cambridge University Press.
Moss, Stepanie (1999). 'Bram Stoker and the London Stage', *Journal of the Fantastic in the Arts*, 10, 124–32.
Mulvey, Laura (1992). 'Visual Pleasure and Narrative Cinema', in *Film Theory*

and Criticism, 4th edn, ed. Gerald Mast, Marchall Cohen and Leo Braudy. Oxford: Oxford University Press, pp. 746–57.

Murray, Paul (2004). *From the Shadow of Dracula*. London: Cape.

Peake, Richard B. (1992). *Presumption, or the Fate of Frankenstein* [1823], in *Seven Gothic Dramas 1789–1825*, ed. Jeffrey Cox. Athens: Ohio University Press, pp. 385–425.

Planché, James (1986). *The Vampire: or, the Bride of the Isles* [1820], in *Plays by James Robinson Planché*, ed. Donald Roy. New York: Cambridge University Press, pp. 45–68.

Richards, Jeffrey (1995). 'Gender, Race, and Sexuality in Bram Stoker's Other Novels', in *Gender Roles and Sexuality in Victorian Literature*, ed. Christopher Parker. Aldershot: Scolar Press, pp. 143–71.

Roy, Donald (1986). 'Introduction to Planché', in *Plays by James Robinson Planché*, ed. Donald Roy. New York: Cambridge University Press, pp. i–xi.

Scott, Clement (1899). *The Drama of Yesterday and Today*, 2 vols. London: Macmillan.

Stevens, John Russell (1992). *The Profession of the Playwright: The British Theatre 1800–1900*. Cambridge: Cambridge University Press.

Stiles, Anne, Stanley Finger and John Bulevich (2010). 'Somnambulism and Trance States in the Works of John William Polidori, Author of *The Vampyre*', *European Romantic Review*, 21, 789–807.

Stoker, Bram (1906). *Personal Reminiscences of Henry Irving*, 2 vols. London: Heinemann.

Stuart, Roxana (1994). *Stage Blood: Vampires of the Nineteenth-Century Stage*. Bowling Green, OH: Bowling Green State University Press.

Szwydky, Lissette Lopez (2010). 'Victor Hugo's *Notre-Dame de Paris* on the Nineteenth-Century London Stage', *European Romantic Review*, 21, 469–87.

Taylor, George (1980). *Henry Irving at the Lyceum*. Cambridge: Chadwick-Healey.

——(1989) *Players and Performances in the Victorian Theatre*. Manchester: Manchester University Press.

Wynne, Catherine (2006). 'Bram Stoker, Genevieve Ward, and the *Lady of the Shroud*: Gothic Weddings and Performing Vampires', *English Literature in Transition, 1880–1920*, 49, 251–72.

Yzereef, Barry (1992). 'Ghostly Appearances: The Vision Scene in *The Corsican Brothers*', *Theatre Notebook*, 46, 4–14.

Chapter 5

Victorian Gothic Poetry: The Corpse's [a] Text

Caroline Franklin and Michael J. Franklin

The thin, clear gaze, the same
Still darts out faun-like from the half-ruin'd face,
Questing and passive . . . 'Ah, poor Jenny's case' . . .

Bewildered that a world
Shows no surprise
At her last maquero's
Adulteries.

Ezra Pound ('Yeux Glauques', ll. 17–24, in Pound, 1921: 57)

Victorian Gothic needs no more emblematically macabre apogee than a scene in the western section of Highgate cemetery on the night of Tuesday 5 October 1869. By the light of a bonfire that also served to dispel noxious graveyard odours, Charles Augustus Howell, unprincipled Pre-Raphaelite 'fixer', watched as two hired gravediggers dug up the coffin of Mrs Dante Gabriel Rossetti. Her loving husband, grief-stricken at both the desecration and the negation of his loving gesture in placing his unpublished poems beside her pale beautiful face, could not bring himself to attend. He had read of the deadly vapours and 'the aqueous part of decomposition, a "fetid sanies"' which exude from the abdomen of the putrefying corpse ('Conductor', 1843: 97).

On unscrewing the coffin lid, the face of Elizabeth Eleanor Siddal, seven years dead, appeared, not 'half-ruin'd', but miraculously preserved; her flaming red-gold hair had grown profusely post-mortem.[1] Such was the report given to Rossetti who spoke of 'That golden *hair* undimmed in death' ('Life-in-Love', l. 14, in Rossetti, 1898: 50). The coffin was actually waterlogged; Lizzie's hair was as wet as that of Ophelia whom she modelled for Millais. Also wet through was the retrieved manuscript book, appropriately bound in ooze leather (rough grey calf) with red edges to the leaves. To his brother Rossetti wrote:

All in the coffin was found quite perfect; but the book, though not in any way destroyed, is soaked through and through, and had to be still further saturated with disinfectants. It is now in the hands of the medical man [Dr Llewellyn Williams] who was associated with Howell in the disinterment, and who is carefully drying it leaf by leaf . . . To others I shall say at present that I have made the rough copies more available than I hoped; but I suppose the truth must ooze out in time. (Rossetti to William Michael Rossetti, 13 October 1869, in Fredeman, 2004: 303)

The truth was that Rossetti's muse/wife and fellow-artist/poet had not a blessed damozel's seven stars in her hair but his own poems oozing aqueous putrefaction. One of these, 'Jenny', he was anxious to rework. For seven years Beata Beatrix had shared a coffin with a prostitute, text by text, 'Two sister vessels' ('Jenny', l. 184) which Dante had inscribed and filled with seed.[2] It is unsurprising that Pound elided the 'case' (body, coffin and text) of Lizzie with 'poor Jenny's case', for the sleeping Jenny, 'Whose eyes are as blue skies, whose hair / Is countless gold incomparable' ('Jenny', ll. 10–11) had rested cheek by jowl with the recumbent Lizzie. Although the body of 'Lazy laughing languid Jenny, / Fond of a kiss and fond of a guinea' (ll. 1–2) is a text easily read, might the pages of her brain ever contain with understanding the thoughts she evokes in her patronising customer/poet?

> Suppose I were to think aloud, –
> What if to her all this were said?
> Why, as a volume seldom read
> Being opened halfway shuts again,
> So might the pages of her brain
> Be parted at such words, and thence
> Close back upon the dusty sense.
> For is there hue or shape defin'd
> In Jenny's desecrated mind,
> Where all contagious currents meet,
> A Lethe of the middle street?
>   (ll. 156–66; Rossetti, 1870: 109–26)

In the contagious Lethe of a middle-earth 'desecrated' Highgate tomb it is the dumb coffin-worm – in a bizarre Marvellian touch – who symbolises Rossetti's 'maquero [pimp/gigolo] adulteries' by penetrating the leaves of 'Jenny'.

A century after the exhumation, Ken Russell's BBC film *Dante's Inferno: The Private Life of Rossetti* (1967) inevitably presented its subject gothically haunted by Lizzie's ghoulish corpse rising from its Highgate grave. But the Victorian Rossetti *was* haunted by his wife, even though he initially comforted himself with a mutually desired revenance, reflecting both approval and artistic dedication:

The truth is, no one so much as herself would have approved of my doing this. Art was the only thing for which she felt seriously. Had it been possible to her, I should have found the book on my pillow the night she was buried; and could she have opened the grave no other hand would have been needed. (Rossetti to Swinburne, 26 October 1869, in Fredeman, 2004: 312)

Intensifying his obsessive guilt concerning his infidelities and neglect, Rossetti was haunted by her paintings, her drawings and her poems, by means of which her suffering returned from beyond the grave. In a diary entry of 6 October 1854, Ford Madox Brown had recorded:

Called on Dante Rossetti, saw Miss Siddal looking thinner and more death-like and more beautiful and more ragged than ever: a real artist, a woman without parallel for many a long year. (W. M. Rossetti, 1899: 19)

Plagued by incipient consumption, neuralgia and stomach pains, addicted to laudanum, and celebrated for an anorexic and pallid beauty, it is unsurprising that the 'ragged' personae of Siddal's poems are instinct with lassitude and longing for the grave. Having been inscribed by Pre-Raphaelite male artists' fascination with the female corpse, it seems almost inevitable that Siddal should prematurely assume that textual role, answering back as a virtual corpse. 'A Year and a Day', written on the back of a letter to Emma Brown, wife of Ford Madox Brown, in 1855, reveals a Gothic melancholia, a study in abjection:

Slow days have passed that make a year,
Slow hours that make a day,
Since I could take my first dear love
And kiss him the old way;
Yet the green leaves touch me on the cheek,
Dear Christ, this month of May.

I lie among the tall green grass
That bends above my head
And covers up my wasted face
And folds me in its bed
Tenderly and lovingly
Like grass above the dead.

Dim phantoms of an unknown ill
Float through my tired brain;
The unformed visions of my life
Pass by in ghostly train;
Some pause to touch me on the cheek,
Some scatter tears like rain.
        . . .
The river ever running down

Between its grassy bed,
The voices of a thousand birds
That clang above my head,
Shall bring to me a sadder dream
When this sad dream is dead.

A silence falls upon my heart
And hushes all its pain.
I stretch my hands in the long grass
And fall to sleep again,
There to lie empty of all love
Like beaten corn of grain.
                    ('A Year and a Day', ll. 1–12; 31–42, in Siddal, 1978: 16–17)

Siddal's title, naming the traditional period after which the corpse could become vocal, might have promised a ballad along the lines of 'The Unquiet Grave':

The twelvemonth and a day being up,
The dead began to speak:
'Oh who sits weeping on my grave,
And will not let me sleep?'
                    (ll. 9–12, in Child, 1882–98, vol. 2: 236)

but corpse and woman 'half in love with easeful Death' share only a desire for the oblivion of sleep. In many respects the title of a poem by her sister-in-law Christina, published in the year of Siddal's suicide, might have been appropriate: 'Dead before Death'. Like straw or thresh, she is devoid of all that is life-giving, yet it is the tall grass above her head that lovingly enfolds her. The pages of her tired brain reveal a pallid Gothic peopled by 'Dim phantoms of an unknown ill', and 'unformed visions' of a haunted half-life. If Siddal's downcast or half-closed eyes emblematise the death-in-life of the Pre-Raphaelite muse, they also represent her boredom with Rossetti's endless dialectic of the beauty of the body and that of the soul. She treated Ruskin's enthusiasm for her art with reserve, suspecting that his generosity was prompted by a desire to patronise Rossetti.[3] Even in offering financial help to rent a 'little cottage in some sheltered Welsh valley', Ruskin managed to sound as if he were performing some act of environmentalism or cultural heritage, objectifying her as 'a beautiful tree', or 'a bit of a Gothic cathedral'.[4] Although it was Jane Morris who had modelled for Rossetti's 'Proserpine', Siddal languorously anticipated the eating of Swinburne's 'Green grapes of Proserpine'– an oneiric Gothic which her life and texts had helped to inspire:

Here, where the world is quiet;
Here, where all trouble seems

Dead winds' and spent waves' riot
In doubtful dreams of dreams;
I watch the green field growing
For reaping folk and sowing,
For harvest-time and mowing,
A sleepy world of streams.
   . . .
I am weary of days and hours,
Blown buds of barren flowers,
Desires and dreams and powers
And everything but sleep.
   ('The Garden of Prosperpine', ll. 1–8, 13–16, in Swinburne, 1866: 196–9)[5]

But if this hypnotic dream of a grassy narcotic bed had been that of Siddal, she had also felt the 'vapours rise from the red-brown mould', a breath-holding spell 'Bending me down to a living death' ('Fragment of a Ballad', ll. 14, 16, in Siddal 1978: 13). Working on the illustrations for William Allingham's projected volume of ballads in May 1854, she produced drawings (and subsequently a watercolour (1857), and a (lost) oil-painting) of intensely angular medievalism to illustrate the 'wild and beautiful' ballad 'Clerk Saunders', first published in Scott's *Minstrelsy of the Scottish Border* (1802). Stabbed to death by Maid Margaret's brothers, Clerk Saunders returns from the grave to beg her release from his trothplight:

My mouth it is full cold, Margaret,
It has the smell, now, of the ground:
And, if I kiss thy comely mouth,
Thy days of life will not be lang.
   (ll. 77–80, in Walter Scott, 1802: 37)[6]

The stark ballad contrast between the mouth of mould and the beautifully moulded mouth is closer to the Death and the Maiden tradition than that of *Laus Veneris*. In the Pre-Raphaelite Gothic of Rossetti's *House of* [death-in-]*Life* he attempts to portray 'the very sky and sea-line' of his sainted model/wife's soul, but a characteristic concentration upon the perfect sensuous line of her mouth ironically blurs distinctions between the immortality and temporality of art, life and death:

   Above the enthroning throat
The mouth's mould testifies of voice and kiss,
The shadowed eyes remember and foresee.
Her face is made her shrine.
   ('The Portrait', ll. 9–12, in Rossetti, 1898: 24)

Unlike Keats, who only fleetingly considers art as 'All breathing human passion far above', Rossetti appears to prefer his pastoral cold; his nightingale muse was 'born for death'. Her immortality is sealed in death-in-life representations: 'They die not, – for their life was death, – but cease; / And round their narrow lips the mould falls close' ('Sonnet LXXI', ll. 13–14, in Rossetti, 1898: 88). The Gothic ambiguities of 'The mouth's mould' focus attention upon the posthumous (humus/mould) voice; although the 'the mould falls close', the dead lips can speak. Throughout centuries of the epitaphic tradition the dramatic *memento mori* of the earth-filled mouth has spoken from the grave to remind the sinner: 'You who look on me must come to this', but the painter/poet of 'The Portrait' – in his immortalising – exercises proprietorial artistic control over text and image, the objet d'art of her body: 'They that would look on her must come to me.'

Christina Rossetti's 'After Death', written on 28 April 1849, portrays a newly dead but totally sentient woman, the epitome of passivity, as a male mourner leans over her bed, bestrewn with rosemary and may. She is intensely aware of surroundings which simultaneously medievalise and subtly suggest liminality: 'half-drawn curtains', 'thro' the lattice ivy-shadows crept', the floor 'strewn with rushes' (or thresh). On the threshold of a dual consciousness of life and death, a death before death, her perspective is one of interiority. This is no near-death, out of body, experience; her consciousness is very much within body, a 'heart in hiding'. The poem as text proceeds from a body as text, rejected in life, but compassionated in death: 'I heard him say: "Poor child, poor child".' He silently weeps but as in life there is no physical contact:

> He did not touch the shroud, or raise the fold
> That hid my face, or take my hand in his,
> Or ruffle the smooth pillows for my head:
> He did not love me living; but once dead
> He pitied me; and very sweet it is
> To know he still is warm tho' I am cold.
>
> (ll. 9–14; Christina Rossetti, 1862: 59)

Her interiority and acute consciousness are not overshadowed by that abiding Victorian Gothic fear of premature burial, but this corpse's text inhabits an ambivalent hinterland between an incommunicable self-abnegating, altruistic love surviving death, and a powerless, but bitterly hostile, resentment of unrecognised or suppressed female sexuality.

The year of Elizabeth Siddal's death and of the publication of 'After Death', in Christina's innovative collection: *Goblin Market and Other Poems* (1862), saw dead lips moving on the other side of the Atlantic.

Emily Dickinson's 'I cried at Pity – not at Pain' might almost have been – were there any evidence that Dickinson had any acquaintance with her exact contemporary – a complex, polysemous and mildly contemptuous riposte to the 'very sweet' comfort Christina's persona might appear to draw from pity and the survival of a sexual warmth she never inspired or shared:

> I cried at Pity – not at Pain –
> I heard a Woman say
> 'Poor Child' – and something in her voice
> Convicted me – of me –
>
> So long I fainted, to myself
> It seemed the common way,
> And Health, and Laughter, Curious things –
> To look at, like a Toy –
>
> To sometimes hear 'Rich people' buy
> And see the Parcel rolled –
> And carried, I supposed – to Heaven,
> For children, made of Gold –
>
> But not to touch, or wish for,
> Or think of, with a sigh –
> And so and so – had been to me,
> Had God willed differently.
>
> I wish I knew that Woman's name –
> So when she comes this way,
> To hold my life, and hold my ears
> For fear I hear her say
>
> She's 'sorry I am dead' – again –
> Just when the Grave and I –
> Have sobbed ourselves almost to sleep,
> Our only Lullaby –
>
> (ll. 1–24, in Franklin, 1998 [hereafter F]: 394 [1862])

Dickinson's infant persona, unaware of the meaning of vivisepulture, though seemingly enduring it, has all the longings of a living child: after a life in which health and happiness were as curiously rare as precious toys wrapped and consigned to exclusive heavenly children as good as (or incorruptible as) gold. She evokes pity even while excoriating it, detesting what has singled her out, convicted her of her unfortunate self. She no more wants her hand held than her life to be held as a text of compassionate sorrow, she wants to stop up 'the access and the passage to' repulsive compunction, seeking the only solace of the sentient corpse – sleep. But 'Sleep', of course, for both the living and the dead, 'is the station grand', the Grand Central for all imaginative journeyings.

The most momentous of all journeys is that to the graveyard for the body which/who is preternaturally aware of the growing corn, red apples on the stubble, harvested pumpkins, the beauty of autumn and the comfort of the quotidian. Though a year and a day have passed all is remembered in distinct clarity:

> 'Twas just this time, last year, I died.
> I know I heard the Corn,
> When I was carried by the Farms –
> It had the Tassels on –
>
> I thought how yellow it would look –
> When Richard went to mill –
> And then, I wanted to get out,
> But something held my will.
>
> ('Twas just this time', ll. 1–8, F344 [1862])

The inability to move – is it the constriction of the coffin with its four-boarded lid, limbs unresponsive to the brain's impulses, or that the persona is imprisoned within its own text, by an author in league with Ancient Death who like 'The Mariner hath h[er] will'? In the black-tasselled hearse she must listen 'like a three years' child' to the corn growing. Such enforced and absolute passivity might seem instinct with Gothic horror did Dickinson not remind us elsewhere that 'Paralysis' is 'our Primer dumb / Unto Vitality!' (ll. 7–8, F284 [1862]). Her hearse is hitched to a star.

Persona, like poet, owns a body of remarkable self-possession and theirs is a trangressive modernist Gothic. She can wryly wonder if at Thanksgiving 'father'd multiply the plates – / To make an even Sum –', or 'would it blur the Christmas glee / My Stocking hang too high / For any Santa Claus to reach / The Altitude of me –' ('Twas just this time', ll. 15–20). For, although this 'felt a Funeral, in [her] Brain', together with the customary six-feet descent, she is soaring high: 'Then Space – began to toll, / As all the Heavens were a Bell' ('I felt a Funeral', ll. 12–13, F344 [1862]). Experience, as Dickinson tells us, involves stepping 'from plank to plank / A slow and cautious way', so it is unsurprising that undergoing life's ultimate experience 'The Stars about my Head I felt, / About my Feet the Sea' ('I stepped from Plank to Plank', ll. 1–4, F926 [1865]). Even when 'a Plank in Reason, broke, / And I dropped down, and down –' she 'hit a World, at every plunge, / And Finished knowing – then –' ('I felt a Funeral', ll. 17–20).[7]

If Gothic is both a product and a critique of the Enlightenment, Dickinsonian Gothic is associated with terrifying mind-expanding revelation. Having been carried past the harvested grain, she is heading

– not like Richard for the mill – but through 'The Starlight Night' of sublime Jesuit Gothic – to 'the barn; withindoors house / The shocks' ('The Starlight Night', ll. 12–13, in Hopkins 1953: 27–8). Welcome to the epistemological and teleological oxymorons of 'Ether Acre'. Having been introduced to a gentlemanly Erl King, who 'kindly stopped' for her under the Amherst alders, she is riding up – on a 'Journey of Down' – to meet her Pantocrator; this is the transcendent and superlative shock to which dead flesh is heir: 'so appalling – it exhilarates –' (l. 1, F341 [1862]):

> Dropped into the Ether Acre –
> Wearing the Sod Gown –
> Bonnet of Everlasting Laces –
> Brooch – frozen on –
>
> Horses of Blonde – and Coach of Silver –
> Baggage a strapped Pearl –
> Journey of Down – and Whip of Diamond –
> Riding to meet the Earl –

(ll. 1–8, F286 [1862])

Dickinson's corpses, as they pause 'before a House that seemed / A Swelling of the Ground' ('Because I could not stop for Death', ll. 17–18, F479 [1862]) care little for the twelfth-century grim and grimy Gothic of 'The Grave', which debased man, as surely as the hell-fire sermons of New England Calvinist, Jonathan Edwards, to the status of his companionate coffin-worm:

> Lathlic is thæt eorth-hus, Loathly is that earth-house,
> And grim inne to wunien And grim to dwell in;
> Ther thu scealt wunien.   There thou shalt dwell
> And wurmes the todeleth. And worms shall share thee.
>   ('The Grave' [*c.* 1150], ll. 29–32; Oxford, Bodleian MS 343, f. 170)

She had read her Emerson, delighting in his poems, and knew that his Aunt Mary had introduced him to the Hindu concept of *ākāsa* (ether), the fifth and subtlest element, replete with invisible energies and intelligences. And 'Ether Acre', yoking the most inaccessible and basest of elements/senses, problematises and glamorises the Gothicism of death in a characteristically surreal and liberating fashion. Transcendentalism acknowledges a world beyond 'dull sublunary' existence and, as Emerson wrote: 'Time dissipates to shining ether the solid angularity of facts.' Beyond even this Emily intuited the concept of time as alien to the unconscious: in the midnight cease 'When everything that ticked has stopped, / . . . space stares, all around' ('It was not death, for I stood up', ll. 17–18, F355 [1862]). The thorny old problem of the time of the resurrection – is it at death or at the second coming's trump? – merely bears witness to the finite mind's incapacity to handle eternity:

> Since then 'tis centuries; but each
> Feels shorter than the day
> I first surmised the horses' heads
> Were toward eternity.
> > ('Because I could not stop for Death', ll. 21–4, F479 [1862])

Yet one does not have to be coy to appreciate a profounder fear than that 'yonder all before us lye / Desarts of vast Eternity', the dread of a soul's being 'admitted to Itself', immediately being made aware of all the soul's self-inscriptions. The Gothic solitudes of space, of sea, of death will constitute 'Society':

> Compared with that profounder site,
> That polar privacy,
> A Soul admitted to Itself:
> Finite Infinity.
> > ('There is a solitude of space', ll. 4–7, F1696 [undated])[8]

The corpse's text acknowledges that, prior to the astounding revelation of the resurrection, the soul trapped – however temporarily – within the decaying body must come face to face in this mind-freezing 'polar privacy' with the awful reality of 'Itself'. This internalised Gothic is of a different order of terror from all the tired paraphernalia of the Gothic imaginary:

> Far safer, through an Abbey – gallop –
> The Stones a'chase –
> Than moonless – One's A'self encounter –
> In lonesome place –
> > ('One need not be a chamber – to be Haunted', ll. 9–12, F407 [1862])

This Dickinson corpse is trapped somewhere between 'science of the grave' and the Gothic science of psychology. In the contemplation of such dread self-realisation there is a need for self-compassion; like Hopkins she might have written: 'let / Me live to my sad self hereafter kind', and the final stanza of ''Twas just this time, last year, I died' shows how Dickinson can 'leave comfort root-room':

> But this sort, grieved myself,
> And so, I thought the other way,
> And just this time, some perfect year –

Themself, should come to me –

(ll. 21–4, F344 [1862])

Thinking 'the other way' is not simply an antidote to grief or terror, a reassurance of heavenly reunion, but a hallmark of her mind-set, prone as it is to destabilising Gothic inversion. We may think of her transgressive female selfhood as anxious to reinscribe the conventional constructions of femininity, but her selfhood is equally anxious to rewrite the corpse's text, unsexed as it might be, or the soul's text, sexless as it is. When the familiar paternoster's ' "Father, thy will be done" to-day' provokes a candid admittance that 'my will goes the other way', it would be limiting simply to regard such candour as rejection of the *pater familias* with his patriarchal Law.[9] We are all equally 'guilty of dust and sin', none more – or less – so than the corpse. One does not need a revolver, it is enough to be forewarned – with a primed imagination – of eschatological ecstasies. It helps to 'read [our] sentence steadily': such matter-of-fact conceiving of shattering shocks at the point where baser 'matter ends' and enlightenment suffuses the soul is more than cathartic:

> I made my soul familiar
> With her extremity,
> That at the last it should not be
> A novel agony,
>
> But she and Death, acquainted,
> Meet tranquilly as friends,
> Salute and pass without a hint –
> And there the matter ends.

('I read my sentence steadily', ll. 9–16; F432: [1862])

Such deceptive simplicity is apparent also in the polite *contretemps* between spirit and dusty Death. At the burial-ground Death conveniently 'argues from the [substantial] ground' of surrounding bodily corruption:

> 'Dissolve,' says Death. The Spirit, 'Sir,
> I have another trust.'
>
> Death doubts it, argues from the ground.
> The Spirit turns away,
> Just laying off, for evidence,
> An Overcoat of Clay.

('Death is a Dialogue', ll. 5–10, F973 [1862])

The Spirit's reluctance to accept dissolution is nothing compromised by its conclusive – and triumphant – doffing earthy vesture. It is the interaction of body and soul, within this 'Vale of Soul-making', that produces indissoluble identity. Dickinson is so preoccupied with writing the corpse's text on account of her fascination with the resurrected state of humanity and her determination to worry away at the details of exactly what overcoat the turning Spirit will don when 'this corruptible must put on incorruption.' She is desperately curious to investigate the dimensions of this celestial Gothic metamorphosis. Lacking authoritative exegesis of the precise differences between the 'natural body' and the 'spiritual body', she must rely upon the intimations of her own elusive soul, moments of mysterious clarity:

> The Shapes we buried, dwell about,
> Familiar, in the Rooms –
> Untarnished by the Sepulchre,
> The Mouldering Playmate comes –
>
> In just the Jacket that he wore
> Long buttoned in the Mold
> Since we – old mornings, Children – played –
> Divided by a world –
>
> The Grave yields back her Robberies –
> The Years, our pilfered Things –
> Bright Knots of Apparitions
> Salute us with their wings –
>
> As we – it were – that perished –
> Themself – had just remained till we rejoin them
> And 'twas they, and not ourself
> That mourned.
>
> ('Of nearness to her sundered Things', ll. 5–20, F337 [1862])

The contrast between 'In just the Jacket that he wore / Long buttoned in the Mold' and 'Bright Knots of Apparitions', complete with saluting wings, highlights her difficulties concerning the imagined degree of 'changed' corpses' corporality. Helen Vendler is undoubtedly right to suggest that Dickinson derives her 'Bright Knots' from Henry Vaughan's 'The Retreat', but this is surely not an unconscious – as Vendler supposes – but a deliberate echo of recaptured 'Angel-infancy' as he 'felt through all this fleshly dress / Bright shoots of everlastingness' ('The Retreat', ll. 19–20). Must the 'Mouldering Playmate' corpse rise on his points in a resurrected *corps de ballet* (Vendler, 2010: 139)? Is the comfortable familiar fleshly body to be despised? Perhaps Dickinson would have felt with Wittgenstein that 'the human body is the best picture of the human soul', or gloried in her fellow modernist botanist's conviction that:

Man's spirit will be flesh-bound when found at best,
But uncumberèd: meadow-down is not distressed
For a rainbow footing it nor he for his bónes rísen.
                    ('The Caged Skylark', ll. 12–14 in Hopkins, 1953: 31–2)

The 'bone-house' of the Anglo-Saxon kenning is no mere container for heart and brain. The rainbow symbolism of divine grace affirms that the 'uncumberèd' body is ultimately no constricting cage for the 'dare-gale' soul. Similarly Dickinson's Gothic concentration upon the corpse's text affords release from a medievalising dualism which regards matter and spirit as irreconcilable, and from the terrestrial Gothic fear of what the corpse might signify or say.

James McIntosh cites a letter of 'about 1878' to an unrecorded recipient revealing her frustrated desire to cross-question Paul concerning what happens to the corpse in that 'twinkling of an eye': 'Were the statement "We shall not all sleep, but we shall all be changed," made in earthly Manuscript, were his Residence in the Universe, we should pursue the Writer until he explained it to us' (McIntosh, 2004: 88). In a letter of October 1880 she sent to her cousin Perez Dickinson Cowan, on receiving a memorial of his baby daughter Margaret who had died the previous November, she writes with acutely sensitive compassion:

It may have been she came to show you Immortality – Her startling little flight would imply she did –. May I remind you what Paul said, or do you think of nothing else, these October Nights, without her Crib to visit? The little Furniture of loss has Lips of Dirks to stab us – I hope Heaven is warm – There are so many Barefoot ones – I hope it is near – the little Tourist was so small – I hope it is not so unlike Earth that we shall miss the peculiar form – the Mold of the Bird. (Johnson and Ward, 1986: 671)

The fragile delicacy of an infant corpse is caught in 'the Mold of the Bird', and the 'startling little flight' of this small 'Tourist' recalls Bede's sparrow fluttering through a lighted hall; this Robin Phoenix exemplifies the journeying soul's immortality.[10] The meaning of the empty crib is as profound as that of the empty sepulchre, but its potential for raw and piercing grief is frighteningly captured in the oxymoronic Gothic of 'Lips of Dirks'.[11]

The poem which this prefaces is little short of astounding in its feverish haste and dramatic immediacy of confirmed revelation. The excitement of gospel news confirmation in floodlit illumination is tangible, electric – she has just received the answer to the question posed in 1 Corinthians 15: 35:

'And with what Body do they come'?
Then they *do* come, Rejoice!
What Door – what Hour-Run – run – My Soul!
Illuminate the House!
'Body'! Then real – a Face – and Eyes –
To know that it is them! –
Paul knew the Man that knew the News –
He passed through Bethlehem –
            (' "And with what Body do they come?" ', ll. 1–8, F1537 [1880])[12]

In the 'The Body grows without' Dickinson had described the body as a 'Temple [that] stands always / Ajar – secure – inviting; / It never did betray / The Soul that asked it's shelter / In solemn honesty' (ll. 4–8, F438 [1862]). If the portals of the temple of the soul stand ajar, likewise did the gates of heaven in the consolatory postbellum sentimentality of an astoundingly popular novel by Elizabeth Stuart Phelps (1844–1911): *The Gates Ajar* (1868).[13] Barton Levi St Armand has linked Dickinson and Phelps, not only in terms of their New England resistance to stern-father-figures, defiance of orthodoxy and their devotion to Elizabeth Barrett Browning's *Aurora Leigh*, but in their 'imaginative way of dealing with a brute reality compounded of the patriarchal nature of American Calvinism and the abiding fact of sudden death' (St Armand, 1984: 15).[14] The loved ones of the 600,000 Civil War dead cried out for comfort – like Phelps whose beau, Lieutenant Samuel Hopkins Thompson, was killed at Antietam, or Phelps's heroine, Mary Cabot, whose beloved brother was shot dead in action. Mary's devoutly heretical aunt, Winifred Forceythe, provided that therapeutic help:

'Roy loved you. Our Father, for some tender, hidden reason, took him out of your sight for a while. Though changed much, he can have forgotten nothing. Being *only out of sight*, you remember, not lost, nor asleep, nor annihilated, he goes on loving. To love must mean to think of, to care for, to hope for, to pray for, not less out of a body than in it.'
    'But that must mean – why, that must mean – '
    'That he is near you. I do not doubt it.' The sunshine quivered in among the ivy-leaves,[15] and I turned to watch it, thinking.
    'I do not doubt,' she went on, speaking low, – 'I cannot doubt that our absent dead are very present with us.' (Phelps, 1868: 87–8)[16]

The feminised, maternal Christianity of *The Gates Ajar* has been seen as relevant to aspects of the development of Dickinson's eschatological thinking, especially 'To the parish night; / Of the separated people / Which are out of sight' ('Three Weeks passed since I had seen Her –', ll. 9–11, F992 [1865]), but little or no attention appears to have been paid to Elizabeth Stuart Phelps's poetry. In her *Songs of the Silent World*

(1885) Phelps features the loving attentiveness of undeparted presences, speaking corpses that abide, anxious to comfort and distressed only by the weakness of living senses, unable to hear or feel them. 'The First Christmas Apart' expresses the pain of the newly-dead's awareness of the impossibility of communication between a living and a resurrected body, of the realisation 'that life is deaf, / And not that death is dumb':

> I cross the old familiar door
> And take the dear old chair.
> You look with desolated eyes
> Upon me sitting there.
>
> You gaze and see not, though the tears
> In gazing burn and start.
> Believe, the living are the blind,
> Not that the dead depart.
>
> ('The First Christmas Apart', ll. 9–16; in Phelps, 1885: 16)

On one level we are presented with the domestication of death, the poem seeks to afford comfort and reassurance to the bereaved, yet we are presented with a Gothic failure of reciprocity, a self isolated, not by premature burial or coffin constriction, but by a paralysing breakdown of loving exchange. This is not like the agonised sense of division felt by Rossetti's 'Blessed Damozel', gazing from 'the rampart of God's house … So high that looking downward thence / She scarce could see the sun', but closer to 'the other way' intuiting of Dickinson: 'As we – it were – that perished – / Themself – had just remained till we rejoin them / And 'twas they, and not ourself / That mourned' ('Of nearness to her sundered Things', ll. 17–20). The physical 'nearness to sundered Things' amplifies the pain:

> I lean above you as before,
> Faithful, my arms enfold.
> Oh, could you know that life is numb,
> Nor think that death is cold!
>
> ('The First Christmas Apart', ll. 21–4)

A Gothic gulf of inches between two consciousnesses proscribes revelation or contact in their Christmas home; the dreadful isolation of lover from beloved is such that she or he would endure a second death:

> Heart of my heart! if earth or Heaven
> Had speech or language fine
> Enough, or death or life could give
> Me symbol, sound, or sign

To reach you – thought, or touch, or eye,
Body or soul – I'd die
Again, to make you understand:
My darling! This is *I!*

('The First Christmas Apart', ll. 31–8)

Phelps's desire to console a living audience by stressing the continuing closeness of the loving deceased is severely compromised by the apocalyptic Gothic of their agonies of separation. To the resurrected body, the living partner seems insensate, as 'dumb', 'deaf', 'blind' and 'numb' as a corpse, and the only mutuality is in mourning. Heaven's gates might be ajar, but the doors of perception are closed at least to earthly senses while the unprofane gaze longingly through the two-way mirror of another dimension.

The trust-repairing teaching of Winifred Forceythe in *The Gates Ajar* underlined that 'Nothing is lost', a text that chimed with both Dickinson's convictions and Victorian science:

The Chemical conviction
That Nought be lost
Enable in Disaster
My fractured Trust –

The Faces of the Atoms
If I shall see
How more the Finished Creatures
Departed me!

('The Chemical conviction', ll. 1–8, F1070 [1865])

But these *Songs of the Silent World* indicate that, prior to that reunion, the resurrected corpse, though clad in a 'life-like' body, has even less power to communicate with – or be viewed by – the living mourner than the tongue-tied cadaver. Although, as Dickinson claims, 'The Shapes we buried, dwell about, / Familiar, in the Rooms', the re-embodied corpse-persona of Phelps's 'The Room's Width' reveals that, in its Gothic isolation from the beloved, resurrection involves profound loss in a Protestant purgatory of absent presence:

I think if I should cross the room,
    Far as fear;
Should stand beside you like a thought –
    Touch you, Dear!

Like a fancy. To your sad heart
    It would seem
That my vision passed and prayed you,
    Or my dream.

Then you would look with lonely eyes –
    Lift your head –
And you would stir, and sigh, and say –
    'She is dead.'

Baffled by death and love, I lean
    Through the gloom.
O Lord of life! am I forbid
    To cross the room?

               (ll. 1–16, in Phelps, 1885: 15)

Is this a divine injunction to forestall any new Lazarus revelation? Certainly Emma Lavinia, now in death as close to Hardy as she had been forty years earlier, experiences the same isolating prohibition. When the grieving husband – 'a dead man held on end' – ventriloquises the calling voice of a dead wife, she is textualised as dedicated to devotion but unable to find 'speech or language fine / Enough' to communicate:

He does not think that I haunt here nightly:
    How shall I let him know
That whither his fancy sets him wandering
    I, too, alertly go? –
Hover and hover a few feet from him
    Just as I used to do,
But cannot answer the words he lifts me –
    Only listen thereto!

      ('The Haunter', ll. 1–8, in Hardy, 2001: 345–6)

Unheard voices from old Wessex and New England each supply an assenting answer to the question posed in Elizabeth Phelps's *Beyond the Gates*: '[W]as it possible to feel desolate in Heaven?' (Phelps 1883: 180).[17] Perhaps it is to obviate such pain that Dickinson's corpse-persona employs her domesticated Gothic, patiently 'lay[ing] the marble tea' whilst waiting to be (re)united with her living lover:

The grave my little cottage is,
Where, keeping house for thee,
I make my parlor orderly,
And lay the marble tea,

For two divided, briefly,
A cycle, it may be,
Till everlasting life unite
In strong society.

              (ll. 1–8, F1784 [undated])

The consolatory Gothic of Elizabeth Phelps's *Gates* novels, rooted in – and intensifying – the enormous post-war growth in spiritualism, conceived of heaven as a perfected version of comfortable antebellum New England, and critics have documented the strength of Dickinson's attachment to spiritualist discourse. Corpse-texts – automatically- or planchette-written – proliferated as obsession with 'crossing-over' embraced both sides of the Atlantic, amidst a welter of self-help table-knocking, occultism, Swedenborgianism, mesmerism and magnetism. In London, among those casting for comfort or 'bogie'-frights in Pre-Raphaelite drawing rooms, was Dante Gabriel Rossetti, who allegedly received regular cryptic corpse 'communications' from Lizzie Siddal through the oak table of Tudor House in Cheyne Walk.

In 1880 Thomas Hall Caine, a young but not uncritical acolyte, described the inaugurator of 'The Fleshly School of Poetry' as having a 'full round face that ought to be ruddy, but is deathly pale . . . the whole outward seeming is that of a man grown old long ages before his due time' (Allen, 1997: 93). Excessive medievalising and addiction to the anaesthetising and hypnotic charms of chloral were familiarising the corpulent Rossetti with the 'pallid innuendoes / And dim approach' of 'the supple Suitor' ('Death is the Supple Suitor', ll. 5–6, F1470 [1878]). He memorialised the woman he had inscribed/textualised/wronged: 'As much as in a hundred years she's dead / Yet is today the day on which she died' (ll. 1–2, in Rossetti, 1911: 239) but, convinced he was dying in the spring of 1876, the morbidly sensitive Rossetti seems terrified at the prospect of Gothic reproof: 'Let me not on any account be buried at Highgate, but my remains burnt as I say' (Fredeman, 2007: 271). Yet reunion remained a devoutly desired consummation; a fragmentary text he enters into a late notebook records his desire to seal 'a bargain to engrossing death':

> Or give ten years of life's most bitter wane
> To see the loved one as she was again.
>
> (ll. 1–2, in Rossetti, 1911: 244)

In 1882, the year that Rossetti's corruptible body was laid in Birchington-on-Sea churchyard under a Celtic cross designed by Ford Madox Brown, Hopkins was completing 'The Leaden Echo and the Golden Echo' to instress Matthew 10: 30 and the 'trumpet crash' miracle of corporeal resurrection. As the earth filled his mouth, perhaps Rossetti was forgetting the Gothic absurdity of a coffin filled with red-gold hair; Elizabeth Siddal's 'beauty-in-the-ghost' might be 'kept / Far with fonder a care':

> See; not a hair is, not an eyelash, not the least lash lost; every hair
> Is, hair of the head, numbered.

Nay, what we had lighthanded left in surly the mere mould
Will have waked and have waxed and have walked with the wind
    what while we slept,
This side, that side hurling a heavyheaded hundredfold
    ('The Leaden Echo and the Golden Echo', ll. 20–4, in Hopkins, 1953: 54)

Notes

1. In Swinburne's 'After Death', published three months after Siddal's death and bogusly sourced as a traditional Breton ballad, the third board of the coffin lid 'spake and said: / "Is red gold worth a girl's gold head?"', *The Spectator*, 35 (24 May 1862), 578–9.
2. It was his painting of 'The Seed of David' triptych, commissioned for the reredos of the restored Llandaff Cathedral by Henry Austin Bruce, later Lord Aberdare, that brought Rossetti not only £400, but ready permission to exhume his wife from Home Secretary Bruce.
3. '[Ruskin] saw and bought on the spot every scrap of design hitherto produced by Miss Siddal. He declared that they were 'far better than mine, or almost than any-one's, and seemed quite wild with delight at getting them' (W. M. Rossetti, 1903: 277).
4. 'Utterly irrespective of Rossetti's feelings or my own, I should simply do what I do, if I could, as I should try to save a beautiful tree from being cut down, or a bit of a Gothic cathedral whose strength was failing. If you would be so good as to consider yourself as a piece of wood or Gothic for a few months, I should be grateful to you' (Ruskin to Siddal, April 1855, in W. M. Rossetti, 1899: 63).
5. Swinburne echoed Wilde, who thought it 'A1', and Theodore Watts-Duncan in their praise of 'A Year and a Day': 'Watts greatly admires the poem, which is as new to him as it is to me. I need not add that I agree with him. There is the same note of originality in discipleship which distinguishes her work in art – Gabriel's influence and example not more perceptible than her own independence and freshness of inspiration' (Lang, 1959–62, vol. 6: 94).
6. Cf. 'You crave one kiss of my clay-cold lips; / But my breath smells earthy strong; / If you have one kiss of my clay-cold lips, / Your time will not be long' ('The Unquiet Grave', ll. 17–20). Siddal's work inspired Sir Edward Burne-Jones's *Clerk Saunders* (1861).
7. Cf. 'The props assist the house / Until the house is built, And then the props withdraw – . . . A past of plank and nail, / And slowness, – then the scaffolds drop – / Affirming it a soul' ('The props assist the house', ll. 1–3, 10–12, F729 [1863]).
8. Cf. 'But were it told to me, to-day, / That I might have the sky / For mine, I tell you that my heart / Would split, for size of me. / The meadows mine, the mountains mine, – / All forests, stintless stars, / As much of noon as I could take / Between my finite eyes' ('Before I got my eye put out', ll. 5–12, F336 [1862]).
9. See 'I have a king who does not speak' (F157 [1860]). In "Heavenly Father", take to thee' she accuses Him of 'The supreme

iniquity' in fashioning the Gothic self-contradiction of the human condition – immortal soul within corruptible body: ' "we are dust." / We apologize to Thee / For Thine own Duplicity' (ll. 6–8, F1500 [1879]).

10. 'I knew a Bird that would sing as firm in the centre of Dissolution, as in it's Father's nest – Phenix, or the Robin?' (Johnson and Ward, 1986: 685).

11. Relevant images of death and dying are also explored by Andrew Smith in Chapter 10 of this volume.

12. Cf. the poem sent on the death of her friend Charles Wadsworth in October 1883 to Charles H. Clark, which draws upon a musical analogy in attempting to capture the enduring harmony of the soul–body symbiosis: 'Below, the Body speaks, / But as the Spirit furnishes – / Apart, it never talks – / The Music in the Violin / Does not emerge alone' ('The Spirit lasts – but in what mode – ', ll. 1–6, F1627 [1883]).

13. Phelps clearly stated her feminist purpose: 'It was written to comfort some few of the women whose misery crowded the land – the helpless, outnumbering, unconsulted women, they whom war trampled down without a choice or protest; the patient, limited, domestic women, who thought little but loved much, and, loving, had lost all' (1897: 98).

14. He might have added their championing of George Eliot; Phelps was the first woman to teach undergraduates at Boston University, foregrounding in a course of lectures on 'Representative Modern Fiction' the novels of her friend and correspondent, Eliot.

15. Contrast Christina Rossetti's 'thro' the lattice ivy-shadows crept', see above p. 77.

16. Winifred Forceythe also has decided ideas about the resurrected corpse: 'What would be the use of having a body that you can't see and touch? A body is a *body*, not a spirit.' She is amused at the notions intelligent people 'have of the heavenly body. Vague visions of floating about in the clouds, of balancing – with a white robe on, perhaps – in stiff rows about a throne, like the angels in the old pictures, converging to an apex, or ranged in semicircles like so many marbles' (1868: p. 117).

17. Interestingly, this novella, dedicated to Phelps's brother Stuart who 'passed beyond August 29, 1883', is now available at www.horrormasters.com/Text/a1727.pdf.

References

Allen, Vivien (1997). *Hall Caine: Portrait of a Victorian Romancer*. Sheffield: Academic Press.

Child, Francis James (ed.) (1882–98). *The English and Scottish Popular Ballads*, 5 vols. London: Henry Stevens; Boston: Houghton Mifflin.

'Conductor' (1843). 'The Principles of Landscape-Gardening and of Landscape Architecture applied to the Laying out of Public Cemeteries and the Improvement of Churchyards', *The Gardener's Magazine*, 9, 93–105, 97.

Franklin, R.W. (ed.) (1998). *The Poems of Emily Dickinson*, 3 vols. Cambridge, MA: Harvard University Press.

Fredeman, William B. (ed.) (2004). *The Correspondence of Dante Gabriel Rossetti*, vol. 4: *The Chelsea Years, 1863–1872*. Woodbridge: D. S. Brewer.

——(ed.) (2007). *The Correspondence of Dante Gabriel Rossetti*, vol. 7: *The Last Decade, 1873–1882*. Woodbridge: D. S. Brewer.

Hardy, Thomas (2001). *Thomas Hardy: The Complete Poems*, ed. James Gibson. Basingstoke: Palgrave.

Hopkins, Gerard Manley (1953). *Poems and Prose of Gerard Manley Hopkins*, ed. W. H. Gardner. Harmondsworth: Penguin.

Johnson, Thomas H. and Theodora Ward (eds) (1986). *The Letters of Emily Dickinson*. Cambridge, MA: Harvard University Press.

Lang, Cecil Y. (ed.) (1959–62). *The Swinburne Letters*, 6 vols. New Haven: Yale University Press.

McIntosh, James (2004). *Nimble Believing: Dickinson and the Unknown*. Ann Arbor: University of Michigan Press.

Phelps, Elizabeth Stuart (1868). *The Gates Ajar*. Boston: Fields, Osgood & Co.

——(1883) *Beyond the Gates*. New York: Houghton, Mifflin.

——(1885). *Songs of the Silent World*. Boston: Houghton Mifflin.

——(1897). *Chapters from a Life*. Boston: Houghton Mifflin.

Pound, Ezra (1921). *Poems 1918–21*. New York: Boni and Liveright.

Rossetti, Christina (1862). *Goblin Market and Other Poems*. London: Macmillan.

Rossetti, Dante Gabriel (1870). *Poems*. London: Ellis.

——(1898). *The House of Life*. London: Ellis and Elvey.

——(1911). *The Works of Dante Gabriel Rossetti*, ed. William M. Rossetti. London: Ellis.

Rossetti, William Michael (ed.) (1899). *Ruskin: Rossetti: Preraphaelitism: Papers 1854–1862*. London: George Allen.

——(1903). 'Dante Rossetti and Elizabeth Siddal: With Facsimiles of Five Unpublished Drawings by Dante Rossetti in the Collection of Mr Harold Hartley', *Burlington Magazine*, 1, 273–95.

St Armand, Barton Levi (1984). *Emily Dickinson and Her Culture: The Soul's Society*. Cambridge: Cambridge University Press.

Scott, Walter (ed.) (1802). *Minstrelsy of the Scottish Border*, 2 vols. Kelso: Ballantyne.

Siddal, Elizabeth (1978). *Poems and Drawings of Elizabeth Siddal*, ed. Roger C. Lewis and Mark Samuels Lasner. Wolfville, NS, Canada: Wombat Press.

Swinburne, Algernon Charles (1866). *Poems and Ballads*. London: Hotten.

Vendler, Helen (2010). *Dickinson: Selected Poems and Commentaries*. Cambridge, MA: Harvard University Press.

Chapter 6

The Victorian Ghost Story
Nick Freeman

Creatures of mist, half credited;
Our faint form flings
No shadow in moonlight on the bed
We visit; noiseless is our tread,
Who come from deserts of the dead,
Where no bird sings.

(Anon. in Dalby, 1995: 1)

During the nineteenth century, the ghost story developed from an embedded narrative in a novel or miscellany into a distinct genre of short fiction which encompassed the brief, spooky anecdote and the technically elaborate and psychologically sophisticated tale. In writing ghost stories, Michael Cox and R. A. Gilbert note that:

> A high degree of purely technical skill is essential, both in plotting and in handling description. Hyperbole lays the literary ghost with deadly finality: it gathers strength through obliquity and operates most powerfully on us, in Elizabeth Bowen's words, 'through a series of happenings whose horror lies in their being just, *just* out of the true'. (Cox and Gilbert, 1986: ix–x)

In the Victorian era, these skills were exercised by major writers and by storytellers who, while they may not have entered the first rank of 'literature', have nevertheless been accorded high praise within their own field. Mrs J. H. Riddell, J. Sheridan Le Fanu, and M. R. James are notable examples. Finally, between 1830 and 1914, the ghost story became increasingly associated with contemporary settings, showing that the technological advances of the time were no defence against the terrifying and inexplicable.

The ghost has a long literary heritage, but roughly speaking, before the Gothic novel placed the 'haunted edifice' as its 'inevitable centrepiece', ghosts were more 'stage device' than 'central character[s]'

(Ashley, 1997: 403). As Mike Ashley notes, Elizabethan and Jacobean dramatists tended to deploy the ghost as 'a melodramatic warning, a harbinger of doom, or an outward manifestation of an individual's guilt' (1997: 403). The historian Owen Davies has shown how these motifs emerged from folklore concerning unquiet spirits seeking vengeance or restitution, guarding treasure or serving as moral exemplars, and they were to remain a rich resource for supernaturalists of all kinds. The crucial distinction between Gothic and earlier literary ghosts is, however, that in fiction from the 1760s onwards, the ghost's purpose was primarily to frighten and horrify rather than to teach moral lessons. Novels such as George Walker's *The Haunted Castle* (1794) and Matthew Lewis's *The Monk* (1796), the latter of which featured the terrifying 'Bleeding Nun', helped evolve a repertoire of 'sheeted spectres, rattling chains and gibbering skeletons' (Ashley, 1997: 403) which led to the types of 'horrid' scene so savoured by Isabella Thorpe in chapter 6 of Jane Austen's *Northanger Abbey* (written 1798, published 1818). Early Gothic fiction often concluded by providing a rational explanation for events that seemed initially to be of supernatural origin, typically exposing them as the fabrications of villainous patriarchs, but Lewis and others exploited the narrative potential of 'proper' ghosts and satanic emissaries. Unfortunately, the law of diminishing returns ensured that these soon became formulaic and open to ridicule: Thomas Love Peacock's *Nightmare Abbey* (1818), like Austen's *Northanger Abbey*, offered memorable satire of the emerging tradition and its uncritical readers.

Gothic writers in Britain, Europe and America soon realised that the most effective ghost stories were reasonably short, for a substantial novel typically struggled to avoid becoming padded out with non-supernatural scenes or degenerating into repetition. As Lewis had shown with his Bleeding Nun, freeing the ghostly encounter from the demands of intricate novelistic plotting allowed for bravura effects which did not need to be dulled by explanation and formal neatness. A dramatic focus on a single event was a central aspect of the success of two of the most artistically successful ghost stories of the pre-Victorian period, Walter Scott's 'Wandering Willie's Tale', an episode in his novel *Redgauntlet* (1824) which adapts a folktale from Joseph Train's *Strains of the Mountain Muse* (1814), and his self-contained 'The Tapestried Chamber' (1828). The latter made good use of a situation widely deployed in later fiction – a character spends a night in a haunted room and has an encounter with something frightening, in this case a malign female spectre. With bedtime reading a growing pastime in an increasingly literate nineteenth-century Britain, the content of stories often echoed the circumstances of their consumption, and transformed the bedroom from the traditional place of safety and repose into a site of unrest and horror.

The 'episode' was gradually supplanted by the self-contained short work, but in skilled hands, the excursion into the supernatural could add new depth and resonance to apparently realist fiction: the apparition of the ghostly Cathy Earnshaw that so terrifies Lockwood in chapter 3 of Emily Brontë's *Wuthering Heights* (1847) is a chilling example. In this sense the ghostly episode was akin to the set-piece nightmare that brought a Gothic element to otherwise realistic works, disrupting the 'normal' world with violent, illogical and, for the novelist, eminently useful symbolic overtones.

The late 1830s saw the publication of two works of key significance for the Victorian ghost story. The first was an episode in Dickens's *The Pickwick Papers* (1836–7), 'The Story of the Goblins who Stole a Sexton', a sketch which acts as a prelude to the visions of Ebenezer Scrooge in *A Christmas Carol* (1843). The second, J. Sheridan Le Fanu's 'A Strange Event in the Life of Schalken the Painter', which appeared in the *Dublin University Magazine* in May 1839, was an altogether darker affair. His 'The Ghost and the Bone-Setter' (1838) had reworked an Irish folktale, but 'Schalken' mixed historical figures such as Gottfried Schalken (1643–1706), a Dutch genre painter who excelled in the representation of candlelight, with the folkloric motif of the Satanic bargain. Schalken's mentor, Gerard Douw, has a ward, the beautiful young Rose Velderkaust, whom Schalken loves. Unfortunately, the customs of the day mean that she is married off to Vanderhausen, a wealthy merchant of repellent aspect who never removes his gloves. Vanderhausen's skin is cadaverous, he has 'two long, discoloured fangs' and his appearance as a whole suggests 'the corpse of some atrocious malefactor, which had long hung blackening upon the gibbet' before its possession by a demon (Le Fanu, 1995: 17). Some months later, Rose returns to Douw's house in a dishevelled and terrified state, crying 'The dead and the living can never be one – God has forbidden it!' (1995: 22). '[T]he darkness is unsafe,' Rose sobs (1995: 23), and she is right, for despite Schalken and Douw's efforts, she is carried off, seemingly by her 'mysterious wooer' (1995: 24), and vanishes without trace.

What gives the story its peculiar horror however is its coda, in which, years later, Schalken visits a church in Rotterdam and has a vision of Rose, wearing 'the same arch smile which used to enchant the artist' in happier days (1995: 25). The vision then climbs into a bed containing 'the livid and demoniac form of Vanderhausen' (1995: 26). Schalken faints at this point, but he has already seen enough to make clear the carnal relationship between Rose and her abductor. Le Fanu's story disdained the providential and refused to explain itself, offering an unsettling fusion of fact and fiction. Through sparing use of horrific description and granting considerable imaginative leeway to readers, it was to prove extremely influential on the ghost story's development.

The appearance of Dickens's *A Christmas Carol* was an equally important moment. Dickens set his novella at Christmas, almost single-handedly creating the vogue for the Yuletide ghost story that continues today, even though uncanny tales with Christmas settings can be traced back to the middle ages and *Gawain and the Green Knight*. He also set it in the homely English present, blending realist social critique with Christian homily, sentimentality, comedy and, in the scenes where Ebenezer Scrooge is visited by the ghost of his old partner Jacob Marley, a mixture of horror and knowingly deployed fictional convention. 'Scrooge then remembered to have heard that ghosts in haunted houses were described as dragging chains', Dickens writes, but such devices have the paradoxical effect of making the transparent Marley, wrapped in a steel chain of 'cash-boxes, keys, padlocks, ledgers, deeds and heavy purses' more rather than less believable (Dickens, 1985: 57). The transformation of a door-knocker into Marley's face, 'like a bad lobster in a dark cellar' (1985: 54) is memorably horrifying, but Dickens wished to entertain and teach rather than merely alarm, as his preface made clear. He hopes his book would 'haunt [his readers] pleasantly, and no one would wish to lay it' (1985: 41), though this lightness of tone ebbed during his career and is notably absent from his late masterpiece, 'The Signalman' (1866), the story of a railwayman haunted by what turn out to be precognitive visions of a fatal accident.

Dickens was a key practitioner of the ghost story, not least since his popularity rubbed off on most of the genres in which he worked and because, as 'conductor' of the magazines *Household Words* and *All the Year Round*, he commissioned individual ghost stories and contributions to shared projects such as *Mugby Junction* (1866), where 'The Signalman' first appeared. Another collaborative work, *The Haunted House* (1859), arose from an argument with the spiritualist William Howitt, and featured stories by Wilkie Collins, Elizabeth Gaskell and Hesba Stretton. A bold if not wholly successful attempt to produce a Christmas portmanteau, the book's conceit was its six writers each spending a week in a (fictional) haunted house, and at the end of that time, telling a tale of the ghostly encounters they had had there. Dickens's contributions 'debunked the idea of haunting by anything other than one's own recollections' (Thomas, 2000: 256) but he remained a keen student of the ghost story, listing its conventions in his essay, 'A Christmas Tree' (1850), and always seeking to develop and innovate.

One of his most prized contributors to *Household Words* was Gaskell, whose supernatural tales offered an amalgam of progressive political attitudes, a sophisticated understanding of Gothic convention, and a willingness to feminise and eroticise the ghostly. Stories such as 'Disappearances' (1851) drew on and occasionally ironised the type of folklore collected in works such as Catherine Crowe's *The Night Side of Nature* (1848), which concentrated less on 'legendary ghosts' than on 'personal experiences and the more subjective types of supranormal encounter' (Bennett, 2000: 13). Dickens reviewed Crowe's book in the *Examiner* and showed both a wide knowledge of ghost lore and a general scepticism about the existence of spirits. Crowe was, however, not simply a collector of folk tales, for, in seeking to investigate 'the probable state of the soul after death' (Crowe, 2000: 23), she maintained that what was presently regarded as supernatural or miraculous would eventually be explained by new scientific doctrines or modes of investigation. As such, Crowe envisaged the later discipline of parapsychology, as well as introducing the term 'poltergeist' into English. Her work was at once an inspiring compendium of source material for future writers and an anticipation of the more scientifically minded ghost stories that would become popular in the early twentieth century.

Gaskell utilised something of Crowe's emphasis on personal experience, but her stories also drew on Gothic notions of the tyrannical father and wicked inheritance ('The Ghost in the Garden Room', later retitled 'The Crooked Branch' 1859, 'The Grey Woman', 1861), and on the dichotomised view of woman as angel or whore prevalent in the mid-Victorian period, even though her stories were often set in earlier times. In 'The Poor Clare' (1856), which opens in December 1747, Lucy is haunted by a shadowy Other who, though seemingly her double, has 'a loathsome demon soul looking out of . . . grey eyes, that were in turn mocking and voluptuous' (Gaskell, 2000: 78). Gaskell's stories were distinguished by their psychological depth; her spectres are all the more disquieting for being rooted in convincing characterisation and everyday settings. Nevertheless, as E. F. Bleiler points out in a discussion of Victorian fictional conventions, even writers of Gaskell's calibre produced work that was in some senses formulaic. The 'writer of a ghost story in the mid-Victorian era demanded very little suspension of disbelief,' he argues. 'There should be only one breach of reality, and this supernaturalism should not grow naturally out of a fantastic background but should be obtrusive in a realistic world' (Bleiler, 1977: xvii). Without being formally spelled out, these principles were reiterated by many writers of the period, though Bleiler makes an exception of Le Fanu, whose work was 'quite different from that of the other Victorians' (1977: xvii) and altogether more sinister in tone.

Ghostly fiction, like other literary modes, typically follows a cycle of innovation, imitation, decline, burlesque and revival. By the late 1850s, this was well established in texts that were, as Bleiler indicates, filled with uncritical repetition. At the end of the 1850s however, the ghost story began to develop in new ways. In Edward Bulwer-Lytton's 'The Haunted and the Haunters, or The House and the Brain' (1859), for instance, a haunted house is investigated by a rationalist who arms himself against 'superstitious fancy' (Bulwer-Lytton, 1944: 120) with a bull terrier and a volume of Macaulay's essays, only to encounter terrifying shadows and apparitions that challenge his no-nonsense credo. The narrator is clearly in agreement with Crowe in venturing that 'what is called the supernatural is only a something in the laws of nature of which we have been hitherto ignorant.' 'The apparition of a ghost is', he says, 'contrary to received opinion, within the laws of nature, and namely, not supernatural' (Bulwer-Lytton, 1944: 126). Such statements have little protective value, however, when the narrator is pursued by 'a darkness shaping itself out of the air' (1944: 127). The story's central situation has been borrowed countless times since, and the dialogue between rationalism and superstition remains at the heart of the genre.

During the 1850s and 1860s, Dickens and Gaskell combined parallel careers as more-or-less realist novelists and writers of Gothic short stories. The arrival of sensation fiction in the late 1850s, which cross-fertilised the dense plotting and contemporary settings of a novel such as Gaskell's *North and South* (1855) with Gothic elements, blurred the boundary between the two forms and invigorated the ghostly tale. Wilkie Collins's *The Woman in White* (1859–60) opens with an encounter with a mysterious apparition on a lonely road, the dramatic impact of which would certainly be diluted without its audience's familiarity with earlier stories. Collins, a close friend of Dickens, wrote a number of supernatural works, including the novel *The Haunted Hotel: A Mystery of Modern Venice* (1878) and short stories such as 'The Dream Woman' (1855) and 'Miss Jéromette and the Clergyman' (1875). Like 'The Signalman', these dramatised the haunted realm between dream, vision and ghostly manifestation. He and Le Fanu often made use of the premonitionary dream or nightmare, employing such devices as 'revelatory codas rather than overtures' (Sullivan, 1986: 259). Incidents of this type destabilised a story's surface realism but greatly enriched its characterisation and atmosphere, as well as generating excitement.

In the 1860s, Collins was rivalled as a sensational writer by Mary Elizabeth Braddon, whose own flair for ghostly fiction is shown in stories such as the much-anthologised 'The Cold Embrace' and 'Eveline's Visitant' (both 1862), and by Le Fanu, who, having been largely inactive during the 1850s, returned to form with a series of ghostly fantasies: 'Squire Toby's Will' (1868), in which a son learns the folly of filial disobedience; 'Dickon the Devil' (1872), a story of a ghost's murderous vengeance; 'The White Cat of Drumgunniol' (1870), in which a banshee takes feline form and brings ruin to an Irish family; and, most originally, the stories collected in *In A Glass Darkly* (1872). In 'Green Tea', Mr Jennings, a clergyman, is haunted by the apparition of a monkey which eventually drives him to suicide. A student of the Swedish mystic Emanuel Swendenborg, Jennings has somehow 'inadvertently opened' the 'inner eye' that allows him to enter the spirit world (Le Fanu, 1993: 39), only for its inherently malicious inhabitants to take note of him and become manifest. 'Mr Justice Harbottle' meanwhile sees a sadistic judge pay the price for his miscarriages of justice when his victims return from beyond the grave and place him on trial. In 1890, another Irish Gothic writer, Bram Stoker, refigured this story in 'The Judge's House', in which a student rents an ancient property in order to revise for his university examinations, only to be menaced and finally murdered by the malign spirit of a 'hanging judge'.

Le Fanu's stories are set in a universe in which no one, not even a baby, is safe: in 'Ghost Stories of the Tiled House', an episode from his novel *The House by the Churchyard* (1863), an entire family is menaced by a 'disembodied "white, fattish hand"' (Sullivan, 1986: 261). His recurrent interest in guilt and inter-generational cruelty make his best stories far from innocent diversions, and distinguish his work from that of his contemporaries. His influence was profound, not least because in Dr Martin Hesselius, the metaphysical physician of *In a Glass Darkly*, Le Fanu created the prototype psychic doctor/detective, a character who inspired Stoker's Van Helsing in *Dracula* (1897), Algernon Blackwood's *John Silence* (1908) and William Hope Hodgson's *Carnacki the Ghost Finder* (1913), all of whom supplement their awareness of folklore and the occult with the latest scientific knowledge.

Gaskell and Braddon were far from being the only women writers of their day to excel in the writing of ghost stories. Rhoda Broughton, Le Fanu's niece by marriage ('Poor Pretty Bobby', 1872), Amelia Edwards ('The Phantom Coach', 1864), Margaret Oliphant, and Mrs J. H. Riddell (*Weird Stories*, 1882) all produced notable tales, some of which, such as Oliphant's late work, 'The Library Window' (1896) have attained classic status. Some of these writers were Scots (Oliphant) or Irish (Riddell) and, as Jenni Calder says, 'exemplify the traditional readiness of the [Celtic] imagination to accommodate the unseen and the unexplainable'

(2000: xiii), but the prevalence of women as ghost story writers from the 1850s onwards is not easily accounted for. Perhaps they benefited from a widely held belief that being 'irrational' or 'intuitive', they were more sensitive to the spirit world – many of the best known spiritualist mediums were women – and could therefore write about it with insight denied to men. More prosaically, in a burgeoning print culture, women were frequent contributors to magazines and journals – Braddon founded *Belgravia* and edited *Temple Bar* – and keenly sensitive less to spirits than to the demands of the marketplace. Finally, fantasy allowed women to write about the mechanics and anxieties of their own world at one remove in fiction that, as Rosemary Jackson argues, 'explores and thereby threatens to dissolve many of the structures upon which social definitions of reality depend', such as 'those rigid boundaries between life and death, waking and dream states . . . reason and madness' (1989: xviii).

By the late 1880s however, the type of ghost story which had brought pleasant frissons to earlier Victorian readers had become stale and was falling victim to parodists. In Oscar Wilde's 'The Canterville Ghost' (1887), an old-fashioned English aristocratic ghost is unable to terrify the Otis family, American parvenus who have purchased his ancestral home complete with tapestried chamber. Wilde somehow combined witty parody with an affecting friendship between the ghost of Sir Simon de Canterville and Virginia Otis, but Jerome K. Jerome's *Told After Supper* (1891) bludgeoned the Yuletide tale without mercy. 'For ghost stories to be told on any other evening than the twenty-fourth of December would be impossible in English society as at present regulated', he observed (Jerome, 1891: 31), before astutely mocking such devices as the ghost who reveals hidden treasure and other staples of Victorian ghostly fiction. In 'My Own Story', the narrator asks a ghost if he 'had a hand in the death of that Italian peasant lad who came to the town once with a barrel-organ that played nothing but Scotch airs?', and is told by the 'fired up' and indignant spectre, 'Had a hand in it? . . . I murdered the youth myself' (Jerome, 1891: 143–4). In Rudyard Kipling's 'My Own True Ghost Story' (1888) meanwhile, the narrator allows an accumulation of circumstantial evidence to terrify him into a belief in ghosts, only to find thoroughly bathetic explanations for events the following morning. H. G. Wells offered in 'The Red Room' (1896) a deliberately over-familiar scenario (the bedroom where no one has ever passed a night safely) which contrived to be parodic and frightening in even measure: few readers can be immune to the terror of being alone in darkness and hearing a sudden and inexplicable movement nearby.

As these parodies show, fictional conventions had become outdated, yet the public appetite for ghost stories remained ravenous: why else go to the bother of ridicule? With readerships growing as a result of the educational reforms of the 1870s and 1880s, and with the new audience being served by a growing number of periodicals printing illustrated short fiction (*The Strand* (1891), Jerome's *Idler* (1892), *Pall Mall* (1893), *Windsor* (1895), *Pearson's* and *Temple* (1896)), the ghost story writer had no shortage of outlets, and the genre thrived in the years leading up to the First World War.

The consequence of this growth of readers and print media was that the ghost story moved into new areas. One road led into short, startling and often horrific tales that could be read at a sitting or indeed, read aloud. Good examples are E. Nesbit's 'Man-Size in Marble' and 'John Charrington's Wedding' from 1893. The first of these featured a young couple who move from London to the countryside. The husband dismisses local legends of walking statues as superstition, only for them to kill his wife in circumstances strongly symbolic of rape – her body is found clutching a marble finger. In the second, Nesbit refigured 'Schalken the Painter' by having a dead man ride off in the honeymoon coach with his bride, a scenario which, like Le Fanu's story, placed a transgressive sexual act at the heart of a supernatural tale. As a politically radical 'new woman', Nesbit turned a sceptical eye on men's marital behaviour and on their faith in rationalism – in 'Man-Size in Marble', the blasé husband and his friend the doctor are far less wise than Mrs Dorman, the countrywoman they regard as a relic of less enlightened times. The horrific conclusion of both stories still leaves something to the imagination but benefits from the increasingly permissive attitudes to the representation of violence and sex seen elsewhere in fiction of the time, and which produced non-ghostly horror stories such as Stoker's 'The Squaw' (1892) or Arthur Machen's *The Three Impostors* (1895).

If Nesbit's fiction was commercially motivated – she had become a professional writer after the ruin of her husband's business – another line of ghostly writing was quite the opposite. M. R. James, a Fellow of King's College, Cambridge, initially wrote ghost stories for his friends and students, reading them aloud at Christmas in memorably spooky performances in his college rooms: an early story, 'Lost Hearts' (1895) used the motif of the murdered boy musician ridiculed by Jerome but transformed it into a horrifying story of ritual sacrifice and black magic. Pestered to publish, he began to do so in the mid 1890s, though his first collection, *Ghost Stories of an Antiquary*, did not appear until 1904. James was an accomplished scholar and his stories frequently feature academics, bibliophiles and antiquarians who encounter the spirit world through texts and objects: mezzotints, binoculars that see through time rather than space, doll's houses, prayer books, ash trees containing spiders covered in 'grayish hair' (James, 1984: 50) even, in 'Oh Whistle and I'll Come to You, My Lad' (1904) an ancient Roman whistle inscribed 'Quis est iste qui venit' – 'who is this who is coming' – which, when blown, summons 'an intensely horrible face of *crumpled linen*' in a hotel bedroom (1984: 81, 90). While other writers used modern, urban settings, James preferred either the pre-Victorian world or, when he did set stories in the present, the desolate East Anglian coast of 'Oh Whistle' or the late work, 'A Warning to the Curious' (1925). Intensely self-conscious in structure and narration, James excelled in producing pastiches of old books and letters which give a remarkable feeling of authenticity to the events and experiences he documents. Asked whether he believed in ghosts, James replied 'I am prepared to consider evidence and accept it if it satisfies me' (1984: 6), a characteristically ambiguous statement from a writer whose best stories left enough unsaid to make them doubly terrifying for imaginative readers. James was instrumental in the rediscovery of Le Fanu, editing a collection of his stories, *Madam Crowl's Ghost* (1923), which unearthed a number of tales not reprinted since their appearances in Victorian periodicals. He also inspired writers such as Arthur Gray, Master of Jesus College, Cambridge, whose *Tedious Brief Tales of Granta and Gramarye* (1919) showed a similar flair for the fabrication of historical incidents.

James's formal experiments are rarely connected with the literary innovations gathered under the term 'modernism' but he was nonetheless aware of the power of the interrupted or discontinuous narrative, fascinated by modes of narration, and quite willing to employ inconclusive and ambiguous endings rather than rationalise or explain his effects. In this he was much like his more famous namesake, Henry James, whose fiction, supernatural and otherwise, pursues these ideas in richly suggestive ways. Henry James began writing ghost stories in the 1860s, but his initial efforts such as 'The Romance of Certain Old Clothes' (1868) were crude in comparison with his later work. It was not until the 1890s that James managed to fuse his interest in what he termed 'the art of fiction' with supernatural narratives. Sometimes, he reworked familiar ingredients, as in 'Owen Wingrave' (1892), in which the protagonist is forced to prove his courage by spending a night in a haunted chamber where one of his ancestors had died, but other works were more original. In 'The Friends of the Friends' (1896), originally entitled 'The Way It Came', James draws on stories of seeing the apparition of a friend or loved one at the moment of their death far away: in November 1918, Harold Owen, brother of Wilfred, apparently saw his brother on *HMS Astraea* off the South African coast a week after the poet had been killed in France. James's story concerns a man and a woman who have both had such experiences. They are repeatedly encouraged to meet by mutual friends but they never do so. When the woman dies, the narrator, who is engaged to the man, discovers her fiancé was visited by her on the night she died. Although the fiancé claims she was alive at that point, the narrator believes instead that he met her ghost, and breaks off the engagement, consumed by a jealousy nothing can dispel. The story's veiled eroticism offers a subtle realignment of Le Fanu's 'the dead and the living can never be one' (Dalby, 1995: 22) and leaves unresolved what actually happened on the night of the woman's death. Leaving his characters nameless, James creates an atmosphere of gossip to produce what would later be termed FOAFF (Friend of a Friend Folklore): the story's narrative frame hints that the tale draws upon actual events. This mode of implicit authentication is quite different from the rationalising principles of many earlier ghost stories, though in other respects, James was building on those which claimed to be true in order to appear more frightening, such as Edwards's 'The New Pass' (1864) or, in the case of Kipling's 'My Own True Ghost Story', to enhance the comic pay-off at the work's conclusion.

Subtlety is the keynote of James's most famous tale, *The Turn of the Screw* (1898), which owed its origins to a ghost story told to him by his friend, Edward White Benson, the Archbishop of Canterbury, in January 1895. Benson, whose three sons also wrote ghost stories (the best of these are the 'spook stories' of E. F. Benson, whose *The Room in the Tower* (1912) contains such horrors as 'Caterpillars', a ghost story about cancer), offered James only a nugget concerning servants who corrupt the children in their charge, and it was three years before James published the finished version in *Collier's Weekly*. The story has prompted a vast array of critical investigations, many concerned with whether the ghosts of Peter Quint and Miss Jessel who haunt Miles and Flora are ghosts or merely the projections of the children's overly protective (and for some, neurotic) governess. However, as Douglas Robillard reminds us, James did intend *The Turn of the Screw* to be a ghost story, and was quite explicit in a later preface about his intention 'To bring the bad dead back to life for a second round of badness' (Sullivan, 1986: 232).

James specialised in refinement and nuance for a highly select audience, but he by no means monopolised the field. His one-time friend Vernon Lee (Violet Paget) 'fuses femininity with the spectral' in fictions that 'leave everything open and without resolution' (Maxwell and Pulham, 2006: 11). In 'A Wicked Voice' (1890), for instance, a young composer visiting Venice becomes gradually possessed by the spirit of a castrato singer, an experience which maddens and unmans him. Like Dickens and Thomas Hardy, whose later poetry frequently concerns itself with 'self-haunting', Lee believed that 'the genuine ghost' is 'one born of ourselves, of the weird places we have seen, the strange stories we have heard' (Lee, 2006: 39), and she used her wide knowledge of history and aesthetics to create works in which realistic detail only emphasises 'the imaginative work of suggestion' (Maxwell and Pulham, 2006: 13). John Meade Falkner's *The Lost Stradivarius* (1895) was less technically radical than the fiction of James or Lee, but the novella offered an inspired combination of historical pastiche (opening in 1867, it goes back to the early 1840s and beyond) and transgressive subject matter such as Neoplatonic occultism and homoeroticism, the latter a taboo subject after the conviction of Oscar Wilde for indecency earlier that year.

Although the ghost story was still not regarded by many as having proper literary credentials, well-written examples by authors with reputations in other fields challenged such assumptions. A case in point is Kipling's 'They' (1904). Inspired by the death of his daughter in 1899, the tale concerns a motorist who gets lost in the Sussex countryside and arrives at a mansion inhabited by a blind old woman and children who watch from the woods; gradually it transpires that the children are ghosts and can only be seen by those who have themselves lost a child. Walter de la Mare was another writer whose reputation outside the genre bolstered the ghost story's literary credibility. The historical novelist Oliver Onions also showed how the form could be as technically and psychologically ambitious as any other, notably in *Widdershins* (1911), a collection containing several impressive stories. The best of these is 'The Beckoning Fair One', a novella concerning the psychological deterioration of a writer, Paul Oleron, as he is slowly possessed by a female spirit in his rented rooms. Onions's masterly use of free indirect style makes it increasingly difficult to distinguish between the thoughts of the narrator and the haunted man, and his witty use of situations from other supernatural fiction, such as the jemmying open of a window seat to reveal a harp's linen case, an allusion to the opening of a vampire's coffin and the finding of its empty shroud, offer additional pleasures for the genre's connoisseurs. Like a number of other stories of the period, for instance Robert Hichens's 'How Love Came to Professor Guildea' (1900), there is an erotic element to the story, with Oleron gradually succumbing to the seductions of the 'Fair One' and accepting 'the shadowy Bridal' she seems to offer (Onions, 1911: 49).

Many writers and publishers during fin de siècle stressed their newness and modernity, and there was, before the Great War undermined such assumptions, a widespread belief in the positive transformative powers of science and technology. Catherine Crowe had hoped that science would eventually be receptive to the study of the paranormal, and her hopes were fulfilled in some ways by the formation of the Society for Psychical Research in 1882. The SPR's aim was (and is) to examine 'without prejudice or prepossession and in a scientific spirit those faculties of man, real or supposed, which appear to be inexplicable on any generally recognised hypothesis', and it attracted a number of influential members, including William James, Henry's brother.[1] The SPR's collection of data concerning ghostly manifestations led to Edmund Gurney and Frank Podmore's *Phantasms of the Living* (1886), which reproduced 700 such accounts, and the Census of Hallucinations (1889–94) which collected 17,000. Using laboratory analysis and fieldwork in its investigations, the SPR's rationalising approach was seen by some as inimical to the ghost story: Vernon Lee's *Hauntings* was prefaced with the defiant claim:

> my four little tales are of no genuine ghosts in the scientific sense; they tell of no haunting such as could be contributed by the Society for Psychical Research, of no spectres that can be caught in definite places and made to dictate judicial evidence. (Lee, 2006: 40)

Lee's stories were set in Europe or in the past, but other writers saw science and technology as offering opportunities rather than threats. Dickens had shown the railways' potential for uncanny events in 'The Signalman'; now a new generation showed that ghosts could haunt not only ancient castles and desolate seashores but also move into a new technological realm. In Onions's 'Roumm' (1911), a crane-driver is haunted by 'The Runner', a spirit that can pass, by some variant of osmosis, into solid matter; the story's dramatic climax takes place on a West End building site, where 'the steel rang with riveters' hammers, and the crane-chains rattled and crashed' (Onions, 1911: 84). In Nesbit's 'The Violet Car' (1910), a father is eventually run down by the same phantom machine that killed his daughter, 'a violet car that moved along the lanes swiftly and silently, and was empty' (Nesbit, 2006: 75). Richard Marsh, whose grandson, Robert Aickman, became a major figure in twentieth-century weird fiction, was always keen to adapt new ideas into remunerative short tales, and in 'The Adventure of the Phonograph' (1898), he used a recording of a woman's murder to terrify her killer – the result was not, strictly speaking, a ghost story, but the motif of the voice from beyond the grave exposing guilt was a familiar one for all its new guise. In 'The Photographs' (1900), an image of a veiled woman appears in a prison photograph of George Solley, a convict jailed for the murder of his wife, even though the photographer did not see her when he took the picture. It transpires that Solley is innocent, and that his wife's ghost has used the photographic medium to provide clues to her actual killer. Again, Marsh was adapting a folkloric motif – the return from the grave to secure justice – to a new world of technology. Far from undermining the ghost story, technological innovation was to prove a valuable invigorating influence.

There are many reasons why the ghost story occupied such a prominent position in Victorian culture. Crucially, the nineteenth century was a time of high mortality rates, very public displays of death and mourning and, at the same time, an increasing scepticism regarding Christian teachings. Even as Darwin and others challenged the notion of the Bible's literal truth, the ghost story allowed writers to explore the mystery of life after death without having to engage in religious controversy. At the same time, the ghost story represented a challenge few writers could resist – how to make new wine from some very familiar, even stale, grapes. This ensured experiment and innovation at key points in the century – the 1830s, the 1860s, the 1890s, – and produced a body of work that remains both popular in itself and a continued inspiration for those working in the genre.

Note

1. For reference please see: www.spr.ac.uk/main/page/spr-publications-para-psychology.

References

Ashley, Mike (1997). 'Ghost Stories', in *The Encyclopedia of Fantasy*, ed. John Clute and John Grant. London: Orbis, pp. 403–7.

Bennett, Gillian (2000). 'Introduction' to Catherine Crowe, *The Night Side of Nature, or Ghosts and Ghost Seers* [1848]. Ware: Wordsworth, pp. 9–14.

Bleiler, E. F. (1977). Introduction to *The Collected Ghost Stories of Mrs J. H. Riddell*, ed. E. F. Bleiler. New York: Dover, pp. v–xxxvi.

Bulwer-Lytton, Edward (1944). 'The Haunters and the Haunted' [1859] in *Tales of Terror and the Supernatural*, ed. Herbert A. Wise and Phyllis Fraser. New York: Random House, pp. 116–46.

Calder, Jenni (2000). Introduction to *A Beleaguered City and Other Tales of the Seen and Unseen*, ed. Jenni Calder. Edinburgh: Canongate, pp. vii–xviii.

Cox, Michael, and R. A. Gilbert (eds) (1986). *The Oxford Book of English Ghost Stories*. Oxford: Oxford University Press.

Crowe, Catherine (2000). *The Night Side of Nature, or Ghosts and Ghost Seers* [1848]. Ware: Wordsworth.

Dalby, Richard (ed.) (1995). *The Mammoth Book of Victorian and Edwardian Ghost Stories*. London: Robinson.

Davies, Owen (2007). *The Haunted: A Social History of Ghosts*. Basingstoke: Palgrave Macmillan.

Dickens, Charles (1849). Review of *The Night Side of Nature* (*Examiner*, 26 February 1848).

——(1985). 'A Christmas Carol' [1843], in *The Christmas Books*, vol. 1, ed. Michael Slater. Harmondsworth: Penguin, pp. 45–133.

Gaskell, Elizabeth (2000). *Gothic Tales*, ed. Laura Kranzler. Harmondsworrth: Penguin.

Jackson, Rosemary (1989). Introduction to *What Did Miss Darrington See: An Anthology of Feminist Supernatural Fiction*, ed. Jessica Amanda Salmonson. New York: The Feminist Press at City University of New York, pp. xv–xxxvii.

James, M. R. (1984). *The Penguin Complete Ghost Stories of M. R. James*. Harmondsworth: Penguin.

Jerome, Jerome K. (1891). *Told After Supper*. London: Leadenhall Press.

Le Fanu, J. Sheridan (1995). 'A Strange Event in the Life of Schalken the Painter' [1839], in *The Mammoth Book of Victorian and Edwardian Ghost Stories*, ed. Richard Dalby. London: Robinson, pp. 5–27.

——(1993). *In a Glass Darkly* [1872], ed. Robert Tracy. Oxford: Oxford University Press.

Lee, Vernon (2006). *Hauntings and Other Fantastic Tales* [1890], ed. Catherine Maxwell and Patricia Pulham. Peterborough, ON: Broadview.

Maxwell, Catherine and Patricia Pulham (2006). Introduction to Vernon Lee, *Hauntings and Other Fantastic Tales* [1890]. Peterborough, ON: Broadview, pp. 9–27.

Nesbit, Edith (2006). *The Power of Darkness: Tales of Terror*, ed. David Stuart Davies. Ware: Wordsworth.

Oliphant, Margaret (2000). *A Beleaguered City and Other Tales of the Seen and Unseen*, ed. Jenni Calder. Edinburgh: Canongate.

Onions, Oliver (1911). *Widdershins*. London: Martin Secker.

Riddell, Mrs J. H. (1977). *The Collected Ghost Stories of Mrs J. H. Riddell*, ed. E. F. Bleiler. New York: Dover.

Smith, Andrew (2010). *The Ghost Story 1840–1920: A Cultural History*. Manchester: Manchester University Press.

Sullivan, Jack (ed.) (1986). *The Penguin Dictionary of Horror and the Supernatural*. Harmondsworth: Penguin.

Thomas, Deborah A. (2000). 'Ghost Stories', in *The Oxford Reader's Companion to Dickens*, ed. Paul Schlicke. Oxford: Oxford University Press, pp. 256–7.

Chapter 7

Victorian Gothic and National Identity: Cross-Channel 'Mysteries'

Avril Horner

The assumption that Gothic became 'domesticated' during the Victorian period is now widely accepted. To a certain extent this is true. Prior to Victoria coming to the throne in 1837, the Gothic text was invariably set in mainland Europe (as in the work of Horace Walpole, Ann Radcliffe, Matthew Lewis, Mary Shelley and Charles Maturin). However, from the 1840s onwards the Gothic comes home to roost, transmogrified as an aspect of the sensation novel and realist fiction. David Punter and Glennis Byron suggest Wilkie Collins's *The Woman in White* (1860), Ellen Wood's *East Lynne* (1861) and Mary Elizabeth Braddon's *Lady Audley's Secret* (1862) as prime examples of this tendency and note also that many ghost stories – an increasingly popular genre during the Victorian period – are set in Britain, rather than abroad (Punter and Byron, 2004: 26–7). Julian Wolfreys agrees; citing *Jane Eyre*, *Wuthering Heights*, *Dombey and Son* and 'The Lifted Veil' as examples, it is, he suggests, the English home which has now become 'unhomely' and uncanny. Noting that critics such as Peter Kitson see Gothic as in a 'transitional' stage between 1840 and 1880 (after which date it burst into lurid life again), Wolfreys describes 'Victorian Gothic' as having an 'evacuated identity', 'bracketed on the one hand by the Gothic-proper and, on the other, the return of the Gothic in the *fin de siècle*' (Wolfreys, 2006: 70–1, 63, 64). While such readings offer valuable overviews of Victorian Gothic, this tendency to describe it as 'domesticated' can result in a neglect of fruitful interchanges between European and British authors of the Gothic during the nineteenth century. It is not for nothing that images of the Bastille and the French Revolution continue to haunt many fictions well into the nineteenth century. In this essay I shall argue that use of Gothic devices heightens an important post-Revolutionary dialogue about social inequality across Eugène Sue's *Les Mystères de Paris* (1842–3), G. W. M. Reynolds's *The Mysteries of London* (1844–8) (both best-sellers in their time) and Dickens's *A Tale of Two Cities* (1859) – the last not usually seen within the 'Mysteries' tradition.

Sue's Paris, a place of 'dark, infectious-looking alleys' and 'fearful haunts' (Sue, n.d.: 9, 125), like London in *Oliver Twist*, consists of murky labyrinthine streets into which an innocent might easily stray from abutting 'respectable' areas. *Les Mystères de Paris* – its title inspired by Ann Radcliffe's *The Mysteries of Udolpho* (1794) – provided a model for G. W. M. Reynolds's *The Mysteries of London* and there is no doubt that Dickens's subsequent portrayal of the city owed much to both Sue and Reynolds. There emerges, then, in the mid-Victorian period, a literary dialogue between French and British authors about the city and social reform. Part of this dialogue concerns itself with the way in which modern bureaucracy enables a new form of power through the processing of secret documents. The effect, as Richard C. Maxwell Jr has remarked, was that such authors pushed 'the city back towards Gothic "mysteries"' in their portrayal of it as threatening and unknowable (Maxwell, 1977: 188). Such 'mysteries', however, served a double purpose for these authors: use of the sensational and the uncanny enthralled newly literate readers of the 'roman feuilleton' or 'penny weekly' while the suffering of the urban poor touched the consciences of the middle and upper classes (who would often buy the publication later in volume form), thereby advancing the cause of progressive liberalism. Interestingly, in 1849, Abel Heywood, who ran a bookshop in Manchester patronised by working-class readers, was selling not only Reynolds's work but translations of fiction by Sue, Dumas, George Sand and Paul Féval (Thomas in Reynolds, 1996: xiv, xv). This cross-channel dialogue went beyond the literary: Sue and Dickens corresponded during 1845, Dickens replying on his behalf to an invitation to address the Manchester Athenaeum, and in 1847 they met in Paris (Chevasco, 2003: 156–7). Indeed, Joseph Milsand, a distinguished French critic, published an essay on Dickens in 1847 in *La Revue Indépendante*, drawing attention to the links between his novels and those of Sue, thus offering a fresh perspective on the French writer whose work had – up till then – been seen within the tradition of novelists such as Samuel Richardson, Ann Radcliffe, Sir Walter Scott and James Fenimore Cooper (Chevasco, 2003: 50–1; James, 2005: 248).

The author of several popular novels published during the 1830s and early 1840s, Eugène Sue was well regarded by French critics who associated him with George Sand, Victor Hugo and Honoré de Balzac. However, his work received mixed reviews in Britain, many critics castigating what they saw as sentimentality and an unhealthy focus on low city life. Opinion turned firmly against him after the 1848 revolutions in Europe; in retrospect, *Les Mystères de Paris* was seen as having fomented political unrest in so far as 'many of the workers on the barricades were ardent readers of Sue's novels' (Prendergast, 2003: 125). Sue was evacuated from British literary history for many decades, despite his influence on authors as diverse as Dickens, Thackeray and Elizabeth Barrett Browning (Chevasco, 2003: 78, 96). Set in 1838, Sue's *Les Mystères de Paris* (serialised between June 1842 and October 1843 in *Le Journal des Débats*) presents the city as threatening and sinister. Its hero, Prince Rodolphe, seeks to avenge social injustice and descends into the underworld of Paris to do so. Adopting a false identity, and presenting himself as a working man whose parents had died of cholera,[1] he befriends a young prostitute, la Goualeuse ('the singer', also known as Fleur de Marie because of her innate goodness), and a convicted murderer, Le Chourineur. Rodolphe rescues Fleur de Marie from her miserable life and places her with other workers he has saved, now living under his protection on a farm outside Paris. It later transpires that Fleur de Marie is his own child, the product of a hasty (and technically invalid) marriage made in his youth. Having separated early from his wife, Rodolphe knew nothing about this young daughter, whom her mother abandoned as a small child to the backstreets of Paris. Near the end of the novel, discovering Fleur de Marie's true identity, the Prince marries her mother in order to legitimise his daughter, at which point she becomes Princess Amélie.

The novel includes several subplots that allow Sue to convey vividly the lives of both underworld criminals and the virtuous poor. Gothic effects are frequently deployed in order to convey the horror of living in the city slums. For example, the description of the garret in which Jerome Morel, a poor jeweller being persecuted by Jacques Ferrand (a corrupt notary), lives with his wife, mother-in-law and five children, recalls some of the ghastly enclaves described in novels by Radcliffe and Lewis:

> A candle, sustained by two sticks of wood on a little square plank, hardly pierces, with its yellow flickering light, the darkness of the garret – a narrow nook, ceiled by the sloping roof, which forms with the floor a very acute angle. The greenish tiles were everywhere visible. The partitions were plastered with mortar, blackened by time, and covered with cracks and rents, through which could be seen the worm-eaten laths: a door off its hinges showed the way to the staircase. The floor, of a colour without a name, tainted, sticky, is covered here and there with bits of decayed straw, with old rags, and with those large bones which the poor buy of the most wretched retailers of rotten meat, to gnaw the cartilages which may yet adhere to them. (Sue, n.d.: 182)

The Morel chapters were 'extraordinarily popular among Sue's lower-class readers' in France (Maxwell, 1992: 198) and the above passage would have been particularly resonant for English readers in 1845, when the Andover workhouse scandal revealed that inmates were so hungry they were eating the marrow from bones they were made to crush (Fowler, 2007: 7–9). In another example of Gothic effects, two of the novel's criminal characters, the Brigand (who has avoided detection by disfiguring his face with vitriol) and La Chouette (who has abused and exploited Fleur de Marie for several years), fight to the death:

> Horrible, frightful events took place in the gloom of the cellar . . . Chained by the leg to an enormous stone placed in the middle of the dungeon, the Brigand, horrible, monstrous, his hair knotted, his beard long, mouth foaming, clothed with bloody rags, turned like a wild beast around his dungeon, dragging after him, by the feet, the corpse of La Chouette, whose head was horribly mutilated, broken, and crushed. (Sue, n.d.: 267–8)

At the end of the novel, and in a slightly different Gothic key, Fleur de Marie refuses the role of Princess and instead enters a convent, where she dies, exhausted by the sorrows of her previous life.

Like Victor Hugo in *Notre Dame de Paris* (1831) – arguably the first 'mysteries' novel (Maxwell, 1992: x) – Sue draws a distinction between the wicked (of whatever class) and the poor who are driven to crime in order to survive. Chapters 2 and 3 are devoted respectively to the 'histories' of Fleur de Marie and Le Chourineur, whose narratives of abuse and starvation go far to explain their immoral lives. Having heard Fleur de Marie's sad story, Rodolphe reflects that 'Misery and poverty, but not crime, had been the ruin of this poor young girl' (Sue, n.d.: 32). This interpolation of autobiographical narratives is a standard feature of work by Sue and Reynolds, allowing the author to 'give a voice to groups usually excluded or repressed: the prostitute, the child-worker, the transported convict, the body-snatcher, the thief' (Thomas, 2000: 65). Hugely popular in France, *Les Mystères* travelled fast to other countries: six translations of the novel were available in Britain alone by 1844 (Chevasco, 2003: 40) and its formula was widely adopted. 'Mysteries' fiction clearly touched a nerve in both countries: its stark portrayal of the way in which vice and social instability accompanied acute poverty reminded the French reader that the utopian vision of the 1789 Revolution had failed to solve the problem of urban deprivation and alerted the nervous English reader to the squalor of parts of London and to the possibility of anarchy and uprising at home.

G. W. M. Reynolds's *The Mysteries of London*, serialised in penny numbers between 1844 and 1848, disappeared from critical view until Montague Summers included it in his *Gothic Bibliography*, published in 1941 (Humpherys and James, 2008: 11). Reynolds, who lived in Paris for six years, taking French citizenship in 1835, prided himself on his republican sympathies. A translator of, and advocate for, French literature (which many English critics saw as a corrupting influence), he published *The Modern Literature of France* in 1839, having returned to London in 1837.[2] An unashamed plagiarist (he had pirated Dickens's *The Pickwick Papers* for his *Pickwick Abroad*), he immediately spotted the potential of *Les Mystères de Paris* for adaptation. Similarities between his work and Sue's are therefore not surprising. Both authors expose, for example, the exploitation of the poor by the rich – Sue's Morel making jewels for the aristocracy in his garret and Reynolds's Ellen Monroe sewing beautiful shawls for the wealthy, earning only sixpence for sixteen hours' work. Both also expose the exploitation of children in such a world: Sue vividly describes La Chouette wrenching a tooth from Fleur de Marie's mouth as punishment for having eaten one of the barley sugars she has been sent out to sell; Reynolds reveals in horrifying detail Bill Boulter's wife's plan to blind her small daughter so as to render her a more effective beggar. Drawing on both Victor Hugo's *Notre Dame de Paris* and Eugène Sue's work, Reynolds's *The Mysteries of London* became a bestseller of the nineteenth century; on his death in 1879 *The Bookseller* reported that whereas Dickens and Thackeray had thousands of readers, 'Mr. Reynolds's were numbered in the hundreds of thousands, perhaps millions' (Burt, 1980: 142). As Maxwell has noted, 'Here was a wonderfully accessible version of Gothic literature, set in familiar London locales but unveiling lurid conspiracies which took place just behind the scenes' (Maxwell, 1977: 191). Later becoming an active Chartist and the proprietor of the left-wing *Reynolds's Weekly Newspaper*, Reynolds maintained his sympathies with French republicanism. Whereas both Sue and Dickens petitioned the aristocracy and the wealthy professional to create a fairer society, Reynolds abhorred the very idea of privileged elitism. While presenting the young Queen Victoria as a kind and charming individual, for example, his narrator fiercely attacks the way in which she is deliberately kept ignorant of the suffering of the poor. As Punter and Byron note, the 'feudal aristocracy' of eighteenth-century Gothic fiction 'is alive and well in his contemporary world' (2004: 161). Indeed, the intolerable gap between the rich and the poor is emphasised throughout *The Mysteries of London*, beginning with its prologue:

There are but two words known in the moral alphabet of this great city; for all virtues are summed up in the one, and all vices in the other: and those words are

WEALTH. | POVERTY. (Reynolds, 1996: prologue; 4)[3]

Reynolds draws attention throughout to the close proximity of elegant and impoverished areas – the 'horrors of Smithfield' existing in the 'midst of a city of so much wealth' (Reynolds, 1996: ch. IX, 28–9), for example. The 'fearful mysteries' of the city have little to do with the supernatural but much to do with the abject living conditions of the poor and the conspiracies of the rich that sustain such inequality. Living in overcrowded houses where incest is not uncommon and corpses quickly decompose ('in four-and-twenty hours myriads of loathsome animalculae are seen crawling about'), the poor are also prey to sudden deadly outbreaks of diseases such as small-pox or scarlatina (Reynolds, 1996: ch. XIII, 38). What Robert Mighall describes as the 'bizarre mixture of radical politics, "sociology", and Gothic sensationalism' (Mighall, 1999: 28) comprising *The Mysteries of London* seems not quite so bizarre when one recognises that its template derives from Sue's most famous work. Indeed, both Sue and Reynolds draw on the contemporary interest in crime and violence, using devices from melodrama and the Gothic mode in order to create complicated plots featuring secret documents, false identities and doppelgangers.

Reynolds, however, must be credited with developing the figure of the doppelganger, a Gothic trope to be richly exploited throughout the century. Setting *The Mysteries of London* between 1831 and 1843, Reynolds uses two brothers in order to illustrate the importance of personal integrity in finding one's way through the moral maze of the city labyrinth. His stark portrayal of their differences in temperament owes much to the conventions of melodrama: 'Eugene was all selfishness and egotism, Richard all generosity and frankness: the former deceitful, astute and crafty; the latter honourable even to a fault' (Reynolds, 1996: ch. V, 19). Both have doubles: Eugene Markham adopts a false identity as the apparently respectable Montague Greenwood, an unscrupulous financier who uses secrets to gain power and control, allowing Reynolds to create a modern type of criminal in the 'City man' (Maxwell, 1977: 192). Eugene's stratagem works, in so far as his wealth and apparent standing (together with corrupt practices) help him to become a Member of Parliament for the constituency of Rottenborough. Other doubles include the aptly named Count Alteroni (the Count is really Prince Alberto, exiled by a despot from the Italian state of Castelcicala), and the appearance during a masquerade of a Carmelite Friar, actually the Reverend Reginald Tracy, a 'libidinous priest' (Reynolds, 1996: ch. CXLIX, 217), through whom Reynolds attacks the hypocrisy of the Church (and whose peeping Tom activities shocked many Victorian readers).

However, the most sinister double in *The Mysteries of London*, the Resurrection Man, belongs to Richard Markham, with whom he shares the initials 'RM'. This ghastly figure, whose real name is the somewhat prosaic 'Anthony Tidkins', plagues Richard Markham from early in the work. Having been framed for passing a counterfeit note, Richard spends some time in prison, where he meets not only Thomas Armstrong, a political philosopher who converts him to democratic idealism, but also the Resurrection Man who, from then on, tries to blackmail and even murder him. As his name ironically suggests, the Resurrection Man makes his living by the grisly trade of grave-robbing. Even he, though, is allowed to tell his own story in the chapter entitled 'The Resurrection Man's History' which – while it does not exonerate him from his dreadful deeds – offers a stark contrast to the privileged upbringing of the Markham brothers while raising interesting questions about class and social determinism. Although grave-robbing rarely occurred after the Anatomy Act of 1832 was passed and plague ships (featured in chapter XXX) were by the 1840s a folk memory (Reynolds, 1996: 68, 228), such scenes allowed Reynolds to portray with Gothic intensity the terrors that still haunted the minds of the poor. Indeed, arguably the Anatomy Act, which gave surgeons access to the unclaimed bodies of workhouse or prison residents, simply replaced the old terror with a chillingly legalised new one. The workhouse, of course, brought its own horrors. Between 1834 – the year in which the Poor Law Amendment Act was passed – and 1884, over 500 new workhouses were built in England and Wales (Fraser, 2009: 64). These institutions were commonly referred to as 'bastilles' or 'pauper bastilles', partly due to their design (often similar to Bentham's 'panopticon') and partly because of their harsh, prison-like conditions (Fowler, 2007: 20, 41, 44, 46). Railing against the Poor Laws, the narrator declares:

> Not even the ingenuity of the Spanish or Italian Inquisitions conceive a more effectual method of deliberate torture and slow death, than the fearful system of mental-abasement and gradient starvation invented by England's legislators. When the labourer can toil for the rich no longer, away with him to the workhouse! (Reynolds, 1996: ch. CLXXXV, 248)

Old Gothic terrors, then, constantly resurface in Reynolds's work. The vile rooms of the Old House in Smithfield, a refuge for thieves and murderers, are likened to 'the cells of the Bastille or the Inquisition'

(Reynolds, 1996: chap. IX, 29) and the constant use of the word 'dungeon' to describe the cellars and underground vaults of ordinary London houses lends an air of Gothic horror to a city at the heart of the British Empire. In one of Reynolds's few evocations of the supernatural, Bill Boulter sees his wife's avenging ghost in the 'terrible dungeon' (Reynolds, 1996: ch. XXVIII, 54) of the Old House in Smithfield and it is in the 'dark dungeon' (Reynolds, 1996: ch. CCLVII, 314) of the Resurrection Man's house in East London that Crankey Jem confines his enemy in a terrible act of vengeance – the episode recalling the fight to the death between the Brigand and La Chouette in Sue's *Les Mystères*.

Reynolds also uses Gothic tropes and devices to critique government espionage in *The Mysteries*. The chapter headings 'The Black Chamber' and 'The Black Chamber Again' might suggest scenes from an eighteenth-century Gothic novel, but in fact they refer to the Black Chamber of the General Post-Office, St Martin's-le-Grand, where a respectable-looking government functionary opens, then reseals, letters from abroad to see if they contain any hint of insurrection (a theme to be developed by Dickens in *A Tale of Two Cities*). Reynolds's Gothicisation of government strategy was no mere fantasy: the private letters of the Italian political exile Mazzini were indeed opened by the Post Office on the authorisation of the Home Secretary, Sir James Graham, leading to a national scandal when this was revealed in the House of Commons in June 1844. Dickens registered his disgust at the practice by writing on envelopes containing letters to Thomas Beard and John Forster: 'It is particularly requested that if Sir James Graham should open this, he will not trouble himself to seal it again' (Dickens, 1977: 151). Furthermore, the chapters depicting Richard's involvement in a revolutionary uprising against a despotic ruler in the imaginary Italian state of 'Castelcicala' and the subsequent establishment of a new democratic social order there, including a minimum wage, were published, as Trefor Thomas points out, 'during the whole of the crucial historical crisis which took place in England between 1844 and 1848' (Thomas, 2000: 68), a crisis fuelled by the rise of Chartism and the Anti-Corn Law League, both founded in 1838. In an issue of *The Mysteries* published in April 1848, Reynolds clearly links the agenda for the new order in Castelcicala with republicanism. As conservative feeling against republicanism hardened in middle England, particularly in the wake of uprisings across Europe, established British authors – including Dickens – began to distance themselves from both Sue and Reynolds while nevertheless continuing to adapt the conventions of the *Mysteries* novel for their own purposes.[4] At the very least, Dickens's comic Gothic version of Reynolds's sinister Resurrection Man in his creation of the spiky-haired grave-robber,

Jeremy Cruncher, implies an engagement with a work he claimed to disdain.

A great admirer of Victor Hugo's work, Dickens also knew Sue's *Les Mystères de Paris* as well as having read Reynolds's *The Mysteries of London*. As Mighall has argued (Mighall, 1999: 69–77), Dickens's stroke of brilliance in *Bleak House* (1853) was to develop the portrayal of the city as a labyrinthine place of dark secrets, violent acts and terrible conspiracies into a full critique of the law and modern bureaucracy as modes of social and governmental control. It is no coincidence, given the purchase of the word 'mysteries' in the mid nineteenth century, that London in that novel is described as a place of 'mysterious symbols' and Mr Tulkinghorn constantly associated with the word 'mysteries' (Maxwell, 1977: 206–7). Not all contemporary critics approved, however, of Dickens's inventiveness, George Brimley commenting in the *Spectator* in 1853 that *Bleak House* was 'meagre and melodramatic, and disagreeably reminiscent of that vilest of modern books, Reynolds' *Mysteries of London*' (Maxwell, 1992: 166). For the purposes of this chapter, however, I shall focus on Dickens's *A Tale of Two Cities* (1859), a novel not usually considered a 'mysteries' fiction. At the heart of this work, set between 1775 and 1794, lie the 'mysteries' of not just one but two cities, London and Paris. In this novel Dickens develops the representation of urban locations as 'mysteries' while also pursuing the more abstract 'mystery' of how the law, society and the individual relate to each other in a democratic system.

Central to the novel is the Bastille, both as an historical reality and as metaphor for the unjust use of legal power. Within it is secreted Dr Manette's letter, written in a mixture of soot, charcoal and his own blood and which attests to the rape of a peasant girl by a member of the aristocratic Evrémonde family that he witnessed many years ago. At that time, in order to guarantee his silence, the Evrémondes had him confined, by a 'lettre de cachet' (in effect, a blank document allowing immediate imprisonment) to the Bastille for almost eighteen years. The novel begins at the point of his release and his journey to England, accompanied by his seventeen-year-old daughter Lucie, who has been brought up there, and by Mr Lorry, who works for Tellson's Bank in London. The tale of Dr Manette allowed Dickens to rehearse yet again his preoccupation with the terrible psychological effects of long imprisonment; at times of stress the good doctor feels the 'shadow of the actual Bastille' falling on him and turns obsessively to shoe-making, an activity that dominated his time in prison, remembering his identity only as 'One Hundred and Five, North Tower' (Dickens, 2003: 83, 44). Indeed, his fear of freedom, on first leaving the Bastille, is vividly expressed in the idea of being 'buried' alive and turning to 'dust' on release. Dickens would have come across this powerful image in both Hogg's *The Private Memoirs and Confessions of a Justified Sinner* (1824) and Victor Hugo's *Notre Dame de Paris*; no doubt his visit to 'The Tombs' prison in Manhattan in 1842 was also in the back of his mind. Even Lucie fears that she will see not her father, but 'his Ghost – not him!' (Dickens, 2003: 28). As many critics have noted, the idea of resurrection to life, enacted most vividly when Sydney Carton's self-sacrifice enables Charles Darnay to escape the guillotine, is a key theme of the novel and derives its power from the Christian tradition. However, Dr Manette and Sydney Carton are men 'resurrected' within a very secular world and as such they demonstrate Dickens's political sensibility.

The Bastille is crucial to the plot of *A Tale of Two Cities*, not least in the centrality of chapter 21, entitled 'Echoing Footsteps', in which Dickens describes the taking of the Bastille in the Gothic idiom; the revolutionaries run through 'gloomy vaults where the light of day had never shone, past hideous doors of dark dens and cages, down cavernous flights of steps' in order to free the prisoners from 'their tomb' (Dickens, 2003: 227). It is at this point that Ernest Defarge, a leader of the Revolution, discovers the letter which is later used to condemn the innocent Charles Darnay. But in a novel in which doubling plays a key role (the plot turns on the uncanny likeness between Darnay and Sydney Carton), the Bastille has its own doppelganger. Tellson's Bank, Mr Lorry's employer, exists as 'a French house, as well as an English one' (2003: 21) and its documents, buried in its many London cellars, evoke the shadow of the Bastille – as does the nearby Temple Bar, where the heads of traitors were once displayed. Dickens thus reminds the reader that barbaric behaviour occurred and still occurs on both sides of the Channel; indeed, the English onlookers at Darnay's trial in London bay for his blood and are disappointed when he is acquitted. Later, Darnay's casual mention of the Tower of London and the inscription to be found in 'an old dungeon' there (2003: 105), indicating secret documents hidden buried nearby, deeply distresses Dr Manette who 'had naturally repressed much' (2003: 201). This mention of the Tower connotes the repressive régimes of both England and France, which readily use spies to maintain their power. The sinister use of 'lettres de cachet' in France is paralleled by the former lazy and corrupt practices of the Old Bailey, 'a kind of deadly inn-yard, from which pale travellers set out continually, in carts and coaches, on a violent passage into the other world' (2003: 63), itself mirrored in La Conciergerie, from which those judged 'guilty' during the Revolution and its aftermath rode to the guillotine in tumbrels, or farm carts.

Doubling thus dispels the supposed differences between England and France and works against the contrasts offered elsewhere in the novel – between, for example, Soho (a quiet, safe, leafy retreat in London) and Saint Antoine (a crowded, dangerous part of Paris, the enclave of spies and revolutionaries). Such 'set' and separated scenes are also undermined by images of fluidity – of water, blood and wine – and of transformation of fluids (of water and wine into blood) that run through the novel, linking the poor of Paris with those of London. The novel's subtext thereby works against its overt narrative of England and France as very different countries. The French capital is both completely unlike its English equivalent, having experienced a revolution followed by mob violence, and yet very much like London. Eleven years after the publication of Marx's *Communist Manifesto* in 1848, which opens with the words 'A spectre is haunting Europe', the problem of the urban poor in London and Paris had been solved by neither country. The 'scarecrows', gaunt with hunger in Dickens's Paris of 1789, who know only 'the taste of . . . black bread and death' (Dickens, 2003: 36), still haunted both capital cities in 1859; 'in short, the period was' in many ways 'like the present period', as the first paragraph of the novel informs us (2003: 5). Ruth Glancy notes that Carlyle and Dickens 'were struck by the similarities in attitude between the members of the *ancien régime* in France and the ruling classes of nineteenth-century England', both impervious to the suffering of the urban poor, whose living conditions had not changed much since the late eighteenth century (Glancy, 2006: 13). The apathy of the British Government in addressing bread shortages and disease in urban areas (particularly the Asiatic cholera epidemic of 1854) appalled Dickens and many other liberal thinkers. A supporter of Chartism, Dickens was dismayed by Parliament's rejection of the 'People's Charter' in 1838, 1842 and 1848, although he had little time for those who used the movement for their own political ends, perceiving Reynolds to be just one such opportunist (Dickens, 1981: 603–4). Dickens's description of a London crowd as potentially 'stopping at nothing' and as 'a monster much dreaded' (2003: 162) at the supposed funeral of Roger Cly indicates an anxiety that the frustrations of the hungry poor and the Chartists might just combine to produce revolutionary conditions (and a version of the Terror) in mid-Victorian England, reflecting his conviction in 1855 that the people's 'discontent . . . is extremely like the general mind of France before the breaking out of the first Revolution' (quoted in Easson, 1993: 100). However, Dickens's portrayal of French revolutionary fervour – both sympathetic to its causes and horrified by the ensuing violence wrought by the vengeful mob (a recurring scene in Gothic fiction of the 1790s) – suggests an ambivalence which, although

resolved at the level of plot by Carton's self-sacrifice, offers no direct
political solution.

Instead, Dickens uses Gothic effects (doubling, ghosting, secrets,
excess of violence) in *A Tale of Two Cities* in order to render disturbing what he sees as modern barbarities: the suffering of the urban poor;
the violence that results from that suffering; the corruption and misuse
of the law. These effects, together with his compression/distortion of
historical events, give the novel a nightmare quality that distinguishes
it from historical fiction. While many 'condition of England' novels by
authors such as Elizabeth Gaskell, Benjamin Disraeli, Charles Kingsley
and George Eliot focused on similar issues, Dickens's decision to distance his subject matter historically and to render it dream-like lends
his treatment of it a particular intensity. As Julian Wolfreys, citing
Wolfgang Iser, notes: 'And if 'the Gothic novel remains unhistorical
precisely because it lacks this link' between the 'historical reality' of the
past and 'the present', then Dickens situates the interconnection explicitly between historical reality and subjective historicity, through the
tropes of Gothic discourse' (Wolfreys, 2010: 19). Certainly the impact
of *A Tale of Two Cities* owes less to the supernatural than to Dickens's
Gothicised representation of past and current injustices and cruelties.
Dismissing within the novel's first page superstitions and the 'supernatural' in a contemptuous rejection of Mrs Southcott's prophecies and
the Cock Lane ghost, and passing immediately to a graphic account –
based on a real historical event – of a youth having 'his hands cut off,
his tongue torn out with pincers, and his body burned alive' as punishment for not having knelt to a procession of monks (Dickens, 2003: 6),
Dickens sets up through his narrator a Gothic agenda that develops the
line of socio-political commentary initiated by Godwin's *Caleb Williams*
(1794) – a novel that represents 'the law in ruins' (Punter, 1998: 36).
In *A Tale of Two Cities*, Dickens marries Paris with London, French
literature and history with those of England, the voices of English historians with those of French writers. Although his main resources in
English were Carlyle's *The French Revolution* (1837), a book he greatly
admired, and Arthur Young's *Travels in France during the Years 1787,
1788, and 1789* (1792), he also used many French sources, including
Jean-Jacques Rousseau's *Confessions* (1782), Louis-Sébastien Mercier's
Tableau de Paris (1782–8) and his *Le Nouveau Paris* (1793–8) (also
used by Sue) as well as Dumas' *Mémoires d'un Médecin* (1846–8).[5]

Dickens's contribution to 'mysteries' fiction – to be continued in
works such as Hugo's *Les Misérables* (1862) and Emile Zola's *Les
Mystères de Marseille* (1867) – was considerable.[6] In *A Tale of Two
Cities*, Dickens exploits the formula in order to explore the very concept

of democracy – a topic with which mid-Victorian England was vitally concerned. For Dickens, however, the private and the public spheres were never separate. In a supremely Gothic chapter entitled 'Night Shadows', the psychological isolation of individuals living in the modern city is communicated through the words 'mystery' and 'secret':

> A wonderful fact to reflect upon, that every human creature is constituted to be that profound secret and mystery to every other. A solemn consideration, when I enter a great city by night, that every one of those darkly clustered houses encloses its own secret; that every room in every one of them encloses its own secret; that every beating heart in the hundreds of thousands of breasts there, is, in some of its imaginings, a secret to the heart nearest it! Something of the awfulness, even of Death itself, is preferable to this. (Dickens, 2003: 14)

Thus the three passengers travelling together in the mail coach are complete 'mysteries to one another' (2003: 17), the narrator later commenting of Dr Manette that 'No human intelligence could have read the mysteries of his mind in the scared blank wonder of his face' (2003: 51). But it is this very individualism that allows 'mysteries' to become 'wonders' at the end of the novel. For Dickens, democracy was not just an ideology but a political system made up of acts and commitments by individuals. Hence the 'wonder' of Sydney Carton's transformation: alienated and made cynical by the corrupt nature of the law, he finds meaning not in his career but in love for Lucie Manette, a love that leads him to sacrifice his own life for her happiness. The character who has described himself as 'like one who died young' (2003: 156) – who has become ghosted to himself – thus feels most alive when about to die. The utopian social system that Carton foresees just before his death, the 'beautiful city and a brilliant people rising from this abyss' (2003: 389), he envisages not only as a democracy that functions more fairly than past and current political systems, but as a system in which individuals will maintain the integrity of the law. In such a society, the son of Lucie and Darnay is to be 'foremost of just judges and honoured men' (2003: 390), thus redeeming the figure of Jacques Ferrand, the immensely powerful and corrupt notary at the heart of Sue's *Les Mystères de Paris*. Only through the integrity of the law, it is implied, will the various repressions charted in the novel – including Dr Manette's repression of his psychological agony and the Marquis's belief in repression as a political system ('The dark deference of fear and slavery, my friend, will keep the dogs obedient to the whip' (2003: 128)) – come to an end. It is perhaps worth remembering here that Dickens was torn between the law and professional writing as careers until the mid 1840s (Chittick,

1990: 12–13). Dickens's use of the phrase 'echoing footsteps' throughout *A Tale of Two Cities* aptly captures the way in which England in 1859 was haunted by a vision of democracy yet to be realised. In England, France's revolutionary cry for 'liberté, egalité, fraternité' inspired Chartism and led eventually to the various social reform initiatives of the 1860s, including the British Reform Act of 1867. In France, the revival of radicalism after 1840 resulted in the formation of the Second Republic in 1848. The invocation of the Bastille by Reynolds and Dickens is thus not simply an empty echo of the Revolution or of late eighteenth-century Gothic novels; nor do Gothic effects in these texts suggest Gothic's 'evacuated identity' at this time. On the contrary, Gothic elements in the works of Sue, Reynolds and Dickens make vivid and sustain an important dialogue concerning the nature of freedom and equality in modern urban society, a dialogue in which the uncanny and the abject are used to interrogate the social and political realities of the time.

Notes

1. There were cholera outbreaks in both London and Paris in 1832.
2. See James (2008), for a full exploration of Reynolds's engagement with French fiction.
3. The full text of Reynolds's *Mysteries* is also available online at: www.victorianlondon.org/mysteries/mysteries-00–chapters.htm. For ease of cross reference between this and Thomas's selection, chapter numbers are given as well as page references to Thomas's edition.
4. Dickens denounced Reynolds as 'a national reproach' for his chairing of the Trafalgar Square Chartist event of 1849 (which resulted in window-breaking) in 'Preliminary Word', the first issue of *Household Words* (30 March 1850), p. 1 (Maxwell: 1992, 166). See Anne Humphreys and Louis James, 'Introduction' (2008), for a useful overview of Reynolds's life and the reception of his work in England.
5. See Glancy (2006), Sanders (1988) and Richard Maxwell's edition of the novel (Dickens, 2003) for detailed accounts of these and other sources used by Dickens.
6. Maxwell points out the similarity between the plots of *A Tale of Two Cities* and *Les Misérables* in the Penguin edition of the novel (Dickens, 2003). See also Maxwell (1992) for a detailed exposition of Hugo's influence on Dickens's writing, and Grossman (1985) and Eco (2006) for explorations of Dickens's influence on Hugo's late work.

References

Burt, Daniel S. (1980). 'A Victorian Gothic: G. W. M. Reynolds's *Mysteries of London*', *New York Literary Forum*, 7, 141–58.

Chevasco, Berry Palmer (2003). *Mysterymania: The Reception of Eugène Sue in Britain 1838–1860*. Oxford and Berlin: Peter Lang.

Chittick, Kathryn (1990). *Dickens and the 1830s*. Cambridge: Cambridge University Press.

Dickens, Charles (1977). *The Pilgrim Edition of the Letters of Charles Dickens*, vol. 4: *1844–1846*, ed. Kathleen Tillotson. Oxford: Clarendon Press.

——(1981). *The Pilgrim Edition of the Letters of Charles Dickens*, vol. 5: *1847–1849*, ed. Graham Storey and K. J. Fielding. Oxford: Clarendon Press.

——(2003). *A Tale of Two Cities* [1859], ed. Richard Maxwell. London: Penguin.

Easson, Angus (1993). 'From Terror to Terror: Dickens, Carlyle and Cannibalism', in *Reflections of Revolution: Images of Romanticism*, ed. Alison Yarrington and Kelvin Everest. London and New York: Routledge, pp. 96–111.

Eco, Umberto (2006). 'Excess and History in Hugo's *Ninety-three*', in *The Novel*, vol. 2: *Forms and Themes*, ed. Franco Moretti. Princeton and Oxford: Princeton University Press, pp. 274–94.

Fowler, Simon (2007). *Workhouse: The People, The Places, The Life Behind Doors*. Kew: The National Archives.

Fraser, Derek (2009). *The Evolution of the British Welfare State*, 4th edn. Basingstoke: Palgrave Macmillan.

Glancy, Ruth (2006). *Charles Dickens's 'A Tale of Two Cities': A Sourcebook*. London and New York: Routledge.

Grossman, Kathryn (1985). 'Satire and Utopian Vision in Hugo, Dickens and Zamiatin', *Journal of General Education*, 37, 177–88.

Humpherys, Anne and Louis James (eds) (2008) *G. W. M. Reynolds: Nineteenth-Century Fiction, Politics and the Press*. Aldershot: Ashgate Press.

James, Sara (2005). 'Eugène Sue, G. W. M. Reynolds, and the Representation of the City as "Mystery"', in *Babylon or New Jerusalem? Perceptions of the City in Literature*, ed. Valeria Tinkler-Villani. Amsterdam: Rodopi, pp. 247–58.

——(2008). 'G. W. M. Reynolds and the Modern Literature of France', in *G. W. M. Reynolds: Nineteenth-Century Fiction, Politics and the Press*, ed. Anne Humpherys and Louis James. Aldershot: Ashgate Press, pp. 19–32.

Maxwell, Richard C., Jr. (1977). 'G. M. Reynolds, Dickens , and the Mysteries of London', *Nineteenth-Century Fiction*, 32/2, 188–213.

——(1992). *The Mysteries of Paris and London*. Charlottesville and London: University Press of Virginia.

Mighall, Robert (1999). *A Geography of Victorian Gothic Fiction*. Oxford: Oxford University Press.

Prendergast, Christopher (2003). *For the People by the People? Eugène Sue's 'Les Mystères de Paris': A Hypothesis in the Sociology of Literature*. Oxford: Legenda.

Punter, David (1998). *Gothic Pathologies: The Text, The Body and The Law*. Basingstoke: Macmillan.

Punter, David and Glennis Byron (2004). *The Gothic*. Oxford: Blackwell Publishing.

Reynolds, G. W. M. (1996). *The Mysteries of London* [1844–8], ed. Trefor Thomas. Keele: Keele University Press.

Sanders, Andrew (1988). *The Companion to 'A Tale of Two Cities'*. London: Unwin Hyman.

Sue, Eugène (n.d. but probably 1989). *The Mysteries of Paris* [1842–3], anonymous translator. Sawtry and New York: Dedalus/Hippocrene.

Thomas, Trefor (2000). 'Rereading G. W. M. Reynolds's *The Mysteries of London*', in *Rereading Victorian Fiction*, ed. Alice Jenkins and Juliet John. Basingstoke: Macmillan, pp. 59–80.

Wolfreys, Julian (2006). 'Victorian Gothic', in *Teaching the Gothic*, ed. Anna Powell and Andrew Smith. Basingstoke: Palgrave Macmillan, pp. 62–77.

——(2010). 'Towards a Phenomenology of Urban Gothic: The Example of Dickens', in *London Gothic: Place, Space and the Gothic Imagination*, ed. Lawrence Phillips and Anne Witchard. London: Continuum, pp. 9–22.

Chapter 8

The Victorian Gothic and Gender
Carol Margaret Davison

Since its inception in the mid eighteenth century and especially during its efflorescence in the late eighteenth century, the Gothic's engagement with gender-related issues has been pronounced and multifarious. Both female and male writers have consciously and adeptly adopted the Gothic – a form that serves as a barometer of socio-cultural anxieties in its exploration of the dark side of individuals, cultures, and nations – to interrogate socially dictated and institutionally entrenched attitudes and laws relating to gender roles, identities and relations. Indeed, the Gothic, which experienced tremendous market success, was often itself gendered as feminine and consequently vilified as vulgar given that the majority of its early producers and consumers were women. Critical assessments of the Gothic in terms of gender questions also date back to the early stages of its production. For example, in a critical essay published posthumously entitled 'On the Supernatural in Poetry' (1802; 1826), Ann Radcliffe, one of the Gothic's most prestigious producers and proponents, advanced a gendered distinction between two types of Gothic literature contingent on what she perceived to be their different impacts on the faculties. While 'terror Gothic' was classified as feminine and tacitly associated with her own work in its aim to expand the soul by bringing it into contact with the terror-inducing sublime, 'horror Gothic' was deemed 'masculine' and associated with the more sensational works of Matthew G. Lewis. In stark contrast to the sublimity of 'terror Gothic', 'horror Gothic' was said to focus on encounters with gruesomely depicted mortality with the effect of contracting, freezing and nearly annihilating the faculties (Radcliffe, 2000). A similar impulse to bring gender to bear on the Gothic in the domain of literary criticism motivated the twentieth-century classification of the 'Female Gothic', a sub-category of the Gothic that takes as its focus female protagonists wrestling with repressed familial histories and problematic social and institutional pressures relating to female sexuality and gender roles.

   Gothic literature into the Victorian period evidences an ongoing fixation with issues of sexuality and gender, extending that genre's range, in tandem with the Victorian novel's forays into social realism, sensation fiction, science fiction, and beyond, to an interrogation of the patriarchal social structures that shaped Britain's political and domestic life. This preoccupation is unsurprising given that Victorian middle-class society deemed sexuality to be 'the key determinant of one's personality' (McLaren, 2002: 3). In this regard, it is important to note that Victorian society conflated the concepts of sex (male/female) and gender (masculinity/femininity), considering gender, as John Stuart Mill lamented in *The Subjection of Women* (1869), to be a natural and inborn quality as opposed to a culturally constructed concept.[1] The Victorian era witnessed unprecedented socio-political changes that radically affected and destabilised the traditional gender roles and relations undergirding marriage and motherhood. Among these developments was the growing number of working- and lower-middle-class women entering the workforce – while some of their middle-class compatriots were clamouring to do the same – coupled with noteworthy legislative changes relating to enfranchisement and such matters as marriage, divorce, child custody and women's property rights.

   The impact and importance of these momentous socio-political shifts is attested to by the fact that a war of words relating to sexuality and gender-related issues may be traced across the entire period, from the Woman Question of the 1840s to the New Woman Question of the 1880s and 1890s. In the face of these substantial changes and their threat to established boundaries of difference, the burgeoning Victorian middle classes compulsively redefined gender relations by underscoring male and female differences (McLaren, 2002: 3). These debates often possessed national implications as their alarmist commentators drew upon medical discourses of disease, degeneration and addiction to declare the erosion of family values and traditional institutions, thus yoking gendered bodies to the national body politic. The explicit battlefield in these debates was the female body and the issue of embattled femininity, with women's social position and behaviour serving as an index of national health. The male subject and masculinity were nevertheless implicated. Men remained the norm against which women and children were measured and 'manliness' served, as the hundreds of Victorian publications devoted to this topic suggest, as one of the key concepts in the Victorian middle-class moral universe (Tosh, 2005: 31). Given the remarkable faith Victorians had in the power of the will (Adams, 1999: 127), manliness became increasingly and inextricably bound up with the concept of self-control, with femaleness raising the spectre of hysteria and a lack of restraint, sexual, moral and otherwise. The hegemonic middle-class Victorian agenda to retain a sense of separate gendered spheres faced ever-increasing challenges as the century progressed.

The Gothic lent itself particularly well to engagement with these controversial issues given its ability to tap deep-seated, sometimes repressed, desires and anxieties, coupled with its fixation on literal and symbolic transgressions. At three particular points in the course of the Victorian period, Gothic novelists weighed in heavily on sex/gender-related debates: the 1840s, during a decade of tremendous social calamity and reform and at the height of debate over the Woman Question; the 1860s, in the aftermath of noteworthy legislation relating to divorce; and the 1880s and 1890s, when anxieties were running high in regard to the New Woman Question, the Decadence Movement, homosexuality and imperialism, and when heated discussion was occurring, particularly in the periodical press, about gender roles and identity. Two principal manifestations of the Gothic may be identified in the Victorian period, the first involving an interfacing between the Gothic and social realism that did not lend credibility to the supernatural; while the second, more fantastic and sensational, Gothic combined with other popular cultural forms such as detective fiction, the boys' adventure novel and science fiction and *did* lend credibility to the supernatural. The Gothic works of the 1840s fall into the first category, the Gothic works of the 1880s and 1890s fall into the second, and the Gothic works of the 1860s offer up a Frankensteinian fusion of both.

The most significant overall developments within the Gothic over the course of the Victorian era are its greater domestication in that Britain serves as a site and source of terror, coupled with its greater internalisation, which involved its adaptation to convey intense emotions and explore, as Gilbert Phelps points out, psychological states of mind (1987: 126). What Frederick Frank has called 'the horror of the fragmented self' (1977: xii) not only took hold post-*Frankenstein*, it underwent some fascinating and experimental narrative surgery. A chronological overview of Victorian Gothic literature in the light of contemporary sex/gender debates evidences the Gothic's role as a unique cultural lens onto these questions. While the intersections of gender and class are paramount in the early and mid-Victorian eras, the issue of gender in relation to sexuality preoccupies writers at the fin de siècle. Regardless of the focus, the concept and conception of the monster, a popular motif that is often bound up with the notion of criminality, serves as a useful heuristic device for considering the Victorian Gothic's shifting fixations vis-à-vis sex/gender issues. The reader witnesses a crucial shift in this period whereby the monster-making Dr Frankenstein becomes largely overshadowed by his monster: the critique of 'monster'-making social conditions and institutions that predominates in the early period is, with a couple of key exceptions, progressively eclipsed by spectacular, commercially popular monsters who embody and express social anxieties relating to various sex/gender issues. Indeed, the spectacular and sensational nature of these monsters and their crimes increases over the course of the period and seems correlated to the severity of their violation of established gender/sex roles and ideals. Notably, while the sexed/gendered monsters in early Victorian Gothic literature remain closeted in the private sphere, thus averting public scandal, late Victorian Gothic monsters are often gender-benders who greatly unsettle the national status quo and its supportive socio-political institutions by threatening to come out of the closet and erupt into the public sphere, an especially acute terror for a society founded on a cult of respectability. As several fin-de-siècle Gothic works suggest, the greatest terror arises when, in a manner in keeping with eyewitness reports about Jack the Ripper who conducted his series of gruesome crimes in Whitechapel in 1888, the imperceptible monster infiltrates the public sphere under the guise of respectability, thus covertly threatening infection and social degeneration.

The 1840s: The Gothic and Social Realism

In what is arguably the most critically respected manifestation of the Gothic in the Victorian period, that form was blended with social realism in the 1840s to produce such fictional classics as Charlotte Brontë's *Jane Eyre* (1847) and *Villette* (1853), Emily Brontë's *Wuthering Heights* (1847), and Anne Brontë's *The Tenant of Wildfell Hall* (1848). As a result of this unique generic fusion, Gothic closets may be found – to adopt a trope suitable to the architecturally obsessed Gothic (Castle, 2005: 689) – in the generally staid and calm manor house of Victorian fiction (a topic explored elsewhere in this volume by Martin Willis). Most of Charles Dickens's works, including *Bleak House* (1852–3) and *Great Expectations* (1861), attest to the success, versatility and tenacity of this narrative union. The dark, sometimes criminal, underbelly of the middle-class domestic sphere, which includes repressed family secrets and histories, is probed and exposed, thus giving the lie, on various grounds, to the Victorians' idealised view of domesticity that was perhaps best captured in John Ruskin's famous essay 'Of Queens' Gardens' (1865) as 'the place of Peace; the shelter, not only from all injury, but from all terror, doubt, and division' (Ruskin, 1866: 87). In the process, middle-class identity, domestic and romantic ideals, and the institutions that grant them authority and protection, are exposed and interrogated.

The Gothic's contribution to the expression of character psychology in social realist fiction has been, for some decades, critically identified and applauded. It was Robert B. Heilman who first coined the term 'New Gothic' in 1958 to describe Charlotte Brontë's use of what he referred to as 'Old Gothic' with its 'relatively crude mechanisms of fear' (Heilman, 1961: 73) to better flesh out character psychology in the burgeoning social realist tradition. Given Brontë's skilful manipulation of the Female Gothic form, however, Ann Radcliffe's use of the explained supernatural to grant expression to her protagonists' anxieties and fears, particularly in relation to sexual propriety and marriage, was probably the primary informing model. Thus did the Gothic help to render social realist fiction more realistic, a rather ironic effect given the generally oppositional drives of those novelistic forms. Notably, however, raising the ghost of the Gothic within the realist tradition also unsettled the certainties – both aesthetic and ideological – of that nascent form: the Gothic upsets the belief that all aspects of our existence are identifiable and representable, and problematises the idea that all aspects of our identity and institutions can withstand logical and moral scrutiny. In mining the complex depths of individual psychology, the Victorian Gothic often conveys what one critic nicely refers to as the 'alterity of subjectivity' (Miles, 2002: 2). Self-estrangement is a realistic, crucial and symbolically loaded stage in these works, especially, for reasons to be discussed, where women are concerned, its annihilation often signalling the protagonist's successful maturation by novel's end.

In keeping with Victorian literature's general preoccupation with the relationship between the individual and society, the exploration of the alterity of subjectivity in Victorian Gothic fiction is usually directed towards social critique. A connection is often drawn between the public and private spheres, social institutions and individuals, whereby, for example, a character's self-estrangement is revealed to be the result of monster-making social institutions that necessitate unnatural self-repression. Thus, the Gothic is often deployed to shed light on the dark side of socio-political realities and institutions whose toll is usually emotional or psychological, resulting in debilitating self-division or the perversion of natural, healthy feeling. In early Victorian Gothic works, many of which are adept reconfigurations of the Female Gothic, Victorian laws and gender ideology repeatedly come under fire. The predominant image that emerges from these texts is of women imprisoned, circumscribed sexually, intellectually and legally, a status that actually reflected women's contemporary socio-political reality. As the jurist William Blackstone explains in his *Commentaries on the Laws of England* (1765), the principal law relating to women in England that obtained well into the Victorian period, was the law of coverture under which a married woman's identity was incorporated and consolidated into that of her husband (quoted in Hoeveler, 1998: 6). E. J. Clery concisely delineates the real consequences of this principle:

> The husband took control of the whole of his wife's property, past, present and future; he had sole rights over their children; a married woman could not enter into any legal agreement or lawsuit on her own behalf; she could not bring proceedings against her husband in common law; and, since her 'very being' was suspended, she no longer held property in her own person, Locke's minimum condition for civil rights. (Clery, 1992: 78)

Thus did women, regardless of their class, as Frances Power Cobbe suggests in her 1868 essay, 'Criminals, Idiots, Women, and Minors', share the same disenfranchised and lowly status as criminals in Victorian society.

Various social commentaries on the status of women drew on the trope of the domestic sphere as prison that was popularised by radical feminist thinker and Female Gothic novelist Mary Wollstonecraft in the 1790s. William Thompson and Anna Wheeler offered up a damning portrait of marriage – 'a system of such iniquitous despotism' (Thompson and Wheeler, 1994: 91) – and of women's pathetic social status in their 1825 commentary, *Appeal of One-Half the Human Race, Women, Against the Pretensions of the Other Half, Men, to Retain Them in Political, and Thence in Civil and Domestic Slavery*. Florence Nightingale's stinging criticism in *Cassandra* (1860) suggests that the middle-class ideology of femininity was likewise constraining, even thirty-five years later. It required that women feign being passionless, don 'intellectual hair-shirt[s]', and quash their desires for a profession or any social relevancy (Nightingale, 1979: 16, 27, 25). In her most damning critique, Nightingale equates marriage with death (1979: 40) and suggests that death is actually a preferable and desired state for Victorian women given their perpetual state of death-in-life (1979: 54–5).

The function of the domestic sphere as 'the eternal prison-house of the wife' (Thompson and Wheeler, 1994: 79) that constituted the driving idea in earlier Female Gothic literature, remains central to Anne Brontë's *The Tenant of Wildfell Hall*, Charlotte Brontë's *Jane Eyre*, and Emily Brontë's *Wuthering Heights*. Anne Brontë's *The Tenant of Wildfell Hall* offers up the decade's most daring exposé of what she suggests are anti-Christian, socially generated and legally sanctioned Victorian domestic crimes. This Gothic temperance novel tackles such taboo phenomena as substance abuse and domestic violence and ultimately rewards its protagonist, who acknowledges her own failings with regard to a love addiction condoned and promoted by the prevailing romantic ideology, with what is represented as a loving, respected Christian marriage between equals. After experiencing abuse at the hands of her upper-middle-class, debauched, alcoholic husband, Arthur Huntingdon, Brontë's compelling protagonist, Helen, struggles to retain custody of her son, escape from an intolerable situation, achieve self-actualisation, and realise a means of financial support by way of her painting. Brontë's indictment of wife abuse, custody issues and the debilitating restraints placed on middle-class women who are disallowed gainful employment and granted love as their only rightful domain, is nothing if not prescient and courageous, drawing on and anticipating Caroline Norton's various writings on infant custody (1839) and women's property rights (1855). Norton experienced a tragic disenfranchisement under English law having been left penniless and without custody of her three sons, one of whom thereafter died while being withheld from his mother and in her husband's care. Although itself a daring denunciation of the socially stigmatised subject of wife abuse, Frances Power Cobbe's 1878 essay devoted to the topic of 'Wife-torture in England' largely resists the idea portrayed candidly and at length in *Tenant* that such abuses also occur among the middle and upper classes.

Charlotte Brontë employs the Gothic to similar ends in *Jane Eyre*, a proto-feminist Gothic fairy tale in which her governess-protagonist resists sexual temptation and rejects existing marital constraints – constraints emblematised, in their worst extreme, in the relationship between Edward Rochester and his mad, incarcerated first wife, Bertha, who are both reduced to the status of slaves in the marital marketplace. In tempering her passions in accordance with Christian precepts that denounce idolatry, and realising a new Christian, companionate marital ideal wherein women are regarded as equal, desiring, vocal subjects and partners with men, Jane Eyre stands out as a singular heroine in defiance of what Brontë suggests are socially dictated acts of female self-annihilation. Charlotte Brontë's *Villette* likewise censures the established Victorian gender ideology which dictates that Lucy Snowe's social 'success' be contingent on the suppression of her voice and the repression of her passionate nature. This containment is rendered symbolically in the story of the buried nun and Lucy's buried letters to Graham Bretton. As Brontë reveals, however, such socially sanctioned repression leads to extreme mental anguish and breakdown. While male characters in early Victorian Gothic fiction, such as Wemmick in Dickens's *Great*

Expectations, are shown to be divided characters who can express different aspects of their character in a healthy manner in different spheres (private/public), no such outlet is available to female characters like Lucy Snowe and Jane Eyre.

The tremendous personal costs of a marital marketplace where economics trump matters of the heart is most memorably and powerfully recounted in Emily Brontë's *Wuthering Heights*, an early Victorian Gothic novel that celebrates the unrestrained joys and passions of an ungendered childhood. The ambitious Catherine Earnshaw, however, subsequently suppresses both her primal identification with and love for Heathcliff along with the joys and passions of girlhood in order to gain social status through a socially sanctioned marriage to Edgar Linton. Thus does Catherine trade in, as Terry Eagleton rightly notes, 'her authentic selfhood for social privilege' (2003: 396) while Emily Brontë daringly denounces the suppression of female passion by way of Catherine's devastating fate. A similar type of Faustian exchange is made by the impoverished orphan Heathcliff who experiences self-loathing in the face of the emasculating power of class privilege (Emily Brontë, 2003: 66). In figuratively selling his soul to attain revenge by beating other capitalists at their own game, Heathcliff becomes a tragic and tormented 'monster' (2003: 143) forged in the crucible of Mary Shelley's *Frankenstein* (1818). A similar tragedy where economics take precedence over ethics and feeling occurs in Pip's case in Dickens's *Great Expectations*. After experiencing a figurative emasculation based on his sense of class powerlessness at the hands of the vengeful Miss Havisham and her monstrously heartless daughter Estella, Pip opts to suppress his better self – his feeling, authentic self – in exchange for social mobility. Dickens ultimately grants Pip some redemption at novel's end, as does Emily Brontë in Heathcliff's case, once he realises the tremendous error and costs, both emotional and spiritual, of his misguided decisions.

It is important to recognise in regard to the intersecting issues of gender and genre, that early Victorian Gothic often advanced a new ideal of masculinity featuring a novel type of gentleman, one free of the class, monetary or criminal associations this figure possessed in the political Godwinian Gothic of the 1790s. Emily Brontë's portrait of Heathcliff is especially provocative in this respect as he comes to emblematise the grotesque transforming power of capitalist enterprise. Originally a penniless orphan, Heathcliff rises to the status of gentleman – a landlord and 'capital fellow' (Emily Brontë, 2003: 25), according to Mr Lockwood, the novel's framing narrator – but his abuses of his wife Isabella, despite being conducted, as he insists, 'strictly within the limits of the law – [avoiding] giving her the slightest right to claim a separation' (2003: 143), position him firmly in the ambiguous category of gentleman-criminal. As Pip's symbolic association with the criminal Magwitch makes clear, he also merits that label in *Great Expectations*. Notably, Dickens reconceptualises gentlemanliness in Pip's uncle, Joe Gargery, a simple blacksmith, whom Dickens celebrates for his possession of 'the wealth of . . . [a] great nature' (Dickens, 1986: 434) given his unflagging love for and dedication to Pip despite that nephew's emotional mistreatment of him. A similar figurative usurpation of power occurs in *The Tenant of Wildfell Hall* where Helen Huntingdon's first husband Arthur, a cruel and careless debauchee who subjects her to horrible humiliations, is replaced by the upright *gentleman*-farmer Gilbert Markham, a man who is duly tested before gaining his marital reward.

The 1860s: The Gothic and Sensation Fiction

The Gothic saw its second major metamorphosis in the domain of the Victorian mainstream novel with the appearance of sensation fiction in the 1860s (discussed in depth in this volume by Laurence Talairach-Vielmas), a form that had its figurative finger on the pulse of contemporary society yet was, ironically, variously denounced as a disease and an 'addictive drug or drink' that engendered a kind of 'unnatural excitement' in its readership (Mansel, 1863: 513, 485, 512). Combining elements from the Gothic, Victorian stage melodrama, the Newgate Novels of the 1830s that took the lives and escapades of notorious criminals as their subject matter, and the burgeoning phenomenon of sensational journalism that traded in illicit passion and criminal activity, sensation fiction saw the joint advent of the detective in British literature and the transgressive Lady-criminal. During an era characterised by mass social and geographic dislocations that saw millions of strangers brought together in unfamiliar urban environments, sensation fiction gave expression to a variety of anxieties around such questions as class mobility, changing marital legislation and the multifaceted nature of identity. Notably, it homed its lens in on the middle-class family – that class which possessed, unlike the working classes, the luxury of privacy. In so doing, like early Victorian Gothic but with different implications, sensation fiction capitalised on the disjunction between public and private/secret selves. In his much-quoted review of Mary Elizabeth Braddon's *Aurora Floyd* (1863), Henry James famously and astutely characterised sensation fiction's fascination with

> those most mysterious of mysteries, the mysteries which are at our own doors
> . . . Instead of the terrors of Udolpho, we [are] treated to the terrors of the

cheerful country house, or the London lodgings. And there is no doubt that these were infinitely the more terrible. (James, 1865: 594)

James's assessment of these tamer, more domesticated terrors seemed to be confirmed by contemporary sensational journalism and is echoed by the young barrister and detective-in-training Robert Audley in Mary Elizabeth Braddon's hugely popular *Lady Audley's Secret* (1862), when he observes that 'in these civilized days all kinds of unsuspected horrors are constantly committed' (Braddon, 1992: 97).

In an effort to magnify the impact of such home-grown horrors, sensation fiction took as its primary point of sight the crimes of ostensibly respectable middle-class women within the institution of marriage, their only available 'career choice'. The decision was hugely commercially successful, especially in the wake of the 1857 Divorce and Matrimonial Causes Act that secured married women some property rights and saw divorce moved from canon to civil law, thus rendering it more accessible to the middle classes. Sensation fiction both represented and registered the fall-out of this law that unsettled the sense of marital security and the stability of gender roles and relations, sometimes serving as a type of cautionary tale, at others exaggerating those social changes for their titillating entertainment value. As Lyn Pykett has underscored, 'gender roles are central here, and uncertainties about gender roles within the family, the differing expectations about marriage held by men and women, and misunderstandings between marital partners are a recurring theme' (Pykett, 1994: 10).

Ironically, divorce is rarely portrayed in this literature. Instead, these dark domestic tales often point up the inadequacies of contemporary marriage and inheritance laws and the justice system, and feature desperate individuals willing to violate those laws in order to attain their goals. Although the figure of the gentleman-criminal husband remains – like Sir Percival Glyde in Willkie Collins's *The Woman in White* (1859–60) who institutionalises his wife and secretly alters her identity in order to retain control over her money – the novel and compelling ingredient in several noteworthy instances is a figurative daughter of William Makepeace Thackeray's Becky Sharp. This resourceful and designing underclass woman who is guilty of deceptively violating her marriage vows seems related to the new socially disruptive race of women that Eliza Lynn Linton denounces in her essay 'The Girl of the Period' (1868), who refuse to fulfil their natural and proper domestic obligations. On this basis, these novels were given the pejorative nickname 'Bigamy Novels' (Mansel, 1863: 490). In the face of the fact that, as Lady Audley realises early, her 'ultimate fate in life depended upon

[her] marriage' (Braddon, 1992: 350), the protagonist of sensation fiction is sometimes a self-centred entrepreneurial femme fatale. Despite the sexual innuendos involved with bigamy, the sexual energies of these femmes fatales tend to be held at bay. These will be granted expression by their more spectacular and sexualised literary sisters at the fin de siècle.

Particularly in the hands of Wilkie Collins, himself a writer trained in the law whose familial/'marital' arrangements to two women were strikingly unorthodox – he married neither, yet fathered three children with them – sensation fiction exhibited a fascination with sexual politics and the often devastating consequences of marriage and inheritance laws on women and children. In portraying individuals driven to extremes and sometimes to criminal activity due to repressive laws, Collins's works are more in keeping with the Gothically inflected social reform novels of the 1840s that point the finger at the monster-making socio-political system. While *No Name* (1862) indicts outdated inheritance laws, *Man and Wife* (1870) engages with the issue of antiquated marriage laws then prevalent in Scotland and Ireland. In a brilliant sleight of hand that turns established Gothic on its head with its demonisation of the foreigner, Collins uses Count Fosco in *The Woman in White* (1860), his most famous work of sensation fiction, to point up serious deficiencies in the British legal system, a system indicted for being in collusion with the monied classes (Collins, 1985: 33). To what he suggests are myopic, hypocritical Britons, Fosco exposes the problematic ambivalence of British laws that serve both as an accomplice to and the enemy of crime (1985: 258). In regard to gender issues, Fosco also praises and confirms Marian Halcombe's suggestion that women remain entirely unprotected under British law (1985: 315), being essentially submissive servants at the mercy of their husbands (1985: 633).

Mary Elizabeth Braddon's *Lady Audley's Secret*, deemed 'one of the most noxious books of modern times' (Rae, 1865: 187), which went through nine editions in only three months after its initial publication in 1862, signalled the beginning of an interesting shift in Victorian Gothic literature in its ambivalence towards the monstrous female criminal. Despite being abandoned with an infant by her first husband, George Talboys, minimal sympathy is extended to Lucy Graham as she undergoes shifts in identity and her crimes escalate from child abandonment and bigamy to attempted murder and arson. There is no critique, as there is in Collins's works, of oppressive social institutions that may engender criminals. Braddon does echo Collins, however, in underscoring the artificiality and performativity of gender roles. In Lady Audley's case, her respectable status and beauty not only, as the young Robert

Audley suggests, render her crimes more horrifying (Braddon, 1992: 271), they enable them, serving as a façade under which she can operate with impunity.

Masculinity is also of key concern, being portrayed as embattled in *The Woman in White*, where a struggle occurs between the logical, masculine Marian Halcombe, a detective-in-training whose moustache provides pseudo-scientific evidence of her gender transgression, and Walter Hartright, whose final marriage to Laura Fairlie decidedly puts Marian in her place and confirms John Stuart Mill's hypothesis in 'The Subjection of Women' (1869) that 'the generality of the male sex cannot yet tolerate the idea of living with an equal' (Mill 1989: 166). A similar battle of the sexes transpires in *Lady Audley's Secret* between the titular heroine and her nephew, the barrister-detective Robert Audley. Just as Walter Hartright's masculinity is confirmed and consolidated at the end of Collins's novel by way of a rugged adventure trip to South America, so too does Robert Audley regain dominance over Lady Audley as signified by the incarceration of her questionably mad and, ultimately, dead, female body. While the Gothic is employed by Braddon to bring bad marriages into sharp relief, Robert and Lady Audley are, like all true Gothic protagonists, variously haunted. Robert's spectres are manipulative women, the prevalence in society of failed marriages at a time when he is falling in love (Braddon 1992: 204) and the unsolved murder and unburied body of his best friend (1992: 401); while Lady Audley is figuratively haunted by the ghost of George Talboys, the first husband she believes she murdered (1992: 265). The asylum in Belgium in which she is finally 'buried alive', a fate paralleling her mother's, serves as an extension of medicalised male power into the domestic sphere. Lady Audley's prime secret may well be that, as Elaine Showalter has claimed, she is actually a '*sane* and, moreover, representative' woman (1977: 167). The novel's most secret and unaddressed crime, however, is her violation of gender codes, a transgression that is pathologised and punished by Robert Audley who turns her over, under the guise of compassion and mercy, to the madhouse doctors. As sensational as Lady Audley was deemed to be – one reviewer declared her 'at once the heroine and the monstrosity' of Braddon's novel (Rae, 1865: 186) – she is extremely tame when compared to her fin-de-siècle counterparts.

The 1880s/1890s: Fin-de-siècle Fantastic Gothic

As the spectacular, supernaturalised Gothic of the fin de siècle suggests, British masculinity came under fire from two primary forces during this period – a new 'race' of sexually voracious, power-hungry and intellectual 'New Women' who insisted on a new sexual contract, and 'the purportedly foreign "abomination" of same-sex desire' (Castle, 2005: 686) that became associated with the Decadence Movement thanks especially to Max Nordau's *Degeneration* (1895), an ostensible work of medical theory that pathologised much fin-de-siècle art. Jointly, New Women and homosexuals/Decadents were considered dreaded subversives who raised the spectre of eugenic dangers and social degeneration (Dowling, 1979: 445, 447). Indeed, in a period fascinated with psychology, particularly women's (Dowling, 1979: 434), that saw the new scholarly field of sexology that propounded new scientific norms of male and female sexuality, both groups were demonised by their respective critics as erotomaniacs. These sexual and psychological monsters challenged traditional notions of 'natural' gender identity and boundaries. The word 'invert', which means 'to turn upside down', was employed in relation to both. While, as Eliza Lynn Linton claimed, New Women were characterised by 'a curious inversion of sex, which does not necessarily appear in the body, but is evident enough in the mind' (1868: 82), doctors used the term 'invert' in the latter decades of the nineteenth century as a noun to refer to a man who was attracted to other men (McLaren, 1997: 177). Especially after Oscar Wilde's prosecution in 1895 under the Labouchère Amendment for 'acts of gross indecency' with a man, the Decadence Movement became more closely associated with homosexuality, a 'condition' that, since its classification in 1869 (McLaren, 1997: 177), was widely regarded, like nymphomania, another prominent 'condition' at the fin de siècle (Bouchereau, 2000: 293), as a form of insanity (McLaren, 1997: 219).

In the face of these significant events and social studies, several major fin-de-siècle Gothic novels register an intense homosexual panic. One can only imagine the impact that 'Carmilla' (1872), J. Sheridan Le Fanu's vampire tale of female same-sex desire, had on its audience given its unmentionable – and, for some, inconceivable – subject matter and its explosion of such accepted theories as physician William Acton's that 'the majority of women . . . are not very much troubled with sexual feeling of any kind' (quoted in Adams, 1999: 126). Unlike Richard Marsh's queer gender-bending monster in *The Beetle* (1897), Robert Louis Stevenson's *The Strange Case of Dr Jekyll and Mr Hyde* (1886), Oscar Wilde's *The Picture of Dorian Gray* (1891) and Bram Stoker's *Dracula* (1897) illustrate that the dreaded queer monster who threatens sexual 'conversion', hysteria, and even death, is frequently male. What Dr Jekyll characterises as his 'undignified' pleasures (Stevenson, 1987: 65) seem to include encounters of the queer kind given the description by his manservant Bradshaw who witnesses Mr Hyde emerging from Dr Jekyll's bedroom in the middle of the night inexplicably attired in Dr Jekyll's ill-fitting clothes (1987: 67). In a similar blackmail narrative riddled with the word 'queer' and fuelled by the threat of public exposure, Robert Holt's dramatic emergence late at night, dressed only in a cloak, from the home of the respected politician Paul Lessingham in *The Beetle*, raises a similar suggestion. Dorian Gray serves as a classic yet queer homme fatal who, while proving lethal to various women, is also 'fatal to young men' (Wilde, 2008: 127). The existence of his curious disguises held in a secret wainscoting press (2008: 135) recalls the case of Ernest Boulton and Frederick William Park, two transvestites and suspected homosexuals who were charged in 1871, after a sensational and widely publicised trial, with 'conspiring and inciting persons to commit an unnatural offence' (Adams, 1999: 135). Count Dracula's near attack on Jonathan Harker and those actually committed against the male sailors aboard the *Demeter* that conducts him to England, notably under the cover of darkness and with no narrative description provided, also attest to a vampire who may be said to suck both ways.

Notably, Stevenson's and Wilde's works are more in keeping with early Victorian Gothic in their attention to society's monster-making role. Without denying Dr Jekyll's and Dorian Gray's accountability for their downfalls, both works suggest that monsters are, in part, products of sexually repressive, hypocritical societies that are particularly exacting, as Dr Jekyll suggests in his concluding Statement, for professionals (Stevenson, 1987: 60) who must, in pursuit of their pleasures, embrace a 'double existence' (1987: 67). Both narratives show that when addictions to those pleasures take hold, the perversion of the addict's sensibility follows, transforming gentlemen into gentlemen-criminals. Dorian Gray's pursuit of a 'new Hedonism' (Wilde, 2008: 111) likewise involves the perverting process of addiction and necessitates a 'double life' (2008: 147) in Britain, a domain he calls 'the native land of the hypocrite' (2008: 128). Thus is a superficial society that equates status and beauty with moral uprightness exposed by Wilde as hypocritical and perverse.

Such degenerate, queer, hyper-sexualised monsters often find themselves racialised in much fin-de-siècle Imperial Gothic (a topic discussed by Patrick Brantlinger in Chapter 13 of this volume). The atavistic Mr Hyde with his 'dusky pallor' (Stevenson, 1987: 67) provides a stellar example, as do H. G. Wells's invading, phallic-female Martians with their 'fungoid . . . oily brown skin' (Wells, 1968: 126) in *The War of the Worlds* (1898). The nation is not only profoundly gendered, therefore, as Ania Loomba has nicely observed (1998: 215), but racialised. In late

Victorian Gothic narratives, patriarchal, white Britain finds itself repeatedly threatened with emasculation and degeneration by the dreaded, queer, hyper-sexualised, 'dark' or Orientalising agents of empire. In this manner, as Patrick Brantlinger has cogently illustrated, Britons projected various sexualities onto the empire and its varied indigenous peoples – 'from superhuman sexual prowess to effeminacy and homosexuality' (2009: 68). While the putative threats in such narratives are conceived as foreign and invasive, the actual dreads are often native and familiar. By way of this strategy of displacement, the empire – which generated its own anxieties and desires at the fin de siècle, particularly in regard to what was perceived as its economic parasitism – served to crystallise ambivalent reactions to other socio-political phenomena. For example, in an era that saw the passing of the Married Women's Property Act of 1882 which significantly altered the common-law doctrine of coverture to allow a married woman to own, buy and sell her own property, New Women were considered a serious threat to the status quo. Labelled by one writer as a 'sublimated Frankenstein's monster' (Caird, 1996: 288), the New Woman called into question the established idea of an essential female nature, women's limited professional and employment opportunities, and their right of choice in relation to marriage, maternity and sexuality. H. Rider Haggard's *She* (1887) provides what is perhaps the most compelling example of the Imperial Gothic's engagement with the New Woman question. Horace Holly's projection of his personal fears and history onto Africa where he encounters She-Who-Must-Be-Obeyed is fascinating given his role as representative imperialist and the tormented, mixed response She engenders in him of desire and repulsion. In the final analysis, however, this immensely beautiful, powerful, two-thousand-year-old femme fatale who rules over a people of mixed race must be destroyed given her threat to invade Britain and overthrow Queen Victoria. Only in such a manner may British manhood, and indeed the very nation, be safeguarded.

British manliness, which was critiqued by Sarah Grand in her 1894 article 'The New Aspect of the Woman Question' as being 'at a premium . . . because there is so little of it' (2007: 208), was also, however, deemed recuperable by way of the empire in the form of physical adventure and homosocial bonding. Rising, ironically, to its most hysterical, fevered pitch, fin-de-siècle Gothic also enacted the recovery of British manhood by way of the graphic, spectacular and ritualised punishment and symbolic sacrifice of New Women. The Beetle's act of humiliating Marjorie Lindon by cropping her hair and forcing her to cross-dress as a boy to facilitate their travels through England (Marsh, 2008: 272–4), thus exposing the masculine propensities of this novel's sole independent and outspoken (New) woman in what is described by Marsh as an 'age of feminine advancement' (2008: 108), is noteworthy but ultimately tame in comparison with the disturbing annihilation of New Women in Haggard's *She* and Stoker's *Dracula*. In memorable and stark contrast, Ayesha (She-Who-Must-Be-Obeyed) undergoes a horrifying figurative sati that precipitates her Darwinian regression into a hideous mass 'no larger than a big monkey' of dark hair and claws (Haggard, 1998: 294), while Lucy Westenra's figurative yet explicitly detailed gang-rape, mutilation and decapitation by a group of putatively heroic crusaders engaged in a national purity and defence campaign is presented as just punishment for their shared crime of expressing sexual desire. Femininity is also presented as recuperable by way of such acts of ritualised, misogynistic violence, a tragic and ironic shift from early Victorian Gothic when women, who were then its principal producers, employed the form to help secure women the right to self-expression and realisation.

Note

1. Mill punctuates his essay with various references to this idea, in one instance stating that 'what is now called the nature of women is an eminently artificial thing – the result of forced repression in some directions, unnatural stimulation in others' (1989: 138).

References

Adams, J. E. (1999). 'Victorian Sexualities', in *A Companion to Victorian Literature and Culture*, ed. H. F. Tucker. Malden, MA and Oxford: Blackwell Publishers, pp. 125–38.

Bouchereau, G. (2000). 'Nymphomania' [1892], in *The Fin de Siècle: A Reader in Cultural History c.1880–1900*, ed. Sally Ledger and Roger Luckhurst. Oxford: Oxford University Press, pp. 293–7.

Braddon, M. E. (1992). *Lady Audley's Secret* [1862]. New York and Oxford: Oxford University Press.

Brantlinger, Patrick (2009). *Victorian Literature and Postcolonial Studies*. Edinburgh: Edinburgh University Press.

Brontë, Emily (2003). *Wuthering Heights* [1847]. Boston, MA and New York: Bedford and St Martin's Press.

Caird, Mona (1996). 'A Defense of the So-called "Wild Women"' [1892], in *'Criminals, Idiots, Women, and Minors': Victorian Writing by Women on Women*, ed. S. Hamilton. Peterborough, ON: Broadview Press, pp. 287–307.

Castle, Terry (2005). 'The Gothic Novel', in *The Cambridge History of English Literature, 1660–1780*, ed. J. Richetti. Cambridge: Cambridge University Press, pp. 673–706.

Clery, E. J. (1992). 'The Politics of the Gothic Heroine', in *Reviewing*

Romanticism, ed. P. W. Martin and R. Jarvis. New York: St. Martin's Press, pp. 69–85.

Cobbe, Frances Power (1868). 'Criminals, Idiots, Women, and Minors', *Fraser's Magazine*, December, 777–94.

——(1878). 'Wife-torture In England', *Contemporary Review*, April, 55–87.

Collins, Wilkie (1985). *The Woman in White* [1860]. Harmondsworth: Penguin.

Dickens, Charles (1986). *Great Expectations* [1861]. New York: Bantam.

Dowling, L. (1979). 'The Decadent and the New Woman in the 1890s', *Nineteenth Century Fiction*, 33, 434–53.

Eagleton, Terry (2003). 'Myths of Power: A Marxist Study on *Wuthering Heights*', in Emily Brontë, *Wuthering Heights*, ed. L. H. Peterson. New York: Bedford and St Martin's Press, pp. 394–410.

Frank, Frederick, F. (1977). 'Introduction', in P. B. Shelley, *'Zastrozzi: A Romance' and 'St. Irvyne: Or, The Rosicrucian'*, ed. G. M. Matthews and K. Everest. New York: Arno Press, pp. ix–xxv.

Grand, Sarah (2007). 'The New Aspect of the Woman Question' [1894], in *Literature and Culture in the Fin de Siècle*, ed. T. Schaffer. New York: Pearson Longman, pp. 205–10.

Haggard, H. Rider (1998). *She: A History of Adventure* [1887]. Oxford: Oxford University Press.

Heilman, Robert B. (1961). 'Charlotte Brontë's "New Gothic"' [1958], in *Victorian Literature: Modern Essays in Criticism*, ed. A. Wright. New York: Oxford University Press, pp. 71–85.

Hoeveler, Diane Long (1998). *Gothic Feminism: The Professionalization of Gender from Charlotte Smith to the Brontës*. University Park: Penn State University Press.

James, Henry (1865). 'Miss Braddon', *The Nation*, 9 November, 593–4.

Linton, E. L. (1868). 'The Girl of the Period', *The Saturday Review*, 14 March, 339–40.

Loomba, A. (1998). *Colonialism/Postcolonialism*. London: Routledge.

Mansel, H. L. (1863). 'Sensation Novels', *Quarterly Review*, 113, 481–514.

Marsh, Richard (2008). *The Beetle* [1897]. London: Penguin.

McLaren, A. (1997). *The Trials of Masculinity: Policing Sexual Boundaries 1870–1930*. Chicago and London: The University of Chicago Press.

——(2002). *Sexual Blackmail: A Modern History*. Cambridge, MA and London: Harvard University Press.

Miles, Robert (2002). *Gothic Writing, 1750–1820: A Genealogy* [1993], 2nd edn. Manchester and New York: Manchester University Press.

Mill, J. S. (1989). 'The Subjection of Women' [1869], in *On Liberty and Other Writings*, ed. S. Collini. Cambridge: Cambridge University Press, pp. 119–217.

Nightingale, Florence (1979). *Cassandra* [1860]. New York: The Feminist Press at the City University of New York.

Norton, C. (1839). *A Plain Letter to the Lord Chancellor on the Infant Custody Bill*. London: James Ridgway.

——(1855). *A Letter to the Queen on Lord Chancellor Cranworth's Marriage and Divorce Bill*. London: Longman Brown, Green and Longmans.

Phelps, G. (1987). 'Varieties of English Gothic' [1982], in *From Blake to Byron*, ed. Boris Ford. Harmondsworth: Penguin, pp. 110–27.

Pykett, Lynn (1994). *The Sensation Novel from The Woman in White to The Moonstone*. Plymouth: Northcote House.

Radcliffe, Ann (2000). 'On the Supernatural in Poetry' [1802; 1826], in *Gothic Documents: A Sourcebook 1700–1820*, ed. E. J. Clery and R. Miles. Manchester: Manchester University Press, pp. 163–72.

Rae, W. F. [unsigned] (1865). 'Sensation Novelists: Miss Braddon', *North British Review*, 43, 180–204.

Ruskin, John (1866). 'Of Queens' Gardens' [1865], in *Sesame and Lilies*. New York: J. Wiley, pp. 81–113.

Showalter, E. (1977). *A Literature of Their Own: British Women Novelists From Brontë to Lessing*. Princeton: Princeton University Press.

Stevenson, Robert Louis (1987). *The Strange Case of Dr Jekyll and Mr Hyde* [1886]. Oxford: Oxford University Press.

Thompson, W. and A. Wheeler (1994). *Appeal of One-Half the Human Race, Women, Against the Pretentions of the Other Half, Men, To Retain Them in Political, and Thence in Civil and Domestic Slavery* [1825]. Bristol: Thoemmes Press.

Tosh, J. (2005). *Manliness and Masculinities in Nineteenth-Century Britain: Essays on Gender, Family and Empire*. Harlow: Pearson Education Limited.

Wells, H. G. (1968). *The War of the Worlds* [1898], in *The Time Machine* and *The War of the Worlds*. New York: Fawcett.

Wilde, Oscar (2008). *The Picture of Dorian Gray* [1891]. Oxford: Oxford University Press.

Chapter 9

Queer Victorian Gothic
Ardel Thomas

In the nineteenth century, most Gothic narratives that can be read as having either overtly or covertly queer themes or characters are bound up in familial worries, medical diagnoses (including scientific experimentation) or legal discourses.[1] In many cases, queer Victorian Gothic can simultaneously explore, defend and, on occasion, interrogate these overarching authoritative institutions and systems of power as they were constantly being re-invented and re-inscribed with the goal of shaping the familial, medical and legal paradigms that still constrain us today. The Victorian family – specifically the Victorian middle-class family – was being rigidly defined in strict nuclear, heteronormative terms; thus, in much Victorian Gothic, the queer elements are part of the family secret. Definitions of disease began to diligently include and pathologise anyone who was not clearly heterosexual and who did not clearly ascribe to a strictly masculine or strictly feminine demeanour. And nineteenth-century British laws – particularly by the fin de siècle – became obsessed with sodomy (the Labouchère Amendment), male cross-dressing (the infamous court case against Ernest Boulton and Frederick Park) and cross-class homosexual liaisons (The Cleveland Street Affair).[2] While medical and legal discourses rendered male homosexuality more visible, there were certainly instances of female homosexuality and bisexuality, as well as various transgender and genderqueer crossings. Boulton and Park often went about publicly in petticoats, for example, but the foundation of their arrest was not a genderqueer worry *per se* but rather that their cross-dressing signalled that they *might* commit sodomy.[3]

As a genre, Gothic allowed authors to explore the landscape of sexual taboos and gender identities. However, Gothic also became a safe location in which authors could investigate ideas about race, interracial desire, cross-class relations, ethnicity, empire, nation and 'foreignness' during the nineteenth century. The strength of Gothic rests upon its being a liminal genre; it allowed many nineteenth-century authors to look at social and cultural worries consistently haunting Victorian Britain even as the official discourse worked tirelessly to silence those concerns. These issues are inextricably linked, which complicates and enriches the field of queer Victorian Gothic.[4]

In the introduction to their collection, *Queering the Gothic*, William Hughes and Andrew Smith explain that 'Gothic has, in a sense, always been queer. The genre . . . has been characteristically perceived in criticism as being poised astride the uneasy cultural boundary that separates the acceptable and familiar from the troubling and different' (2009: 1). 'Gothic' and 'queer' are aligned in that they both transgress boundaries and occupy liminal spaces, and in so doing, they each consistently interrogate ideas of what is 'respectable' and what is 'normal'. As Hughes and Smith argue, 'to be queer is to be different, yet it is also to be unavoidably associated with the non-queer, the normative . . . The two states exist in reciprocal tension' (2009: 3). 'The queer' has to function within heteronormative culture while at the same time calling the idea of 'the norm' into question. Gothic is also 'different' because it, like 'the queer', straddles the boundary between 'acceptable' and 'troubling'; Gothic often gets defined against other more 'normative' types of fiction. George Haggerty points out that 'the cult of gothic fiction reached its apex at the very moment when gender and sexuality were beginning to be codified for modern culture . . . gothic fiction offered a testing ground for many unauthorized genders and sexualities' (2006: 2). Between the 1850s and the 1870s, numerous authors utilised the Gothic as this 'testing ground' to explore queer constructions of monstrosity – sometimes in a completely sympathetic vein and, at other times, with a deep sense of ambivalence toward their queer subjects. Three authors who exemplify this are Wilkie Collins, Elizabeth Gaskell and J. Sheridan Le Fanu.[5]

Wilkie Collins and Elizabeth Gaskell approached subjectivities deemed 'degenerate', 'perverse' and/or racially 'other' sympathetically through the complex mechanism of Gothic and the construction of monstrosity. For both of these authors, the precise characters who 'should' be monstrous within typical Victorian Gothic frameworks are given great sympathy as well as crucial roles within the narrative. Wilkie Collins's *The Woman in White* (1860) and *The Moonstone* (1868) play upon mid-Victorian worries about the 'surplus of women' (that is, the spinster), gender non-conformity (numerous 'freak sideshows' had cropped up in London in the 1850s)[6] as embodied by the bearded ladies, Julia Pastrana and Madame Clofuillia, and concerns over race and empire following the 1857 Indian Revolution (at that time termed a Mutiny).

Early in the narrative of *The Woman in White* the reader is set up to think of such 'oddities' as the bearded ladies when, in his initial narrative, Walter Hartright (the compiler of the split narratives that make up Collins's novel) briefly mentions the London 'show-room' in reference to his Italian friend, Pesca, being incredibly short (Collins, 2006: 52). Soon after this reference to the 'freak shows', Walter leaves London to take up residence as a drawing master for two young ladies (half-sisters) in Cumberland at Limmeridge House. In a scene famous for its Gothic suspense, Walter Hartright first meets Marian Halcombe, the spinster of the house. However, the 'flutter of expectation' (2006: 73) that agitates Hartright's emtions is rapidly suceeded not so much by bathos as disbelief. Hartright recalls:

> The lady's complexion was almost *swarthy* and the dark down on her upper lip was almost a moustache. She had a large, firm, masculine mouth and jaw; prominent, piercing, resolute brown eyes; and thick, coal-black hair, growing unusually low down on her forehead. Her expression – bright, frank, and intelligent – appeared, while she was silent, to be altogether wanting in those feminine attractions of gentleness and pliability, without which the beauty of the handsomest woman alive is beauty incomplete. To see such a face as this set on shoulders that a sculptor would have longed to model – to be charmed by the modest graces of action through which the symmetrical limbs betrayed their beauty when they moved, and then *to be almost repelled by the masculine form and the masculine look* of the features in which the perfectly shaped figure ended – was to feel a sensation oddly akin to the helpless discomfort familiar to us all in sleep, when we recognize yet cannot reconcile the anomalies and contradictions of a dream. (2006: 73–4, my emphasis)

With this description of the beautiful feminine body and the swarthy masculine face, Collins sets his audience up to expect that Marian Halcombe will become the queer Gothic monstrosity of the book. While Halcombe certainly maintains her queer position in this sensational Gothic novel, she never becomes evil. Rather, Wilkie Collins utilises Marian Halcombe's queer positionality to make a subversive point about family structures, heroism, strong marital relations that are not heteronormative and socially acceptable; he even sets the motif of the so-called 'Angel in the House' on its proverbial head.

Not only does Marian's questionable gender identity render her queer in the context of *The Woman in White*, but her relationship with her half-sister, Laura, is (even for a Victorian audience) overtly homoerotic. In one instance, Marian's diary records that Laura, 'put her lips to mine, and kissed me. "My own love," she said softly, "you are so much too fond of me and so much too proud of me"' (2006: 192). And, prior to Laura's disastrous marriage to Sir Percival Glyde, Marian writes,

Before another month is over our heads, she will be *his* Laura instead of
mine! ... I am as little able to realize the idea ... my mind feels almost as
dulled and stunned by it, as if writing of her marriage were like writing of her
death. (2006: 211)

Marian's anxiety is not without merit. As the story progresses, the
reader learns that Glyde is not the gentleman he passes himself off as,
and that he and his nefarious Italian friend, Count Fosco, are plotting
to kill Laura in order for Glyde to inherit her fortune. This is the point
when the legal as well as the familial structure enters into the queer
Gothic narrative because it is Marian Halcombe and *not* any of the
male relatives *nor* Laura's other love (Walter) who stand up to defend
her when she is asked to sign legal documents that will, in essence, strip
her of all of her rights and cede them to her husband, Sir Percival Glyde.
Marian Halcombe, alone, questions the legal document. Later in the
course of the novel, it is Marian Halcombe, again, who saves Laura
from the confines of the insane asylum after Glyde and Fosco's plot to
murder her has failed.

What can actually be read as Collins's most subversive point in this
1860 Gothic sensation novel is the re-construction of the family unit
by the story's conclusion. Walter and Laura have been able to get
married, have a baby and return to Cumberland as the rightful owners
of Limmeridge House. That being said, Marian Halcombe is also
there with them in a committed relationship. Interestingly, Laura gets
exactly what she wants: a lifetime commitment from *both* Walter and
Marian. Collins ends his novel by asking the reader to think of Marian
Halcombe, the genderqueer spinster as the 'good angel of our lives'
(2006: 617).[7]

Just as Marian Halcombe becomes the queer hero of *The Woman in
White*, Wilkie Collins creates yet another admirable queer character in
his Gothic detective novel *The Moonstone*, in the form of Ezra Jennings,
a biracial genderqueer doctor's assistant. Since much of the narrative
before the introduction of Jennings has centred around racial and imperial concerns – the evil John Herncastle's original theft of the Indian
diamond as part of British colonial booty and the three Hindu priests
roaming the English countryside in an attempt to retrieve and restore
the diamond to its rightful place in India – the initial description of Ezra
Jennings draws attention to his biraciality, which would make him suspicious to a nineteenth-century audience:

His complexion was of a gipsy darkness ... His nose presented the fine
shape and modelling so often found among the ancient people of the East,
so seldom visible among the newer races of the West ... From this strange

face, eyes, stranger still, of the softest brown – eyes dreamy and mournful, and deeply sunk in their orbits – looked out at you, and (in my case, at least) took your attention captive at their will. Add to this a quantity of thick closely-curling hair, which, by some freak of Nature, had lost its colour in the most startlingly partial and capricious manner. Over the top of his head it was still of the deep black which was its natural colour. Round the sides of his head – without the slightest gradation of grey to break the force of the extraordinary contrast – it had turned completely white . . . I looked at the man with a curiosity which, I am ashamed to say, I found it quite impossible to control. (Collins, 1999: 390)

What compounds the suspicion of Jennings's character is that his gender (and with that his sexuality) is as ambiguous as his ethnic identity. During their meeting at Dr Candy's house, Jennings shares his story of misfortune with Franklin Blake. He proclaims that 'physiology says, and says truly, that some men are born with female constitutions – and I am one of them!' and then further warns Blake that 'You are in bad company' (1999: 441, 446). Etymologically, 'bad' and 'badling' come from the Old English word *baeddel* which refers to either an effeminate man or a hermaphrodite.[8] Although he will not tell Blake the exact nature of the accusation against him, Jennings does confide that he suffered 'at the merciless treatment' of his own family and 'the enmity to which I have fallen a victim' (1999: 447).

Just as Marian Halcombe needed to intervene on Laura's behalf where misogynous Victorian legal matters were concerned, Ezra Jennings must make a medical intervention on behalf of Franklin Blake and Rachel Verinder's failing relationship. Because Jennings does not cleanly fit into any binary – Eastern/Western, male/female or heterosexual/homosexual – his scientific opium experiment that will reveal the truth about the theft of the Indian diamond out of Rachel's cabinet incorporates an amalgamation of Eastern and Western medicine and experimentation. Jennings takes this burden on, knowing that whilst he will be contributing to a more positive future for the young couple he will also, once and for all, be shunned by all men of authority (doctors and lawyers) in Yorkshire. As the go-between who blesses the reconciliation and thus paves the way for the forthcoming heterosexual union, Ezra Jennings embodies a *hijra*-like identity – an Indian identity that describes people who are neither male nor female.[9] Although Collins's depiction of Jennings is completely sympathetic, he – unlike Marian Halcombe – cannot find a place to survive and thrive in a Victorian Gothic framework. While the spinster was beginning to gain some cultural respect and was allowed a modicum of room to make a life for herself, a biracial, genderqueer figure could have no such place. Ezra Jennings is ultimately buried in an unmarked grave and his journals are burned. The historic record of his existence, like the historic record of many queer people throughout the nineteenth century, is completely erased.

Elizabeth Gaskell also employs gender ambiguity in her queer Gothic that critiques the confines of abusive heteronormative relations and the victimisation of women. In her short story 'The Grey Woman' (1861), Gaskell cleverly places the Victorian reader outside England in order to explore ways that gender, race, class and subversions of 'normative' heterosexual family structures can function together to create a transgressive narrative.[10] Gaskell's unconventional narrative style – she often ends her tales abruptly – functions much like her setting the action outside England in that she breaks the bounds of confinement (which is also particular to Gothic), reiterating on a structural level the layered possibilities for complex queer readings.

In 'The Grey Woman', Gaskell relates the story of Anna Scherer, a young German woman, who falls into a disastrous marriage with a sadistic Frenchman, Monsieur de la Tourelle. When Anna accidentally finds out that her husband is a murderer (she is hidden in a room where la Tourelle deposits a murdered body), her companion Amante, a Norman woman described as 'tall and handsome', saves her life by helping her escape from the isolated Gothic castle known as 'The Rocks' (Gaskell, 1992: 265). At one point in the narrative when Amante and Anna are trapped in a loft at a miller's house, Amante insists that the two women cross-dress so that when they escape out into public again they will be seen as a tailor and his wife. (It is important to note that, for Anna, the cross-dressing is not so much one of gender but of class.) Part of the queer space Amante and Anna have entered into is that of a heterosexual couple. Shortly after their becoming 'man and wife', Anna writes, 'I became attached to Amante. I have sometimes feared since, lest I cared for her only because she was so necessary to my own safety; but no! it was not so; or not so only, or principally' (1992: 287).

It becomes clear that, through the course of their wanderings as husband and wife, Amante and Anna do have a love relationship. While a lesbian undertone certainly exists between Anna and Amante, their cross-dressing as a heterosexual married couple brings a more complex layer to the queer reading of this tale. Throughout the story, Gaskell consistently utilises phrases like 'she entered the house, and boldly announced herself as a travelling tailor, ready to do any odd jobs of work that might be required, for a night's lodging and food for *herself and wife* (1992: 288, my emphasis) or else, 'I close behind her, sewing at another part of the same garment, and from time to time [was] well scolded by my . . . husband' (1992: 288), and 'she [Amante] brought him to see me, her sick wife' (1992: 299). Through the use of 'her wife' and the constant switching between 'her' and 'husband' Gaskell creates a space where gender categories elide, creating neither a specifically heterosexual nor a specifically homosexual marriage. Gaskell gracefully utilises this genderqueer space in her Gothic narrative to carry out her critique of women's roles as wives in Victorian culture. When Anna gives birth to her baby, it is Amante, and not the biological father, who is the first father the baby comes to know.

In a tragic conclusion, Amante is tracked down and killed by la Tourelle's men. Interestingly, her biological sex is not 'found out' until the medical men arrive to examine the body. Once stripped of the male dress, Amante's sex (not necessarily her gender) is revealed to everyone out on the public street. The juxtaposition of Amante's biological sex and her gender identity are *not* treated as part of the Gothic horror of the situation. (Many nineteenth-century authors would have made this revelation the horrifying climax of the queer Gothic story.) Instead, Gaskell writes the scene in an incredibly poignant way, leaving the reader in mourning alongside Anna as she grieves for her dead husband. Of course, she had no way of knowing this at the time, but Gaskell has written what has, sadly, too often become a reality for transgender and genderqueer people – that the need to 'pass' due to oppression is so great they are often not known as transgender until there is some sort of medical intervention – some sort of 'discovery of the truth' – and it is almost always sensationalised.[11] Gaskell treats Amante with respect – and in a beautiful and moving scene, foreshadows the wrongs and disrespect often meted out to those who embody a transgender identity.

In his famous lesbian vampire tale 'Carmilla' (first published in serial form in *The Dark Blue* from 1871–2), J. Sheridan Le Fanu does not necessarily cast a sympathetic eye on the queer situation which becomes underlined with family secrets and incestuous possibilities. That being said, Le Fanu does not employ the Gothic as a means of creating a thoroughly detestable queer Gothic monster. Le Fanu's work marks a turning point in queer Victorian Gothic because 'Carmilla' sits on the precipice of medical and legal 'innocence' concerning queer subjectivity. This novella predates the explosion of sexological writings by medical experts like Richard von Krafft-Ebing, conducted in works such as his 1886 tome, *Psychopathia Sexualis*. In particular, the 'General Pathology' as well as the 'Special Pathology' sections of the *Psychopathia Sexualis* linger on fetishism, sado-masochism and other forms of perversion, consistently tying them in with masturbation and homosexuality, both of which were seen as detrimental to one's physical and mental wellbeing.[12] Although 'Carmilla' predates Krafft-Ebing's text, it certainly foreshadows much of the queer behaviours seen more and more as 'psychopathic' in the latter part of the century.

As Victor Sage argues, 'Carmilla' is a 'powerfully ambiguous text, which represents several taboos at once' (2004: 178). In the case of 'Carmilla', the vampire is aggressive (though romantically so through Laura's nostalgic narrative); but Laura, the 'victim', is herself an embodiment of miscegenation (her father is English and her mother was Eastern European) which has nothing to do with the vampire's attack. (By 1897, when Bram Stoker created *Dracula*, vampirism had become synonymous with miscegenation.) Some of the deep ambivalence in Le Fanu's tale lies within the homoerotic scenes between Carmilla and Laura:

> Sometimes after an hour of apathy, my strange and beautiful companion would take my hand and hold it with a fond pressure, renewed again and again; blushing softly, gazing in my face with languid and burning eyes, and breathing so fast that her dress rose and fell with the tumultuous respiration. It was like the ardour of a lover; it embarrassed me; it was hateful and yet overpowering; and with gloating eyes she drew me to her, and her hot lips travelled along my cheek in kisses; and she would whisper, almost in sobs, 'You are mine, you *shall* be mine, you and I are one for ever.' Then she has thrown herself back in her chair, with her small hands over her eyes, leaving me trembling. (Le Fanu, 2009: 23)

In this near pornographic rendering of queer sex and mutual masturbation, the reader *almost* forgets that this is supposed to be a frightening moment in the story. Oddly, it is immediately following this incredibly vivid homoerotic passage that Le Fanu includes gender confusion as Laura wonders to herself: 'was there here a disguise and a romance? What if a boyish lover had found his way into the house and sought to prosecute his suit in masquerade?' (2009: 23). The reader is left to wonder if Laura is truly so naïve to think that because her encounter is overtly sexual, her pursuer must be male. Laura's musing about Carmilla's gender epitomises the way that same-sex desire often gets mapped back onto the heterosexual paradigm; it also demonstrates Le Fanu's uncertainty towards the homoeroticism at the heart of his tale.

The conclusion to 'Carmilla' is, perhaps, the most ambiguous moment in the story on at least two different levels. Although Carmilla's head has been removed and her body burned by the band of patriarchs lead by Laura's father, we are left to wonder if Laura has undergone any sort of medical treatment after having been vamped; or, upon her death, is she, too, going to become a lesbian vampire? The other point of uncertainty at the novella's conclusion lies with Le Fanu's description of Laura daydreaming about Carmilla whom she nostalgically remembers as 'sometimes the playful, languid, beautiful girl; sometimes the writhing fiend I saw in the ruined church; and *often* from a reverie I have started, *fancying* I heard the light step of Carmilla at the drawing-room door' (2009: 83, my emphases). It is as though Laura is actually a bit hopeful that Carmilla will return.

Le Fanu's erotic, tender *and* ambivalent tale offers us a way to look back, historically, at the change that the fin de siècle was going to bring to queer Gothic writings. By the late 1880s, once *Psychopathia Sexualis* had been published and the Labouchère Amendment passed, much queer Victorian Gothic set about demonising the queer 'other'. Richard Marsh's classic reverse-colonisation novel *The Beetle* (1897) – which actually outsold Stoker's *Dracula* – offers an outstanding example of the ways that queer subjectivity and racial difference combine to become the main ingredients for creating queer Gothic monstrosity. In Marsh's harrowing tale, the queer Gothic monster is an Egyptian figure that constantly fluctuates across the gender spectrum (most characters wonder if 'it' is male or female) as well as shape-shifts across species categories. More frightening than the Beetle's ability to straddle several subjectivities at once is its ability to wreak havoc through the destruction of heteronormative relationships and the eradication of the gender binary. The monster molests English men and women of all socio-economic classes as both a male and female entity and *forces* its victims to expose themselves in public either naked or cross-dressed. No Western science can seem to understand or contain it, and nobody is safe whilst the Beetle roams the streets of London.

While there are numerous fin-de-siècle Gothic stories like Marsh's that clearly demonise 'the other' – a monster who usually embodies multiple subject positions at once – there are still others that attempt to break through some of the hegemonic discourse of the late Victorian era, although the attempt may be quite subtle. Florence Marryat's *The Blood of the Vampire* (1897) exemplifies a story that, on the surface, reads as yet another re-inscription of the queer colonial subject as monstrous (please note that this novel is also discussed at length in Chapter 14 of this volume by Victoria Margree and Byrony Randall). As in 'Carmilla', however, there are moments of deep ambivalence where the reader is asked to interpret a more subversive reading of the author's purpose.

The Blood of the Vampire is the story of a young Jamaican woman, Harriet Brandt, who is a 'half-breed' – her father was a cruel British vivisectionist and her mother the daughter of a Jamaican witch who practiced *obeah*. Harriet's grandmother was bitten by a vampire bat while pregnant, so her granddaughter, unknowingly, harbours a vampiric contagion. The first person we meet whom Harriet emotionally 'vamps' is Margaret Pullen, a married Englishwoman – the mother of an infant daughter – vacationing without her husband (who is in military service) in Heyst, Belgium. Like Laura in 'Carmilla', we are left to wonder at the same-sex attraction felt by the 'victim'. The following is Pullen's description of a look from Harriet immediately following her having extricated herself from the Jamaican woman's embrace:

> Margaret Pullen, glancing up once was struck by the look with which Harriet Brandt was regarding her – it was so full of yearning affection – almost of longing to approach her nearer, to hear her speak, to touch her hand! It amused her to observe it! She had heard of cases, in which young unsophisticated girls had taken unaccountable affections for members of their own sex. (Marryat, 2009: 27)

Mrs Pullen, the epitome of a good English mother and wife, *recognises* Harriet's queer gaze. She, too, participates in the flirtation and homoerotic dance. Pullen is also, seemingly, punished for her transgression because her daughter languishes and dies from Harriet's affection.

The English medical practitioner Dr Phillips arrives just in time to diagnose the affliction, but not in time to save the baby's life. Oddly enough, Dr Phillips's medical 'authority' on the matter of Harriet Brandt as a half-breed, queer vampire is predicated on Jamaican folklore and *not* on a Western medical education, although he passes his authoritative diagnosis off as completely sound and scientific. Before the novel's conclusion, Dr Phillips takes it upon himself to explain to Harriet the nature of her disease. His intervention with Harriet's 'disease' can be read as Michel Foucault's definition of 'an act of violence if it is not subjected strictly to the ideal ordering of nosology' (Foucault, 1975: 8). In intervening, Dr Phillips uses his authority as a man of medicine to claim an understanding of the classification of Harriet's 'disease'. This diagnosis (and the death of Harriet's husband which she believes to be her fault) moves Harriet to commit suicide by the novel's conclusion. The final scene is tragic and quite sympathetic to the emotional agony Harriet experiences once a medical authority has definitively told her (as so many queer people are still told) the nature of her 'disease'. As in Le Fanu, Marryat's ambivalence in *The Blood of the Vampire* gives us room for sympathy and room to wonder about the author's ultimate intent.

The terms 'genderqueer' and 'queer' are undeniably useful when looking at Victorian Gothic because they connote a sense of flexibility; they hold the multiple gender identities and sexual behaviours of a Victorian culture that was *beginning* to rigidly define the connection between identity and behaviour. Within these legal and medical constructions of the 'normal', however, there was still room for flexibility and complexity. For example, it is not at all unusual that Oscar Wilde had a wife and children whilst he also enjoyed numerous sexual encounters with both elite, educated men like Lord Alfred Douglas as well as with working-class male prostitutes. The Victorians understood, far more than we give them credit for, such intricate erotic possibilities and the functions of complicated as well as compartmentalised lives.

As evidenced by these various authors' approaches to marginalised queer and genderqueer characters and situations, it is possible to argue that queer Victorian Gothic itself, as a sub-genre, operates as a sort of thermometer measuring the waning of cultural tolerance from the mid to the late nineteenth century. As Katrien Bollen and Raphael Ingelbien have argued in their comparison of Collins's mid-century work to Stoker's fin-de-siècle *Dracula*, Collins worked to combat British xenophobia whilst Stoker's novel illuminates 'the gradual decline of Liberal politics' as the century progressed (Bollen and Ingelbien, 2009: 418). The radical critiques of 'proper' gender and sexual identities and behaviours put forward by Wilkie Collins and Elizabeth Gaskell in the 1850s and 1860s reflect a less restrictive moment in popular Victorian culture before more constrained heteronormative legal and medical discourses became prevalent within societal systems of power as well as within the popular press.

One of the problems in understanding and defining queer people has been the way that, historically, we are taught that this particular identity really was not recognised as such until after the 1969 Stonewall Riots in New York City – and this current understanding of what became the beginning of the *modern-day* LGBT movement has actually got in our way and made it more difficult to look into the past. To their credit, some fin-de-siècle authors such as Marryat wrestled with ambiguity in their queer Gothic, just as they struggled with 'normative' ideas about sexuality and gender identity. Taken together, all of these queer Gothic narratives can help us call into question the monolithic ideas we might have about Victorian culture and Victorian attitudes. The Victorian era was teeming with queer possibilities and Queer Victorian Gothic gives us a crucial lens through which we can begin to explore these various social and cultural issues of the nineteenth century in more depth.

Notes

1. I utilise the term 'queer' on numerous levels: in its nineteenth-century historical context to point to the generally weird, odd or ill (the words 'odd', 'curious' and 'strange' continually come up within queer Victorian Gothic),

as well as in the early twentieth-century evolution of the term as it was applied (quite negatively) to homosexuality. In my theoretical framework, I also employ the term 'queer' in the complex, politically charged late twentieth- and early twenty-first-century reclamation of the term. Unlike the gender specificity found in gay and lesbian theories and historiographies, queer theory – especially given the historical definitions of 'queer' – supplies room for multiple, potentially polyvalent positions, conveying gender, sexuality, race, class and familial structures beyond heteronormative (and often bourgeois) social constructs. I read gender ambiguity as transgender or genderqueer when it challenges the gender binary. 'Genderqueer' has only recently fully come into use as a term that goes beyond the gender binary. Some theorists and activists have suggested it as an alternative to 'transgender', a term rooted in Western dichotomies and one that still implies a crossing from one fixed gender position to the opposite pole of the binary. See Thomas (2012).

2. In early August 1885, the radical MP, Henry Labouchère, introduced Section 11 of the Criminal Law Amendment Act. The following morning, on 7 August 1885, *The Pall Mall Gazette* published an account of the new law:

> Mr. Labouchère moved . . . to insert a clause which dealt with outrages on public decency, and which provided that any male person who in public or private committed or procured the commission by any male person of any act of gross indecency with another male person, should be guilty of a misdemeanour, and, on being convicted, should be liable to be imprisoned for any term not exceeding one [*sic*] year, with or without hard labour. (*The Pall Mall Gazette*, 7 August 1885, Issue 6364, from the Nineteenth-Century British Library Newspapers online archives, accessed on 14 June 2010)

It is interesting to note that *The Pall Mall Gazette* actually got the term for imprisonment wrong – the actual amendment reads *two* years. See also Cocks (2003), Cook (2003), Kaplan (2005) and Weeks (1979). Labouchère's amendment did not, in many ways, do anything 'new' since Henry VIII's 1533 edict had already outlawed sodomy in public and private. What these authors *do* note is that Labouchère's amendment made the legal move to equivocate sodomy to male homosexual sex. For an in-depth account of the cross-dressers, Boulton and Park, see Kaplan (2005: 19–101). Finally, the Cleveland Street Affair refers to the 1889 police raid on a male homosexual brothel located off Tottenham Court Road, where young working-class men were 'servicing' Victorian gentleman. The above authors have all done extensive work on Cleveland Street as well. See also Simpson, Chester and Leitch (1976).

3. See Kaplan (2005: 23). In the public imagination, cross-dressing and homosexuality were not necessarily linked; however, the prosecutor on this case chose to make that link, which from this case forward shifted views of cross-dressing to equate it with sodomy.

4. Publicly, the male homosexual (the sodomite) was the figure most focused upon; however, there are numerous queer Gothic stories that are just that

– fully queer in that the entire spectrum of queer options can be explored. Up to this point, most of the attention of Queer Studies and even Queer Gothic Studies has been paid to male homosexuality. It is my hope that this essay will aid scholars to see a much broader spectrum of queer possibilities in Victorian Gothic.

5. Collins and Gaskell both originally published their queer Gothic pieces for Charles Dickens's *All The Year Round*. Interestingly, Dickens had already created a lesbian monster out of his character Miss Wade in *Little Dorrit* (1855–7). In writing their stories directly after Dickens's novel, Collins and Gaskell both pick up the pen to sympathetically defend their queer characters in direct opposition to Dickens.

6. See Richard Collins (2003).

7. In his own life, Wilkie Collins was in two committed relationships with Martha Rudd and Caroline Graves. Collins's secret life with two women and two full households could very well have enabled him to write about unconventional relationships more knowingly and less judgementally. See Clarke (1988), Gasson (1998).

8. Definition of 'bad' and 'badling' from the *Oxford English Dictionary* at www.oed.com/bad and badling, accessed 2 April 2011.

9. *Hijras* are incredibly complex gender-variant figures in Indian culture; they are still looked on with fear and disdain. See Nanda (1990: 23).

10. It is important to remember that 'Mrs' Gaskell was a woman author at a time when it was even risky for male authors like Collins to be creating sympathetic and positive depictions of queer characters. Here in the twenty-first century, we can certainly complain that Gaskell was 'playing it safe' by setting her stories outside England. However, her placement of the queer action outside national boundaries might very well have given her the room she needed to create her subversive queer Gothic tales.

11. See, for example, Feinberg (1996: 89). Feinberg discusses the necessity for transgender people to 'pass' in order to remain safe in a virulently transphobic society.

12. See Krafft-Ebing (1920).

References

Bollen, Katrien and Raphael Ingelbien (2009). 'An Intertext that Counts? *Dracula, The Woman in White*, and Victorian Imaginations of the Foreign Other', *English Studies*, 90/4, 403–20.

Clarke, William M. (1998). *The Secret Life of Wilkie Collins*. London: Allison & Busby.

Cocks, H. G. (2003). *Nameless Offences: Homosexual Desire in the Nineteenth Century*. London: I. B. Tauris Publishers.

Collins, Richard (2003). 'Marian's Moustache: Bearded Ladies, Hermaphrodites, and Intersexual Collage in *The Woman in White*', in *Reality's Dark Light: The Sensational Wilkie Collins*, ed. M. Bachman and D. R. Cox. Knoxville: University of Tennessee Press, pp. 131–72.

Collins, Wilkie (2006). *The Woman in White* [1861]. Peterborough, ON: Broadview Press.

——(1999). *The Moonstone* [1868]. Peterborough, ON: Broadview Press.

Cook, Matt (2003). *London and the Culture of Homosexuality, 1885–1914*. Cambridge: Cambridge University Press.

Feinberg, Leslie (1996). *Transgender Warriors: Making History from Joan of Arc to Dennis Rodman*. Boston: Beacon Press.

Foucault, Michèl (1975). *The Birth of the Clinic: An Archaeology of Medical Perception*, trans. A. M. Sheridan Smith. New York: Vintage Books.

Gaskell, Elizabeth (1992). 'The Grey Woman' [1861], in *A Dark Night's Work and Other Stories*. Oxford: Oxford University Press, pp. 249–303.

Gasson, Andrew (1998). *Wilkie Collins: An Illustrated Guide*. Oxford: Oxford University Press.

Haggerty, George (2006). *Queer Gothic*. Urbana and Chicago: University of Illinois Press.

Hughes, William, and Andrew Smith (2009). 'Introduction: Queering the Gothic', in *Queering the Gothic*, ed. William Hughes and Andrew Smith. Manchester and New York: Manchester University Press, pp. 1–10.

Kaplan, Morris B. (2005). *Sodom on the Thames: Sex, Love, and Scandal in Wilde Times*. Ithaca: Cornell University Press.

Krafft-Ebing, Richard von (1920). *Psychopathia Sexualis: With Especial Reference to the Antipathic Sexual Instinct – a Medico-Forensic Study* [1886], trans F. J. Rebman. New York: Medical Art Agency.

Le Fanu, J. Sheridan (2009). *Carmilla* [1871–2], ed. and introduction Jamieson Ridenhour. Kansas City: Valancourt Books.

Marryat, Florence (2009). *The Blood of the Vampire* [1897]. Kansas City: Valancourt Books.

Marsh, Richard (2004). *The Beetle* [1897], ed. and introduction Julian Wolfreys. Kansas City: Valancourt Books.

Nanda, Serena (1990). *Neither Man Nor Woman: The Hijras of India*. Belmont, CA: Wadsworth Publishing Company.

Sage, Victor (2004). *Le Fanu's Gothic: The Rhetoric of Darkness*. Basingstoke: Palgrave Macmillan.

Simpson, Colin, Lewis Chester and David Leitch (1976). *The Cleveland Street Affair*. Boston: Little, Brown and Company.

Thomas, Ardel (2012). *Queer Others in Victorian Gothic: Transgressing Monstrosity*. Cardiff: University of Wales Press.

Weeks, Jeffrey (1979). *Coming Out: Homosexual Politics from the Nineteenth Century to the Present*. London: Quartet.

Chapter 10

Victorian Gothic Death
Andrew Smith

Representations of death in the Victorian Gothic are closely aligned to models of subjectivity. How to read death, and the anxieties that it provokes, indicates just how far notions of the self are founded on discourses about death. By the end of the century there emerges a clear separation between ideas of a sustainable (quite possibly post-mortem) inner life and the corrupted and finite physical body. However, before examining this bifurcation and its manifestation in Victorian Gothic texts it is necessary to outline how death and subjectivity became related, and this entails an exploration of its roots in the Romantic Gothic.[1]

Terry Castle's account of *The Mysteries of Udolpho* (1794) moves beyond the critical commonplace which has noted Radcliffe's 'explained supernatural' in order to examine how, at a more subtle and profound level, the novel anticipates Freud's notion of the uncanny by addressing an anxiety that the living may be dead (as in Emily St Aubert's concerns for her absent paramour Valancourt), and by suggesting also that the living are haunted by the dead (as in Emily's dead father's controlling influence over her sensibility). In this way ghostliness becomes an aspect of introspection which is defined by its introjection of a new anxiety about death and dying so that 'Ghosts and spectres retain their ambiguous grip on the human imagination; they simply migrate into the space of the mind' (Castle, 1995: 135). That this is a new conceptualisation is confirmed for Castle by Philippe Ariès' account of changing burial and mourning rituals where he notes that by the late eighteenth century a Romantic understanding of mourning emerged which was predicated on a denial of the horror of the putrefying dead body (Ariès, 1981). This retreat from the body into the mind was in accord with a Romantic sensibility that focused on ideas of the lost self of the other. This apparent sanitising of death nevertheless created new feelings of psychological trauma in which 'The everyday [had] come to seem fantastic; and the fantastic more and more real' (Castle, 1995: 137). This emphasis on inner anxiety also brought with it an idea about vision which would dog later Victorian Gothic accounts of death. As Castle claims: 'The successful denial of mortality . . . requires a new spectralized mode of perception, in which one sees through the real person, as it were, towards a perfect and unchanging spiritual essence' (1995: 136). Whilst one may become aware of the spirits of others one also becomes aware of physical mortality. Mary Shelley in 'On Ghosts' (1824), for example, reminisces on the death of a friend and concludes that we are all just the living dead because 'the earth is a tomb, the gaudy sky a vault, we but walking corpses' (Shelley, 2000: 282). *Frankenstein* (1818) addresses these issues in ways which underpin later Gothic accounts of death.

Frankenstein, at one level, represents a triumph over death. Victor's science is a fundamentally creative one which enables him to create life out of death. This language of creativity aligns him, as Maurice Hindle has noted, with images of the creative scientist of the period as represented by the experimental ambitions of Humphrey Davy.[2] It also aligns Victor with a model of the Romantic poet who orchestrates a particular language of nature in his construction of the creature – even if the creature is ultimately an aesthetic disappointment. There are many points of contact between the creature and Edmund Burke's idea of sublime terror in his *Philosophical Enquiry* (1757), notably images of monstrosity and associations with death, but Shelley moves beyond any attempt to naturalise such images by challenging the Romantic conception of nature on which, from the late eighteenth century, they have come to depend.[3] The issue of vision is key here, as the Romantic gaze is forced away from its usual props in order to contemplate an alternative model of imminence which is psychological (and so non-transcendent) in origin. The crucial moment occurs in the dream Victor has, having collapsed with exhaustion after the fevered creation of the creature. Victor's pursuit of rest is disrupted:

> I thought I saw Elizabeth, in the bloom of health, walking in the streets of Ingolstadt. Delighted and surprised, I embraced her, but as I imprinted the first kiss on her lips, they became livid with the hue of death; her features appeared to change, and I thought that I held the corpse of my dead mother in my arms; a shroud enveloped her form, and I saw the grave-worms crawling in the folds of the flannel. (Shelley, 1985: 106)

On waking Victor is confronted by the creature and flees. The dream articulates a truth about Victor which he has to painfully acknowledge, which is that he harbours a latent hostility towards his fiancée Elizabeth and that the image of the dead mother compounds his negative feelings towards domestic responsibilities. That this dream is followed by an encounter with the baby-like creature in which 'His jaws opened, and he muttered some inarticulate sounds, while a grin wrinkled his cheeks' (1985: 106), augments the dream's demonised images of family life. The novel suggests that the creature is produced from Victor's inner life and that it enacts his horror of domesticity by killing those who are associated with it. By representing the relationship between the creature and Victor in psychological terms it indicates the need to develop both a new language of introspection (one which replaces the Romantic Sublime), and acknowledges the central role which images of death and dying play in this new subjectivity. How to account for death and its relationship to introspection became important themes addressed by Edgar Allan Poe.

Poe's 'Mesmeric Revelation' (1844) develops an argument about the relationship between the body and soul which is couched in a philosophical language of transcendence that suggests a Romantic influence. The narrator, who practises mesmerism on the dying Vankirk, regards that practice as one which conjures the subject into 'an abnormal condition, in which the phenomena resemble very closely those of death, or at least resemble them more nearly than they do the phenomena of any other normal condition within our cognizance' (Poe, 1982b: 88). Vankirk, who is close to death, is thus an eminently suitable subject for exploring the possible experiences of the soul. Vankirk tells the narrator that he has not asked him to help with his bodily ailment (he is dying of a tubercular illness), but 'to satisfy me concerning certain psychal impressions which, of late, have occasioned me much anxiety and surprise' (1982b: 89). The anxiety relates to the presence of the soul which Vankirk can only corroborate the existence of whilst on the point of death. The problem is how to find a language in which to express the soul's engagement with the physical world and this relocates *Frankenstein*'s pursuit of a new language of introspection. However, Vankirk is looking for an impersonal universal truth rather than describing personal dilemmas and their impact on behaviour. For Vankirk, his disembodied soul becomes synonymous with mind, which has its provenance within the mind of God because 'All created things are but the thoughts of God' (Poe, 1982b: 92). At the end the narrator notes that Vankirk has physically died and wonders if he had 'been addressing me from out the region of the shadows?' (1982b: 95). The tale thus posits the ultimate experience of introspection as taking place after (or perhaps during) death in which mind finds its home within the mind of God. Death is thus not about the body, it is about a new moment of transition in which the self discovers its immortality.

Poe returned to these issues in 'The Facts in the Case of M. Valdemar' (1845) which records the placing of Valdemar into a mesmeric trance at the point of death, at which the narrator notes how 'The glassy roll of the eye was changed for that expression of uneasy *inward* examination' (Poe, 1982a: 99, original italics). However, the tale lacks the philosophical focus of 'Mesmeric Revelation' and culminates in two moments of horror. The first is when Valdemar shouts out 'For God's sake! – quick! – quick! – put me to sleep – or, quick! – waken me! – quick! – *I say to you that I am dead!*' (1982a: 103, original italics). The second is what they are left with at the end, 'a nearly liquid mass of loathsome – of detestable putrescence' (1982a: 103). The uplifting disquisition on the soul in 'Mesmeric Revelation' is now replaced by a scene of metaphysical and physical horror. These two quite different conclusions map the directions which subsequent Gothic narratives would take in which there is either a view that the corruption of the body can be transcended (perhaps most clearly typified by the ghost story), or that there is the horror of dead undead bodies (as in the vampire, for example). However, there is a consistent theme which aligns images of death with models of subjectivity and the links which Mary Shelley made earlier to creativity are reworked by George Eliot in 'The Lifted Veil' (1859), which also explores some of the themes mined by Poe.

Eliot's tale begins with 'The time of my end approaches', and this opening paragraph concludes with 'I foresee when I shall die, and everything that will happen in my last moments' (Eliot, 1999: 9). Latimer, Eliot's narrator, has been periodically subject to visions throughout his life. Initially he had regarded such visions as possibly supporting his ambitions to become a poet. A vision of Prague that he has leads him to wonder 'was it the poet's nature in me, hitherto only a troubled yearning sensibility, now manifesting itself suddenly as spontaneous creation?' (1999: 10). However these fleeting visions do not constitute poetic inspiration. Indeed often such visions appear to be random or focused around limited revelations. Latimer, for example, is able to read the thoughts of certain individuals but he is unable to read the thoughts of Bertha, his wife. On marriage to Bertha there is some change but crucially he is unable to discern that Bertha, trapped in a loveless marriage, intends to poison him. He is, however, haunted by the moment when he will really die (of heart failure) because 'continually recurring, was the vision of my death – the pangs, the suffocation, the last struggle, when life would be grasped at in vain' (1999: 36). Unlike in Poe's 'Mesmeric Revelation', his visions cannot be assimilated into a religious vision because all he discerns is the mindless unhappiness of others, so that the 'continual suffering had annihilated religious faith within me' (Eliot, 1999: 36). The emphasis is therefore not on life after death but on the horror of a death foretold.

The narrative does however include an image of possible resurrection when Bertha's maid, Mrs Archer, dies and is briefly restored to life by Latimer's medical friend Meunier, who revives her with a blood transfusion. Mrs Archer on revival looks at Bertha, and Latimer recounts that 'The dead woman's eyes were wide open, and met hers in full recognition – the recognition of hate' (1999: 41). She then confesses that she had played a part in the attempt to poison Latimer, before dying for a second time. In 'The Lifted Veil' the universe is essentially secular and the blood transfusions rework the idea of life after death in strictly physical terms. Ideas about death and dying also underpin some of the essential contextual material that the Gothic responded to and this can be witnessed in the quite different writings of Eliot's partner George Henry Lewes and the work of Herbert Mayo on trances, primitive beliefs and vampires.

Mayo in *On the Truths Contained in Popular Superstitions with an Account of Mesmerism* (1851) interprets vampirism as a projected psychological phenomenon. Mayo, professor of anatomy and physiology at King's College London, also developed an account of mesmerism which accords with that of Poe. He identifies a particular level of trance which he terms the 'death-trance' in which 'the action of the heart, and of the breathing, and of voluntary motion; generally likewise feeling and intelligence, and the vegetative changes in the body, are suspended' (Mayo, 2003: 28–9). It is whilst in this pseudo-death-like state that the soul is released and becomes aware of its place in a wider spiritual universe. However, because the subject now appears to be dead there is the possibility of live burial. This leads Mayo to read folklore on vampires found 'alive' in their graves as analogies about the anxiety of being buried alive. Also accounts of visitations from vampires can be related to the same plight because they indicate that the buried subject is attempting to transmit a message about his or her predicament to close friends or relations. Mayo argues that in such moments:

> The soul of the buried man is to be supposed to be brought into communication with his friend's mind. Thence follows, as a sensorial illusion, the apparition of the buried man. Perhaps the visit may have been an instinctive effort to draw the attention of his friend to his living grave. I beg to suggest that it would not be an act of superstition now; but of ordinary humane precaution, if one dreamed pertinaciously of a recently buried acquaintance, or saw his ghost, to take immediate steps to have the state of the body ascertained. (2003: 49)

However, such visitations are not without their dangers. Vampirism might, according to folklore, be a contagious condition but then so is, according to Mayo, the death trance sent by the entombed subject.

This latter might place the receiver into a similar trance so they too are mistaken for dead and consequently buried, so that 'The visit was fatal to the party visited' (2003: 77). What is significant is how Mayo reads vampirism as a sign of psychological trauma. Whilst this is different in kind to Freud's reading of symptoms and indeed fantasies (because there is no sexual element to Mayo's reading), it does share with it a version of the subject who transforms inner anxiety into an externalised form (the narrative of the vampire). Burke's model of the sublime, which has the fear of death as one of its principal characteristics, is also implicitly evoked here.

There is a conundrum in Mayo's treatise because at one level he wants to argue that the soul is released at the point of physical death and that therefore we do not actually die (and that trances give us a foretaste of what it might be like to be disembodied), but at another level he registers a Victorian horror of live burial in which the signs of physical death are misread. For Mayo:

> The entire absence of the ordinary signs of life is insufficient to prove the absence of life. The body may be externally cold; the pulse not be felt; breathing may have ceased; no bodily motion may occur; the limbs may be stiff (through spasm); the sphincter muscles relaxed; no blood may flow from an opened vein; the eyes may have become glassy; there may be partial mortification to offend the sense with the smell of death, and yet the body may be alive. (2003: 32)

Mayo's treatise vacillates between the body and the inner world of the subject. As we have seen, in the Gothic from the late eighteenth century onwards there is a reiterated interest in models of introspection – ones which either regard death as a source of anxiety or as a means of release. Mayo's focus on when death might physically occur is clearly tied to an anxiety relating to live burial. It also, however, addresses a scientific issue of the day concerning how one pinpoints the exact moment of death. These are issues which George Henry Lewes explored with some vigour in his *The Physiology of Common Life* (1860).

Lewes's book explores a number of ways in which life might be prolonged and his discussion of the possibility of blood transfusions may well have influenced Eliot's representation of just such an experiment in 'The Lifted Veil'. Lewes's emphasis is, as reflected in the title of his book, on how one might evaluate death (and indeed life) in physical terms. He moves beyond Mayo's account of the physical pseudo-symptoms of death in order to problematise the moment at which death might have occurred. Lewes notes that:

Yet, although the organism may be dead, many of the organs may be living: the interruption may have taken place, and the unity be destroyed, but the units are not destroyed. Hours after a man is dead, his muscles live, and will contract; his glands live, and will secrete; his heart lives, and will beat; his stomach lives and will digest. (1860, vol. 2: 446)

This leads Lewes to the conclusion that considered in molecular terms:

There can be no such thing as matter essentially dead; there can be no such thing as matter essentially living. That which to-day we class as dead, will to-morrow be classed as living, and that which is living to-day will be dead to-morrow. Living and dead are terms which indicate certain groups of *phenomena*; and these phenomena are dependent upon certain groups of *conditions*. (1860, vol. 2: 416, original italics)

For Lewes, the whole issue of what is living and what is dead is blurred by a consideration that matter (chemically conceived) cannot be properly considered 'dead'. Also, he hints at the possibility of organs renewing themselves, which would prolong life beyond what would be considered a typical term, leading him to speculate that people might live to '400, and so on until some *necessity* be shown for the termination' (1860, vol. 2: 440, original italics).

Lewes deals solely in externals and his deliberations seem to be far removed from the links between death and introspection that we have so far considered. However, he is also moving beyond, or at least complicating, the notion of 'death' and his idea of a possible physical (rather than spiritual) immortality helps shape a reading of death in H. Rider Haggard's *She* (1887), which will be discussed below.[4] Also of interest are the metaphors which Lewes employs, as they incorporate an image of the body politic. He argues, for example, that 'Molecular death, or waste of substance consequent on vital activity, is incessant; but the organism lives on, surviving this death of the organs, as the nation survives though men perish daily' (1860, vol. 2: 445). This conflation of bodies with images of society is also elaborated when Lewes claims that:

The growth and decay of an organ, is like the growth and decay of a nation . . . the individual cells composing the organ grow and perish, as the individual men . . . grow and perish. There is a certain aggregate unity, but it is made up of distinct units. Just as the life of a nation . . . is the sum total of the lives of all its individual parts, so is the life of an organism the sum total of the lives of its individual cells. (1860, vol. 2: 428)

Discussions that conflate ideas about the body with the political body of the nation are not new, but they do inform a particular strand of the Imperial Gothic which is evidenced by Haggard's *She* and they implicitly inform much of the discussion which takes place between the narrator, Holly, and Ayesha, which centres on moral and political issues.

Holly's first sight of Ayesha manifests her as an erotic embodiment of the living dead:

> a tall figure stood before us. I say a figure, for not only the body, but also the face was wrapped in a soft white and gauzy material in such a way as at first sight to remind me most forcibly of a corpse in its grave-clothes. And yet I do not know why it should have given me this idea, seeing that the wrappings were so thin that one could distinctly see the gleam of the pink flesh beneath them. (Haggard, 1995: 106)

For Holly, she is both dead and alive and his tantalising glimpse of her pink flesh will later be elaborated into a profoundly felt desire. She tells Holly that she has lived for two thousand years and mocks his credulity by stating ' "Dost thou believe that all things die . . .? I tell thee that nothing dies. There is no such thing as Death, though there be a thing called Change" ' (1995: 111). This position is close to Lewes's view that the only real change is molecular transformation. Revealingly Holly, writing after the event, recalls in a footnote that:

> Ayesha was a great chemist, indeed chemistry appears to have been her only amusement and occupation. She had one of the caves fitted up as a laboratory, and, although her appliances were necessarily rude the results that she attained were, as will become clear in the course of this narrative, sufficiently surprising. (1995: 146)

Ayesha's ability to control nature has an overt political edge to it. Over two thousand years she has created and let die many different races, which at one level also indicates just how far the novel examines the (quite literal) construction of racial categories. Shawn Malley has noted of Ayesha that she:

> is not depicted as a mystic, but as a scientist who . . . approaches psychic phenomena as objects of rational, psychological study. The universe Ayesha inhabits and explores as a eugenicist, astronomer, chemist, physicist, geologist, and archaeologist is a decidedly Darwinian one. (1997: 290)

Ayesha tells Holly that the key to her long life is the flame of life which grants an extended if not infinite life:

> Life is wonderful, ay, but that it should be a little lengthened is not wonderful. Nature hath her animating spirit as well as man, who is Nature's child, and he who can find that spirit, and let it breathe upon him, shall live with her life. (Haggard, 1995: 113)

This is a view which also accords with Lewes's view of how life may be protracted.

Ayesha is the ultimate empire builder who controls through fear, ruling 'by terror. My empire is of the imagination' (Haggard, 1995: 132), but also through eugenics. Bodies and empires are closely aligned as she outlines her theory of the body politic which is fundamentally Darwinian, telling Holly that 'Those who are weak must perish; the earth is to the strong, and the fruits thereof' (1995: 153). For Holly this is a disappointment because instead of wisdom he sees her long life as having atrophied any moral sensibility, and is concerned that if her view was 'carried to its logical conclusion [it], would absolutely destroy all morality' (1995: 153). Bodies replace the inner life in Ayesha's vision, but the novel's rejection of this (via Holly) works as a critique of colonialist racist ideologies which saw the body as a marker of racial identification. At another level the novel also argues that images of Empire never quite die in the way that Ayesha suggests: rather they have a continuing if fragmentary presence which is linked to images of death. Elsewhere in the novel Holly discovers the embalmed bodies of the denizens of the now lost city of Kôr and such is their multitude that they are used to light a dance – one that Holly recollects through an image of a recycled Empire:

> There was something very terrible, and yet most fascinating, about the employment of the remote dead to illumine the orgies of the living; in itself the thing was a satire, both on the living and the dead. Caesar's dust – or is it Alexander's? – may stop a bunghole, but the functions of these dead Caesars of the past was to light up a savage fetish dance. (1995: 164)

Holly's analogy is instructive, as it not only develops the novel's theme of reincarnation, but also links with an idea of recycling that Thomas Huxley outlined in *Lessons in Elementary Physiology* (1868), where he argues that:

> The sun's rays, acting through the vegetable world, build up some of the wandering molecules of carbonic acid, of water, of ammonia, and of salts, into the fabric of plants. The plants are devoured by animals, animals devour one another, man devours both plants and other animals; and hence it is very possible that atoms which once formed the busy brain of Julius Caesar may now enter into the composition of Caesar the negro in Alabama, and of Caesar the house-dog in an English homestead. (1898: 21)

So, as in Lewes's formulation, the dead never really die. In *She* death focalises the discussion about what it means to be human. For Holly this relates to the inner life, a world of morality and introspection in which a type of ethical evolution might become possible, whereas Ayesha represents an alternative image of death which sees no experience possible beyond the body, telling Holly to 'live for the day, and endeavour not to escape the dust which seems to be man's end' (Haggard, 1995: 165). Ultimately Ayesha cannot escape her history as her second entry into the flame of life sees her regress into a 'monkey' (1995: 222). This pull between the needs of the body and morality was returned to by Haggard in three sequels to *She*, which suggest that he regarded the first novel as unfinished business. *Ayesha: The Return of She* (1905) is told from the point of view of the now-dying Holly, who encounters Ayesha in the 'hall of shades' where 'She seemed a Queen of Death receiving homage from the dead' (Haggard, 1998: 211).[5]

Freud in *The Interpretation of Dreams* (1900) recounts discussing *She* in a dream where he refers to it as addressing 'the immortality of our emotions'. He sees this, within the context of his dream, as referring to his yet to be published works that would grant his own immortality if only he would be prepared to offer them up to the public – all of which becomes a conceit for the need to subject himself to self-analysis (Freud, 1991: 587). *She* thus takes Freud into an account of introspection, one founded on the idea of transcending death through writing. This suggests a move beyond the Darwinian vision of Ayesha, but that this has a continuing presence is clear in the work of F. W. H. Myers who explored links between the subliminal mind, the spirit and death from an evolutionary perspective.

F. W. H. Myers was a president of the Society for Psychical Research (SPR) and the culmination of his extensive research on psychic phenomena was the posthumously published (he died in 1901) *Human Personality and its Survival of Bodily Death* (1903, revised 1907). Myers's work can be seen within the context of Mayo's idea that spirits can communicate with the living and that such communication can take place before death. Myers, however, wanted to explore a number of case histories, submitted to the SPR, which confirmed for him the possibility of life after death. For Myers the subliminal mind is where our spirit resides and this is a faculty which enables thought transference during life, but which also survives our death. Whilst, according to Myers, the subliminal mind has always been in existence, it is only at the end of the nineteenth century that its presence began to be felt as it evolved into a form of communication that had gained visibility (as testified by the numerous case histories submitted for scrutiny to the SPR). This leads Myers to claim that '*Spiritual evolution:* . . . is our destiny, in this and other worlds; – an evolution gradual with many gradations, and rising to no assignable close' (1907: 344, original italics). Myers goes further by claiming that the subject is divided into physical and spiritual entities which are developed through evolutionary principles which are specific to them, so that he argues 'Let us suppose that whilst incarnate men have risen from savagery into intelligence, discarnate men have made on their part a like advance' (1907: 345). It is also important to Myers that this subliminal self represents a positive spiritual presence and is related to ideas of creativity, intelligence and morality – there are thus no genuinely evil spirits in his cosmology because we are involved in an 'endless evolution of wisdom and love' (1907: 350) which will transcend materialism because we will see 'a mind use a brain' (1907: 332).

The idea of a brain being controlled by a mind was central to Mayo's conception of vampirism as a symptom of psychological projection. Poe explored how the mesmeric trance enables a possible communion with the spirit world and the idea that the dead speak to us is clearly central to Myers's thinking. However, access to this subliminal self can also be found via hypnotic suggestion because it enables access to a subliminal trance in which messages may be received. It is an idea that Stoker exploits in *Dracula* (1897).

That Count Dracula possesses some form of hypnotic ability is suggested in his influence over Lucy Westenra when she is made to sleep-walk to him whilst in Whitby.[6] For Myers it is in sleep that an alternative, subliminal, version of ourselves is manifested and sleep-walking demonstrates that presence as the conscious self is effectively possessed by an alternative inner self. Van Helsing is aware of this when he tells Seward regarding the dying Lucy that 'It will be much difference, mark me, whether she dies conscious or in her sleep' (Stoker, 1996: 160). This might appear to invite a conventional psychoanalytical reading which associates vampirism with sexualised subconscious desires, but considered in Myers's terms it implies that the inner life represents an alternative form of existence which symbolically (to evoke Mayo) links vampirism with the 'dead undead' of the self that both survives death and which is subject to its own laws of evolution. Van Helsing is the principal agent in the novel for introducing an intellectual context for these ideas when he challenges Seward for accepting Charcot's account of hypnotism but rejecting 'thought-reading', whereas Van Helsing, crucially, sees such ideas as part of an evolution of knowledge in which 'there are things done to-day in electrical science which would have been deemed unholy by the very men who discovered electricity' (Stoker, 1996: 191). This language of evolutionary change shares with Myers the vision of an evolution that has taken place within the inner self. Trance-like states thus represent in the novel, as they do in Mayo and Myers, the preservation of the dead as well as a means of gaining access to the inner life of the other, as Van Helsing tells Seward of Lucy's infection that 'in trance could he best come to take more blood. In trance she died, and in trance she is Un-Dead, too' (Stoker, 1996: 201). This conception of the inner life stands in contrast to the novel's overt engagement with theories of degeneration which are mapped onto the Count's body. This indicates that whilst the novel addresses a language of decline (degeneration), it also explores a troubled language of evolution.[7]

The central issue relates to the brain and how it is perceived. The emphasis on the brain illustrates how ideas about evolution are trans-ferred to the mind. Van Helsing, for example, admires Mina's exercise of logic and refers to her 'man's brain – a brain that a man should have were he much gifted' (1996: 234). Van Helsing also acknowledges of the Count that:

> in him the brain powers survived the physical death; though it would seem that memory was not all complete. In some faculties of mind he has been, and is, only a child; but he is growing, and some things that were childish at the first are now of man's stature. (1996: 302)

He therefore needs to be destroyed before he evolves into a danger-ous adult form. Revealingly the Count mocks Mina with 'you, like the others, would play your brains against mine' (1996: 287), which indi-cates just how significant the mental battle is.

Mina allows herself to be put in a hypnotic trance when her associates know the Count must be asleep, and through this she can enter his body and hear sounds (such as the lapping of waves) which provide clues as to his whereabouts. She is able to journey subconsciously because 'Sleep has no place to call its own' (1996: 312), meaning that she can mentally travel to him.

Dracula thus gives credence to the ideas entertained by Myers and Mayo that vampirism can be seen in symbolic terms as representing a resurrection of the inner (Un-Dead) life. However, such an evolutionary possibility is demonised in the novel because, as in *She*, it is associated with amoral occult forces. As Van Helsing says 'The very place where he have been alive, Un-Dead for all these centuries, is full of strangeness of the geologic and chemical world' (Stoker, 1996: 319), which – with the Count's alchemical studies – represents a forbidden science. *Dracula* can thus be seen as engaging with wider discourses about death and sub-jectivity at the end of the nineteenth century, and its ambivalence about such theories of the mind is neatly captured in Renfield's rebuttal of Van Helsing's ideas: 'I wish you would take yourself and your idiotic brain theories somewhere else' (1996: 256).

Death in the Victorian Gothic is an underexplored area of enquiry.

An investigation of it reveals how images of death are closely linked to models of subjectivity. It would seem that what it means to be human during the period is fraught with concerns about the frailty of the physical body, but 'humanity' is also freighted with a model of the inner life which transcends that frailty. There appear to be two linked versions of events, one in which the dead do not really die (as witnessed from Radcliffe through to Stoker), but also a concurrent fear that the dead will not stay dead (as in the vampire, but also arguably in the odd half-life of the ghost). It is typical of the Gothic that it vacillates between these positions as it explores how death shapes the subject's sense of what it means to be a person.

Notes

1. There is the earlier tradition of the 'Graveyard Poets' of the 1740s and 1750s which shaped the Romantic model of death: however, space precludes a proper discussion of their influence. Also, a key text during the period is Tennyson's *In Memoriam* (1850), but it sits outside the specifically Gothic tradition discussed here, even if it has links to that tradition.
2. See Hindle's introduction to *Frankenstein* (Shelley, 1985: 24–5).
3. See Burke (1998), especially sections on 'Terror' (pp. 53–4), 'Vastness' (p. 66) and 'Ugliness' (pp. 108–9).
4. My reading of Haggard's novel explores specific representations of death and dying which I have also explored in a colonial context in Smith (2003).
5. The other novels in the series are *She and Allan* (1921) and *Wisdom's Daughter: The Life and Love Story of She-Who-Must-be-Obeyed* (1923).
6. See also the discussion of mesmerism in Hughes (2000: 170–7).
7. The novel makes explicit reference to Lombroso and Nordau.

References

Ariès, Philippe (1981). *The Hour of Our Death*, trans. Helen Weaver. New York: Alfred A. Knopf.

Burke, Edmund (1998). *A Philosophical Enquiry into the Origin of our Ideas of the Sublime and Beautiful* [1757], ed. Adam Phillips. Oxford: Oxford University Press.

Castle, Terry (1995). 'The Spectralization of the Other', in *The Female Thermometer: Eighteenth-Century Culture and the Invention of the Uncanny*. Oxford: Oxford University Press, pp. 120–39.

Eliot, George (1999). *The Lifted Veil and Brother Jacob* [1859], ed. and introduction Helen Small. Oxford: Oxford University Press.

Freud, Sigmund (1991). *The Interpretation of Dreams* [1900], trans. and ed. J. Strachey. The Penguin Freud Library, vol. 4. Harmondsworth: Penguin.

Haggard, H. Rider (1995). *She* [1887]. Ware: Wordsworth.

——(1998), *Ayesha: The Return of She* [1905]. Polegate: Pulp Fictions.

Hughes, William (2000). *Beyond Dracula: Bram Stoker's Fiction and its Cultural Context*. Basingstoke: Macmillan.

Huxley, Thomas (1898). *Lessons in Elementary Physiology* [1868, revised 1885]. London: Macmillan.

Lewes, George Henry (1860). *The Physiology of Common Life*, 2 vols. Edinburgh and London: Blackwood, vol. 2.

Malley, Shawn (1997). ' "Time Hath No Power Against Identity": Historical Continuity and Archaeological Adventure in H. Rider Haggard's *She*', *English Literature in Transition 1880–1920*, 40/3, 275–97.

Mayo, Herbert (2003). *On the Truths Contained in Popular Superstitions with an Account of Mesmerism* [1851]. Westcliff-on-Sea: Desert Island Books.

Myers, F. W. H. (1907). *Human Personality and its Survival of Bodily Death*. London: Longmans.

Poe, Edgar Allan (1982). 'The Facts in the Case of M. Valdemar' [1845], in *The Complete Tales and Poems of Edgar Allan Poe*. Harmondsworth: Penguin, pp. 96–103.

——(1982). 'Mesmeric Revelation' [1844], in *The Complete Tales and Poems of Edgar Allan Poe*. Harmondsworth: Penguin, pp. 88–96.

Shelley, Mary (1985). *Frankenstein* [1818], ed. and introduction Maurice Hindle. Harmondsworth: Penguin.

——(2000). 'On Ghosts' [1824], in *Gothic Documents: A Sourcebook 1700–1820*, ed. E. J. Clery and Robert Miles. Manchester: Manchester University Press, pp. 280–5.

Smith, Andrew (2003). 'Beyond Colonialism: Death and the Body in H. Rider Haggard', in *Empire and the Gothic: The Politics of Genre*, ed. Andrew Smith and William Hughes. Basingstoke: Palgrave, pp. 103–17.

Stoker, Bram (1996). *Dracula* [1897], notes and introduction Maud Ellmann. Oxford: Oxford University Press.

Chapter 11

Science and the Gothic
Kelly Hurley

There is no longer any doubt as to the fact – the ability of a strong will thus to enslave another's weaker mind and reduce it to a canine automatonism. It has, indeed, been repeatedly proved that this astounding power may be exercised without, and even against, the consent of the subject. Behold the appalling possibility!

(Gould, 1890: 2174)

I was not living a true life; I was living a dual life. A power extraneous to myself, and yet possessing me, made me a mere machine . . . I resisted, I struggled. And still I was bound in chains; still I was held by a mysterious occult power.

(Hocking, 1890: 176)

In Joseph Hocking's novel *The Weapons of Mystery* (1890), Justin Blake finds himself in thrall to Herod Voltaire, 'a fiend in human form'. An unscrupulous cosmopolite of mysterious origins, and the narrator's sworn enemy and rival for the woman he loves, Voltaire has hypnotised him, and now Blake is no longer himself. He has blackouts and hallucinations. He is controlled by Voltaire's 'terrible eye' and his potent 'will-force' when they are face to face (Hocking, 1890: 168, 95). What is more, the hypnotist can command Blake from a distance, forcing him to speak and act in accordance with Voltaire's wishes, or paralysing and silencing Blake when he attempts to break free. The narrator has become 'a slave to a deep designing villain, held fast in his power by some secret nervous or brain forces which he possessed' (1890: 85). Blake's worst nightmare is that he might be compelled to violate his own moral character while under hypnotic influence: that Voltaire 'might make me do things which would be altogether opposed to what I believed right and true' (1890: 85). This nightmare seems to become reality when Blake awakens from a blackout clutching a knife and a bloody neckcloth belonging to Kaffar, Voltaire's Egyptian accomplice. All Blake can remember is a long, elaborate hallucination in which he wandered through a surreal Egyptian landscape and then fought savagely with Kaffar. 'What had I done?' he asks in terror. 'Could it be that I had murdered this man? Had I? Had I?' (1890: 146).

Not too surprisingly, such overheated rhetoric is typical of the late Victorian Gothic literature of criminal hypnosis. But one finds similarly charged language in late Victorian scientific articles like the one excerpted above, written by George M. Gould, a medical doctor, and also exploring the 'appalling possibility' of magnetised subjects behaving like murderous automatons. As another doctor-author noted ironically, 'the excitement with which the phenomena and apparent results of hypnotism have been accepted in England' makes it 'almost seem as if the hypnotic influence had obtained sway over the scientific minds of the nineteenth century' (Thomson, 1890: 624). At the fin de siècle, both scientists and Gothic authors explored a scenario that even the former might characterise as 'creepy' and 'uncanny' (Gould, 1890: 2172): criminal hypnotists gain absolute control over their hapless subjects, maliciously tampering with their minds, implanting terrible suggestions, substituting their own will and desires for those of the victims. The victims are then lost to themselves, becoming deranged, 'canine', machinic, enslaved.

During the 1880s and 1890s, British, Continental, and American popular and medical journals contributed to a sensational debate about hypnotism: how to define it, its proper uses, and its potential dangers, particularly the dangers posed by hypnotic and post-hypnotic suggestion.[1] The debate was fuelled by a notorious rivalry between two competing French schools of experimental psychology, one associated with the Salpêtrière Hospital in Paris, the other with the University in provincial Nancy; the first led by Jean-Martin Charcot and the second by Hippolyte Bernheim, both physician-neurologists. The experiments of the Salpêtrière and Nancy psychologists were well publicised in French newspapers and journals in the 1880s (Hillman, 1965: 166–8, 170–80), and became of increasing interest in Britain as the decade progressed. An 1890 *Contemporary Review* article described the often acrimonious debate between Charcot and Bernheim and their disciples as 'a full wave' of controversy from the Continent which 'has at last broken on our shores' (Innes, 1890: 555).

Late Victorian Gothic authors seized upon this controversy with great enthusiasm, quick to exploit the narrative possibilities opened up by experimental psychology. Hypnosis might be represented as a weird supernatural force, as a scientifically explicable process that was nonetheless uncanny in its working and effects, or as a quasi-occult phenomenon that troubled the distinction between science and supernaturalism. Such strategies are typical of the fin-de-siècle Gothic, which consistently attempted to figure monstrosity within scientific terms. Its monsters might develop according to the laws of evolutionary biology, or be modelled on the pathological types (perverts, regressives, the insane) described in nineteenth-century human sciences such as sexology, degeneration theory and psychology. For instance, the vampire in Bram Stoker's *Dracula* (1897) is not only a supernatural being. Count Dracula, the text suggests, may also be one of the atavistic 'criminal types' described by criminal anthropology. Or perhaps the vampire is the product of strange 'geologic and chemical' processes – 'occult ... forces of nature' that direct evolution in unexpected ways, and are as yet only imperfectly understood (Stoker, 1997: 296, 278). *Dracula*'s vampires are also hypnotists.[2] In contrast to Van Helsing, for whom hypnotism is a physician's tool to be deployed in the service of righteousness, they are criminal hypnotists, using their powers to seduce and debauch their victims.

The monstrosity of the criminal hypnotist is particularly figured by the eyes. Dracula's 'red, gleaming eyes' shine in the moonlight (Stoker, 1997: 88). In Arthur Conan Doyle's 'John Barrington Cowles' (1886), Kate Northcott, who disturbingly admixes male and female traits, has eyes that are notable for both 'their feminine softness' and their 'steely hardness, ... power of command', and 'penetrating intensity' (Doyle, 1979: 250). The otherwise handsome Herod Voltaire is a kind of Cyclops; his strange grey-green eyes are 'placed very close together, and, the bridge of the nose being narrow, they appeared sometimes as if only one eye looked upon you' (Hocking, 1890: 15). Dick Donovan's 'The Woman with the "Oily Eyes"' (1899) describes vampire eyes 'illumined ... by a violet light', with 'a peculiar, glistening appearance like oil' (Donovan, 1899: 32, 45). The eponymous shape-shifter of Richard Marsh's *The Beetle* (1897) has enormous eyes that 'ran, literally, across the whole of the upper portion of his face' (Marsh, 2004: 53).

Under the power of those eyes, Robert Holt finds himself being slowly drained of subjectivity by the Beetle-person. '[S]omething was going from me', he says, 'the capacity, as it were, to be myself' (Marsh, 2004: 54, 56). Hypnotised victims are no less Gothic than their tormenters: they become 'spectralized' (Luckhurst, 2002: 213), rendered uncanny to themselves and to the reader. They often narrate their own transformation into a state of spectral otherness – whether that state is insubstantiality, libidinal excess or murderous rage – in the first person, underscoring the terror of the loss of self-possession. 'At that moment I felt gripped by an unseen power, and I was irresistibly drawn towards the door ... like a man in a sleep', says Blake (Hocking, 1890: 78). At Castle Dracula, beset by seductive female vampires, the ultra-rational Jonathan Harker finds himself regressing to a primitive mental state, 'struggling to awake to some call of my instincts' (Stoker 1997: 48), and runs screaming from the room. After chaste Mina Harker falls under Dracula's spell, she admits unhappily, 'Strangely enough, I did not want to hinder him' (1997: 251). The scientist-narrator of Doyle's 'The Parasite' (1894), suddenly possessed and animated by the strong will of his magnetiser, finds himself 'tearing' out of the house and running down a muddy road in what seems a 'misty and strange and unnatural' dream-reality (Doyle, 1981: 58).

Such uncanny hypnotised subjects had already appeared a century earlier, in the practice known as 'mesmerism' or 'animal magnetism'. The two terms are roughly synonymous, the former deriving from Franz Anton Mesmer, the German physician who was the self-proclaimed discoverer and most famous practitioner of animal magnetism in the late eighteenth century. Mesmer's work centred on the phenomenon of magnetic fluid, an invisible force said to circulate within and between all living beings, and whose blockage was the cause of ill health. The magnetic fluid 'could be stored up, concentrated, and communicated at a distance to restore an individual's mental and bodily harmony' (Bourne Taylor and Shuttleworth, 1998: 6). It might be concentrated in tubs of water, for instance, and its energies transferred to human beings across a rope or metal rod. But this mysterious life-force was most powerfully transmitted by means of human touch, moving like a charge of electricity from patient to patient – or more typically, back and forth between the patient and the skilled operator who manipulated and focused the fluid. The patient undergoing treatment might fall into a deep, therapeutic sleep, erupt into healing convulsions, or slip into a trance and experience visions.

Here, in embryo, we find a characteristic scenario that would be repeated across the nineteenth century in scientific, journalistic and literary accounts of mesmerism (and later, hypnotism).[3] A powerful magnetiser with dangerously compelling eyes controls his subject with a series of mesmeric 'passes', that is, sweeping strokes across or just above the body and face. In George du Maurier's novel *Trilby* (1894), for instance, the evil Svengali looms over and stares fixedly at Trilby, making 'passes and counterpasses on her forehead and temples and down her cheek and neck'. Within this scenario the mesmerised subject is then spectralised – perhaps breaking into violent fits of hysterical delirium, perhaps enjoying ecstatic visions, perhaps becoming paralysed and 'spellbound' like the hapless Trilby, who 'could not move' after Svengali's ministrations (du Maurier, 1978: 54).

Mesmer's influence spread across the Continent and eventually reached Great Britain in the 1830s.[4] Sessions featuring displays of animal magnetism, often called *séances* to denote their exotic Continental origins, became more and more common in Great Britain in the years that followed. Mesmerism was practised in Great Britain for therapeutic reasons, as an experimental discipline that might further the advancement of knowledge about the human mental apparatus, and as a form of popular entertainment. From its inception mesmerism was subject to stern criticism, despite, or perhaps because of, its extravagant promises to benefit humankind. Mesmerists were charlatans and criminals, or they were fools and self-deceivers. Mesmerism was an immoral practice, a seducer's art. However, many believed that mesmerism had 'discovered a new form of invisible force which was yet to be identified, and unveiled new potentialities of the mind' (Bourne Taylor and Shuttleworth, 1998: 6).

As Alison Winter has argued convincingly, Victorian mesmerism was not a risible 'fringe' phenomenon in its times, but rather one of the 'central . . . preoccupations of Victorian culture' (Winter, 1998: 4). It was extensively discussed in the pages of the most important new medical journal, *The Lancet*. Most ordinary Victorians had read about, heard about or even attended a magnetic *séance*, which might take place in an exhibition hall, a hospital theatre or a private home. Nor should Victorian mesmerism be dismissed as a pseudo-science. 'Definitions of science were malleable during these years', and the practice of mesmerism 'became the occasion for contests over authority in science, medicine, and intellectual life alike', authority which was 'more insecure than historians appreciate' (Winter, 1998: 6, 4). In particular, nineteenth-century psychology 'was an emergent profession', lacking a methodological orthodoxy and 'eager to consolidate its own power base' (Bourne Taylor and Shuttleworth, 1998: 228). Whether the study of mesmerism would advance or prove detrimental to that goal remained to be seen.

The alternate term 'hypnotism' was promulgated by James Braid, a surgeon, who challenged Mesmer's theory that magnetic trance was caused and guided by the circulation of an invisible fluid. In his *Neurypnology; or, the Rationale of Nervous Sleep, Considered in Relation with Animal Magnetism* (1843), Braid defined hypnotism as a trance-state achieved by manipulating the nervous system with external stimuli and through suggestion.[5] Braid's work, which introduced the phrase 'hypnotic influence' (Crabtree 1993: 158), would help shift the discussion towards such concepts as mental influence, will force and suggestibility. These concepts would be crucial in the Salpêtrière–Nancy debate several decades later.

How did one define hypnotism? Who was susceptible to hypnotic trance? How dangerous were hypnotic and post-hypnotic suggestion? These were the chief points of difference between the Salpêtrière and Nancy schools. For Charcot, hypnotism was closely related to hysteria, which he believed was of physiological rather than psychological origins. '[T]he persons . . . who are susceptible of hypnotization, are nervous creatures, capable of becoming hysterical, if not actually hysterical at the beginning of the experiments', so that 'fit subjects' for hypnotism 'are by no means so plentiful as some authors would have us believe' (Charcot, 1890: 160, 163). Only defective individuals could be hypnotised, in other words. Most readers would have found this reassuring, for it meant that ordinary citizens need have no fear of falling into an unscrupulous hypnotist's power. Charcot defined three stages of hypnotism: lethargy, catalepsy and somnambulism; and though in the third stage somnambules were open to hypnotic suggestion, it was highly unlikely that they could be forced to commit actual crimes, as opposed to 'laboratory crimes' induced in experimental theatres (1890: 164).

Charcot's three stages nonetheless produced phantasmatic subjects. In 'the lethargy' and 'the catalepsy . . . there is absolute unconsciousness; the subject is motionless, his will is in abeyance' (1890: 161). An unsigned article in *The Lancet* describes an unlucky waitress hypnotised by an amateur who fell into 'so profound' a sleep that she could not be roused for hours (Anon., 1890a: 615). Here we have the uncanny spectacle of a living, breathing human evacuated of subjectivity, like the 'spellbound' Trilby. In Doyle's 'The Parasite', Austin Gilroy becomes frantic when his fiancée is turned into a kind of blank-faced wax figure by the 'mesmeric sleep':

> [Agatha] might have been dead for all the impression that I could make. Her body was there on the velvet chair. Her organs were acting, her heart, her lungs. But her soul! It had slipped from beyond our ken. Whither had it gone? What power had dispossessed it? (Doyle, 1981: 46)

Bernheim did not link hypnotism to hysteria or any other pathological state: 'I define hypnotism as the induction of a peculiar psychical condition which increases the susceptibility to suggestion' (1973: 15). This 'peculiar psychical condition' could be induced in anyone. Some subjects were more readily suggestible than others, and the depth of, and behaviour under, hypnotic trance varied from individual to individual, but

all persons were suggestible to some extent. Bernheim began by studying the therapeutic possibilities of hypnotism, the treatment 'of both
functional and organic diseases by suggestion during hypnotic sleep'
(Hillman, 1965: 168). And had Bernheim's experiments at Nancy been
limited to this kind of work, what he called 'suggestive therapeutics',
hypnosis might never have sparked such widespread public interest in
the 1880s. But in 1884 Bernheim and Jules Liégeois, Professor of Law
at the University of Nancy, undertook a series of dramatic experiments
on the forensic ramifications of hypnotic suggestion. These experiments attempted to demonstrate just how far the subject's openness to
suggestion might go. The results were troubling. Hypnotised subjects
were asked to lie, steal and even commit hypothetical murder, and they
readily complied.

Critics of the Liégeois experiments pointed out that the crimes he had
documented were merely crimes of the laboratory, and that Liégeois'
subjects would not have attempted murder so cheerfully had they been
supplied with daggers of steel rather than paper, or had they been asked
to return home and serve arsenic to their families. In actual rather than
laboratory situations, they argued, no hypnotised individual could be
persuaded to commit an act that went against his or her basic moral
character. William Newbold, affirming that hypnotised subjects almost
never performed acts that ran contrary to conscience, added that:

> in the few cases where it seems probable that the [hypnotised] patient has
> really committed what he believes to be a crime, it is often not shown that the
> crime would have been especially abhorrent to his normal self. (1888: 238)

However, many psychologists and journalists disagreed. Breaking
from their mentor Charcot, Alfred Binet and Charles Féré affirmed that
'the hypnotic subject may become the instrument of a terrible crime, the
more terrible since, immediately after the act is accomplished, all may be
forgotten – the crime, the impulse, and its instigator' (1888: 768).

Gould wrote that a hypnotised person is 'at the mercy' of the hypnotist, whose 'suggestions and implanted ideas fill the vacant and enslaved
consciousness with abnormal and illogical data, and direct its energies
with mechanical rigidity' (1890: 2173). The Nancy experiments had
produced a different phantasmatic subject than Charcot's wax figure:
this one first evacuated of self-ness, and then set in automatic motion
by the hypnotic suggestion, moving and speaking like a machine. The
phenomenon of *post*-hypnotic suggestion made the matter even worse.

> Not only is it possible to make a man feel or do, while in the hypnotic sleep,
> whatever is suggested to him; it is possible to suggest or order him, while he

is in that condition, to feel or do something after he has come out of it, and *is in his ordinary state*. (Innes, 1890: 556, emphasis added)

In 'The Parasite', Miss Penelosa says that during the mesmeric sleep she had 'set' Agatha to go off like 'the alarum of a clock' by means of post-hypnotic suggestion, and a blank-faced Agatha in fact executes Penelosa's command at the exact time named, remembering nothing afterwards. 'If six months instead of twelve hours had been suggested, it would have been the same' (Doyle, 1981: 51).[6]

The hypnotised automaton is not necessarily blank or stiffly robotic. Propelled by 'fixed ideas, irresistible impulses' implanted by the hypnotist, the victim may erupt 'suddenly' and violently into action (Binet and Féré, 1888: 767–8). Marsh's Holt finds himself 'whirled around, and sped hastily onwards' like a horse 'with a bridle in its mouth'. Here uncanniness results from the scenario of a subject animated by an impulse or motive that does not originate from the self – like a mechanised Holt being jerked along 'helter-skelter' through the London streets (Marsh, 2004: 70, 82). This scenario is even more uncanny for the subject who experiences it first hand. For Doyle's Gilroy, hypnotic suggestion is simultaneously an external coercion and an interpolated motive that sets his body into frantic motion. 'Suddenly I was gripped – gripped and dragged from the couch. It is only thus that I can describe the overpowering nature of the force which pounced upon me' (Doyle, 1981: 64). As the line between external and internal blurs, one cannot even be sure if the hateful impulse does not come from within after all. Hocking's Blake worries that his own violent temper, and not hypnotic suggestion, might have led him to kill Kaffar during his blackout. 'How did I know it was Voltaire's power . . .? Might not my blind passion have swept me on to this dark deed?' (Hocking, 1890: 177).

The Salpêtrière and Nancy physicians did agree on two things. The first was that hypnotism should only be practised by professionals, by physicians and psychologists rather than amateurs and popular magnetisers, who were likely to cause ill health and 'nervous derangement' in their subjects (Anon., 1890b: 699).[7] The second concerned sexual abuses by hypnotists. Though he did not allow for crime by suggestion, Charcot believed that hypnotising in order to seduce, like hypnotising for entertainment or profit, constituted a form of criminal hypnosis. He emphasised the perilous attractions of an utterly passive female body to an unscrupulous operator: 'during the periods when the will is in abeyance and the sleep complete', a hypnotised woman is 'so much lifeless matter offered to the lechery of the magnetizer' (1890: 161–2).

Hypnotic seduction might involve other things besides outright assault, however. The physical and emotional intimacy of the encounter meant that 'somnambulist subjects often display a kind of attraction for the experimenter who has hypnotized them' (Binet and Féré, 1888: 767). The mesmeric exchange in itself created a sensual bond between operator and subject, a bond that was only intensified by further sessions. As Charcot wrote, 'a woman who in the waking state would have been chaste, may during the somnambulism give herself up to the one who has hypnotised her, especially if the hypnosis has been repeated many times' (1890: 162). Note how such a formulation complicates the already troublesome problem of whether one's basic moral character can or cannot be violated by hypnotic suggestion, for how is one to know if a woman '*would have* been chaste' before falling prey to the hypnotist?

A still more disturbing question was whether complex emotions could be interpolated into another subjectivity by means of magnetism. An unsigned *Saturday Review* article related an 'actual case' from 1865 of a 'respectable young woman living with her father' who was hypnotised by Castellan, 'a vagabond mesmeriser'. Castellan 'compelled her to leave her home, follow him, and live with him, though he was a filthy and repulsive creature' (Anon., 1890b: 699). The magnetiser might well be able to command an emotional bond with his victim – even if that emotional bond is ambivalent, like the 'fascination of repulsion' Rosa Bud feels for John Jasper in Charles Dickens's *The Mystery of Edwin Drood*' (1870), and which 'had been upon her so long . . . that she felt as if he had power to bind her by a spell' (Dickens, 1974: 234). Trilby is 'haunted by the memory of Svengali's big eyes and the touch of his soft, dirty finger-tips on her face'. Like Rosa, Trilby feels 'fear' mixed with 'repulsion' when she thinks of her tormenter, but becomes increasingly in thrall to him (du Maurier, 1978: 58). All three texts describe a 'repulsive' man, but even the most disgusting magnetisers might be capable of implanting erotic desire, perhaps love, in their unwilling victims.

In 'The Parasite', Gilroy is violated by just such a loss of emotional integrity: 'I must come when she wills it. I must do as she wills. Worst of all, *I must feel as she wills*' – that is, he must love the unattractive Miss Penelosa when she so commands, though 'the very sight' of her 'fills me with horror and disgust' (Doyle, 1981: 59, 66, emphasis added). In the late Victorian Gothic, the compelling magnetiser is frequently female and her victim male, inverting the more traditional sexual dynamic described above. Male characters' loss of volition and integral subjectivity through hypnotic suggestion is figured as a loss of essential masculinity in stories like 'The Woman with the "Oily Eyes"' and 'The Parasite'. Gilroy is a self-proclaimed 'materialist' and positivist, 'a man who is

devoted to exact science' (Doyle, 1981: 42), and his descent into subjection and raving irrationality is devastating.[8] Jack Redcar is a 'brawny
giant' with 'a masterful nature', but he is drained and exhausted by the
'repellent' Annette, Donovan's oily-eyed woman. The ultra-masculinity
Jack represents is literally shattered by the end of the story when Annette
throws him over a cliff. 'His head had been battered to pieces against
the rocks as he fell, and every bone in his body was broken' (Donovan,
1899: 3, 22, 38).

Conversely, the erosion of masculinity, traditionally the gender of the
'universal' human subject, contributes to the spectralisation of fin-de-
siècle subjectivity through hypnosis more generally. Criminal hypnosis
empties out the subject, bizarrely animates the subject, divides the
subject and estranges it from itself. As a French journalist wrote in 1885,
hypnosis 'will demonstrate that the personality is neither really defined,
nor permanent, nor stationary; that the sense of free will is essentially
floating and illusive, memory multiple and intermittent, and that character is a function of these variable qualities and can be modified'.[9]

Since its inception the Gothic had been concerned with dream-states,
irrationality, insanity, hysteria, delusions and mental breakdown. As
discussed earlier, the Victorian Gothic was opportunistic in its relation
to science, borrowing from any number of scientific discourses, psychology included, in order to further its project of the making-strange
of human identity. The debate on criminal hypnosis provided new,
panic-inducing models of self and intersubjectivity for the Gothic, new
language and frameworks for producing spectral identities, new possibilities for plot and narration. The Gothic absorbed these things quickly
but not without certain formal difficulties. As I conclude, I wish to look
at two stories' sometimes uneven attempts at incorporation, beginning
with Doyle's 'John Barrington Cowles' (1886), published just before
news of the Salpêtrière–Nancy debates became widely circulated in
Britain.

The story's Kate Northcott is in many ways a traditional Gothic villainess, snaky and sensuous, a man-eater who leaves behind a string of
dying fiancés. 'She is the devil!' mutters one of her victims. 'Beautiful
– beautiful; but the devil!' (Doyle, 1979: 255). Kate has an appalling
secret that is never revealed to the reader, only to her fiancés. This secret
is clearly sexual in nature since Kate must impart it before her wedding-
night, and since each horrified fiancé immediately breaks off the engagement and begins to rave hysterically, as John raves to his friend Bob,
the narrator. The secret 'is too dreadful' to be told, he cries, 'too . . .
unutterably awful and incredible!' First John, and the text, deploys a
characteristic Gothic rhetoric of obfuscation, whereby an otherworldly

or excessive Gothic phenomenon is designated *unspeakable*, so that its content can only be figured by means of allusion or indirection. John then draws from a bewildering *mélange* of familiar Gothic monsters. Kate is a 'fiend', a werewolf, a child-eater. She is a 'ghoul from the pit! A vampire soul behind a lovely face!' (1979: 269). Some, but not all, of these monsters are traditionally associated with Gothic femininity, with gender-neutral epithets like 'fiend' and 'ghoul' further confusing our speculations about what it is, exactly, that makes Kate unspeakable.

Midway through the story we learn that Kate is also a criminal hypnotist, 'possess[ing] extraordinary powers over the minds, and through the minds over the bodies, of others' (1979: 274). When Dr Messinger, a famous mesmerist, comes to Edinburgh for a public exhibition, he lectures about the dangers posed by the criminal hypnotist:

> a mesmerised subject is entirely dominated by the will of the mesmeriser. He loses all power of volition, and his very thoughts are such as are suggested to him by the master-mind . . . A strong will can, simply by virtue of its strength, take possession of a weaker one, even at a distance, and can regulate the impulses and the actions of the owner of it. (1979: 263–4)

Kate certainly seems to have all of the makings of such a mesmeric 'master-mind'. She has the characteristic hypnotist's eyes, and a dominating, even sadistic, personality, as we see when she beats her cringing terrier with a heavy whip. And as any skilled hypnotist would be, Kate is attracted to the sensitive and suggestible John Barrington Cowles, a 'slim', somewhat feminine young man with 'dark, tender eyes' and a 'highly nervous temperament' (1979: 249, 264).

That Kate is in fact a skilled hypnotist is made clear at Dr Messinger's lecture. Proposing to demonstrate the phenomenon of hypnotic suggestion on a stranger, Messinger chooses John from the audience and focuses his will-force and his 'singularly intense and penetrating' gaze upon him. Kate, however, counter-mesmerises the professional mesmerist, gazing back 'with such an expression of concentrated power upon her features as I have never seen on any other human countenance'. Messinger collapses in exhaustion and must bring the performance to an abrupt end (1979: 264).

Structurally this quite dramatic scene occupies a central place in the tale. And yet mesmerism as a theme remains oddly unintegrated, its relation to the theme of Gothic female sexuality obscure. It is not even clear that Kate uses her hypnotic abilities for the purpose of seduction. It is true that she stares intently at John when she first meets him, but when John turns around and meets her eyes, she drops hers demurely, and it is John who then keeps his 'fixed' gaze on Kate 'for some moments', drawn by her beauty and not by any hypnotic power. If we are to believe her dying, drunken fiancé Archibald Reeves when he claims that a ghostly Kate sits by his bed 'with her great eyes watching and watching hour after hour', this seems more like traditional demonic possession than newfangled criminal hypnotism. And if we are to believe that it was Kate who induced John's suicide, this was a spirit-Kate, with a 'shimmering form' like a phantom's and a 'strange wild' laugh like a banshee's, who used witchery rather than mesmerism to lure John over the cliffs (1979: 252, 255, 272–3).

In Kate, says the narrator, 'some even more fiendish and terrible phase of character lay *behind*' her powers as a hypnotist – some 'horrible trait', some 'dreadful . . . mystery' (1979: 274, emphasis added). In this odd formulation, the unspeakable, whatever its traumatic content, is the primary source of Gothic *frisson*, and criminal hypnotism is secondary, though their exact relations to one another are not specified. What does it mean to say that the Gothic unspeakable lies 'behind' the phenomenon of criminal hypnosis? Perhaps the hypnotism plot merely masks and obscures a more primal terror of female sexuality, just as John's hysterical ravings about 'unutterably awful' things seem to do. Perhaps the hypnotism plot mirrors or runs parallel to the plot of female sexual terrorism, Kate's masculine-inflected powers of mental domination reinforcing her characterisation as a succubus who 'saps all the strength and manhood out of' her victims (1979: 255). Perhaps the introduction of criminal hypnosis as a new, very modern, source of terror serves to augment more traditional Gothic representations, just as John's multiplication of Gothic epithets for Kate confuses our understanding of her as a sheerly sexual monster but intensifies her uncanny affect.

In a similar tale, 'The Woman with the "Oily Eyes"', plot elements inspired by experimental psychology are superimposed on a story of Gothic female sexuality, with the former standing in sometimes ambiguous relation to the latter. Like 'John Barrington Cowles', Donovan's tale tells of a succubus-like monster who drains and destroys her male victims. And like 'John Barrington Cowles', it has difficulty specifying just what it is that makes its villainess so unspeakably dreadful. Annette is 'an unnatural woman', 'a she-devil', 'a diabolical creature', 'a malignant fiend'. She is a 'basilisk' who sucks the life out of babies. She is a serpentine femme fatale, with 'oily eyes that gleamed and glistened, and . . . seemed to have in them that sinister light which is peculiar to the cobra, and other poisonous snakes' (Donovan, 1899: 8–9, 15, 10).

In this case, the source of Annette's monstrosity finally *seems* to be identified. 'She was a human vampire, and my worst fears were confirmed!' Donovan's story climaxes with two vivid accounts of blood-sucking, one suffered by the narrator, Peter Haslar, the other by his best friend, Jack. Its descriptions of etiolated victims, 'hideous' neck-wounds, and blood-stained mouths would have been familiar to any reader of the just-published *Dracula* (Donovan, 1899: 39, 33).

I write 'seems', because Annette's Gothic identity is complicated, like Kate's, by her characterisation as a criminal hypnotist. Using the famous eyes, Annette seduces the narrator as well as Jack. She tampers with Jack's emotions so that he becomes enslaved to her and spurns his beloved wife, Maude. She hypnotises Maude so that she can only behave 'mechanically', like an automaton, while Annette kills her baby (1899: 14–15). Under her hypnotic influence the once-honourable Jack beats his wife unconscious and breaks his best friend's arm.

By 1899 the character of the Gothic hypnotist-vampire was well enough established, but this story stumbles in its attempts to represent it. It is not that the criminal hypnosis plot is not fully integrated with the Gothic femininity plot, as was the case in the earlier 'Cowles'. Here hypnosis and Gothic femininity are seamlessly conjoined at the climax, when hypnotist-Annette's 'marvellous eyes glowing with violet light' leave the narrator helplessly 'subdued to her will', and vampire-Annette's 'hot breath' on his neck fills him with 'ecstacy' and 'a delightful sense of dreamy langour' (1899: 32).

Rather, the two discursive realms of science and Gothicism are not fully integrated. Annette is a vampire-hypnotist – both a traditional monster and a figure from real-time experimental psychology – but the text cannot decide whether this means she is a supernatural being or a human anomaly that might be explicable within the human sciences. This confusion over Annette's identity manifests itself at the level of narration, beginning on the first two pages. The doctor-narrator, like any good Gothic storyteller, promises to tell a tale that is 'grim', 'ghastly' and 'weird', but quickly adds that he publishes 'in the interest of science'. His version of the story, he insists, is the correct and factual one. He includes 'all the peculiar circumstances of the case' in order to counter 'certain garbled versions [that have] crept into the public journals' (1899: 1–2). Though his account is filled with breathless horror and exclamation marks, Dr Haslar often cannot help approaching his best friend's death from a more clinical perspective, for 'from the psychological point of view it was a study' (1899 13). And in fact, 'The Woman with the "Oily Eyes"' often reads like a psychological or sexological case study.[10] The basilisk-eyed Annette may be a 'rare' freak of nature, but Dr Haslar can cite 'several well authenticated cases' of others like her (1899: 37).

'The Woman with the "Oily Eyes"' concludes with a 'note by the author', presumably Donovan himself, explaining that the story was inspired by traditional folkloric tales of 'ghouls and vampires' from the Pyrenees, Styria, Turkey, Russia and India. Or rather, it seems to conclude here. Ten more pages follow, and these detail 'the story of Annette *from official records*' (Donovan, 1899: 40, 41, emphasis added). Like the formal case studies of late Victorian clinical medicine, this text within the text includes details of the aberrant subject's parentage, childhood, earliest deviant behaviours and manifestations of perversity in adulthood, thereby providing a scientific rationale for Annette's many outrageous behaviours. The effect is disorienting, to say the least. We cannot even tell who is supposed to have written this 'sequel' to the story proper. It is not 'the author', for the appended case study of Annette, proposing science rather than folkloric supernaturalism as an explanation for the vampire-hypnotist, negates the 'author's note'. And the sequel's calm, chilly formality distinguishes it from Haslar's excitable, often disjointed narrative style.

Whatever it is that makes Annette unspeakable – her vampiric sexuality, her hypnotic powers, her very plausibility *within* a scientific framework – the story cannot contain it. It breaks apart in its attempt to conjoin science and supernaturalism. But the story is interesting for precisely that reason. 'John Barrington Cowles' and 'The Woman with the "Oily Eyes"' are not artistic failures but narrative experiments, whose struggles help us understand the late Victorian Gothic's struggles to incorporate the new and strange paradigms of human identity provided by experimental psychology and other sciences.

Notes

1. At least four articles entitled 'The Dangers of Hypnotism' came out in 1890 alone: in *The Lancet* (reprinted in *Science*), *The Saturday Review*, *The Spectator*, and *Westminster Review* (Anon. 1890a, 1890b, 1890c; Thomson, 1890). Whenever possible, I have worked with articles from mainstream rather than medical journals. For articles on hypnotism and criminal hypnosis in the *British Medical Journal* between 1880 and 1893, see Leighton (2006: 206–11).
2. For *Dracula*'s engagement with Victorian writings on mesmerism and hypnotism, see Hughes (2000: 167–77) and Luckhurst (2002: 210–13).
3. For the Gothic's representations of mesmerism earlier in the century, see Willis (2006: 28–62, 113–32).
4. For a full account of mesmerism's reception in Great Britain, see Winter (1998), especially pp. 15–59.
5. If Braid had hoped to take the terms 'mesmerism' and 'animal magnetism' out of circulation, this did not happen. 'Hypnotism', 'mesmerism' and 'animal magnetism' continued to be used almost interchangeably, particularly in popular fiction. In *The Weapons of Mystery*, the narrator describes

himself as 'mesmerized or hypnotized, whatever men may please to call it' (Hocking, 1890: 94).

6. As *The Spectator* reported, post-hypnotic suggestion might even be administered by telephone or letter (Anon., 1890c: 507).

7. Mary Elizabeth Leighton describes this position as an anxious one: physicians and psychologists attempted to consolidate 'professional authority', and deflect criticism of their own work, by denouncing 'charlatans and unqualified professionals' (Leighton, 2006: 211).

8. For the breakdown of masculine rationality in Doyle's fin-de-siècle writings, see Smith (2004: 127–41) and Wynne (2006).

9. Philippe Daryl, quoted in Hillman (1965: 175). Philippe Daryl was a pseudonym for Jean François Paschal Grousset, a science-fiction writer as well as journalist.

10. In Case Twenty-three of *Psychopathia Sexualis* (1886), sexologist Richard von Krafft-Ebing discusses Sergeant Bertrand, a cannibalistic necrophiliac who is compared to a vampire.

References

Anon. (1890a). 'The Dangers of Hypnotism', *The Lancet*, 15 March, 615–16.

——(1890b). 'The Dangers of Hypnotism', *The Saturday Review*, 69, 699–700.

——(1890c). 'The Dangers of Hypnotism', *The Spectator*, 12 April, 507–8.

Bernheim, H. (1973). *Hypnosis and Suggestion in Psychotherapy: A Treatise on the Nature and Uses of Hypnotism* [1884]. Northvale, NJ and London: Jason Aronson Inc.

Binet, A. and C. Féré (1888). 'Hypnotism in Disease and Crime', *The Popular Science Monthly*, 32, 763–9.

Bourne Taylor, Jenny Shuttleworth and Sally Shuttleworth (eds) (1998). *Embodied Selves: An Anthology of Psychological Texts, 1830–1890*. Oxford: Clarendon Press.

Charcot, Jean-Martin (1890). 'Hypnosis and Crime', *Forum*, 9, 159–68.

Crabtree, Adam (1993). *From Mesmer to Freud: Magnetic Sleep and the Roots of Psychological Healing*. New Haven and London: Yale University Press.

Dickens, Charles (1974). *The Mystery of Edwin Drood* [1870], ed. Arthur J. Cox. New York: Penguin Books.

Donovan, Dick (1899). *Tales of Terror*. London: Chatto and Windus.

Doyle, Arthur Conan (1979). *The Best Supernatural Tales of Arthur Conan Doyle*, ed. E. F. Bleiler. New York: Dover Publications.

——(1981). *The Edinburgh Stories of Arthur Conan Doyle*. Edinburgh: Polygon Books.

du Maurier, George (1978). *Trilby* [1894]. London: J. M. Dent.

Gould, George M. (1890). 'The Ethics of Hypnotism', *The Open Court*, 4, 2172–4.

Hillman, Robert G. (1965). 'A Scientific Study of Mystery: The Role of the Medical and Popular Press in the Nancy-Salpêtrière Controversy on Hypnotism', *Bulletin of the History of Medicine*, 39, 163–82.

Hocking, Joseph (1890). *The Weapons of Mystery*. London and Melbourne: Ward, Lock & Co.

Hughes, William (2000). *Beyond Dracula: Bram Stoker's Fiction and its Cultural Context*. New York: St Martin's Press.

Innes, A. Taylor (1890). 'Hypnotism in Relation to Crime and the Medical Faculty', *Contemporary Review*, 58, 555–66.

Leighton, Mary Elizabeth (2006). 'Under the Influence: Crime and Hypnotic Fictions of the *Fin de Siècle*', in *Victorian Literary Mesmerism*, ed Martin Willis and Catherine Wynne. Amsterdam and New York: Rodopi, pp. 203–22.

Luckhurst, Roger (2002). *The Invention of Telepathy, 1870–1901*. Oxford: Oxford University Press.

Marsh, Richard (2004). *The Beetle* [1897], ed. Julian Wolfreys. Peterborough, ON: Broadview Press.

Newbold, William Romaine (1888). 'Posthypnotic and Criminal Suggestion', *The Popular Science Monthly*, 32, 230–41.

Smith, Andrew (2004). *Victorian Demons: Medicine, Masculinity and the Gothic at the Fin-de-Siècle*. New York: Palgrave.

Stoker, Bram (1997). *Dracula* [1897], ed. Nina Auerbach and David J. Skal. New York: W. W. Norton & Company.

Thomson, St Clair (1890). 'The Dangers of Hypnotism', *Westminster Review*, 134, 624–31.

Willis, Martin (2006). *Mesmerists, Monsters, and Machines: Science Fiction and the Cultures of Science in the Nineteenth Century*. Kent, OH : Kent State University Press.

Winter, Alison (1998). *Mesmerized: Powers of Mind in Victorian Britain*. Chicago and London: University of Chicago Press.

Wynne, Catherine (2006). 'Arthur Conan Doyle's Domestic Desires: Mesmerism, Mediumship and *Femmes Fatales*', in *Victorian Literary Mesmerism*, ed. Martin Willis and Catherine Wynne. Amsterdam and New York: Rodopi, pp. 223–43.

Chapter 12

Victorian Medicine and the Gothic
William Hughes

In an influential 1998 study of Bram Stoker's *Dracula* (1897), Robert Mighall argues that, as well as persisting as a flourishing literary genre, Gothic had become a functional component of professional medical writing by the time of the Victorian fin de siècle. The rise of a clinical sexology, which relocated the physical and moral basis of human sexual activity away from religion and into the secular discourses of physiology and psychology, was to underwrite a new era in the cultural expression of monstrosity and deviance. Under this fearful regime of human introspection, the devil as a gross external tempter was finally vanquished by more subtle temptations whose origins were concealed within the contemporary body – by desires, obsessions and fixations nascent within the self, rather than proffered by an already deviant Other. The threat of abstract, punitive damnation in the future was likewise dispersed by the now-perceptible presence of mental and physical disabilities, the origin of which could likewise be traced to the participation of an ancestor in such transparently deviant practices as masturbation, homosexuality, polyandry and incest. As Mighall concludes, this was a discursive process 'that transformed the supernatural into the pathological, and monsters into perverts' (1998: 63). It might be added that its introspective gaze expanded the focus of deviance potentially to *all* human beings, the unseen psychology and the weakened body implicating the virtuous as well as the dissolute and, perhaps more problematically, the practitioner as well as the patient.

If the type of materialist response pioneered by Mighall and his contemporaries provided a refreshing – if not revitalising – correction of the long-standing psychoanalytic domination of Gothic criticism (Baldick and Mighall, 2000; Hughes, 2006), it was not without its own characteristic faults. These faults were perhaps most concentrated in the domination of this branch of Gothic criticism by the study of a single historical period, and its further preoccupation with a specific medical discipline rather than with the broader implications of the medico-chirurgical field as a whole. Medical criticism of the Gothic – quite possibly because of the enhanced topicality of *Dracula* at the time of that novel's centenary in 1997 – became fixated upon the Victorian fin de siècle. The tenor of criticism published around this time – most notably Kelly Hurley's *The Gothic Body* (1996) and Mighall's *A Geography of Victorian Gothic Fiction* (1999) – exemplifies the closing decades of the nineteenth century as a time in which the discourses of medicine, anthropology, imperialism, urban planning and residual religious apologetics collide with popular fiction, producing works which seemingly express both the fearful unease of an era perceived as closing, and the prospect of a future rendered decidedly uncertain.

If *Dracula* is by far the most critically exploited work in this context, Stoker's novel surely has significant compatriots in Arthur Machen's *The Great God Pan* (1894), H. G. Wells's *The Island of Dr Moreau* (1896), and Richard Marsh's *The Beetle* (1897), all of which consider the mutability of the familiar human body, as much as they discern the abiding mystery of the mind in the early years of clinical psychology. These canonical fin-de-siècle works, though, are neither unique nor truly innovative in that tradition which might aptly be termed the medical Gothic. In this respect, acknowledgement is also due to earlier works within the Gothic which successfully and systematically imbricated the medical and the generic. If the rather sparse clinical context exposed by the pre-Victorian *Frankenstein* (1818) enforces that novel's protracted encounter with medical ethics and the philosophy of human development, then other writings more firmly grounded in early and mid-Victorian thought might be considered as specific considerations of contemporary medical practice.

Medicine, in both its orthodox and speculative guises, informs countless Gothic short stories, from the mesmeric revelations of Edgar Allan Poe's 'The Facts in the Case of M. Valdemar' (1845), to the often humorous episodes originally written for *Blackwood's Edinburgh Magazine* by Samuel Warren in the 1830s but reprinted in volume form throughout the Victorian era as *Passages from the Diary of a Late Physician*. These latter are an undoubted influence upon the content of J. Sheridan Le Fanu's medically framed collection *In A Glass Darkly* (1872; see Haslam, 1998: 282, n. 8). More substantial explorations of the discourses, as well as the ethics, of Victorian medicine are to be found in novels originally serialised and in many cases dramatised also. Notable examples include, inevitably, the representation of alienism and medico-jurisprudence in Wilkie Collins's *The Woman in White* (1860), though *Heart and Science* (1883) by the same author is a considerably more disturbing study in speculative vivisection and systematic abuse. This latter work has potentially as much to say about experimental medicine and the human subject as the considerably better known *The Strange Case of Dr Jekyll and Mr Hyde* (1886), by Robert Louis Stevenson.

Historically, Gothic criticism has been inclined to regard the fictionalised human subject as primarily a psychological entity. Though the psychological cannot be ignored in Victorian Gothic, the physiological rightly deserves a critical acknowledgement in proportion to its pervasive presence in the genre. The mind, with its normalities as much as its deviances, cannot function in the Victorian novel without due deference to the containing body that carries and sustains it. The illusory separation of mind and body is a post-Victorian conception, and one with little grounding in the physiological medicine of the nineteenth century, as Collins's Count Fosco makes abundantly clear in *The Woman in White*, 'Mind, they say, rules the world. But what rules the mind? The body' (Collins, 1996b: 617). Fosco, a chemist, is but one of many Gothic villains who intervene into the integrity of the human body, introducing dis-order and dis-ease in tandem with drugs and delusions. The Satanic, theologically informed tempter of the first phase of the genre is in many respects eclipsed in Victorian medical Gothic by the astute but irresponsible secular medical practitioner – variously a doctor, surgeon, chemist, asylum keeper, vivisectionist, or else a more humble institutional assistant – whose function is to make change in the holistic well-being of a subject who usually trusts in the probity of such professional figures.

That professional figure, possibly no longer a tempter but certainly an agent of profound change in the physical, mental and moral well-being of the patient, is likewise a body to be scrutinised. In the place of the attenuated body of Radcliffe's Schedoni or the baleful and dim eye of Maturin's Wanderer – theological transgressors both – the Victorian medical Gothic substitutes the introspective agony of Stoker's moral vivisectionist, John Seward, who perceives himself as the psychological doppelganger of his own degenerate patient (Stoker, 2007: 115), or else the 'fleshless face' (Collins, 1996a: 99) and skeletonised form of Collins's literal experimenter upon the living integument, Nathan Benjulia. 'Sin', as Wilde contended, is commonly in fiction 'a thing which writes itself across a man's face' (Wilde, 1985: 164–5): likewise, in Gothic, the morbid pathology perversely shared by both physician and patient is as commonly manifested in the physiognomy of the latter as it is on the body of the former, and seemingly parallel qualities of mind typify the uneasy psychologies of both.

The casuistry of rhetoric, rather than the mystery of the human body, is what lies at the heart of the discourse of medicine. Medicine as a practice may be concerned with the body, but it is justified, explained and transmitted by way of authorising languages and structures in much the same way as the civil jurisprudence with which it became associated as the nineteenth century progressed. The intricacies of language, the power of testimony and evidence, as Victor Sage asserts in *Horror Fiction in the Protestant Tradition* (1988), link medicine, law and theological apologetics. A medical intervention, in other words, has to be not merely demonstrated but *justified*, its implications and moral dilemmas extracted and duly presented, as it were, to the practitioner's peers – or, else, to the reader who temporarily assumes that ethical mantle. Criminal law, rather than professional ethics, may practically and literally condemn those practitioners who fail to observe its orthodoxies and limitations. The reader, likewise, may exercise empathy or be guided to condemn professional arrogance or inhuman thoughtlessness. It might be added that, in nineteenth-century Gothic fiction, medical practice is seldom undertaken without hesitation, and is almost invariably characterised by a sense of crisis, or even panic, on the part of the practitioner that parallels (and at times exceeds) the contemporary danger faced by the prone and tremulous body of the patient.

J. Sheridan Le Fanu's *In A Glass Darkly* is perhaps the most extreme representation of the interfacing of medicine, law, ethics and apologetics characteristic of Victorian medical Gothic. It purports to be, simultaneously, an edited collection of medical case studies, as well as a description and justification of treatments administered and clinical decisions made therein. In the great tradition of Gothic documentation, of course, Le Fanu's collection fails to achieve the promise of its authoritative structure, for the seemingly confident rhetoric of editor and practitioner are brittle, illusory and at times conflicting. The selection of case studies is, likewise, specious, and their individual outcomes far from satisfactory. Where *Frankenstein*, for example, raises identifiable concerns regarding the ethical responsibility of the individual practitioner in an age of technology, and *The Woman in White* highlights the abuses which may be committed by too crude an application of medicine through law, *In a Glass Darkly* retreats from any polemical encounter with the institutions of medicine. In place of polemic, perversely, the reader finds merely a dilettante appreciation of events which may yet be deemed of profound significance to the patient affected by them. As Le Fanu's fictional – and unnamed – editor informs the reader in the opening prologue which prefaces both 'Green Tea' and the whole volume, these tales have been selected not to inform or instruct, nor even to exemplify, but merely to 'amuse or horrify' a casual or 'lay reader' (Le Fanu, 1993: 6) as they once apparently entertained a fellow professional.

In a Glass Darkly, indeed, oscillates uneasily between the secular empiricism of medical observation and the more relaxed standards of supernatural entertainment. If the presiding physician, Martin Hesselius, is compromised here, it is less because of his medical malpractice – though his incompetence is *not* passed over – and more because of his persistence as a practitioner reminiscent of pre-Victorian professionalism, an exemplar of the departed age of the polymath rather than the contemporary world of the specialist. Hesselius, as represented by the editor in the prologue to 'Green Tea', embodies the ambivalence of an age, just on the margins of living memory, which may be paradoxically typified by its interests in both Enlightenment and Romanticism. Scripted as a convinced reader of the Christian mystic Emmanuel Swedenborg (Le Fanu, 1993: 16) and the author of a treatise on metaphysical medicine (1993: 9), Hesselius is also a physician practising a secular discipline in eighteenth-century London, and an empiricist whose own rhetorical inclinations are as apparently divided as his public persona. As the editor, purportedly writing after the death of Hesselius in the nineteenth century, notes,

> He writes in two distinct characters. He describes what he saw and heard as an intelligent layman might, and when in this style of narrative he had seen the patient either through his own hall-door, to the light of day, or through the gates of darkness to the caverns of the dead, he returns upon the narrative, and in the terms of his art, and with all the force and originality of genius, proceeds to the work of analysis, diagnosis and illustration. (Le Fanu, 1993: 5–6)

Convenient though this strategy may be for a reader not formally trained in the language and conceptuality of institutional medicine, it fails to adequately conceal the tension which fractures the presiding physician's authority. The gaze of the 'intelligent layman' could arguably be considered broadly analogous to the understanding of the non-clinical reader, who necessarily relies upon empirical observation and a common-sense projection from cause to likely effect. The somewhat purple prose of the editor which divides the two voices of Hesselius introduces a more speculative – possibly even a more fanciful – aspect of the German physician which subtly disrupts his status as a medical professional. The (lay) reader, implicitly, undertakes his own process of 'analysis, diagnosis and illustration' from the symptoms so unadornedly presented by Hesselius. He is thus rendered able to distinguish how the physician's practice veers sharply from a medical focus upon the corporeal to a philosophical speculation which freely associates the mind with abstract spirit.

It is this conflation of the secular and the spiritual which permits what might otherwise be a symptom of physiological disorder to become the harbinger of exquisite spiritual torments apparently prompted not by the excessive ingestion of green tea (Le Fanu, 1993: 39) but rather by the patient's inclination to consume pagan philosophy as a late-night intellectual delicacy. If the prompt as to the cause of the patient's delusion – he is haunted by a spectral monkey – is not conveyed strongly enough in the story's title, the character himself, the Reverend Mr Jennings, makes the obvious diagnosis quite plain. Recalling the first day of his visual affliction, he tells Hesselius:

> I tried to comfort myself by repeating again and again the assurance, 'the thing is purely disease, a well known physical affection, as distinctly [*sic*] as small-pox or neuralgia. Doctors are all agreed on that, philosophy demonstrates it. I must not be a fool. I've been sitting up too late, and I daresay my digestion is quite wrong, and with God's help, I shall be all right, and this is but a symptom of nervous dyspepsia.' Did I believe all this? Not one word of it. (1993: 25–6)

Jennings's vain explanations irresistibly recall those proffered by Dickens's dyspeptic arch-materialist Ebenezer Scrooge, almost thirty years earlier, when confronted by the ghost of Jacob Marley. The detailed appearance of Marley's ghost, a thoroughly recognisable figure whose dress and features are recounted at length by the ironic and humorous narrator of *A Christmas Carol* (1843), is in itself not sufficient to convince the curmudgeonly Scrooge of it enjoying any reality beyond the sensorium of his presumably disordered nervous system. The ghost, realising this, confronts the miser with the question 'Why do you doubt your senses?':

> 'Because', said Scrooge, 'a little thing affects them. A slight disorder of the stomach makes them cheats. You may be an undigested bit of beef, a blot of mustard, a crumb of cheese, a fragment of an underdone potato. There's more of gravy than of grave about you, whatever you are!' (Dickens, 1910: 23)

Scrooge's somewhat lame pun, and his envisioning of a physical regime besieged by partially digested morsels of food, mask Dickens's fiction's participation in a contemporary medical debate which saw mental health as intimate to physical vitality. Hesselius, it might be added, is likewise inclined to associate the visual and aural delusion of Jennings's phantom monkey with 'physical, though *subtle* physical, causes' (Le Fanu, 1993: 33, original italics). To a reader versed in Victorian medicine, even at the level of lay interest, the behaviour of these two spectre-smitten dyspeptics would be both familiar and logical.

There is, however, a touch of irony in the involuntary disturbances purportedly suffered by Scrooge and Jennings as a consequence of ingesting substances seemingly so innocuous as a roast dinner or a pot of green tea respectively. The ostensibly medical debate at mid-century, with which Dickens, Le Fanu and Collins also were most likely familiar, was conducted in popular as well as clinical publications, and was acutely concerned with the contemporary abuse of alcohol and opium, supplemented by the unprecedented consumption of *Cannabis Indica* or Indian Hemp – the 'hachisch' favoured by the Indian cult of assassins.[1] This specific concern with intoxicants and narcotics forms part of the wider Victorian debate upon adulteration and contamination – a debate which was to transfer itself from temperance and a concern regarding foodstuffs to a nascent racial (and racist) science of eugenics as the century progressed towards the fin de siècle.[2] The rhetoric of *quality* is crucial here. Indulgence is a dangerous thing, and the mere act of consuming irresponsibly may threaten the self with inner demons as potent as any external tempter.

Jennings, certainly, makes clear the congruence between eating and thinking as inexorable processes the nature of which may imperil the individual. Confessing his woes to Hesselius, in a perverse inversion of his role as a Protestant minister, he fearfully notes that

> as food is taken in softly at the lips, and then brought under the teeth, as the tip of the little finger caught in a mill crank will draw in the hand, and the arm, and the whole body, so the miserable mortal who has been once caught firmly by the end of the finest fibre of his nerve, is drawn in and in, by the enormous machinery of hell, until he is as I am. (1993: 31)

Jennings, of course, is inclined to read his affliction – the grinning phantom ape who distracts him in the clergyman's pulpit and mouths blasphemies in his chambers – as a spiritual punishment for his 'degrading fascination' (1993: 21) with paganism. Perversely, though, it is a doctor whom he consults, not a fellow cleric, and the published account of their interviews – implicitly distilled by the editor from Hesselius's own notes upon the case – stress rather the progressive and indulgent sensualism of the clergyman in his consumption of tea in ever-increasing strength, 'the ordinary black tea' being succeeded by its green equivalent which 'cleared and intensified the power of thought so' (1993: 22). Just as Jennings stresses how 'Paganism is all bound together in essential unity' (1993: 21), religion being intimate to art and to manners as well as concerned with ceremonial practice, 'Green Tea' acutely imbricates the relationship between an irresponsible indulgence in substances and the development of habits of thought and belief which might be termed abnormal by the nineteenth-century philosophy contemporaneous with the editor's milieu.

Habitual indulgence, as the influential British physician William B. Carpenter argues, in an 1874 revision of a study of mental pathology first published in his *Principles of Human Physiology* in 1852, weakens moral as much as mental fibre. Carpenter's sixteenth chapter, entitled 'Of Intoxication and Delirium', makes this abundantly clear. Outlining a perceived '*weakening* [original italics] of Volitional control' which inculcates 'the incoherence of thought, the incongruity of the imaginary creations and the extravagance of the feelings', Carpenter states:

> this weakening is still more obvious, when not merely the quality of the Blood, but the nutrition of the Brain, has been deteriorated by the prolonged action of 'nervine stimulants'; the Will becoming, as it were, paralysed, so that the mental powers are not under its command for any exertion whatever, while even its controlling power over bodily movement may be greatly diminished. (1874: 636–7)

In Victorian medical Gothic, the deviant pathological focus of the text is almost always an individual who indulges in addictive, speculative or sensual practices. These practices, though they may retain recognisable implications appropriate to contemporary discourses of ethics and spirituality, are however characteristically linked by plot and rhetoric to the medical processes of diagnosis, prognosis and – occasionally – cure. If the tempter as an actual, discrete being is for the most part a concept obsolete in Victorian fiction – Marie Corelli's Prince Rimânez in *The Sorrows of Satan* (1895) is a rare exception – the tempted subject, he who fails to resist his own uncontrolled desires, is still scripted as an imbiber of substances external to the body. Irresponsible indulgence and abject addiction are close companions in this rhetoric of the abnegation of the will. There is but a short conceptual hiatus which separates the supposedly innocuous tastes of Le Fanu's Jennings from the more serious drug abuse associated with Dickens's John Jasper in *The Mystery of Edwin Drood* (1870) and Stevenson's Henry Jekyll – the latter, though his habitual indulgence in what is an impure or adulterated drug (Stevenson, 2006: 66), as dissipated a figure as the doppelganger through which he enacts his repressed tendency to violence and excess, the 'original evil' hitherto held in check (2006: 54).

Dangerous if taken but once, such extraneous substances are in themselves inclined to contaminate the body in a subtle form of osmosis, the impure substance leaching into the blood by way of the digestive and circulatory systems, becoming a contaminant which compromises the integrity of the body. If the quality of the blood is thus compromised, the reciprocal relationship which that intensely symbolic fluid bears to the body within which it circulates ensures a further burden of signification upon the contaminated self. Carpenter's remarks regarding the nutrition of the brain are crucial here. A body, whose sanguine integrity has been compromised through ingestion or injection, is inevitably given guidance and volition by an equally contaminated brain. Carpenter is clear regarding this:

> The states of Mind temporarily produced by *intoxicating agents*, – Alcohol, Opium, Hachisch, and the like, – are closely akin to one another in this fundamental character; as they are also to the *delirium* of fevers or other diseases, which is due to the introduction of a morbid matter into the Blood, whereby a zymosis or fermentation of its own materials is produced, which gives it a poisonous action on the brain. (1874: 637, original italics)

This has an obvious implication for vampire narratives, whereby the process of sanguine extraction is also one of injection, the surface of the skin being necessarily ruptured by the bite of the revenant. If the analogy of sexual penetration were not sufficient to render this scenario sufficiently taboo, the matter of contamination – in a pathological as well as a sexual sense – is ever present.

Perhaps most notably, in Stoker's *Dracula* (1897) the vampirised Mina Harker complains that 'There is a poison in my blood, in my soul, which may destroy me, which must destroy me; unless some relief comes to us' (Stoker, 2007: 373). That poison has entered Mina's circulation not simply through the vampire's bite, but more emphatically because she has herself *consumed* his blood (2007: 92). This violent event has conventionally been interpreted as a displaced though obvious representation of oral sexuality.[3] Yet Mina's recollection – upon which this interpretation in part depends – retains a more literal function in its description of what is a bodily process of ingestion as much as a symbolic enactment of forced fellatio. She recalls that the vampire

> opened a vein in his breast. When the blood began to spurt out, he took my hands in one of his, holding them tight, and with the other seized my neck and pressed my mouth to the wound, so that I must either suffocate or swallow some of the – Oh, my God! my God! What have I done? (2007: 331)

This is *not* an unspeakable act, for Mina *does* name the substance she consumes. The focus, indeed, is arguably less the substance than the involuntary swallowing, and the consequences impendent upon ingestion. Blood, here, is a poison, and the rhetoric of *Dracula* arguably draws as much upon the medical discourse of temperance as it does upon sexual symbolism. Charles Mercier, writing on alcohol-induced insanity in an 1890 guide to mental pathology, states, for example:

> It has been shown how the alcohol that is taken into the stomach is absorbed into the blood, and carried by it into actual contact with the nerve elements, upon which it acts as a direct stress of very urgent and powerful character. (1890: 313)

As Mercier contends, 'a prolonged course of drinking extending over years' (1890: 314) renders an individual pathological. If the self is debilitated, so too are other family members brutalised in consequence. Mina, knowing the addictive nature of vampirism, may rightly fear that she now poses such a risk to those closest to her.

As she admits, her relationship to her husband has utterly changed: 'I must touch him or kiss him no more. Oh, that it should be that it is I who am now his worst enemy and whom he may have most cause to fear' (Stoker, 2007: 328). The very essence of the poison is seemingly concentrated upon her lips, or else carried upon her breath – which may ultimately be as 'rank' (2007: 59) as that of the vampire who has inducted her. Volition, it would seem, means nothing here: those who are led involuntarily, unknowingly even, into the thrall of addiction are potentially as dangerous to others as those who embrace vice willingly and wholeheartedly.[4] Her position parallels the working men of London, who are depicted as remarkably thirsty in *Dracula* (2007: 200, 272, 305, 307). Their alcoholism, funded at times by the Count's *largesse*, is congruent to that of the fledgling vampire, and just as likely to damage those closest to them – their wives, children and other dependents.

Those who actively seek to ingest their chosen poison in Victorian Gothic, it might be added, are subject to a similar rhetoric. 'Henry Jekyll's Statement of the Case', effectively the doctor's deathbed confession as well as his clinical commentary upon his chemically induced condition, is suggestive of the shameful and reflective rhetoric which might be adopted by an embattled individual struggling to resist a more conventional craving. Having chosen to remain in the body of Jekyll, and eschew the pleasures of Hyde, the Doctor reflects:

> For two months . . . I was true to my determination; for two months, I led a life of such severity as I had never before attained to, and enjoyed the compensations of an approving conscience. But time began at last to obliterate the freshness of my alarm; the praises of conscience began to grow into a thing of course; I began to be tortured with throes and longings, as of Hyde struggling after freedom; and at last, in an hour of moral weakness, I once again compounded and swallowed the transforming draught. (Stevenson, 2006: 60)

Once the self has become habituated, it may be added, any attempt to disengage the addiction is fraught with risk, for the already compromised self is weak, easily led, full of cravings. As Jekyll confirms, addiction fuels irresponsibility:

> I do not suppose that, when a drunkard reasons with himself upon his vice, he is but once out of five hundred times affected by the dangers that he runs through his brutish, physical insensibility; neither had I, long as I had considered my position, made enough allowance for the complete moral insensibility and insensate readiness to evil, which were the leading characters of Edward Hyde. (2006: 60)

Jekyll's resistance, however well meaning, is futile. Contemporary medical rhetoric again illustrates how fragile abstinence can be:

> If persons whom drink effects in this way are wise, and have sufficient self control, they entirely abjure the use of alcohol after an experience of this kind, and so long as they keep from it they are useful members of society. If, however, they are deficient in determination, and cannot keep from the bottle, they pass their lives going in and out of lunatic asylums. (Mercier, 1890: 316)

Of course, the vast majority of habitual drinkers do *not* shuttle periodically between the saloon-bar and the madhouse, but rather maintain an infectious example to those around them, apparently enjoying – albeit with an unsteady gait – the freedom of the streets. Jekyll, likewise, in the persona of Hyde may riot with his veneer of civility eroded to a greater or lesser extent. Mercier, again, strikingly anticipates Stevenson:

> Let us suppose that the toper has taken distinctly more than is good for him; that instead of the thin film taken off his highest centres, a paring of appreciable thickness has had its function removed by the alcohol. The consequence of this loss is that his conduct becomes more conspicuously defective. He is excited into a quarrel by a provocation which would have no such effect on him in his normal condition, and he conducts the quarrel in an unseemly manner. He uses language which he would never permit himself to use when sober, and displays his passion before strangers and servants in a way that would horrify him at other times. (Mercier, 1890: 317)

Recall here how Hyde, Jekyll's pared-down double, assaults the 'aged and beautiful' Sir Danvers Carew despite the latter's 'pretty manner of politeness' (Stevenson, 2006: 20), how he uses language which Utterson deems 'not fitting' (2006: 15), and how he cries, and makes his craving for his contaminant obvious even to his respectable manservant (2006: 37).

The recurrent failure of medical science in Victorian Gothic is far more, however, than a mere dwelling upon the incompetence of the individual practitioner – who is a fictional construction, after all. Incompetence, ambition, ignorance or sheer dogmatism may provide intrigue and colour at the level of the individual plot, but are arguably reflective also of a pervasive perception of the greater profession. If there is a dominant focus for this perception within Victorian Gothic, then it would seem to be the overwhelmingly materialist – rather than simply secular – attitude to the patient (and indeed to the human species generally) progressively adopted in institutional medicine. The philosophical intimacy between Hesselius and Jennings compromises somewhat the firm demarcation between patient and practitioner which is nominally both enforced and policed through formal rhetoric, the right to authoritatively diagnose and make credible prognosis, and the power to inhibit or prevent movement and communication. His more orthodox fictional counterparts are in contrast more emphatic in their deployment of such restrictive and (for their patients) disempowering practices. The powerlessness of the patient is a consistent feature of medical Gothic. Where the pre-Victorian excesses of Victor Frankenstein recalled the practice of the anatomist, who disturbs only dead bodies and living emotions, later figures in fiction violate the living body, shaping and modifying it to achieve ambitions as radical as they are unethical.

H. G. Wells's Dr Moreau is perhaps the best-known exemplar of this aspect of Victorian medical Gothic. However, an equally compelling example may be found in an earlier novel by Wilkie Collins, the ethical implications of which are arguably as complex as those in Wells's 1896 novella. *Heart and Science* is a narrative of human rather than animal experimentation, leavened with Collins's usual intrigues regarding legitimacy, inheritance and marriage. As its title suggests, the soul has apparently become an irrelevance in late Victorian medical thought, and the heart is likewise merely a physiological pump rather than the repository of emotions or compassion. It is within this context that the vivisectionist, Dr Nathan Benjulia, both observes and fosters the brain disease of the orphaned Carmina Graywell, exposing her to a similar risk of needless death as animals subjected to laboratory experimentation. If vivisection is, as Edward Carpenter and Edward Maitland suggest in a hostile pamphlet on the practice, 'the logical outcome and last expression of the scientific materialism of the day' (1893: 14), then the ultimate extension of that philosophy ought rightly to be the experimental deployment of human subjects. Indulgence and irresponsibility would here again appear to be central components in the demonisation of a certain type of medical practitioner. It is, indeed, the practitioner, rather than medical practice itself, that is at fault, as Carpenter and Maitland assert:

> Knowledge is power. In itself it is neither good nor bad. It all depends in whose hands it is. In the hands of a good man power is good; in the hands of a bad and cruel man power is devilish; in the hands of an idiot it destroys him who uses it. Let us beware lest our knowledge serve only to destroy us. (1893: 16)

Given, however, that Victorian medicine is a collegiate and regulated practice, the implication persists that the greater institution is somehow morally negligent, and this implication is delivered so as to rhetorically manoeuvre the outraged lay reader into implicitly opposing *all* vivisection. If a collegiate academic such as Lewis Carroll could argue that vivisection demoralises and renders its practitioners callous (quoted in Collins, 1996a: 345–6), then a lay contemporary such as the pseudonymous 'Mercy's Voice' might with equal vigour claim that British vivisectors are 'by unserviceable cruelty, rudely robbing the medical profession of its dignity' (Mercy's Voice, 1876: 7). The latter commentator, notably, forecasts that vivisection in medical schools will in some way contribute to 'a lowering of the moral standard of the nation, that must fill our minds with grave apprehensions for its future' (1876: 8). The actions of the few impact upon the morals of the many.

Benjulia experimentally abuses his patient in much the same way as Stoker's Seward stimulates the lunatic R. M. Renfield to satisfy his own 'scientific' curiosity (Hughes, 2007) in *Dracula*. However, the sense of outrage in *Heart and Science* is, crucially, magnified on account of the gendered nature of medical practice, and the threat posed by the *male* doctor to the physically prone or legally powerless woman placed under his care (Depledge, 2007). Though the implications of the sexual interference which may occur as an abuse of such power seldom attain those associated with the pseudo-medical control which Svengali exercises over his mesmerised subject in George du Maurier's *Trilby* (1894), sexuality remains an understated though present context for much of the nineteenth century. It is perhaps exposed to its greatest extent not in *Dracula* but in Machen's *The Great God Pan*, where Dr Raymond's practical brain surgery – 'a slight lesion in the grey matter . . . a trifling rearrangement of certain cells' (Machen, 2005: 184) – temporarily lifts the supposed veil between the material and transcendent worlds. There is a suggestion of vivisection here, again, to be sure. Raymond, when reproached with the guilt he might feel should the operation fail (or, rather, should it succeed in excess of his expectations), contends, casually:

No, I think not, even if the worst happened. As you know, I rescued Mary from the gutter, and from almost certain starvation, when she was a child; I think her life is mine, to use as I see fit. (2005: 186)

But if Raymond is easy with regard to the ethical utility of the 'purchased' human body in experimental surgery, he is utterly irresponsible in his failure to face the implications of what might happen should his subject indeed *see* the god Pan during a successful operation. Given the lascivious reputation the Goat-Foot God enjoyed in classical art and letters, Raymond seems negligent in his actions to say the least. Rendered 'a hopeless idiot' (2005: 189–90) during her five minutes of artificially induced unconsciousness, and thus not able to even communicate what she has seen, Mary is also physiologically compromised – implicitly by the horny Pan – and returns pregnant to the doctor who, *in loco parentis*, ought rightly to have cared for her physical well-being and moral probity. Though the remainder of the story focuses upon the disastrous events which accompany any contact with Mary's daughter, Helen, an intimate of Pan and of the satyrs, its conclusion returns the narrative to Raymond, his patient and the issues of egotism, ethics and responsibility. Raymond, finally, is forced to admit that 'It was an ill work I did that night' (2005: 232), and his conclusions are advanced with a somewhat scriptural chastening of tone. Admitting that he 'broke open the door of the house of life, without knowing or caring what might pass forth or enter in', Raymond concludes that 'when the house of life is thus thrown open, there may enter in that for which we have no name, and human flesh may become the veil of a horror one dare not express' (2005: 232).[5] Science, in other words, may reveal phenomena, but can still lack the conceptual mechanisms necessary to comprehend or control such things. Medicine, likewise, in seeking to understand the broader field of humanity, may imperil the intellect of the practitioner as much as it threatens the body of the patient. The desires of speculative science, and the ambitions of the practitioner hungry for fame or for power, are seldom successfully negotiated against the dangers prototypically faced by the fictional patient.

Medicine is certainly analogous to broader science in Gothic fiction – though it is not utterly congruent. The doctor and the mad scientist may map over each other, but the former enjoys a more substantial intimacy with the human body than the latter could ever hope to attain. If the scientist prototypically considers the general and the generic, the doctor's domain is surely that of the individual – the patient. It is when the two epistemological drives come to combine in the practice of a single individual – when the doctor treats his patient not for his or her own disorder but as the facility from which a generalisation might be made or a theory tested – that the characteristic difficulties arise that dissociate the doctor from his patient. Ultimately, in Gothic, the medical practitioner is a figure who inculcates or accelerates rather than curing disease, and he is thus a source of suspicion, a distortion of the culturally idealised image of altruistic professionalism. In Gothic, if a doctor is theoretically inclined, he is also, apparently, egotistical; if altruistic, he may as equally be incompetent. His access to the body is privileged, but this privilege as often as not depends upon the verification of the law as much as it does upon the ability or trustworthiness of the fictional practitioner. It is often his title as a doctor that facilitates his practice, rather than his demonstrable ability. In Victorian Gothic, the medical practitioner is as compromised and as problematic as the subject he purports to diagnose and cure. The devil is now in the detail of the doctor's practice: he no longer walks among us.

Notes

1. See, for example, Anon. (1858), Anon. (1885), The Dwarf of Blood (1888).
2. See Anon. (1898: col. 2).
3. See, for example, Sage (1988: 180).
4. This, certainly, would seem to be the message of Stoker's 1875 Gothic temperance serial narrative, 'The Primrose Path', where an Irish carpenter is easily led from drink into selfish irresponsibility and finally to murder and suicide (Stoker, 1999: 52, 82–3, 104).
5. The allusion to Luke 8, vv. 26–39 should be obvious here, though the Bible admits to no human agency in demonic possession.

References

Anon. (1858). 'Law and Police Intelligence', *The Englishwoman's Review and Home Newspaper*, issue 50 (26 June), 704.
Anon. (1885). 'How we Dissipate Now', *Funny Folks*, issue 572 (14 November), 365.
Anon. (1898). 'Drink and Degradation', *Wings* 16/10 (1 October), 139.
Baldick, Chris, and Robert Mighall (2000). 'Gothic Criticism', in *A Companion to the Gothic*, ed. David Punter. Oxford: Blackwell Publishing, pp. 209–28.
Carpenter, Edward and Edward Maitland (1893). *Vivisection*. London: Wm Reeves.
Carpenter, William B. (1874). *Principles of Mental Physiology, with their Applications to the Training and Discipline of the Mind, and the Study of its Morbid Conditions*. London: Henry S. King & Co.
Collins, Wilkie (1996a). *Heart and Science: A Story of the Present Time* [1883]. Peterborough, ON: Broadview Press.
——(1996b). *The Woman in White* [1860]. Oxford: Oxford University Press.

Depledge, Greta (2007). '*Heart and Science* and Vivisection's Threat to Women', in *Wilkie Collins: Interdisciplinary Essays*, ed. Andrew Mangham. Newcastle: Cambridge Scholars Publishing, pp. 149–63.

Dickens, Charles (1910), *A Christmas Carol* [1843], in *The Christmas Books*. London: Cassell, pp. 11–86.

Dwarf of Blood, The [pseud.] (1888). 'Calcutta on the Job', *The Sporting Times*, Issue 1,270, 21 January, p. 5.

Haslam, Richard (1998). 'Joseph Sheridan Le Fanu and the Fantastic Semantics of Ghost-Colonial Ireland', in *That Other World*, ed. Bruce Stewart. Gerrards Cross: Colin Smyth, vol. 1, pp. 268–86.

Hughes, William (2006). 'Gothic Criticism: A Survey, 1764–2004', in *Teaching the Gothic*, ed. Anna Powell and Andrew Smith. Basingstoke: Palgrave, pp. 10–28.

——(2007). 'Habituation and Incarceration: Mental Physiology and Asylum Abuse in *The Woman in White* and *Dracula*', in *Wilkie Collins: Interdisciplinary Essays*, ed. Andrew Mangham. Newcastle: Cambridge Scholars Publishing, pp. 136–48.

Hurley, Kelly (1996). *The Gothic Body: Sexuality, Materialism, and Degeneration at the Fin de Siècle*. Cambridge: Cambridge University Press.

Le Fanu, J. Sheridan (1993). 'Green Tea' [1869], in *In A Glass Darkly* [1872], ed. Robert Tracy. Oxford: Oxford University Press, pp. 5–40.

Machen, Arthur (2005). *The Great God Pan* [1894], in *Late Victorian Gothic Tales*, ed. Roger Luckhurst. Oxford: Oxford University Press, pp. 183–233.

Mercier, Charles (1890). *Sanity and Insanity*. London: Walter Scott.

Mercy's Voice [pseud.] (1876). *Vivisection*. Toronto: Copp, Clark & Co.

Mighall, Robert (1998). 'Sex, History and the Vampire', in *Bram Stoker, History, Psychoanalysis and the Gothic*, ed. William Hughes and Andrew Smith. Basingstoke: Macmillan, pp. 62–77.

——(1999). *A Geography of Victorian Gothic Fiction: Mapping History's Nightmares*. Oxford: Oxford University Press.

Sage, Victor (1988). *Horror Fiction in the Protestant Tradition*. Basingstoke: Macmillan.

Stevenson, Robert Louis (2006). *The Strange Case of Dr Jekyll and Mr Hyde* [1886] *and Other Tales*. Oxford: Oxford University Press, pp. 1–66.

Stoker, Bram (1999). *The Primrose Path* [1875]. Westcliff-on-Sea: Desert Island Books.

——(2007). *Dracula* [1897]. Bath: Artswork Books.

Wilde, Oscar (1985). *The Picture of Dorian Gray* [1890]. Harmondsworth: Penguin.

Chapter 13

Imperial Gothic
Patrick Brantlinger

'Romance is the cry of the time', novelist Hall Caine declared in 1890 (Caine, 1979: 480). Reacting against fictional realism and its epistemological twin, scientific materialism, many late Victorian writers turned to romanticism and, more specifically, to the themes and literary conventions of Gothic romances. The advocates of romance paradoxically cite as a key reason for its revival its disappearance from the modern world. H. Rider Haggard, for example, lamented the vanishing of 'the ancient mystery of Africa'. Where, he wondered, 'will the romance writers of future generations find a safe and secret place, unknown to the pestilent accuracy of the geographer, in which to lay their plots?' (quoted in Etherington, 1984: 66). The protagonists in Joseph Conrad's stories and novels, though they typically experience disillusionment, are seekers of adventure and romance, which Conrad also thought were rapidly disappearing. And in Sir Arthur Conan Doyle's *The Lost World* (1911), a newspaper editor tells one of the heroes, 'the big blank spaces in the map are all being filled in, and there's no room for romance anywhere' (Doyle, 1912: 13). This chapter explores how an understanding of the romance helps contextualize the popular appeal of the imperial Gothic in the period.

The romance seemingly represents an adventure into the unknown, 'As the visible world is measured, mapped, tested, weighed,' wrote Andrew Lang in 1905, 'we seem to hope more and more that a world of invisible romance may not be far from us' (Lang, 1970: 279). Lang makes this remark in an essay entitled 'The Supernatural in Fiction', which connects not only to the romance revival but also to late Victorian interest in the occult, in which many novelists, artists and intellectuals took a keen interest (Killeen, 2009: 124–59; Oppenheim, 1985). Doyle, for example, although the creator of that highly rational detective Sherlock Holmes, became a convert to Spiritualism and, after World War I, wrote a history of that alternative religion. The uncanny workings of the supernatural have always been one of the hallmarks of Gothic fiction. Many late Victorian adventure tales with imperial themes and settings also contain hints, and sometimes much more than hints, of the supernatural, as in Haggard's 1887 bestseller *She* or in Rudyard Kipling's 1890 tale 'The Mark of the Beast', in which the protagonist is turned into a werewolf. Such stories make up the literary sub-genre of imperial Gothic fiction.[1]

While the sub-genre includes Gothicised adventure stories set in unfamiliar, faraway places, it also includes stories in which characters, creatures or uncanny objects from those faraway places invade Britain, threatening domestic peace and harmony, as in Bram Stoker's *Dracula* (1897). Although Stoker's Transylvanian Count does not come from some distant part of the British Empire, he is himself an imperialist who is descended from a long line of bloodthirsty conquerors, back to Attila the Hun. Published in the same year as *Dracula*, and at first an even more popular horror story, Richard Marsh's *The Beetle* also involves an alien intruder, this time from Egypt. The title character, a shapeshifter who is both a hideous human and a living scarab, comes to England seeking fresh victims as human sacrifices for the secret cult of Isis to which he – or she – belongs. The Beetle, notes Glennis Byron, 'is both human and animal, animal and insect, male and female, and, perhaps most shockingly of all, heterosexual and homosexual' (Byron, 2000: 140).

Marsh's 'diabolical Asiatic' is an even more extreme version than the vampire of what Kelly Hurley, in her study of the Gothic body, calls 'the abhuman' (1996: 3–20). The Beetle is polymorphously perverse with no clear sexual preference, although it is especially keen on kidnapping a young Englishwoman to sacrifice to Isis. When it assaults its victims, both female and male, in its scarab form, the attacks seem to be some horrific type of rape. '*The Beetle* inverts the issue of colonization by pre-senting the East/West conflict in terms of Oriental aggression', Hurley claims. She adds that it describes

> an Oriental incursion, with white slavery and genocide as its end, into the very heart of London; and [it] distorts the issue further by presenting Egypt as a site not of relatively stable English rule during Lord Cromer's occupation, but of Oriental misrule, under which innocent white tourists are kidnapped, tortured, and murdered with impunity. (1996: 127–8)

Hurley's point about 'relatively stable English rule' suggests that impe-rial Gothic fiction, though it deals with innumerable threats to the power and glory of the British Empire, at a time when that Empire was the largest and most powerful the world had ever known, expresses anxieties about decline and fall that always seem to haunt political, military and economic success.

There is no ambiguity concerning the sexuality and sexual preference of Haggard's femme fatale Ayesha or She-Who-Must-Be-Obeyed. The heroine of *She* threatens to come to Britain and conquer its empire by usurping the throne from that most powerful woman in the world, Queen Victoria. Haggard's bewitching femme fatale is gorgeous rather than abhuman, but nevertheless monstrous for several reasons. She is a necrophiliac, in love with the embalmed corpse of the man she murdered two thousand years ago. She is also a tyrant, ruling over the inferior race of the Amahaggers, who are themselves cannibals, much inferior to the denizens of the lost civilization of Kôr. Nearly immortal, She appears to Leo Vincey and Horace Holly to wear the wrappings of a mummy, although she easily doffs these wrappings in a striptease that causes Holly to fall head over heels for her. Haggard, Stoker and Doyle, moreover, all contributed to the craze for Gothic tales in which Egyptian mummies come to life and threaten murder and mayhem.[2]

Major themes of imperial Gothic fiction include going native – Mr Kurtz's 'infernal' fate in Conrad's *Heart of Darkness* (1899), for instance; insanity, which is how going native is often interpreted; reverse invasion or colonisation, as in *Dracula* (the Count travels to London and threatens to vampirise all of England); racial, civilisational or psychological degeneration, as in both *Heart of Darkness* and *Dracula* and also in Robert Louis Stevenson's *Dr Jekyll and Mr Hyde* (1886); 'sexual anarchy,' as Elaine Showalter (1990) calls it, or anxieties about both feminism and homosexuality, as in *She* and *The Beetle*; and the possible reality of hauntings and other occult phenomena, as in mummy stories, *Jekyll and Hyde* or *Dracula*. Besides evocations of the uncanny and supernatural, imperial Gothic tales utilise a number of conventions drawn from older Gothic romances such as Matthew Lewis's *The Monk* (1796) and Mary Shelley's *Frankenstein* (1818, revised 1831). These conventions include editorial frames and fragmented narratives (*Dracula* and *Heart of Darkness*, among others); accounts of nightmares, sometimes suggesting that the story as a whole is a nightmare; ghostly or demonic apparitions; the diabolical twin or doppelganger, most famously in *Jekyll and Hyde*; and the rendering of characters and actions in Manichaean terms, treating good and evil as warring, irreconcilable absolutes.

Like the emergence of other literary genres and sub-genres, imperial Gothic was culturally overdetermined. Its authors were reacting to many factors besides what they saw as the exhaustion of fictional realism and, with the exploration and mapping of the last mysterious places on the planet, the diminishing chances for adventure. Among those factors were Darwinism and other scientific discoveries such as entropy or the Second Law of Thermodynamics; the lure of alternative religions, including Spiritualism, occultism and Buddhism, and Theosophy. The form also addressed the threat posed by new rivals to British imperial hegemony, particularly the United States and a recently unified Germany, unrest in Ireland, and the early stirrings of nationalism in India and other parts of the Empire. In addition the imperial Gothic explored the emergence of the 'New Woman' and artistic and literary 'decadence', as well as new inventions such as telegraphy, the phonograph, the telephone, radio and motion pictures, all of which appeared to have uncanny properties and effects (Menke, 2008; Wicke, 1992).

Besides the Gothic romances that appeared between the 1790s and 1830s, aspects of many Victorian novels – Dickens's *Bleak House* (1853) for example, or *The Mystery of Edwin Drood* (1870) – have Gothic features. A central figure in the production of Victorian Gothic fiction was Dickens's friend, William Harrison Ainsworth (Killeen, 2009: 34–52). The forerunners of late Victorian and Edwardian imperial Gothic fiction include Charlotte Brontë's *Jane Eyre* (1847), Wilkie Collins's *The Moonstone* (1868) and Edward Bulwer-Lytton's *The Coming Race* (1871). In Brontë's tale, both Mr Rochester and his mad wife Bertha Mason are threatening intruders from the colonies and it is noteworthy that Rochester has made his fortune through slavery. Bertha in particular is portrayed in Gothic terms, as an apparition haunting Thornfield Hall. *The Moonstone*, too, concerns a threat from abroad, this time in the form of a fabulous but cursed diamond from India. And *The Coming Race* not only anticipates the flourishing of imperial Gothic fiction starting in the 1880s, but also the 'scientific romances' of H. G. Wells, which themselves are versions of imperial Gothic. Bulwer-Lytton's fantasy deals with an underground race of monsters, the Vril-ya, that may supplant humanity in the Darwinian 'struggle for survival'.

In the 1880s, George Saintsbury, Andrew Lang, Haggard and Stevenson all contended that the literary genre of the romance was superior to the fictional realism that had dominated the first four decades of the Victorian era. They tended to identify the romance with imperial adventure fiction, which might or might not have Gothic overtones – Robert Ballantyne's *The Coral Island* (1858), for example, or Stevenson's *Treasure Island* (1883), which Haggard sought to outdo in writing *King Solomon's Mines* (1886). Though the plucky English lads in Ballantyne's bestseller confront cannibals and pirates, it is not, in contrast to the tales by Stevenson and Haggard, noticeably Gothic. In any event, the advocates of romance saw it as simultaneously more basic, more primitive or childlike, and more universal than fictional realism. Saintsbury defined 'the pure romance of adventure' as 'the earliest form of writing', related to heroic mythology and the epic (1979: 396). The realist novel deals with passing manners and characters; the romance deals with universal 'passions and actions'. 'For the romance is of its nature eternal and preliminary to the novel', Saintsbury contends; 'The novel is of its nature transitory and is parasitic on the romance' (1979: 397).[3] So, too, in 'Realism and Romance', Lang declared that, while he appreciated good realistic novels, 'the natural man within me, the survival of some blue-painted Briton or of some gipsy', is at least 'equally pleased with a *true* Zulu love story', such as those Haggard had begun to write.[4] Lang added that 'the advantage of our mixed condition, civilized at top with the old barbarian under our clothes, is just this, that we can enjoy all sorts of things' (1887: 689–90).

Developing ideas that he found in Edward Burnett Tylor's *Primitive Culture* (1872), Lang calls romances '"savage survivals", but so is the whole poetic way of regarding Nature' (1887: 690). Tylor defined 'survivals' as vestiges of past beliefs and customs that continued to influence present beliefs and customs. Superstitions about ghosts and the occult are examples. Tylor also held that poetry in general was a holdover from primitive times, and Lang argued that the romance was more poetic as well as more primitive (and therefore more basic) than fictional realism. He agreed with Saintsbury that it was the earliest and hence most universal form of storytelling, evident in myths, legends, epics and the fairy tales he collected and published.

Lang's comments express several of the themes and motifs in the late-century revival of romance writing and, more specifically, of imperial Gothic fiction. The idea that his civilised self conceals an 'old barbarian' is a version of the doppelganger motif evident in many late Victorian romances, including *Jekyll and Hyde*. Although Lang views his 'barbarian' inner self in positive terms, since it allows him to 'enjoy all sorts of things', the surfacing of buried, primitive selves in Gothic romances is usually a sign of psychological and physical atavism, of criminality, and of racial degeneration. Often it is also, as in *Jekyll and Hyde*, at least metaphorically demonic or diabolical.

In 'A Gossip on Romance' (1882), Stevenson defines romance as 'the poetry of circumstance' as opposed to character and manners (Stevenson, 1999b: 54). He adds that:

> the great creative writer shows us the realisation and the apotheosis of the day-dreams of common men. His stories may be nourished with the realities of life, but their true mark is to satisfy the nameless longings of the reader, and to obey the ideal laws of the day-dream. (1999b: 56)

And he proceeds to say that 'true romantic art . . . makes a romance of all things' (1999b: 60). In 'A Humble Remonstrance', Stevenson's response to Henry James's 'The Art of Fiction' (1884), he like Lang associates romance-writing with primitive storytelling: 'The real art that dealt with life directly was that of the first men who told their stories round the savage camp-fire' (Stevenson, 1999b: 85). And also like Lang, who had declared that the aim of the adventure tale was to appeal to 'the Eternal Boy' in its readers, Stevenson held that 'the novel of adventure' was more basic and universal than Jamesian realism. James had stated that he could not properly judge *Treasure Island* because, although he 'had been a child', he had 'never been on a quest for buried treasure'. Stevenson responded to this remark by declaring that what it really shows is that James had never been a child:

> There never was a child (unless Master James) but has hunted gold, and been a pirate, and a military commander, and a bandit of the mountains; but has fought, and suffered shipwreck and prison, and imbrued its little hands in gore, and gallantly retrieved the lost battle, and triumphantly protected innocence and beauty. (1999b: 86)

For the adventure romance, 'danger' and action are what matter, not 'character', which 'to the boy is a sealed book; for him, a pirate is a beard, a pair of wide trousers and a liberal complement of pistols' (1999b: 87).

Jekyll and Hyde is set in London, and hence seemingly does not fit the category of imperial Gothic fiction, as exemplified by *Treasure Island* or by Haggard's adventure tales set in southern Africa, Egypt, Mexico and elsewhere. Yet Hyde is an atavistic, apelike figure whose abhuman features suggest the stereotype of the Irish hooligan. Stevenson was well aware of Fenianism, a close-to-home rebellion against Britain's imperial domination of Ireland. David Punter notes that 'Hyde's behaviour is an urban version of "going native"' (1980: 241), attributing his depiction to anxieties about imperial and racial degeneration. *Jekyll and Hyde* can thus be read as a version of the imperial Gothic motif of reverse invasion, in which something or someone alien and monstrous threatens to wreak havoc in the very heart of London.

Besides *Jekyll and Hyde*, Stevenson makes use of Gothic conventions – the recounting of nightmares, for example – in many of his other stories. 'Thrawn Janet' (1881) deals with witchcraft, and 'Markheim' (1885) with a demonic doppelganger. At the outset of *Treasure Island*, Jim Hawkins does the bidding of the mysterious 'captain' by keeping a lookout for 'the seafaring man with one leg', who then 'haunted my dreams', a phrase that evokes the Gothic figures of ghosts and nightmares:

> On stormy nights, when the wind shook the four corners of the house, and
> the surf roared along the cove and up the cliffs, I would see him in a thousand
> forms, and with a thousand diabolical expressions. Now the leg would be cut
> off at the knee, now at the hip; now he was a monstrous kind of a creature
> who had never had but the one leg, and that in the middle of his body. To
> see him leap and run and pursue me over hedge and ditch was the worst of
> nightmares. (Stevenson, 1981: 5)

Treasure Island has some of the characteristics of imperial Gothic
fiction, but it more obviously fits into the burgeoning category of boys'
adventure stories, harking back to Captain Frederick Marryat's mid-
shipman novels and, even farther, to Daniel Defoe's *Robinson Crusoe*
(1719). Such fiction typically features youthful heroes doing battle
against a wide range of foreign enemies, from the French at the time of
the Napoleonic Wars to ferocious cannibals during the exploration of
Central Africa.

As a powerful expression of the doppelganger theme, *Jekyll and
Hyde* merits comparison with older versions, including such classics of
early Gothic fiction as *Frankenstein* and James Hogg's *Confessions of
a Justified Sinner* (1824). It also merits comparison to Stevenson's later
doppelganger romance, *The Master of Ballantrae* (1889). Written while
Stevenson was recuperating in the South Seas, it is a tale about 'fraternal enemies' (Stevenson, 1983: xxxiv), similar to Sir Walter Scott's
historical romances. Set mainly in Scotland during and after the Battle
of Culloden in 1745, some of its events take place in France, India and
North America. After Prince Charles lands in Scotland, the noble Durie
family has to decide whether to fight for him or to remain loyal to King
George. With a coin toss, one of the Durie brothers is sent to do battle
for the Prince, while the other supports the King. The first brother, the
Master of Ballantrae, is believed slain at Culloden. But he survives and
makes his way into exile in France. This is the Master's first narrow
escape from death. Even before Culloden, the Master has earned a reputation for diabolical behavior, while his stay-at-home brother Henry is
a bit dull and conventional. When the Master returns to Scotland, the
differences and quarrels between the two brothers magnify, leading to a
duel in which Henry apparently kills the Master. But when Henry leaves
what he thinks is his brother's corpse to seek help, the Master again
escapes death and, though gravely wounded, is taken away by a gang of
smugglers. After learning that his brother has survived the duel, Henry
declares: 'nothing can kill that man. He is not mortal. He is bound upon
my back to all eternity' (1983: 135).

After he recovers, the Master travels to India, where he acquires a
sinister follower, Secundra Dass, who is described by the main narrator,

land steward Ephraim Mackellar, as 'the black man' and a 'black deil' (1983: 158, 241). When he first sees Dass, Mackellar tells the Master: 'This time you have brought the black dog visibly upon your neck', suggesting that the Master is in league with the devil (1983: 153). Mackellar also says that the Master himself 'had all the gravity and something of the splendour of Satan in the "Paradise Lost"' (1983: 159). And he calls the Master a 'bloodsucker' who acts against Henry's feelings and interests from 'devilish malice' (1983: 75).

To escape the Master's 'devilish malice', Henry and his family migrate to New York. The Master soon follows them, however, along with Mackellar and Secundra Dass. There, the Master and Dass, with a gang of backcountry roughs, go in search of the treasure he had previously buried in the forest. Believing the roughs will kill him after he has led them to the treasure, the Master, with Dass's help, feigns death, and Dass buries him alive. Pursuing the Master, Henry and Mackellar come upon the grave where Dass digs him up and attempts to revive him. The Master begins to show signs of life and opens his eyes. The shock of witnessing what appears to be his third miraculous or demonic escape from death kills Henry. But Dass has been too late; the Master also dies.

The motif of the doppelganger and the many diabolical metaphors, reinforced by the Master's seemingly miraculous escapes from death, indicate the Gothic nature of Stevenson's story of 'fraternal enemies'. Its settings in Scotland, India, and colonial New York connect it to British imperialism. And the sinister Secundra Dass represents an alien invasion from the imperial periphery into the metropole (in this case, Scotland). As the Master is weasling his way into Henry's son's confidence, Mackellar calls him 'a diabolical Aeneas', adding to the imperial resonance of the story. The Master slyly tells Alexander tales of his adventures in 'the ancient cities' of India and elsewhere. Mackellar speculates, as if commenting on boys' adventure fiction like *Treasure Island*: 'what an empire might be so founded, little by little, in the mind of any boy, stood obviously clear to me' (1983: 164).

While in the South Seas, Stevenson wrote a number of stories in a realist vein that foreshadow Joseph Conrad's critique of imperialism in *Heart of Darkness*, *Lord Jim* (1900), and some of Conrad's other novels and short stories. *Heart of Darkness* is undoubtedly the masterpiece both of imperial Gothic fiction and of the realist critique of turn-of-the-century European imperialism. Stevenson also almost has it both ways at once in some of his South Sea stories, including 'The Beach of Falesá' (1892), *The Wrecker* (1892) and *Ebb-Tide* (1894). He also wrote a few Gothicised stories that feature South Seas characters, similar to some of Rudyard Kipling's stories featuring Indian characters. Thus, Stevenson's

'The Bottle Imp' (1891) has several Gothic characteristics including the story of how Keawe, the Hawaiian protagonist, comes into the possession of a magic bottle, similar to Aladdin's lamp in *The Arabian Nights*. The demon inside the bottle grants the owner's wishes, but the owner must sell the bottle for less than he paid for it; if he dies while still owning it, his soul will go to hell. The man, presumably an American or European, who sells it to Keawe, explains:

> Long ago, when the devil brought it first upon earth, it was extremely expensive, and was sold first of all to Prester John for many millions of dollars; but it cannot be sold at all, unless sold at a loss. If you sell it for as much as you paid for it, back it comes to you again like a homing pigeon. (Stevenson, 1999a: 75)

The imp grants several of Keawe's wishes, though he and his new wife have trouble trying to sell the bottle. They finally sell it to a drunken sailor in Tahiti, and thus regain their happiness. Keawe and his wife may be innocent of the ways of the world, but Stevenson does not attribute the magic of the bottle to Hawaiian superstitions: the devil is plainly the one Christians of all races believe in. In contrast, in 'The Beach of Falesá', the villain Case has spooked the natives by stringing up wind harps and fake demons in the jungle. The protagonist Wiltshire dynamites Case's fakery and, in a final tussle, kills Case. The natives are superstitious – there are no demons; but the Europeans, most of them anyway, are evil.

Imperial Gothic fiction emerged in late Victorian culture together with other sub-genres of popular romantic narrative, including detective stories and science fiction. Many of Doyle's Sherlock Holmes tales are simultaneously detective stories and imperial Gothic romances. And Wells's 'scientific romances', as he called them, including *The Time Machine* (1895), *The Island of Doctor Moreau* (1896), and *The War of the Worlds* (1898) are also examples of imperial Gothic fiction. With its frequent themes of alien invasions and the exploration of other worlds, science fiction has continued to share many of the properties of imperial Gothic romance.

In several of Holmes's 'adventures', characters have returned from the far reaches of the Empire bringing trouble and sometimes murder with them. Dr Watson himself was wounded in warfare in Afghanistan. In 'The Five Orange Pips' (1891), a letter arrives from Pondicherry, India, containing five orange pips and the letters K.K.K. The recipient of the letter is murdered several weeks later. The initials refer to the Ku Klux Klan; the recipient had been a plantation owner and had fought for the south in the American Civil War. In 'The Speckled Band' (1892), Dr

Grimsby Roylett has returned from India with a poisonous snake that
he uses as a murder weapon. And in 'The Boscombe Valley Mystery'
(1891), John Turner has made a fortune through highway robbery in
Australia, where he was known as 'Black Jack of Ballarat'.

There are many ties to the Empire and to other places around the
world in the mysteries that the highly cosmopolitan Holmes solves. The
most significant of the imperial ties occur in *The Sign of Four* (1890). In
that novella, Holmes is on the trail of 'the great Agra treasure', which
has come into the possession of the Sholto brothers. After Dr Watson
explains matters to them, Mrs Forrester declares:

> 'It is a romance! . . . An injured lady, half a million in treasure, a black can-
> nibal, and a wooden-legged ruffian. They take the place of the conventional
> dragon or wicked earl.'
> 'And two knight-errants to the rescue', added Miss Morstan, with a bright
> glance at me. (Doyle, 1993: 70–1)

Both of the Sholto brothers live like nabobs in their separate houses,
waited on by Indian servants, in the suburbs of London. Their deceased
father stole the treasure from the convict Jonathan Small and his three
Sikh partners (the four original thieves) and brought it from India to
England. The Gothic trappings of the story include Watson's depictions
of London at night, with crowds flitting 'eerie and ghost-like' along the
streets (1993: 19), and of the suburbs, 'the monster tentacles which the
giant city was throwing out into the country' (1993: 21). At Pondicherry
Lodge, peering through a keyhole at the corpse of Bartholomew Sholto,
Holmes remarks, 'There is something devilish in this, Watson' (1993:
37). And Holmes stresses the imperial context of the story when he tells
Watson that the strange 'ally' of the man with the wooden leg 'breaks
fresh ground in the annals of crime in this country, – though parallel cases suggest themselves from India, and . . . Senegambia"' (1993:
41).

The 'ally' is the ferocious Andaman Islander Tonga, who has slain
Bartholomew Sholto with a poison dart. Holmes later reads to Watson
a passage from a 'gazeteer' dealing with the Andaman Islanders: they
are:

> fierce, morose, and intractable, though capable of forming most devoted
> friendships when their confidence has once been gained. . . . They are natu-
> rally hideous, having large, misshapen heads, small, fierce eyes, and distorted
> features . . .They have always been a terror to shipwrecked crews, braining
> the survivors with their stone-headed clubs, or shooting them with their poi-
> soned arrows. These massacres are invariably concluded by a cannibal feast.
> (1993: 68–9)

In pursuit of Jonathan Small and his 'ally' on the Thames, Watson describes Tonga as a Gothic monstrosity:

> Never have I seen features so deeply marked with all bestiality and cruelty. His small eyes glowed and burned with a somber light, and his thick lips were writhed back from his teeth, which grinned and chattered at us with a half animal fury. (1993: 86–7)

Tonga is an 'unhallowed dwarf with [a] hideous face' (1993: 86–7). Holmes and Watson shoot him before he can blow a poison dart at them. After his capture, Jonathan Small says:

> I never raised hand against Mr. Sholto. It was that little hell-hound Tonga who shot one of his cursed darts into him . . . I welted the little devil with the slack end of the rope for it, but it was done . . . (1993: 89)

Small's account of how he and his three Sikh accomplices came by the Agra treasure deals with that most Gothic of imperial catastrophes, 'the great mutiny' or Indian Rebellion of 1857–8: 'One month India lay as still and peaceful, to all appearance', Small says, 'as Surrey or Kent; the next there were two hundred thousand black devils let loose, and the country was a perfect hell' (1993: 97–8). After the mutineers kill Small's fellow employee Dawson and his wife and and set the plantation owner's bungalow on fire, Small watches: 'the flames beginning to burst through the roof . . . From where I stood I could see hundreds of the black fiends, with their red coats still on their backs, dancing and howling round the burning house' (1993: 98). In these and other passages, Small utilises the Gothic rhetoric that characterises many accounts of the Rebellion in newspapers, histories, novels and other genres. 'The city of Agra is a great place', Small avers, 'swarming with fanatics and devil-worshippers of all sorts' – but these are Indians in general rather than the mutineers (1993: 99). Small teams up with three Sikh soldiers to steal the treasure from a mutinous rajah, whose servant Achmet they murder. They are arrested for the murder, however, and sent to a prison colony in the Andaman Islands, which is where Small acquires his devilish sidekick Tonga.

If detective fiction can have some of the characteristics of imperial Gothic, it can also have some of the characteristics of science fiction. Holmes, after all, is a scientific investigator and an experimental chemist. He has written expert treatises on footprints as clues and on the different types of tobacco ash. The metaphoric links between science and magic, however, help to give his adventures a Gothic twist. Thus, at the outset of 'A Scandal in Bohemia' (1891), Watson, amazed as always by Holmes's powers of deduction, tells him that, if he had lived several centuries ago, he might have been taken for a wizard and burned at the stake.

Science and magic are also twinned, like Gothic doubles, in Wells's 'scientific romances'. That was Wells's phrase for what soon came to be called 'science fiction'. Though he had been trained in science, Wells said of his romances:

> It occurred to me that instead of the usual interview with the devil or a magician, an ingenious use of scientific patter might with advantage be substituted. I simply brought the fetish stuff up to date, and made it as near actual theory as possible. (quoted in Aldiss, 1976: 8–9)

The invading Martians in *The War of the Worlds* are, like Bulwer-Lytton's Vril-ya, monsters with advanced technology. The narrator describes both the Martians and their machines in abhuman, Gothic terms, hideous to behold. They arrive in 'vast spider-like machines, nearly a hundred feet high, capable of the speed of an express-train, and able to shoot out a beam of intense heat' (Wells, 2003: 103). Inside they carry 'handling machines', also like metallic spiders or crabs. Although there are 'controlling', 'cerebral' Martians within the machines, the mechanisms seem to be their bodies, as if they were cyborgs. They are, moreover, vampires, seeking human blood for their food.

The Gothic abhuman appears also in *The Island of Doctor Moreau* (1896), in the form of the Beast People. Although Moreau is a scientist, the science he practises seems to Prendrick like black magic. Moreau is trying to improve on evolution, using surgery reminiscent of vivisection to carve animals into human beings. Like Frankenstein's monster, the monstrous creatures Moreau fashions rebel and kill him in revenge for their pain and suffering. And science in *The Time Machine* also seems magical. The Time Traveller is transported some 800,000 years into the future, where he encounters what he interprets as the ultimate outcome of human progress and evolution. Humanity has split into two abhuman species, the effete Eloi who have lost all traces of civilisation, and the underground, cannibalistic Morlocks, who feed on the Eloi.

In his analysis of the late Victorian romance revival, Nicholas Daly contends that it is more closely allied to literary modernism than to the eighteenth-century Gothic. Daly also argues that imperial Gothic romances such as *King Solomon's Mines* have little to do with anxieties about the decline and fall of the British Empire, which between the 1880s and World War I was at the peak of its power and glory. Certainly there are themes in late Victorian romances – the stress on evolution and futuristic technology in Wells's scientific romances, for example – that point ahead to Modernism. As one of the pioneers of science fiction,

Wells was also, in a sense, a pioneer Modernist. And Jennifer Wicke has called *Dracula* 'the first great modern novel in British literature' (1992: 467). Conrad, moreover, is typically seen as a Modernist author.

Yet the Gothic themes and conventions Conrad utilises in *Heart of Darkness* and some of his other narratives are present in many earlier Gothic romances. And while the focus of that great novella is specifically on Belgian King Leopold's scandalous private empire in the Congo, it can be read as a critique of the rapaciousness of imperialism in general. The narrator of *Heart of Darkness*, Marlow, declares: 'The conquest of the earth, which mostly means the taking it away from those who have a different complexion or slightly flatter noses than ourselves, is not a pretty thing when you look into it too much' (Conrad, 2006: 7). Further, Conrad clearly intended Kurtz's going native to exemplify what can happen to even the best and brightest products of European civilisation when they encounter their own primitive impulses and desires. Civilisation and progress are fragile and perhaps even fraudulent, *Heart of Darkness* tells us, and can easily degenerate into their opposites. That is a message apparent in many other examples of imperial Gothic fiction. Within every civilised self lurks an 'old barbarian', to quote Andrew Lang again. Evolution is random, not necessarily progressive, and even the white race – even Anglo-Saxons – can degenerate, perhaps into the Eloi and Morlocks Wells's Time Traveller discovers. Both imperial Gothic and much modernist literature – T. S. Eliot's *The Waste Land* (1922), for example – suggest that civilisation is only skin deep. At the bottom of the abyss, in the heart of darkness, and in imperial Gothic fiction, lurks what Kurtz discovers within himself: 'The horror, the horror!' (Conrad: 2006, 69).

Notes

1. I first discussed imperial Gothic fiction in *Rule of Darkness* (Brantlinger, 1988: 227–53).
2. Haggard's mummy tales include *She* (1887) and *The Yellow God* (1908). In Stoker's *The Jewel of Seven Stars* (1903, revised 1912), the mummy of Queen Tera is revivified in Cornwall. Doyle authored 'The Ring of Thoth' (1890) and 'Lot No. 249' (1892). Nicholas Daly points out that fictional mummies frequently become love objects rather than destructive monsters (1999: 84–116). Ayesha or She loves the embalmed corpse of Kallikrates, for example, and the protagonist in Haggard's 'Smith and the Pharoahs' falls in love with a beautiful mummy.
3. Several twentieth-century critics echo Saintsbury's judgement about the priority of the romance over the novel. See, for example, Northrop Frye, *The Secular Scripture*:

Romance is the structural core of all fiction: being directly descended from folktale, it brings us closer than any other aspect of literature to the sense of fiction, considered as a whole, as the epic of the creature, man's vision of his own life as a quest. (Frye, 1976: 15)

4. In 1887, Haggard had not yet written adventure tales in which the main characters were Zulus, as he would later do with *Nada the Lily* (1892) and several other romances set in southern Africa. Besides *King Solomon's Mines* (1885) and *She*, Lang probably had Haggard's 1884 novel *The Witch's Head* in mind, a tale he commended to Stevenson, telling him that he had recently met Haggard, who 'has done another boy's romance', *Allan Quatermain*, also published in 1887. Lang tells Stevenson that he admires 'the fights in the *Witch's Head*, and the Zulu. [Haggard] is good at Zulus' (Lang: 1990: 90).

References

Aldiss, Brian (1976). *Billion Year Spree: The True History of Science Fiction.* New York: Schocken.

Brantlinger, Patrick (1988). *Rule of Darkness: British Literature and Imperialism, 1830–1914.* Ithaca: Cornell University Press.

Byron, Glennis (2000). 'Gothic in the 1890s', in *A Companion to the Gothic*, ed. David Punter. Oxford: Blackwell Publishing, pp. 132–41.

Caine, Hall (1979). 'The New Watchwords of Fiction' [1890], in *A Victorian Art of Fiction: Essays on the Novel in British Periodicals*, vol. 5: 1870–1900, ed. John Charles Olmsted. New York: Garland, pp. 471–80.

Conrad, Joseph (2006). *Heart of Darkness* [1899]. New York: Norton.

Daly, Nicholas (1999). *Modernism, Romance and the Fin de Siècle: Popular Fiction and British Culture, 1880–1914.* Cambridge: Cambridge University Press.

Doyle, Sir Arthur Conan (1912). *The Lost World.* New York: Review of Reviews.

——(1993) *The Sign of Four* [1890]. Oxford: Oxford University Press.

Etherington, Norman (1984). *Rider Haggard.* Boston: Twayne.

Frye, Northrop (1976). *The Secular Scripture: A Study of the Structure of Romance.* Cambridge, MA: Harvard University Press.

Hurley, Kelly (1996). *The Gothic Body: Sexuality, Materialism, and Degeneration at the Fin de Siècle.* Cambridge: Cambridge University Press.

Killeen, Jarlath (2009). *Gothic Literature 1825–1914.* Cardiff: University of Wales Press.

Lang, Andrew (1887) 'Realism and Romance', *Contemporary Review*, 52 (November), 683–93.

——(1970) 'The Supernatural in Fiction' [1905], in *Adventures among Books.* Freeport, NY: Books for Libraries Press, pp. 273–80.

——(1990). *Dear Stevenson: Letters from Andrew Lang to Robert Louis Stevenson with Five Letters from Stevenson to Lang*, ed. Marysa Demoor. Leuven: Uitgeverij Peeters.

Menke, Richard (2008). *Telegraphic Realism: Victorian Fiction and Other Information Systems.* Stanford: Stanford University Press.

Oppenheim, Janet (1985). *The Other World: Spiritualism and Psychical*

Research in England, 1850–1914. Cambridge: Cambridge University Press.

Punter, David (1980). *The Literature of Terror: A History of Gothic Fictions from 1765 to the Present Day.* London: Longman.

Saintsbury, George (1979). 'The Present State of the Novel I' [1887], in *A Victorian Art of Fiction: Essays on the Novel in British Periodicals*, vol. 5: *1870–1900*, ed. John Charles Olmsted. New York: Garland, pp. 391–8.

Showalter, Elaine (1990). *Sexual Anarchy: Gender and Culture at the Fin de Siècle.* New York: Viking.

Stevenson, Robert Louis (1981). *Treasure Island* [1883]. New York: Bantam Books.

——(1983). *The Master of Ballantrae* [1889]. Oxford: Oxford University Press.

——(1999a).'The Bottle Imp' [1891], in *South Sea Tales*. Oxford: Oxford University Press, pp. 73–102.

——(1999b). *R. L. Stevenson on Fiction: An Anthology of Literary and Critical Essays*, ed. Glenda Norquay. Edinburgh: Edinburgh University Press.

Wells, H. G (2003). *The War of the Worlds* [1898]. Peterborough, ON: Broadview Press.

Wicke, Jennifer (1992). 'Vampiric Typewriting: *Dracula* and its Media', *English Literary History*, 59, 467–93.

Chapter 14

Fin-de-siècle Gothic
Victoria Margree and Bryony Randall

In Margaret Oliphant's 'Old Lady Mary' (1884) a doctor and a vicar argue about a child's apparent vision of ghosts. Each is manoeuvring not to claim the phenomenon for his own sphere of expertise, but rather to disclaim the responsibility of pronouncement. This drama of epistemological uncertainty speaks to a wider crisis of knowledge experienced by the late Victorians and produced by the progressive displacement of a religious by a secular worldview throughout the nineteenth century. Suspended between supernatural and scientific explanations of the world, it is little surprising that the fin de siècle should have produced an explosion of literatures of the fantastic, including many Gothic fictions whose icons continue to haunt popular imagination today. These texts, with their frequently limited and uncertain narrative perspectives, evince the anxious recognition that even – or indeed, especially – in late nineteenth-century Britain, realities may be in evidence that no existing body of knowledge is adequate to the task of explaining.

The term 'fin de siècle' signifies themes of cultural decline. By the 1890s, Victoria was in her sixth decade on the throne and it was clear to her contemporaries that an older Victorian social order was being dismantled. Processes of modernisation had eroded many of the certainties of an earlier period, particularly mid-century confidence in the prospect of ongoing progress. The late Victorians were intensely aware of themselves as being modern, and yet a sense permeated culture that this modernity, while it had delivered improvements in standards of living, had also brought about forms of misery and deprivation worse even than those seen in the past; as witnessed, for example, in impoverished areas of London – at the time the most modern metropolis on the globe. The fin de siècle marked a period of transition from old to new, without the assurance that the future would bring continued enlightenment and improvement. This has led Sally Ledger and Roger Luckhurst usefully to describe fin-de-siècle culture as characterised by the 'ambivalence of modernity' (2000: xiii). Such ambivalence proceeded, they argue, from the strange commingling, at the brink of a new epoch, of fears of cultural degeneration with hopes for regeneration and emancipation. In this context, Gothic fiction provided a vehicle for exploring social transformations and the ambivalence they evoked.

Major themes of the Gothic fin de siècle include the growth of the city and the rise of an urban poor, challenges to older Victorian ideologies of gender and sexuality, doubts about the validity and stability of Empire, and fears about immigration. Underpinning all these themes is the issue of developments in science during the period. The scientist is a familiar figure in fin-de-siècle Gothic fiction, as are those monsters produced by scientific experimentation, or presented as capable of being known and revealed by science. As Andrew Smith observes (2004), this testifies to the way in which science itself took on a somewhat Gothic quality in the popular imagination of the period. One reason for this was the publication in 1859 of Charles Darwin's *The Origin of Species*. This work had at first appeared to support mid-Victorian ideas of progress by suggesting the perfectibility of species: the subsequent recognition, however, that evolution could consist in a movement from complexity to a more simple form of organism led to the development of the pseudoscience of degeneration theory. According to this, evolution could in certain circumstances work in reverse, returning a complex and civilised being to the state of primitivism from which it had emerged. Degeneration theory, in the hands of, for example, the criminologist Cesare Lombroso or the physician Max Nordau, assumed important ideological functions, offering a way of explaining all that seemed to ail Victorian society and threaten progress. Crime, poverty, mental illness; the existence of the 'pervert', the homosexual, the New Woman; decadent art and philosophy; the vulnerability of Empire to rebellion in the colonies – all these phenomena could be explained by the hypothesis of the existence a subgroup of human beings in whom evolution was working backwards. The biological decline of the individual organism, as it was assumed to be communicable, threatened the decline of civilisation. Paradoxically, civilisation itself was held to be at fault, since civilisation had created the degenerate and enabled his propagation through its suspension of the mechanism of natural selection. Fin-de-siècle Gothic fictions abound with descriptions of degenerate physiognomies, of abhuman bodies in which the unclear boundary between the human and the animal is made manifest (Hurley, 2004: 3 and *passim*), and often operate as exhortations that civilisation protect itself from itself by eliminating the degenerate type. Darwinism and its (mis)interpretations provided fertile ground for texts that revelled in the destruction of religious orthodoxies about the divine origin of man and his absolute separation from the beasts.

At the same time, however, this was a period in which fiction traced 'strange realignments of the relationship between science and religion' (Botting, 2006: 136). As Fred Botting notes, much of this fiction works by presenting divergent tendencies within science. A materialistic science is contrasted with a transcendental science capable of 'disclos[ing] new natural miracles and powers' (2006: 138). This transcendental science, represented by such figures as Stevenson's Dr Jekyll and Stoker's Van Helsing, oddly recombines with aspects of religion, mythology or mysticism, by providing confirmation of the 'supernatural' while insisting that it is not really outside of the natural world at all, but is instead an aspect of 'a mysterious natural dimension beyond the crude limits of rationality and empiricism' (Botting, 2006: 136). In this respect Gothic fictions were responding to a contemporary debate about the proper contours of science; about whether such putative phenomena as spirits, mesmerism or telepathy really existed and, if they did, could be investigated and known by scientific methods (see Chapter 11 in this volume on this topic). That modern science might confirm beliefs previously abandoned as superstitions, helps to explain the uncanny character so frequently attributed it by Gothic fictions of the period. Interestingly, Botting suggests that while science's disclosure of 'threatening natural forces' (2006: 137) could be a source of horror, it could also prove 'spiritually elevating' (2006: 136) by offering 'grander visions of a mysterious and sacred universe' (2006: 149) to be counterpoised to the narrow rationality of bourgeois Victorian life. This observation recalls Gothic's original affinity, a century earlier, with the Romantic Movement's affirmation of passion, imagination and faith, in protest against the disenchantment produced by industrialisation and Enlightenment. It also helps to account for one of the distinctive features of much Gothic literature of the period; these fictions persistently, even lovingly, project the destruction of civilisation and Empire, only to restore their precarious order at the final hour. This suggests that Gothic at the fin de siècle is able to combine two divergent impulses: one for the sublimity of the imagined destruction of all social normality; the other for the reassurance of its restoration.

This ambivalence towards threatened catastrophe contributes to what Roger Luckhurst has identified as the frequent difficulty of deciding the politics of fin-de-siècle Gothic fictions (2005: xi). If, as he observes, a text is often conservative and subversive simultaneously, this might be in part because of the contradictory investment of authors and readers in both destruction and preservation of the order of everyday realities.

Frequently, the monster that menaces bourgeois normality is strangely alluring. In the remainder of this chapter, we will be attentive to the – often ambiguous – politics of the fictions we discuss, particularly around gender. Nicholas Ruddick claims that: 'that almost all the important fantastic fiction of the fin de siècle is by male authors suggests that the period was characterised by intense desires and anxieties of a specifically masculine kind' (2007: 192). Nonetheless, beyond the now-canonical works of male writers such as Stevenson, Stoker, Wilde, James and Wells, much Gothic output of the period was female-authored and until recently has been neglected or ignored. By arguing for the importance, too, of this fantastic fiction, we shall seek to show how the literature of the period also reveals desires and anxieties of a specifically feminine kind. What might be monstrous to the male literary imagination may represent a figure of emancipation for women writers. We will proceed by considering some major figures in fin-de-siècle Gothic: the vampire, the man of science and the ghost.

The vampire

Bram Stoker's *Dracula* (1897) gives us undoubtedly the most famous of literary vampires, in a period in which vampires and creatures with vampiric qualities pervade.[1] The text updates the Gothic romance of the late eighteenth and early nineteenth centuries by relocating horror from the past, and from the margins of human habitations, into modern Britain. This is enacted when the narrative shifts from the putative boundary of civilisation in Eastern Europe, to the heart of the modern metropolis when the Count arrives in London, hell-bent on reverse-colonising the centre of Empire by buying up its land and vampirising its women. The narrative thus mobilises a plethora of contemporary anxieties surrounding urban spaces in which degenerate immigrants are able anonymously to roam. That Count Dracula is a degenerate is rendered explicit when the novel's scientist-scholar Van Helsing refers to his 'child-brain' (Stoker, 2000: 343), a verdict later echoed by Mina Harker when she declares 'The Count is a criminal and of criminal type. Nordau and Lombroso would so classify him' (2000: 383). The presence in the modern city of a centuries-old feudal aristocrat, whose primitivism is writ large across his physiognomy, signals precisely that anachronistic presence of the past in the present that Robert Mighall suggests is central to the Gothic mode (Mighall, 2003). At the same time, the presentation of the vampire as a creature that is not truly supernatural, but a part of the natural world and therefore capable of being known by modern science, brings about that strange realignment of science and superstition remarked upon by Botting.

Dracula has gained a reputation for being one of the most misogynistic texts in a frequently anti-feminist genre. This proceeds from the novel's treatment of a new sort of female personage much discussed in fin-de-siècle culture. The 'New Woman' was the epithet given to a generation of women who, dissatisfied with Victorian gender roles, sought legal and political parity with men as well as increased sexual freedoms. So great was the perceived threat posed by this early feminism to an order based upon male privilege that late Victorian culture proliferated images of monstrous females. In *Dracula*, neither of the two central female characters are straightforwardly New Women, but both have characteristics of the type: in Mina, her determination to continue her employment in married life; in Lucy, her sexual desirousness (signalled first by her desire to marry three suitors, and then in her 'voluptuous' and 'wanton' qualities as a vampire). Stoker, fascinated yet terrorised by the subversive figure of the New Woman, splits her into two. Mina functions as an acceptable version since her qualities can be put to the service of men. Lucy's desires, however, cannot be accommodated by the social order, so she is punished and killed (by being staked by her husband Arthur in the presence of her other suitors, clearly suggesting a scene of gang rape). In so employing the figure of the vampire to explore the problem of the modern woman, Stoker was drawing upon a much-used fin-de-siècle trope. A male-dominated medical establishment often held the biology of women to be essentially degenerate; a particular belief being that the loss of nutrients in menstruation led women to seek replenishment from men's semen. As Bram Dijkstra has demonstrated (1988), scientific discourse colluded with a misogynistic culture to envision women as essentially vampiric – as drainers of the vitality of men.

Such ideas are at work, albeit in complicated ways, in Florence Marryat's *The Blood of the Vampire* (1897), which, published in the same year as *Dracula*, shares its concern with the dangers posed by a distinctly modern type of young woman. The novel tells the story of a young heiress, Harriet Brandt, newly emerged into society following a secluded convent upbringing consequent upon her parents' death in an uprising by servants on their Jamaican estate. After several of Harriet's friends have mysteriously sickened and died it is eventually revealed to her that she is the daughter of a sadistic scientist father and a mixed-race mother thought to practice voodoo; and that her grandmother, a slave bitten by a vampire bat during pregnancy, has passed on to Harriet the inheritance of both black, and vampire, blood. The consequence of this biological inheritance is, she is told, that she will drain the energy of all those who love her and whom she loves, so that they will be debilitated by her while she herself grows strong. To avoid this prospect, she must live a solitary life and forgo romance, marriage and motherhood.

Harriet is therefore not a vampire in the sense that Stoker's Lucy is: there is no biting and bloodsucking, but instead a form of psychic vampirism by which Harriet unwittingly drains the life-force from others. Indeed, the supernatural explanation of Harriet's fatal influence is never confirmed but remains hearsay, with characters vacillating over whether it is the vampire bat's bite, or just the misalliance of her mixed-race and vicious-natured parents, that dooms her. But the conceit of psychic vampirism enables Marryat to explore a version of female subjectivity both troublingly transgressive and alluring (as well as a range of fin-de-siècle anxieties around syphilitic contamination, degeneration and racial miscegenation). The most persistent characterisation of Harriet is in terms of her *appetitive* nature. She is introduced to us through description of her blood-red lips (Marryat, 2009: 4) – also a central image in *Dracula* – which in addition to titillating the reader with the (unfulfilled) promise of a more conventional vampire, signify her sensuousness and capacity to consume. She devours food with an obvious enjoyment that other characters find distasteful; just as she unashamedly devours with her eyes the handsome young man with whom she will begin a sexual dalliance.

Harriet's embodiment of sensual appetites that offend conventional proprieties aligns her with the figure of the New Woman, and connects her with Stoker's Lucy among other dangerously sexual female characters from Gothic texts of the period.[2] Does Marryat, then, exploit the trope of the female vampire to produce less conservative ideological results than do male writers of Gothic? Marryat has indeed been read as internalising male fears about the sexually transgressive woman, and there is much in the text that supports this.[3] The trajectory of the narrative confirms Harriet's dismal prognosis, as all those to whom she becomes close do indeed succumb to illness and in some cases death, including a baby, linking Harriet to the ranks of the vampire women in *Dracula* whose monstrous inversion of femininity is exemplified by their feeding upon children. The novel therefore seems to endorse the fin-de-siècle fear that there is a certain type of woman who presents an extreme danger to others, with Marryat adopting a biologically determinist framework to contain the social threat posed by the figure of alterity that Harriet presents. The narrative's denouement in her suicide seems, in this reading, to suggest that the author can envisage no better outcome for her than an early death.

While Marryat frames Harriet within scientific explanations, there is, however, something in her presentation that exceeds these terms, marking Marryat's text as atypical in its presentation of Gothic femininity. This has to do with the enormous sympathy for Harriet generated in the implied reader, making the story a tragic tale of a young woman doomed in her quest to love and be loved. In this novel, most unusually, we are given access to the interiority of the Gothicised woman, and this reveals frequently not the vengefulness and cruelty that is prophesised for her, but only a passionate enthusiasm that offends a rigidly conventional society (as when she 'should like to tear up and down this road as hard as ever I could throwing my arms over my head and screaming aloud!' (Marryat, 2009: 10)). Harriet's dominating motivation is, it appears, not primarily physical or sexual pleasure but emotional intimacy; we are frequently told of her need for love, and that she is 'really and truly fond of' the man she agrees to marry (2009: 151). Nor does Harriet come off badly in the frequent comparisons between herself and the eminently proper Elinor Leyton – another young unmarried woman and to some extent Harriet's opposite – who is frequently depicted as sneering and curling her lip in disgust at others, in contrast to Harriet's warmth towards those around her. This sympathy generates the grounds for a critique of a society so remorselessly conventional that it refuses to accommodate the passion, enthusiasm and joyfulness of a young woman such as Harriet.

Marryat also dramatises the vulnerability of the young woman in the hands of the medical establishment. Harriet's condition is diagnosed by a broadly sympathetically presented family physician, Dr Phillips. Early in the narrative, we hear Dr Phillips tantalise other characters by recounting the rumours of Harriet's vampire blood and her mother's witchcraft. He does so, however, without explicitly affirming them, ultimately relying upon the 'scientific' discourse of heredity to explain her malign personality. When revealing to Harriet her condition, he takes a slightly different position again, explaining that some people '*give out*' to those around them, while some people '*draw*', and that Harriet's 'temperament [is] more of the *drawing* than the yielding *order*' (2009: 162). Our suspicions that the doctor's rational, scientific paradigm might, nevertheless, accommodate the supernatural, are magnified by these words of his explanation: 'you will, in fact, have *sucked them dry*' (2009: 162). But while the text implies that he delivers this diagnosis as gently as possible, the reader may perceive what the doctor apparently does not: the absolute devastation caused to a young woman by hearing that love, family, and even friendship, must forever remain beyond her grasp. Marryat's indebtedness to scientific theories in a context where, as we have seen, women had good reason to be suspicious of male-authored scientific scripts, while simultaneously alerting her readers to the inability of even the most sympathetic family doctor adequately to empathise with a female patient, amplifies our reading of this text as exemplifying the political ambiguity (*per* Luckhurst) of the Gothic. That Marryat herself led an unconventional life and must have suffered from the strictures of so censorious a social world, only supports the textual evidence for a degree of authorial equivocation in this complex work.

The man of science

That two infamous antiheroes of the fin-de-siècle Gothic canon are men of science destroyed by their own creations is symptomatic of the anxiety surrounding scientific developments in the late nineteenth century discussed earlier. But ambiguity frequently adheres to even the most unsympathetic of such figures. In H. G. Wells's *The Island of Doctor Moreau* (1896) a scientist who has been vivisecting animals in an attempt to turn them into human beings is beaten to death by one of his experimental subjects. While Moreau might appear to be an unequivocally malign figure, Wells's own defence of vivisection for medical purposes (see Harris, 2009: 44–57), together with the narrator's reluctant admiration for Moreau (alongside horror at his practices), as well as 'Prendick's confused anxieties for a conclusion' (Harris, 2009: 55), all give this text that other key characteristic of Gothic – undecidability.

Robert Louis Stevenson's *The Strange Case of Dr Jekyll and Mr Hyde* (1886) gives us perhaps the period's most famous Gothic double, as well as the clearest articulation of the emerging contrast between different scientific orientations.[4] As Botting notes, Jekyll mocks his friend Dr Lanyon's 'narrow and material views', as he demonstrates to the astonished Lanyon the outcome of his experiments in 'transcendental medicine' (Stevenson, 1998: 58; Botting, 2006: 139), his transformation into the 'ape-like' (Stevenson, 1998: 26, 75, 76) Mr Hyde. Dr Jekyll's demise is more complex than is Dr Moreau's, the self-slaughter of Hyde also necessarily involving the murder of his alter ego. But in both cases, the dangers of a science that goes beyond its acceptable bounds – that is, in Botting's definition of Gothic, excessive – are clear. In this respect, both are modernisations of Mary Shelley's *Frankenstein* (1818), with this key difference: in the fin-de-siècle texts the use of science to create new human beings reveals the unpalatable proximity of the human to the animal and the Gothic possibility of degenerating into a state of bestiality.

Jekyll's potion solves for the good doctor the distinctly upper-middle-class professional problem of how to 'body forth social virtue' while enjoying 'certain kinds of personal freedom' (Punter, 1996: 3). While the text is famously coy as to what these freedoms consist in, critics have read them as being of a sexual nature and possibly involving prostitution and homosexuality.[5] It is clear, however, that the pleasures and dangers of these freedoms are the prerogatives of a distinctly masculine world, in which men wander the streets of London at night and the all-male professional sphere provides ample opportunities for homosocial bonding. Implicit, yet clearly apparent from this text, is a sexual double standard. For men a degree of departure from strict Victorian morality is tolerated, even expected, provided it does not risk being made public outside the limits of the world of male clubs and their code of secrecy. But as we have seen with *Dracula*'s Lucy, and will see with Machen's Helen Vaughan, for women no degree of sexual impropriety is permitted but is instead severely punished.

In Arthur Machen's *The Great God Pan* (1894) 'central Gothic themes converge on the figure of one elusive yet monstrous woman' (Luckhurst, 2005: xxix). Helen Vaughan is born as the result of an experiment by Dr Raymond, a 'transcendental' scientist whose 'trifling rearrangement of certain cells' (Machen, 1995: 184) in the brain of his protégée Mary 'lift[ed] the veil' between this world and the 'real' world of the spirits – of Pan; Helen is the offspring of Mary and (it is implied) Pan himself. In this story, an atavistic power associated with the Greek gods is accessed from a clandestine laboratory in rural Wales, only to invade the modern metropolis. Having terrorised London, incognito, by apparently seducing well-to-do men in a manner which drives them to kill themselves, Helen, like Harriet, herself commits suicide, though in her case she is forced to take her own life under threat of legal intervention and/or possible violence. In contrast to *The Blood of the Vampire* the 'monstrous' woman is, however, never given a voice in *The Great God Pan*. The silence of the central female character is part of the text's misogyny, but also of its narrative effect. What it means to have seen 'the Great God Pan' remains hidden – is, the text implies, ineffable – adding to the mystery and terror at the heart of the story, linked to a predatory female sexuality.

Doctors and scientists appear frequently in the Gothic short stories of Edith Nesbit. In several stories, the differing attitudes of characters towards the possibility of supernatural phenomena lead to crises in what have appeared to be idyllic heterosexual relationships; providing Nesbit with a way – as Nick Freeman (2008) has observed – of critiquing a social order that allows for the systematic rejection of female perspectives in favour of male ones. For example, in 'Man Size in Marble' (1893), a young husband dismisses as superstition the fears of his wife and their housekeeper produced by a local legend, but on realising that their fears are justified is prevented from possibly saving his wife from murder by his friend Dr Kelly ('six feet of solid common sense' (Nesbit, 2006b: 27)), who insists on detaining him to disabuse him of his apparent delusion. 'Hurst of Hurstcote' (1893) offers another version of the split between the transcendental scientist-scholar and the more prosaic medical man, where both fail the woman they love. John Hurst is introduced as having something 'strange and secret' about him, whose superior manner together with his interest in 'Black Magic' made him unpopular with his peers, while women, however, 'all lik[ed] him' (Nesbit, 2006a: 101). The narrator, a medical doctor still in love with Hurst's new wife, Kate, accepts an invitation to visit the couple at Hurst's newly inherited ancestral home. Kate affirms that her husband is 'very, very wise' (2006a: 104) but confides to the narrator her disquiet about his researches into the occult, saying (somewhat contradictorily) that while she does not believe in Black Magic she thinks such things 'wicked' and believes that there are some things one 'is meant *not* to know' (2006a: 105). When Kate suddenly succumbs to 'marsh fever', Hurst repeatedly insists she is not dead, and eventually admits that before they were married he hypnotised her and 'forbade her soul to leave its body till [his] time came to die' (2006a: 108). Telling the narrator in horror that he has seen Kate return to him, begging 'Let me go, John – let me go!' (2006a: 109), Hurst urges his friend to open her coffin to ensure that she is at rest. The narrator, however, believes Hurst mad and only pretends that he has done as he was asked. The story ends with a tableau of the couple lying dead in each others' arms, Hurst having discovered his friend's deception and killed himself in order to release his wife's soul.

The narrator and Hurst represent different poles of a 'masculine' relationship to the supernatural, leading each to fail the woman both men love. That Kate is nearly condemned to a horrific fate by the narrator's refusal to credit the supernatural, recalls 'Man Size in Marble'. However, the belief that the narrator directly dismisses is not Kate's but Hurst's. Thus, Hurst himself is placed in the feminised position of being a believer in the marvellous whose judgement is dismissed by masculine, scientific, rationality (we remember that he has always been more popular with women than men). But Hurst, while a believer in the supernatural, uses this knowledge for purposes he should not, lacking the feminine wisdom to see that there are secrets one should not expose. Though ultimately recognising his responsibility to sacrifice himself, the fact that he took advantage of having placed Kate 'completely under

[his] control' (2006a: 108) to meddle with so profound a matter as the relationship between body and soul signals a critique of attempts by men, even tenderly devoted husbands, to assert their power over women. Here as elsewhere in Nesbit's fiction, masculine approaches to the supernatural are presented as particularly problematic, providing Nesbit with a way of addressing the problems of male–female relationships in patriarchal culture.

Ghosts

There is no shortage, in the fin de siècle, of literary ghosts, many of the terrifying, inexplicable, and sometimes murderous variety. M. R. James, considered by many a master of the genre, published the first of his celebrated stories of revenants and the undead in 1895; other phantasms range from the demonic hanging judge who takes up residence in the body of a rat in Bram Stoker's 'The Judge's House' (1891), the victims of sacrificial rites dating back millennia in Grant Allen's 'Palinghurst Barrow' (1892), and even a racehorse and his trainer in Lettice Galbraith's 'The Trainer's Ghost' (1893). But there was a gendered aspect to the realm of the ghostly in late-nineteenth-century culture. The spiritualist movement had been an important factor in Victorian cultural life since its arrival from America in the mid-century, and one which attributed to women an unusual degree of authority and privilege (Owen, 1989). But the foundation in 1882 of The Society for Psychical Research, which Emma Liggens argues gave 'new resonance' to the genre, by seeking real-life stories of hauntings (2009: iii), was formed largely of scientific men searching for material proof of the claims of spiritualists about such alleged phenomena as spirit apparitions, mediumship and mesmerism. Here our focus on two notable types of fin-de-siècle literary ghost, the 'benign' ghost, and the psychological ghost, continues our explorations of these (interrelated) themes of gender and science.

Many working women writers of the late nineteenth century such as Margaret Oliphant, Charlotte (Mrs J. H.) Riddell and B. M. Croker turned to the ghost story in the 1880s and 1890s, attesting to the popularity and commercial success of the genre at that time. There is, however, a notable prevalence of benign ghosts in the work of these writers, returning to earth to right a wrong or protect the vulnerable. What is more, the manner of narration and/or the reaction of the characters frequently tends to the phlegmatic, taking the appearance of the supernatural almost as part of the normal vicissitudes of everyday life. The shock, terror or drama associated with the spine-tingling ghost story is attenuated. To this extent, they may appear not to contain the features which we have argued characterise a fin-de-siècle Gothic text, and might rather be seen as a continuation of the Victorian realist mode. Yet Gothic elements of fear, vengefulness, violence or corruption do appear prominently in the stories of Riddell and Croker, but in human, or natural, rather than supernatural form.

Many of Croker's ghost stories depict a colonised India from the point of view of the colonisers, often (and unusually for the genre) through a first-person female narrator. A striking aspect of these texts is the manner in which the women who see the ghosts take it in their stride; while we are told that they experience fear and dread, even physical ill effects, there is also something of the stiff upper lip about their reactions. In Croker's 'To Let' (1893) the narrator and her sister-in-law, after witnessing the ghostly apparition of a horse and rider plunging to their deaths off the veranda of the house they are renting, find themselves able not only to eat and sleep but to play a little tennis. In 'The Dâk Bungalow at Dakor' (1893) two women react to the ghost they have seen with as much indignation as fear, commanding their menfolk to dig up the veranda of the bungalow to reveal what the ghostly apparition implied, namely that a young Englishman had been murdered by two sinister native servants. In these stories, the ghostly appearances, while central to the narrative, are presented as no more and indeed perhaps less threatening than many other challenges facing the Englishwoman in India, such as the colonised racial other (insubordinate servants as in 'The Dâk Bungalow at Dakar') or uncomfortable and even dangerous climatic conditions (the fever-inducing heat or the torrential rains in 'To Let'). In Croker's colonial fictions the supernatural becomes a way of both expressing and containing anxieties around the colonial experience, their tone and plot structure revealing a desire to assert the strength of women confronted with what are seen as its more threatening practical aspects.

Riddell's ghosts appear predominantly as benevolent seekers of justice or protectors of the vulnerable living. Most of the stories have a similar formal framework, in which a male protagonist takes on a reputedly haunted house and on investigating the mystery uncovers a crime (such as a murder or homicidal neglect). The haunting thus exorcised, the property may now be safely and rightfully occupied. Riddell's stories are particularly concerned with the judicious use of wealth and with men's economic responsibility to women. Riddell shifts the focus of anxiety in these stories from the supernatural to the actual, using the popular and alluring mode of the fantastic ultimately to remind the reader of the cruelty, selfishness and avarice of ordinary human beings. The fact that in one instance – 'Walnut Tree House' (1882) – a house remains haunted while being happily occupied by the protagonist and his family emphasises that the supernatural is far from being the most threatening aspect of the world Riddell depicts. Her tales of benevolent ghosts Gothicise everyday domestic space – as did the sensation fiction of the 1860s – exposing how the very privacy of this space enables abuses, in particular (but not exclusively) of women and children.

One of Riddell's haunted-house stories, however, stands out from her usual pattern. In 'Old Mrs Jones' (1882), the ghost is not experienced as benign, but scares off lodgers taken in by the Tippenses, tenants of a house previously inhabited by a Doctor Jones and his wife, Zillah. When a young woman cousin of the Tippenses is eventually led, sleep-walking, by the ghost to a nearby house in which the body of a woman is found in a laboratory, it appears that the doctor – rumoured to have been a brutal man who mistreated the wife he married for her money – has murdered Zillah before assuming a disguise as a German chemist. On the day that the Tippenses are forced to leave the house, a woman is spotted running from window to window as the house is destroyed in a mighty conflagration. This story contains a number of key fin-de-siècle Gothic themes. The murderous Dr Jones is evidently another instance of the malign man of science and – anticipating Stevenson's Dr Jekyll – is a debauched doctor. Furthermore, that the discovery of the crime does not, in this instance, exorcise the ghost or render the house habitable, signifies a disturbance at once unfathomable and excessive. This excess is presumably linked both to the designation of Old Mrs Jones by locals as a 'witch' (Riddell, 2009: 137, 173) and a 'blackamoor' (2009: 149; although the narrator corrects this saying that she is 'not black, only exceedingly brown', 2009: 149). She is therefore aligned with Harriet Brandt as an ambivalent figure of Gothicised racial otherness, in a text which evokes an earlier novel with Gothic aspects, *Jane Eyre* (1847). Importantly, however, the theme of female vulnerability and the dependency of wives upon husbands is not restricted to this overtly Gothic couple, but extends to the otherwise contented marriage of the Tippenses. While Mrs Tippens quickly recognises the reality of the haunting and its threat to their family, Mr Tippens thinks only in terms of his three-year tenancy and rejects his wife's pleas to move. As contractor of the tenancy and head of the family, authority is his alone. Here, as often in Nesbit's fiction, women's greater capacity for accommodating the supernatural into their worldview is of little aid in a social world which vests power in the hands of men.

Elsewhere in the literature of the period we find ghosts who make their narrative entrance with little commotion on the part of characters or narrator. In Henry James's 'Sir Edmund Orme' (1891) the ghost, if not exactly benign, has a decorous, gentlemanly demeanour and ability to blend in with his surroundings, and rouses curiosity rather than terror in the narrator-protagonist. Sir Edmund's existence as a ghost is never questioned. Conversely, and perhaps unexpectedly, in James's most celebrated 'ghost' story (indeed probably the most celebrated of the period), the whole narrative turns on the question of whether the ghosts are real, or are a projection of the disturbed mind of a young governess, and yet the effect of the story is much more chilling than that of 'Sir Edmund Orme'. While most contemporary reviews read *The Turn of the Screw* (1898) as a ghost story, subsequent criticism emphasised the psychological aspect of the story, with Freudian approaches flourishing in the mid twentieth century. More recent work tends to resist a reading which eliminates the famous epistemological uncertainty of the text, rather insisting on this aspect of the novella as central to its disturbing effect. The narrator can be seen as another example of the female victim of, specifically male, intransigence and selfishness (in this case embodied in the figures of the bachelor gentleman who abandons his orphaned nephew and niece to the care of an inexperienced governess, and his demonic double, the valet, Peter Quint). Indeed, that, as T. J. Lustig notes, the phrase 'The turn of the screw [*sic*] connotes various forms of restriction, intensification, enclosure, enforcement or constraint' (1999: 258) reminds us of the comparisons to be made between the governess and the imprisoned heroines of other Gothic texts; she may not be physically locked in, but she is placed in a position where her options in response to apparent haunting (or at the very least, traumatised children) are severely limited. That she can also be interpreted as a disturbed and obsessive young woman wielding a destructive influence on her young charges makes sure that this text retains the ambiguity which is, perhaps, its most Gothic aspect.

James's friend and sometime acolyte Vernon Lee (Violet Paget) also wrote what Luckhurst calls 'the subtle terrors of the *psychological* Gothic [as distinct from] the body horrors of the *physiological* Gothic' (Luckhurst, 2005: xii). Lee's ghosts are far from being benign, and it is not just murderous phantasms that mark her work out as recognisably Gothic: there are mysterious portraits; (derelict) ancient buildings, mortal passions, and femmes fatales. There are, however, two specific ways in which Lee revises the ghost story for the fin de siècle; and both of these are congruent with the anti-scientific strand we have detected in much Gothic women's writing from the period. Firstly, these stories allow Lee to explore non-normative sexual desires and identities. Gender ambiguity features frequently, as in the cross-dressing Alice Oke in 'Oke of Okehurst' (1886/1890), or the ambiguously gendered singer of 'A Wicked Voice' (1889). In a period in which 'sexologists' were claiming human sexuality for the authority of scientific discourse, Lee's work evidently connects to the pervasive debate around the limits of science. As Stefano Evangelista puts it, 'Identifying sexual desire with the supernatural, Lee implicitly exposes the inadequacy of science as a medium to analyse sexual behaviour' (Evangelista, 2006: 107). Where a scholar falls in love with a long-dead Italian aristocrat, or a young wife with the poet-lover of one of her ancestors, such desires cannot be contained within a scientific epistemology. Secondly, but relatedly, Lee challenges the authority of 'modern ghost experts' – who are parodied in her preface to her 1890 collection of ghostly short stories, *Hauntings*, as 'highly reasoning men of semi-science' – to pronounce upon 'the ghostly' (Lee, 2006: 38). Here, as in the stories themselves, the existence of the supernatural is not discounted altogether, but its provenance and ontological status is emphatically outside the purview of the 'logical' or scientific, being something that can be conveyed only by an aesthetic capable of retaining ambiguity. Lee wonders whether the 'genuine ghosts' are not those of the mundane type, evidenced by the Society for Psychical Research, but instead those vague ones 'of whom I can affirm only one thing, that they haunted certain brains' (2006: 40). With her suggestion that the genuine ghost may be 'this one born of ourselves' (2006: 39), Lee anticipates the Freudian insight – which is also the insight of much Gothic fiction of the period – that our most uncanny possessions originate in the places of strangeness within our own selves. In Lee's work, this uncanniness is particularly associated with the power of the past to erupt in the imagination of the modern mind, charging the present with terror, mystery and erotic effect.

Lee's insistence on aesthetic ambiguity correlates with the political ambiguity characteristic of the Gothic literature of this period. While female-authored texts address the same themes and anxieties of the male-authored Gothic canon – around sexuality, race, economics, and in particular science – they frequently evince an alienated female sensibility in relation to these issues. While this may at times modulate into overt feminist criticism, more often these texts share with those of the male-authored canon an uncertainty as to what if any epistemological frame can make sense of the phenomena with which they are dealing. This undecidability – at once epistemological and political – is key to the unsettling quality of Gothic fin-de-siècle literature.

Notes

1. For a wide-ranging survey of vampires in fin-de-siècle culture, including poetry, painting and sculpture as well as fiction, see Dijkstra (1988). Other quasi-vampiric figures can be found in, for example, H. G. Wells's *The War of the Worlds* (1898), George MacDonald's *Lilith* (1895) and Mary Elizabeth Braddon's 'Good Lady Ducayne' (1896).
2. See for example, the dangerous female characters in H. Rider Haggard's *She* (1887), Arthur Machen's *The Great God Pan* (1894), Marie Corelli's *Ziska* (1897) and Richard Marsh's *The Beetle* (1897).
3. See for example Depledge (2009), Hammack (2008) and Malchow (1996).
4. Almost equally well known as a fin-de-siècle novel of doubles is Oscar Wilde's *The Picture of Dorian Gray* (1890).
5. See for example Showalter (2001).

References

Allen, Grant (1995). 'Palinghurst Barrow' [1892], in *Late Victorian Gothic Tales*, ed. Roger Luckhurst. Oxford: Oxford University Press, pp. 151–70.

Botting, Fred (2006). *Gothic*. London and New York: Routledge.

Croker, B. M. (2005). 'The Dâk Bungalow at Dakor' [1893] in *Late Victorian Gothic Tales*, ed. Roger Luckhurst. Oxford: Oxford University Press, pp. 96–108.

Depledge, Greta (2009). 'Introduction' to Florence Marryat, *The Blood of the Vampire*. Brighton: Victorian Secrets.

Dijkstra, Bram (1988). *Idols of Perversity: Fantasies of Feminine Evil in Fin-De-Siècle Culture*. New York and Oxford: Oxford University Press.

Evangelista, Stefano (2006). 'Vernon Lee and the Gender of Aestheticism', in *Vernon Lee: Decadence, Ethics, Aesthetics*, ed. Catherine Maxwell and Patricia Pulham. Basingstoke: Palgrave, pp. 91–111.

Freeman, Nick (2008). 'E. Nesbit's New Woman Gothic', *Women's Writing*, 15/3, 454–69.

Hammack, Brenda Mann (2008). 'Florence Marryat's Female Vampire and the Scientizing of Hybridity', *Studies in English Literature 1500–1900*, 48/4, 885–96.

Harris, Mason (2009). 'Introduction' to H. G. Wells, *The Island of Doctor Moreau*. Peterborough, ON: Broadview.

Hurley, Kelly (2004). *The Gothic Body: Sexuality, Materialism and Degeneration at the Fin de Siècle*. Cambridge: Cambridge University Press.

Ledger, Sally and Roger Luckhurst (2000). 'Introduction: Reading the "Fin de Siècle"', in *The Fin de Siècle: A Reader in Cultural History, c.1880–1900*, ed. Sally Ledger and Roger Luckhurst. Oxford: Oxford University Press, pp. xiii–xxiii.

Lee, Vernon (2006). 'Preface to *Hauntings*' [1890], in *Hauntings and Other Fantastic Tales*, ed. Catherine Maxwell and Patricia Pulham. Peterborough, ON: Broadview, pp. 37–40.

Liggens, Emma (2009). 'Introduction' to Charlotte Riddell, *Weird Stories* [1882]. Brighton: Victorian Secrets.

Luckhurst, Roger (2005). 'Introduction', in *Late Victorian Gothic Tales*, ed. Roger Luckhurst. Oxford: Oxford University Press, pp. ix–xxxi.

Lustig, T. J. (1999). 'Henry James and the Ghostly', extracted in Henry James, *The Turn of the Screw*. New York: Norton.

Machen, Arthur (1995). *The Great God Pan* [1894], in *Late Victorian Gothic Tales*, ed. Roger Luckhurst. Oxford: Oxford University Press, pp. 183–233.

Malchow, H. L. (1996). *Gothic Images of Race in Nineteenth-Century Britain*. Stanford: Stanford University Press.

Marryat, Florence (2009). *The Blood of the Vampire* [1897]. Brighton: Victorian Secrets.

Mighall, Robert (2003). *A Geography of Victorian Gothic Fiction: Mapping History's Nightmares*. Oxford: Oxford University Press.

Nesbit, Edith (2006a). 'Hurst of Hurstcote' [1893], in Edith Nesbit, *The Power of Darkness: Tales of Terror*. Ware: Wordsworth Editions, pp. 101–11.

——(2006b). 'Man-Size in Marble' [1893], in Edith Nesbit, *The Power of Darkness: Tales of Terror*. Ware: Wordsworth Editions, pp. 17–28.

Owen, Alex (1989). *The Darkened Room: Women, Power and Spiritualism in Late Victorian England*. London: Virago.

Punter, David (1996). *The Literature of Terror: A History of Gothic Fictions from 1765 to the Present Day*, 2 vols, vol. 2. Harlow: Pearson Education.

Riddell, Charlotte (2009). 'Old Mrs Jones' [1882], in Charlotte Riddell, *Weird Stories*. Brighton: Victorian Secrets, pp. 129–73.

Ruddick, Nicholas (2007). 'The Fantastic Fiction of the Fin de Siècle', in *The Cambridge Companion to the Fin de Siècle*, ed. Gail Marshall. Cambridge: Cambridge University Press, pp. 189–206.

Showalter, Elaine (2001). *Sexual Anarchy: Gender and Culture at the Fin de Siècle*. London: Virago.

Smith, Andrew (2004). *Victorian Demons: Medicine, Masculity and the Gothic at the Fin-de-Siècle*. Manchester: Manchester University Press.

Stevenson, Robert Louis (1998). *The Strange Case of Dr Jekyll and Mr Hyde* [1886], in *'The Strange Case of Dr Jekyll and Mr Hyde' and 'Weir of Hermiston'*, ed. Emma Letley. Oxford: Oxford University Press, pp. 1–76.

Stoker, Bram (2000). *Dracula* [1897]. Peterborough, ON: Broadview.

Bibliography

Adams, J. E. (1999). 'Victorian Sexualities', in *A Companion to Victorian Literature and Culture*, ed. H. F. Tucker. Malden, MA and Oxford: Blackwell Publishers, pp. 125–38.

Aldiss, Brian (1976). *Billion Year Spree: The True History of Science Fiction*. New York: Schocken.

Allen, Grant (1995). 'Palinghurst Barrow' [1892], in *Late Victorian Gothic Tales*, ed. Roger Luckhurst. Oxford: Oxford University Press, pp. 151–70.

Allen, Vivien (1997). *Hall Caine: Portrait of a Victorian Romancer*. Sheffield: Academic Press.

Altick, Richard (1991). *The Presence of the Present: Topics of the Day in the Victorian Novel*. Athens: Ohio State University Press.

Amigoni, David (2011). *Victorian Literature*. Edinburgh: Edinburgh University Press.

Andrew, Donna T. (1980). 'The Code of Honour and Its Critics: The Opposition to Duelling in England, 1700–1850', *Social History*, 5, 409–34.

Anglo, Michael (1977). *Penny Dreadfuls and Other Victorian Horrors*. London: Jupiter Books.

Anon. (1837). 'The Execution of Greenacre', *Morning Chronicle*, no. 21,053.

——(1843). 'The Principles of Landscape-Gardening and of Landscape Architecture applied to the Laying out of Public Cemeteries and the Improvement of Churchyards', *The Gardener's Magazine*, 9, 93–105, 97.

——(1858). 'The Byways of Literature: Reading for the Millions', *Blackwood's Magazine*, vol. 84, 200–16.

——(1858). 'Law and Police Intelligence', *The Englishwoman's Review and Home Newspaper*, issue 50 (26 June), 704.

——(1859). 'Subterranean Switzerland', *All the Year Round*, 2 (5 November), 25–32.

——(1860). 'Natural selection', *All the Year Round*, 3/63 (7 July), 293–9.

——(1863). 'Not a New Sensation', *All the Year Round*, 9 (July 25), 517–20.

——(1885). 'How we Dissipate Now', *Funny Folks*, issue 572 (14 November), 365.

——(1890). 'The Dangers of Hypnotism', *The Lancet*, 15 March, 615–16.

——(1890). 'The Dangers of Hypnotism', *The Saturday Review*, 69, 699–700.

——(1890). 'The Dangers of Hypnotism', *The Spectator*, 12 April, 507–8.

——(1894). 'Madame Rachel', *Notes and Queries*, 8/6, 322–4.

——(1898). 'Drink and Degradation', *Wings* 16/10 (1 October), 139.

Archer, William (1882). *English Dramatists of Today*. London: Sampson.

Ariès, Philippe (1981). *The Hour of Our Death*, trans. Helen Weaver. New York: Alfred A. Knopf.

Ashley, Mike (1997). 'Ghost Stories', in *The Encyclopedia of Fantasy*, ed. John Clute and John Grant. London: Orbis, pp. 403–7.

Baker, William (2002). *Wilkie Collins's Library: A Reconstruction*. Westport, CT and London: Greenwood Press.

Baldick, Chris, and Robert Mighall (2000). 'Gothic Criticism', in *A Companion to the Gothic*, ed. David Punter. Oxford: Blackwell, pp. 209–28.

Barker-Benfield, G. J. (1992). *The Culture of Sensibility: Sex and Society in Eighteenth-Century Britain*. Chicago: University of Chicago Press.

Beer, Gillian (2000). *Darwin's Plots: Evolutionary Narrative in Darwin, George Eliot and Nineteenth-Century Fiction*. Cambridge: Cambridge University Press.

Belford, Barbara (1996). *Bram Stoker: A Biography of the Author of Dracula*. New York: Knopf.

Bending, Lucy (2000). *The Representation of Bodily Pain in Late Nineteenth-Century English Culture*. Oxford: Clarendon Press.

Bennett, Gillian (2000). 'Introduction' to Catherine Crowe, *The Night Side of Nature or Ghosts and Ghost Seers* [1848]. Ware: Wordsworth, pp. 9–14.

Bernheim, H. (1973). *Hypnosis and Suggestion in Psychotherapy: A Treatise on the Nature and Uses of Hypnotism* [1884]. Northvale, NJ and London: Jason Aronson Inc.

Binet, A. and C. Féré (1888). 'Hypnotism in Disease and Crime', *The Popular Science Monthly*, 32, 763–9.

Bleiler, E. F. (1977). Introduction to *The Collected Ghost Stories of Mrs J. H. Riddell*, ed. E. F. Bleiler. New York: Dover, pp. v–xxxvi.

Bollen, Katrien and Raphael Ingelbien (2009). 'An Intertext that Counts? *Dracula*, *The Woman in White*, and Victorian Imaginations of the Foreign Other', *English Studies*, 90/4, 403–20.

Boone, Troy (2005). *Youth of Darkest England: Working-Class Children at the Heart of Victorian Empire*. New York and London: Routledge.

Booth, Michael (1965). *English Melodrama*. London: Herbert Jenkins.

——(1981) *Victorian Spectacular Theatre 1850–1910*. Boston, MA: Routledge.

Botting, Fred (2006). *Gothic*. London and New York: Routledge.

Bouchereau, G. (2000). 'Nymphomania' [1892], in *The Fin de Siècle: A Reader in Cultural History c.1880–1900*, ed. Sally Ledger and Roger Luckhurst. Oxford: Oxford University Press, pp. 293–7.

Boucicault, Dion (1996). *The Corsican Brothers: A Dramatic Romance in Three Acts* [1852], ed. George Taylor. Oxford: Oxford University Press, pp. 87–125.

Bourne Taylor, Jenny and Sally Shuttleworth (eds) (1998). *Embodied Selves: an Anthology of Psychological Texts, 1830–1890*. Oxford: Clarendon Press.

Braddon, Mary Elizabeth (1862). *Lady Audley's Secret, Sixpenny Magazine*, vol. 3.

Brantlinger, Patrick (1988). *Rule of Darkness: British Literature and Imperialism, 1830–1914*. Ithaca and London: Cornell University Press.

——(2009). *Victorian Literature and Postcolonial Studies*. Edinburgh: Edinburgh University Press.

Bondeson, Jan (2002). *Buried Alive: The Terrifying History of Our Most Primal Fear*. New York: Norton.

Bronfen, Elisabeth (1992). *Over Her Dead Body: Death, Femininity and the Aesthetic*. Manchester: Manchester University Press.

Brontë, Emily (2003). *Wuthering Heights* [1847]. Boston and New York: Bedford and St. Martin's Press.

Buckley, Jerome H. (1966). *The Triumph of Time: A Study of the Victorian Concepts of Time, History, Progress, and Decadence*. Cambridge, MA: Harvard University Press.

——(1984). *The Turning Key: Autobiography and the Subjective Impulse since 1800*. Cambridge, MA: Harvard University Press.

Bulwer-Lytton, Edward (1944). 'The Haunters and the Haunted' [1859], in *Tales of Terror and the* Supernatural, ed. Herbert A. Wise and Phyllis Fraser. New York: Random House, pp. 116–46.

Burke, Edmund (1998). *A Philosophical Enquiry into the Origin of our Ideas of the Sublime and Beautiful* [1757], ed. Adam Phillips. Oxford: Oxford University Press.

Burt, Daniel S. (1980). 'A Victorian Gothic: G. W. M. Reynolds's *Mysteries of London*', *New York Literary Forum*, 7, 141–58.

Butler, E. M. (1956). *Byron and Goethe: Analysis of a Passion*. London: Bowes and Bowes.

Byerly, Alison (1997). *Realism, Representation, and the Arts in Nineteenth-Century Literature*. Cambridge: Cambridge University Press.

Byron, Glennis (2000). 'Gothic in the 1890s', in *A Companion to the Gothic*, ed. David Punter. Oxford: Blackwell, pp. 132–41.

Caine, Hall (1979). 'The New Watchwords of Fiction' [1890], in *A Victorian Art of Fiction: Essays on the Novel in British Periodicals*, vol. 5: *1870–1900*, ed. John Charles Olmsted. New York: Garland, pp. 471–80.

Caird, Mona (1996). 'A Defense of the So-called "Wild Women"' [1892], in *'Criminals, Idiots, Women, and Minors': Victorian Writing by Women on Women*, ed. S. Hamilton. Peterborough, ON: Broadview Press, pp. 287–307.

Calder, Jenni (2000). Introduction, in *A Beleaguered City and Other Tales of the Seen and Unseen*, ed. Jenni Calder. Edinburgh: Canongate, pp. vii–xviii.

Carpenter, Edward and Edward Maitland (1893). *Vivisection*. London: William Reeves.

Carpenter, William B. (1874). *Principles of Mental Physiology, with their Applications to the Training and Discipline of the mind, and the Study of its Morbid Conditions*. London: Henry S. King & Co.

Carroll, David (1996). 'Introduction' to George Eliot, *Silas Marner*, ed. David Carroll. London: Penguin, pp. vii–xxv.

——(2005). 'The Gothic Novel', in *The Cambridge History of English Literature, 1660–1780*, ed. J. Richetti. Cambridge: Cambridge University Press, pp. 673–706.

Castle, Terry (1995). 'The Spectralization of the Other', in *The Female Thermometer: Eighteenth-Century Culture and the Invention of the Uncanny*. Oxford: Oxford University Press, pp. 120–39.

Chadwick, Edwin (1984). *Report on the Sanitary Conditions of the Labouring Population* [1842]. Edinburgh: Edinburgh University Press.

Charcot, Jean-Martin (1890). 'Hypnosis and Crime', *Forum*, 9, 159–68.

Chevasco, Berry Palmer (2003). *Mysterymania: The Reception of Eugène Sue in Britain 1838–1860*. Oxford and Berlin: Peter Lang.

Child, Francis James (ed.) (1882–98). *The English and Scottish Popular Ballads*, 5 vols. London: Henry Stevens; Boston: Houghton Mifflin.

Chittick, Kathryn (1990). *Dickens and the 1830s*. Cambridge: Cambridge University Press.

Clarke, William M. (1998). *The Secret Life of Wilkie Collins*. London: Allison & Busby.

Clery, E. J. (1992). 'The Politics of the Gothic Heroine', in *Reviewing Romanticism*, ed. P. W. Martin and R. Jarvis. New York: St Martin's Press, pp. 69–85.

Cobbe, Frances Power (1868). 'Criminals, Idiots, Women, and Minors', *Fraser's Magazine*, December, 777–94.

——(1878). 'Wife-torture In England', *Contemporary Review*, April, 55–87.

Cocks, H. G. (2003). *Nameless Offences: Homosexual Desire in the Ninteenth Century*. London: I. B. Tauris Publishers.

Clover, Carol (1992). *Men, Women, and Chainsaws: Gender in the Modern Horror Film*. Princeton: Princeton University Press.

Collins, Richard (2003). 'Marian's Moustache: Bearded Ladies, Hermaphrodites, and Intersexual Collage in *The Woman in White*', in *Reality's Dark Light: The Sensational Wilkie Collins*, ed. M. Bachman and D. R. Cox. Knoxville: University of Tennessee Press, pp. 131–72.

Collins, Wilkie (1985). *The Woman in White* [1860]. Harmondsworth: Penguin.

——(1992). *The Law and the Lady* [1875]. Oxford: Oxford University Press.

——(1994). *Heart and Science* [1883]. Stroud: Alan Sutton.

——(1999). *The Moonstone* [1868]. Peterborough, ON: Broadview Press.

Conrad, Joseph (2006). *Heart of Darkness* [1902]. New York: Norton.

Cook, Matt (2003). *London and the Culture of Homosexuality, 1885–1914*. Cambridge: Cambridge University Press.

Cox, Jeffrey (ed.) (1992). *Seven Gothic Dramas 1789–1825*. Athens: Ohio University Press.

Cox, Michael, and R.A. Gilbert (eds) (1986). *The Oxford Book of English Ghost Stories*. Oxford: Oxford University Press.

Crabtree, Adam (1993). *From Mesmer to Freud: Magnetic Sleep and the Roots of Psychological Healing*. New Haven and London: Yale University Press.

Croker, B. M. (2005). 'The Dâk Bungalow at Dakor' [1893], in *Late Victorian Gothic Tales*, ed. Roger Luckhurst. Oxford: Oxford University Press, pp. 96–108.

Crowe, Catherine (2000). *The Night Side of Nature or Ghosts and Ghost Seers* [1848]. Ware: Wordsworth.

Dalby, Richard (ed.) (1995). *The Mammoth Book of Victorian and Edwardian Ghost Stories*. London: Robinson.

Daly, Nicholas (1999). *Modernism, Romance and the Fin de Siècle: Popular Fiction and British Culture, 1880–1914*. Cambridge: Cambridge University Press.

Davies, Owen (2007). *The Haunted: A Social History of Ghosts*. Basingstoke: Palgrave Macmillan.

Depledge, Greta (2007). '*Heart and Science* and Vivisection's Threat to Women', in *Wilkie Collins: Interdisciplinary Essays*, ed. Andrew Mangham. Newcastle: Cambridge Scholars Publishing, pp. 149–63.

——(2009). 'Introduction' to Florence Marryat, *The Blood of the Vampire*. Brighton: Victorian Secrets.

Dickens, Charles (1849). Review of *The Night Side of Nature*, *Examiner*, 26 February 1848.

——(1974). *The Mystery of Edwin Drood* [1870], ed. Arthur J. Cox. New York: Penguin Books.

——(1977). *The Pilgrim Edition of the Letters of Charles Dickens*, vol. 4: *1844–1846*, ed. Kathleen Tillotson. Oxford: Clarendon Press.

——(1981). *The Pilgrim Edition of the Letters of Charles Dickens*, vol. 5: *1847–1849*, ed. Graham Storey and K. J. Fielding. Oxford: Clarendon Press.

——(1985). *A Christmas Carol* in *The Christmas Books* [1843], vol. 1, ed. and introduction, Michael Slater. Harmondsworth: Penguin, pp. 45–134.

——(1996). *Bleak House* [1853]. London: Penguin.

——(1996). *Great Expectations* [1861]. London: Penguin.

——(2003). *A Tale of Two Cities* [1859], ed. Richard Maxwell. London: Penguin.

Dijkstra, Bram (1988). *Idols of Perversity: Fantasies of Feminine Evil in Fin-De-Siècle Culture*. New York and Oxford: Oxford University Press.

Dircks, P. T. (1976). 'James Robinson Planché and the English Burletta Tradition', *Theatre Survey*, 17, 68–81.

Disraeli, Benjamin (1985). *Sybil, or the Two Nations* [1845]. London: Penguin.

Donovan, Dick (1899). *Tales of Terror*. London: Chatto and Windus.

Dowling, L. (1979). 'The Decadent and the New Woman in the 1890s', *Nineteenth Century Fiction*, 33, 434–53.

Doyle, Arthur Conan (1912). *The Lost World*. New York: Review of Reviews.

——(1979). *The Best Supernatural Tales of Arthur Conan Doyle*, ed. E. F. Bleiler. New York: Dover Publications.

——(1981). *The Edinburgh Stories of Arthur Conan Doyle*. Edinburgh: Polygon Books.

——(1993). *The Sign of Four* [1890]. Oxford: Oxford University Press.

Drotner, Kirsten (1988). *English Children and Their Magazines, 1751–1945*. New Haven: Yale University Press.

du Maurier, George (1978). *Trilby* [1894]. London: J. M. Dent.

Eagleton, Terry (2003). 'Myths of Power: A Marxist Study on *Wuthering Heights*', in Emily Brontë, *Wuthering Heights*, ed. L. H. Peterson. New York: Bedford and St. Martin's Press, pp. 394–410.

Easson, Angus (1993). 'From Terror to Terror: Dickens, Carlyle and Cannibalism', in *Reflections of Revolution: Images of Romanticism*, ed. Alison Yarrington and Kelvin Everest. London and New York: Routledge, pp. 96–111.

Eco, Umberto (2006). 'Excess and History in Hugo's *Ninety-three*', in *The Novel*, vol. 2: *Forms and Themes*, ed. Franco Moretti. Princeton and Oxford: Princeton University Press, pp. 274–94.

Eliot, George (1999). *'The Lifted Veil'* and *'Brother Jacob'* [1859], ed. and introduction Helen Small. Oxford: Oxford University Press.

——(1996). *Silas Marner* [1861]. London: Penguin.

Emmet, Alfred (1980). 'The Vampire Trap', *Theatre Notebook: A Journal of the History and Technique of the British Theatre*, 34, 128–9.

Etherington, Norman (1984). *Rider Haggard*. Boston: Twayne.

Evangelista, Stefano (2006). 'Vernon Lee and the Gender of Aestheticism', in *Vernon Lee: Decadence, Ethics, Aesthetics*, ed. Catherine Maxwell and Patricia Pulham. Basingstoke: Palgrave, pp. 91–111.

Farnell, Gary (2009). 'The Gothic and the Thing', *Gothic Studies*, 11/1, 113–23.

Feinberg, Leslie (1996). *Transgender Warriors: Making History from Joan of Arc to Dennis Rodman*. Boston: Beacon Press.

Filon, Augustin (1897). *The English Stage: Being an Account of the Victorian Drama*, trans. Frederic Whyte. London: Milne.

Fitzball, Edward (1834). *Esmeralda: or, The Deformed of Notre Dame: A Drama in Three Acts*. London: Lacy.

Flanders, Judith (2011). *The Invention of Murder*. London: HarperCollins.

Fletcher, Kathy (1987). 'Planché, Vestris, and the Transvestite Role: Sexuality and Gender in Victorian Popular Theatre', *Nineteenth Century Theatre*, 15, 9–33.

Forry, Steven Earl (1990). *Hideous Progenies: Dramatizations of 'Frankenstein' from Mary Shelley to the Present*. Philadelphia: University of Pennsylvania Press.

Foucault, Michèl (1975). *The Birth of the Clinic: An Archaeology of Medical Perception*, trans. A. M. Sheridan Smith. New York: Vintage Books.

——(1977). *Discipline and Punish: The Birth of the Prison*, trans. Alan Sheridan. Harmondsworth: Penguin.

Fowler, Simon (2007). *Workhouse: The People, The Places, The Life Behind Doors*. Kew: The National Archives.

Frank, Frederick F. (1977). 'Introduction', in P. B. Shelley, *'Zastrozzi: A Romance' and 'St. Irvyne: or, The Rosicrucian'*, ed. G. M. Matthews and K. Everest. New York: Arno Press, pp. ix–xxv.

Frank, Lawrence (2009). *Victorian Detective Fiction and the Nature of Evidence: The Scientific Investigations of Poe, Dickens, and Doyle*. London: Palgrave Macmillan.

Franklin, R. W. (ed.) (1998). *The Poems of Emily Dickinson*, 3 vols. Cambridge, MA: Harvard University Press.

Fraser, Derek (2009). *The Evolution of the British Welfare State*, 4th edn. Basingstoke: Palgrave Macmillan.

Fredeman, William B. (ed.) (2004). *The Correspondence of Dante Gabriel Rossetti*, vol. 4: *The Chelsea Years, 1863–1872*, Woodbridge: D. S. Brewer.

——(ed.) (2007). *The Correspondence of Dante Gabriel Rossetti*, vol. 7: *The Last Decade, 1873–1882*, Woodbridge: D. S. Brewer.

Freedgood, Elaine (2006). *The Ideas in Things: Fugitive Meaning in the Victorian Novel*. Chicago: University of Chicago Press.

Freeman, Nick (2008). 'E. Nesbit's New Woman Gothic', *Women's Writing*, 15/3, 454–69.

French, Richard D. (1975). *Antivivisection and Medical Science in Victorian Society*. Princeton: Princeton University Press.

Freud, Sigmund (1990). 'The Uncanny' [1919] in *Art and Literature: Jensen's 'Gradiva', Leonardo Da Vinci and Other Works*, vol. 14 in the Penguin Freud Library, ed. Albert Dickson. Harmondsworth: Penguin, pp. 335–76.

——(1991). *The Interpretation of Dreams* [1900], trans. and ed. J. Strachey. The Penguin Freud Library, vol. 4. Harmondsworth: Penguin.

Frye, Northrop (1976). *The Secular Scripture: A Study of the Structure of Romance*. Cambridge, MA: Harvard University Press.

Gaskell, Elizabeth (1992). 'The Grey Woman' [1861], in *A Dark Night's Work and Other Stories*. Oxford: Oxford University Press, pp. 249–303.

——(2000). *Gothic Tales*, ed. Laura Kranzler. Harmondsworth: Penguin.

Gasson, Andrew (1998). *Wilkie Collins: An Illustrated Guide*. Oxford: Oxford University Press.

Gatrell, V. A. C. (1994). *The Hanging Tree: Execution and the English People, 1770–1868*. Oxford: Oxford University Press.

Gibson, Wilker (1958). 'Behind the Veil: A Distinction Between Poetic and Scientific Language in Tennyson, Lyell, and Darwin', *Victorian Studies*, 11, 60–8.

Ginsburg, Carlo (1992). *Clues, Myth, and the Historical Method*. Baltimore: Johns Hopkins University Press.

Glancy, Ruth (2006). *Charles Dickens's 'A Tale of Two Cities': A Sourcebook*. London and New York: Routledge.

Gliserman, Susan (1974–5). 'Early Science Writers and Tennyson's *In Memoriam*: A Study in Cultural Exchange', *Victorian Studies*, 18, 277–308; 437–59.

Gould, George M. (1890). 'The Ethics of Hypnotism', *The Open Court*, 4, 2172–4.

Grand, Sarah (2007). 'The New Aspect of the Woman Question' [1894], in *Literature and Culture in the Fin de Siècle*, ed. T. Schaffer. New York: Pearson Longman, pp. 205–10.

Greenwood, James (1874). *The Wilds of London*. London: Chatto and Windus.

Grossman, Kathryn (1985). 'Satire and Utopian Vision in Hugo, Dickens and Zamiatin', *Journal of General Education*, 37, 177–88.

Groth, Helen (2007). 'Reading Victorian Illusions: Dickens's *The Haunted Man* and Dr Pepper's "Ghost"', *Victorian Studies*, 50, 43–65.

Hadley, Elaine (1995). *Melodramatic Tactics: Theatricalized Dissent in the English Marketplace, 1800–1885*. Stanford: Stanford University Press.

Haggard, H. Rider (1998). *She: A History of Adventure* [1887]. Oxford: Oxford University Press.

Haggerty, George (2006). *Queer Gothic*. Urbana and Chicago: University of Illinois Press.

Halttunen, Karen (1995). 'Humanitarianism and the Pornography of Pain in Anglo-American Culture', *The American Historical Review*, 100, 2, 303–34.

Hammack, Brenda Mann (2008). 'Florence Marryat's Female Vampire and the Scientizing of Hybridity', *Studies in English Literature 1500–1900*, 48/4, 885–96.

Hardy, Thomas (2001). *Thomas Hardy: The Complete Poems*, ed. James Gibson. Basingstoke: Palgrave.

Harris, Mason (2009). 'Introduction' to H. G. Wells, *The Island of Doctor Moreau*. Peterborough, ON: Broadview.

Harse, Katie (2001). 'Melodrama Hath Charms: Planché's Theatrical Domestication of Polidori's "The Vampyre"', *Journal of Dracula Studies*, 3, 3–7.

Haslam, Richard (1998). 'Joseph Sheridan Le Fanu and the Fantastic Semantics of Ghost-Colonial Ireland', in *That Other World*, ed. Bruce Stewart. Gerrards Cross: Colin Smyth, vol. 1, pp. 268–86.

Hillman, Robert G. (1965). 'A Scientific Study of Mystery: The Role of the Medical and Popular Press in the Nancy–Salpêtrière Controversy on Hypnotism', *Bulletin of the History of Medicine*, 39, 163–82.

Hoeveler, Diane Long (1998). *Gothic Feminism: The Professionalization of Gender from Charlotte Smith to the Brontës*. University Park, PA: Penn State University Press.

Heilman, Robert B. (1961). 'Charlotte Brontë's "New Gothic"' [1958], in *Victorian Literature: Modern Essays in Criticism*, ed. A. Wright. New York: Oxford University Press, pp. 71–85.

Hocking, Joseph (1890). *The Weapons of Mystery*. London and Melbourne: Ward, Lock & Co.

Hogle, Jerrold E. (1999). 'Introduction: Gothic Studies Past, Present and Future', *Gothic Studies*, 1/1, 1–9.

Hollingsworth, Keith (1963). *The Newgate Novel, 1830–1847: Bulwer, Ainsworth, Dickens, and Thackeray*. Detroit: Wayne State University Press.

Hopkins, Gerard Manley (1953). *Poems and Prose of Gerard Manley Hopkins*, ed. W. H. Gardner. Harmondsworth: Penguin.

Houston, Gail Turley (2005). *From Dickens to Dracula: Gothic, Economics and Victorian Fiction*. Cambridge: Cambridge University Press.

Hughes, William (2006). 'Gothic Criticism: A Survey, 1764–2004', in *Teaching the Gothic*, ed. Anna Powell and Andrew Smith. Basingstoke: Palgrave, pp. 10–28.

——(2007). 'Habituation and Incarceration: Mental Physiology and Asylum Abuse in *The Woman in White* and *Dracula*', in *Wilkie Collins: Interdisciplinary Essays*, ed. Andrew Mangham. Newcastle: Cambridge Scholars Publishing, pp. 136–48.

——(2009). *Bram Stoker: Dracula*. New York: Palgrave.

Hughes, William, and Andrew Smith (2009). 'Introduction: Queering the Gothic', in *Queering the Gothic*, ed. William Hughes and Andrew Smith. Manchester and New York: Manchester University Press, pp. 1–10.

Humpherys, Anne and Louis James (eds) (2008). *G. W. M. Reynolds: Nineteenth-Century Fiction, Politics and the Press*. Aldershot: Ashgate Press.

Hurley, Kelly (1996). *The Gothic Body: Sexuality, Materialism, and Degeneration at the Fin de Siècle*. Cambridge: Cambridge University Press.

——(2002). 'British Gothic fiction, 1885–1930', in *The Cambridge Companion to Gothic Fiction*, ed. Jerrold E. Hogle. Cambridge: Cambridge University Press, pp. 189–207.

Huxley, Thomas (1898). *Lessons in Elementary Physiology* [1868, revised 1885]. London: Macmillan.

Ignatieff, Michael (1978). *A Just Measure of Pain: The Penitentiary and the Industrial Revolution, 1750–1850*. Basingstoke: Macmillan.

Innes, A. Taylor (1890). 'Hypnotism in Relation to Crime and the Medical Faculty', *Contemporary Review*, 58, 555–66.

Jackson, Rosemary (1989). Introduction to *What Did Miss Darrington See: An Anthology of Feminist Supernatural Fiction*, ed. Jessica Amanda Salmonson. New York: The Feminist Press at City University of New York, pp. xv–xxxvii.

James, Henry (1865). 'Miss Braddon', *The Nation*, 9 November, 593–4.

——(1948). *The Scenic Art: Notes on Acting and Drama, 1872–1901*. New Brunswick, NJ: Rutgers University Press.

James, M. R. (1984). *The Penguin Complete Ghost Stories of M. R. James*. Harmondsworth: Penguin.

James, Louis (1974). *Fiction for the Working Man, 1830–50: A Study of the Literature Produced for the Working Classes in Early Victorian Urban England*. Harmondsworth: Penguin.

James, Sara (2005). 'Eugène Sue, G. W. M. Reynolds, and the Representation of the City as "Mystery"', in *Babylon or New Jerusalem? Perceptions of the City in Literature*, ed. Valeria Tinkler-Villani. Amsterdam: Rodopi, pp. 247–58.

——(2008). 'G. W. M. Reynolds and the Modern Literature of France', in *G. W. M. Reynolds: Nineteenth-Century Fiction, Politics and the Press*, ed. Anne Humpherys and Louis James. Aldershot: Ashgate Press, pp. 19–32.

Jerome, Jerome K. (1891). *Told After Supper*. London: Leadenhall Press.

Johnson, Thomas H. and Theodora Ward (eds) (1986). *The Letters of Emily Dickinson*. Cambridge, MA: Harvard University Press.

Jones, Darryl (2002). *Horror: A Thematic History in Fiction and Film*. London: Arnold.

Kaplan, E. Ann (2005). *Trauma Culture: The Politics of Terror and Loss in Media and Literature*. New Brunswick, NJ: Rutgers University Press.

Kaplan, Morris B. (2005). *Sodom on the Thames: Sex, Love, and Scandal in Wilde Times*. Ithaca: Cornell University Press.

Kendrick, Walter (1991). *The Thrill of Fear: 250 Years of Scary Entertainment*. New York: Grove.

Killeen, Jarlath (2009). *Gothic Literature 1825–1914*. Cardiff: Wales University Press.

Krafft-Ebing, Richard von (1920). *Psychopathia Sexualis: With Especial Reference to the Antipathic Sexual Instinct – a Medico-Forensic Study*, [1886], trans F. J. Rebman. New York: Medical Art Agency.

Lang, Andrew (1887). 'Realism and Romance', *Contemporary Review*, 52 (November), 683–93.

——(1970). 'The Supernatural in Fiction' [1905], in *Adventures among Books*. Freeport, NY: Books for Libraries Press, pp. 273–80.

——(1990). *Dear Stevenson: Letters from Andrew Lang to Robert Louis Stevenson with Five Letters from Stevenson to Lang*, ed. Marysa Demoor. Leuven: Uitgeverij Peeters.

Lang, Cecil Y. (ed.) (1959–62). *The Swinburne Letters*, 6 vols. New Haven: Yale University Press.

Laqueur, Thomas W. (1989). 'Bodies, Details, and the Humanitarian Narrative', in *The New Cultural History*, ed. Lynn Hunt. Berkeley: University of California, pp. 176–204.

——(1989). 'Crowds, Carnival and the State in English Executions, 1604–1868', in *The First Modern Society: Essays in Honour of Lawrence Stone*, ed.

A. E. Beier, David Cannadine and James S. Rosenheim. Cambridge: Cambridge University Press, pp. 305–56.

Ledger, Sally and Roger Luckhurst (2000). 'Introduction: Reading the "Fin de Siècle"', in *The Fin de Siècle: A Reader in Cultural History, c.1880–1900*. Oxford: Oxford University Press, pp. xiii–xxiii.

Lee, Vernon (2006). *Hauntings and Other Fantastic Tales* [1890], ed. Catherine Maxwell and Patricia Pulham. Peterborough, ON: Broadview.

——(2006). 'Preface to *Hauntings*', [1890] in *Hauntings and Other Fantastic Tales*, Catherine Maxwell and Patricia Pulham. Peterborough, ON: Broadview, pp. 37–40.

Le Fanu, Sheridan (1993). 'Green Tea' [1869], in *In A Glass Darkly* [1872], ed. Robert Tracy. Oxford: Oxford University Press, pp. 5–40.

——(1993). *In a Glass Darkly* [1872], ed. Robert Tracy. Oxford: Oxford University Press.

——(1995). 'A Strange Event in the Life of Schalken the Painter' [1839], in *The Mammoth Book of Victorian and Edwardian Ghost Stories*, ed. Richard Dalby. London: Robinson, pp. 5–27.

——(2009). *Carmilla* [1871–2], ed. and introduction Jamieson Ridenhour. Kansas City: Valancourt Books.

Leighton, Mary Elizabeth (2006). 'Under the Influence: Crime and Hypnotic Fictions of the *Fin de Siècle*', in *Victorian Literary Mesmerism*, ed. Martin Willis and Catherine Wynne. Amsterdam and New York: Rodopi, pp. 203–22.

Levine, Caroline (2003). *The Serious Pleasure of Suspense: Victorian Realism and Narrative Doubt*. Charlottesville: University of Virginia Press.

Levine, George (1981). *The Realistic Imagination: English Fiction from Frankenstein to Lady Chatterley*. Chicago: University of Chicago Press.

Lewes, George Henry (1860). *The Physiology of Common Life*, 2 vols. Edinburgh and London: Blackwood, vol. 2.

Liggens, Emma (2009). 'Introduction' to Charlotte Riddell, *Weird Stories* [1882]. Brighton: Victorian Secrets.

Linton, E. L. (1868). 'The Girl of the Period', *The Saturday Review*, 14 March, 339–40.

Lloyd, Tom (1997). *Crises of Realism: Representing Experience in the British Novel, 1816–1910*. Lewisburg: Bucknell University Press.

Loomba, A. (1998). *Colonialism/Postcolonialism*. London: Routledge.

Luckhurst, Roger (2002). *The Invention of Telepathy, 1870–1901*. Oxford: Oxford University Press.

——(2005). 'Introduction' to *Late Victorian Gothic Tales*, ed. Roger Luckhurst. Oxford: Oxford University Press, pp. ix–xxxi.

Ludlam, Harry (1962). *A Biography of Dracula: The Life Story of Bram Stoker*. London: Foulsham.

Lustig, T. J. (1999). 'Henry James and the Ghostly', extracted in Henry James, *The Turn of the Screw*. New York: Norton.

Macdonald, David Lorne (1991). *Poor Polidori: A Critical Biography of the Author of 'The Vampyre'*. Toronto: University of Toronto Press.

Machen, Arthur (2006). *The Great God Pan*, in *The Great God Pan and The Hill of Dreams*. New York: Dover, pp. 9–66.

Malchow, H. L. (1996). *Gothic Images of Race in Nineteenth-Century Britain*. Stanford: Stanford University Press.

Malcolmson, Robert W. (1973). *Popular Recreations in English Society 1700–1850*. London: Cambridge University Press.

Malley, Shawn (1997). ' "Time Hath No Power Against Identity": Historical Continuity and Archaeological Adventure in H. Rider Haggard's *She*', *English Literature in Transition 1880–1920*, 40/3, 275–97.

Mansel, H. L. (1863). 'Sensation Novels', *Quarterly Review*, 113, 481–514.

Marryat, Florence (2009). *The Blood of the Vampire* [1897]. Kansas City: Valancourt Books.

Marsh, Richard (2008), *The Beetle* [1897]. London: Penguin.

Maxwell, Catherine and Patricia Pulham (2006). Introduction to *Hauntings and Other Fantastic Tales* [1890]. Peterborough, ON: Broadview, pp. 9–27.

Maxwell, Richard C., Jr. (1977). 'G. M. Reynolds, Dickens , and the Mysteries of London', *Nineteenth-Century Fiction*, 32/2, 188–213.

——(1992). *The Mysteries of Paris and London*. Charlottesville and London: University Press of Virginia.

Mayo, Herbert (2003). *On the Truths Contained in Popular Superstitions with an Account of Mesmerism* [1851]. Westcliff-on-Sea: Desert Island Books.

McFarland, Ronald E (1987). 'The Vampire on Stage: A Study in Adaptations', *Comparative Drama*, 21, 19–33.

McGowen, Randall (1994). 'Civilizing Punishment: The End of the Public Execution in England', *Journal of British Studies*, 33, 257–82.

McIntosh, James (2004). *Nimble Believing: Dickinson and the Unknown*. Ann Arbor: University of Michigan Press.

McLaren, A. (1997). *The Trials of Masculinity: Policing Sexual Boundaries 1870–1930*. Chicago and London: University of Chicago Press.

——(2002). *Sexual Blackmail: A Modern History*. Cambridge, MA and London: Harvard University Press.

Mearns, Andrew (1970). *The Bitter Cry of Outcast London*. Leicester: Leicester University Press.

Meisel, Martin (1983). *Realizations: Narrative, Pictorial, and Theatrical Arts in Nineteenth-Century England*. Princeton: Princeton University Press.

Menke, Richard (2008). *Telegraphic Realism: Victorian Fiction and Other Information Systems*. Stanford: Stanford University Press.

Mercier, Charles (1890). *Sanity and Insanity*. London: Walter Scott.

Mighall, Robert (1998). 'Sex, History and the Vampire', in *Bram Stoker, History, Psychoanalysis and the Gothic*, ed. William Hughes and Andrew Smith. Basingstoke: Macmillan, pp. 62–77.

——(1999). *A Geography of Victorian Gothic Fiction: Mapping History's Nightmares*. Oxford: Oxford University Press.

——(2008). 'Dickens and the Gothic', in *A Companion to Charles Dickens*, ed. David Paroissien. Oxford: Blackwell, pp. 81–96.

Milbank, Alison (1992). *Daughters of the House: Modes of Gothic in Victorian Fiction*. Basingstoke: Macmillan.

——(2002). 'The Victorian Gothic in English Novels and Stories, 1830–1880', in *The Cambridge Companion to Gothic Fiction*, ed Jerrold E. Hogle. Cambridge: Cambridge University Press, pp. 145–65.

Miles, Robert (2002). *Gothic Writing, 1750–1820: A Genealogy* [1993], 2nd edn. New York and Manchester: Manchester University Press.

Mill, J. S. (1989). 'The Subjection of Women' [1869], in *On Liberty and*

Other Writings, ed. S. Collini. Cambridge: Cambridge University Press, pp. 119–217.

Mitchell, Margaret E. (2003). 'Preface to Special Issue on Victorian Realism: "The Mirror is Doubtless Defective"', *Literature Interpretation Theory*, 14, 179–84.

Moody, Jane (2000). *Illegitimate Theatre in London, 1770–1840*. Cambridge: Cambridge University Press.

Moss, Stepanie (1999). 'Bram Stoker and the London Stage.' *Journal of the Fantastic in the Arts*, 10, 124–32.

Mulvey, Laura (1992). 'Visual Pleasure and Narrative Cinema', in *Film Theory and Criticism*, 4th edn, ed. Gerald Mast, Marchall Cohen and Leo Braudy. Oxford: Oxford University Press, pp. 746–57.

Murray, Paul (2004). *From the Shadow of Dracula*. London: Cape.

Myers, F. W. H. (1907). *Human Personality and its Survival of Bodily Death*. London: Longmans.

Nanda, Serena (1990). *Neither Man Nor Woman: The Hijras of India*. Belmont, CA: Wadsworth Publishing Company.

Nesbit, Edith (2006). 'Hurst of Hurstcote' [1893], in Edith Nesbit, *The Power of Darkness: Tales of Terror*, ed. David Stuart Davis. Ware: Wordsworth Editions, pp. 101–11.

——(2006). 'Man-Size in Marble' [1893], in Edith Nesbit, *The Power of Darkness: Tales of Terror*, ed. David Stuart Davis. Ware: Wordsworth Editions, pp. 17–28.

Nestor, Pauline (2003). 'Introduction' to Emily Brontë, *Wuthering Heights*, ed. Pauline Nestor. London: Penguin, pp. xv–xxxv.

Newbold, William Romaine (1888). 'Posthypnotic and Criminal Suggestion', *The Popular Science Monthly*, 32, 230–41.

Nichol, John Pringle (1839). *Views of the Architecture of the Heavens: In a Series of Letters to a Lady*, 3rd edn. Edinburgh: William Tait.

Nightingale, Florence (1979). *Cassandra* [1860]. New York: The Feminist Press at the City University of New York.

Norton, C. (1839). *A Plain Letter to the Lord Chancellor on the Infant Custody Bill*. London: James Ridgway.

——(1854). 'English Laws for Women in the Nineteenth Century'. London: Printed for Private Circulation.

Oliphant, Margaret (2000). *A Beleaguered City and Other Tales of the Seen and Unseen*, ed. Jenni Calder. Edinburgh: Canongate.

Onions, Oliver (1911). *Widdershins*. London: Martin Secker.

Oppenheim, Janet (1985). *The Other World: Spiritualism and Psychical Research in England, 1850–1914*. Cambridge: Cambridge University Press.

Owen, Alex (1989). *The Darkened Room: Women, Power and Spiritualism in Late Victorian England*. London: Virago.

Peake, Richard B (1992). *Presumption, or the Fate of Frankenstein* [1823], in *Seven Gothic Dramas 1789–1825*, ed. Jeffrey Cox. Athens: Ohio University Press, pp. 385–425.

Phelps, Elizabeth Stuart (1868). *The Gates Ajar.* Boston: Fields, Osgood & Co.

——(1883) *Beyond the Gates*. New York, Houghton, Mifflin.

——(1885). *Songs of the Silent World*. Boston: Houghton Mifflin.

——(1897). *Chapters from a Life*. Boston: Houghton Mifflin.

Phelps, G. (1987), 'Varieties of English Gothic' [1982], in *From Blake to Byron*, ed. Boris Ford. Harmondsworth: Penguin, pp. 110–27.

Planché, James (1986). *The Vampire: or, the Bride of the Isles* [1820], in *Plays by James Robinson Planché*, ed. Donald Roy. New York: Cambridge University Press, pp. 45–68.

Plumb, J. H. (1975). 'The New World of Children in Eighteenth Century England', *Past and Present*, 67, 64–95.

Poe, Edgar Allan (1982). 'The Facts in the Case of M. Valdemar' [1845], in *The Complete Tales and Poems of Edgar Allan Poe*. Harmondsworth: Penguin, pp. 96–103.

——(1982). 'Mesmeric Revelation' [1844], in *The Complete Tales and Poems of Edgar Allan Poe*. Harmondsworth: Penguin, pp. 88–96.

Porter, Roy (2000). *London: A Social History*. Harmondsworth: Penguin.

Pound, Ezra (1921). *Poems 1918–21*. New York: Boni and Liveright.

Prendergast, Christopher (2003). *For the People by the People? Eugène Sue's 'Les Mystèresde Paris': A Hypothesis in the Sociology of Literature*. Oxford: Legenda.

Punter, David (1980). *The Literature of Terror: A History of Gothic Fictions from 1765 to the Present Day*. London: Longman.

——(1998). *Gothic Pathologies: The Text, The Body and The Law*. Basingstoke: Macmillan.

Punter, David and Glennis Byron (2004). *The Gothic*. Oxford: Blackwell Publishing.

Pykett, Lynn (1994). *The Sensation Novel from The Woman in White to The Moonstone*. Plymouth: Northcote House.

Radcliffe, Ann (2000). 'On the Supernatural in Poetry' [1802; 1826], in *Gothic Documents: A Sourcebook 1700–1820*, ed. E. J. Clery and R. Miles. Manchester: Manchester University Press, pp. 163–72.

Rae, W. F. [unsigned] (1865). 'Sensation Novelists: Miss Braddon', *North British Review*, 43, 180–204.

Reynolds, G. W. M (1996). *The Mysteries of London* [1844–8], ed. Trefor Thomas. Keele: Keele University Press.

——(2006). *Wagner the Werewolf* [1846–7], ed. and introduction by Dick Collins. London: Wordsworth.

Richards, Jeffrey (1995). 'Gender, Race, and Sexuality in Bram Stoker's Other Novels', in *Gender Roles and Sexuality in Victorian Literature*, ed. Christopher Parker. Aldershot: Scolar Press, pp. 143–71.

Richards, Thomas (1990). *The Commodity Culture of Victorian England: Advertising and Spectacle, 1851–1914*. London: Verso.

Riddell, Mrs J. H. (1977). *The Collected Ghost Stories of Mrs J. H. Riddell*, ed. E. F. Bleiler. New York: Dover.

——(2009). 'Old Mrs Jones' [1882], in Charlotte Riddell, *Weird Stories*. Brighton: Victorian Secrets, pp. 129–73.

Ritvo, Harriet (1987). *The Animal Estate: The English and Other Creatures in the Victorian Age*. Cambridge, MA: Harvard University Press.

Robbins, Ruth and Julian Wolfreys (eds) (2000). *Victorian Gothic: Literary and Cultural Manifestations in the Nineteenth Century*. Basingstoke: Palgrave Macmillan.

Rossetti, Christina (1862). *Goblin Market and Other Poems*. London: Macmillan.

Rossetti, Dante Gabriel (1870). *Poems*. London: Ellis.

——(1898). *The House of Life*. London: Ellis and Elvey.

——(1911). *The Works of Dante Gabriel Rossetti*, ed. William M.Rossetti. London: Ellis.

Rossetti, William Michael (ed.) (1899). *Ruskin: Rossetti: Preraphaelitism: Papers 1854–1862*. London: George Allen.

——(1903). 'Dante Rossetti and Elizabeth Siddal: With Facsimiles of Five Unpublished Drawings by Dante Rossetti in the Collection of Mr. Harold Hartley', *Burlington Magazine*, 1, 273–95.

Roy, Donald (1986). 'Introduction to Planché', in *Plays by James Robinson Planché*, ed. Donald Roy. New York: Cambridge University Press, pp. i–xi.

Ruddick, Nicholas (2007). 'The Fantastic Fiction of the Fin de Siècle', in *The Cambridge Companion to the Fin de Siècle*, ed. Gail Marshall. Cambridge: Cambridge University Press, pp. 189–206.

Ruskin, John (1866). 'Of Queens' Gardens' [1865], in *Sesame and Lilies*. New York: J. Wiley, pp. 81–113.

Rymer, James Malcolm (2008). *Varney the Vampire* [1845–7], introduction and notes by Curt Herr. Crestline, CA: Zittaw Press.

Sage, Victor (1988). *Horror Fiction in the Protestant Tradition*. Basingstoke: Macmillan.

——(1994). 'Gothic Laughter: Farce and Horror in Five Texts', in *Gothic Origins and Innovations*, ed. Allan Lloyd Smith and Victor Sage. Amsterdam: Rodopi, pp. 190–203.

——(2004). *Le Fanu's Gothic: The Rhetoric of Darkness*. Basingstoke: Palgrave Macmillan.

Saintsbury, George (1979). 'The Present State of the Novel I' [1887], in *A Victorian Art of Fiction: Essays on the Novel in British Periodicals*, vol. 5: *1870–1900*, ed. John Charles Olmsted. New York: Garland, pp. 391–8.

Sala, George Augustus (1895). *The Life and Adventures of George Augustus Sala, Written by Himself*, vol. 1. New York: Charles Scribner's Sons.

Sanders, Andrew (1988). *The Companion to 'A Tale of Two Cities'*. London: Unwin Hyman.

Scarry, Elaine (1987). *The Body in Pain: The Making and Unmaking of the World*. Oxford: Oxford University Press.

Scott, Clement (1899). *The Drama of Yesterday and Today*, 2 vols. London: Macmillan.

Scott, Walter (ed.) (1802). *Minstrelsy of the Scottish Border*, 2 vols. Kelso: Ballantyne.

Scull, Andrew (ed.) (1981). *Madhouses, Mad-Doctors, and Madmen: The Social History of Psychiatry in the Victorian Era*. London: Athlone.

Shapiro, Stephen (2008). 'Introduction: Material Gothic', *Gothic Studies*, 10/1, 2–3.

Shelley, Mary (1985). *Frankenstein* [1818], ed. and introduction Maurice Hindle. Harmondsworth: Penguin.

——(2000). 'On Ghosts' [1824], in *Gothic Documents: A Sourcebook 1700–1820*, ed. E. J. Clery and Robert Miles. Manchester: Manchester University Press, pp. 280–5.

Showalter, E. (1977). *A Literature of Their Own: British Women Novelists From Brontë to Lessing*. Princeton: Princeton University Press.

——(1990). *Sexual Anarchy: Gender and Culture at the Fin de Siècle*. New York: Viking.

Siddal, Elizabeth (1978). *Poems and Drawings of Elizabeth Siddal*, ed. Roger C. Lewis and Mark Samuels Lasner. Wolfville, NS, Canada: Wombat Press.

Simmel, Georg (1950). 'Metropolis and Mental Life' [1903], in *The Sociology of Georg Simmel*, trans. Kurt Wolff. Glencoe, IL: The Free Press, pp. 409–24.

Simpson, Colin, Lewis Chester and David Leitch (1976). *The Cleveland Street Affair*. Boston: Little, Brown and Company.

Smith, Andrew (2002). 'Rethinking the Gothic: What do we mean?', *Gothic Studies*, 4/1, 79–85.

——(2003). 'Beyond Colonialism: Death and the Body in H. Rider Haggard', in *Empire and the Gothic: The Politics of Genre*, ed. Andrew Smith and William Hughes. Basingstoke: Palgrave, pp. 103–17.

——(2004). *Victorian Demons: Medicine, Masculinity and the Gothic at the Fin-de-Siècle*. New York: Palgrave.

——(2010). *The Ghost Story 1840–1920: A Cultural History*. Manchester: Manchester University Press.

Spierenburg, Pieter (1984). *The Spectacle of Suffering: Executions and the Evolution of Repression; From a Preindustrial Metropolis to the European Experience*. Cambridge: Cambridge University Press.

Springhall, John (1999). *Youth, Popular Culture and Moral Panics: Penny Gaffs to Gangsta Rap, 1830–1996*. New York: St Martin's Press.

St. Armand, Barton Levi (1984). *Emily Dickinson and Her Culture: The Soul's Society*, Cambridge: Cambridge University Press.

Stevens, John Russell (1992). *The Profession of the Playwright: The British Theatre 1800–1900*. Cambridge: Cambridge University Press.

Stevenson, Robert Louis (1981). *Treasure Island* [1883]. New York: Bantam Books.

——(1983). *The Master of Ballantrae* [1889]. Oxford: Oxford University Press.

——(1987). *The Strange Case of Dr Jekyll and Mr Hyde* [1886]. Oxford: Oxford University Press.

——(1999).'The Bottle Imp' [1891], in *South Sea Tales*. Oxford: Oxford University Press, pp. 73–102.

——(1999). *R. L. Stevenson on Fiction: An Anthology of Literary and Critical Essays*, ed. Glenda Norquay. Edinburgh: Edinburgh University Press.

Stiles, Anne, Stanley Finger and John Bulevich (2010). 'Somnambulism and Trance States in the Works of John William Polidori, Author of *The Vampyre*', *European Romantic Review*, 21, 789–807.

Stoker, Bram (1906). *Personal Reminiscences of Henry Irving*, 2 vols. London: Heinemann.

——(1995). 'The Judge's House' [1891], in *The Mammoth Book of Edwardian and Victorian Ghost Stories*, ed. Richard Dalby. London: Robinson, pp. 274–90.

——(1996). *Dracula* [1897], notes and introduction Maud Ellmann. Oxford: Oxford University Press.

——(1999). *The Primrose Path* [1875]. Westcliff-on-Sea: Desert Island Books.

Stuart, Roxana (1994). *Stage Blood: Vampires of the Nineteenth-Century Stage*. Bowling Green, OH: Bowling Green State University Press.

Sue, Eugène (n.d. but probably 1989). *The Mysteries of Paris* [1842–3], anonymous translator. Sawtry and New York: Dedalus/Hippocrene.

Sullivan, Jack (ed.) (1986). *The Penguin Dictionary of Horror and the Supernatural*. Harmondsworth: Penguin.

Swinburne, Algernon Charles (1866). *Poems and Ballads*. London: Hotten.

Szwydky, Lissette Lopez (2010). 'Victor Hugo's *Notre-Dame de Paris* on the Nineteenth-Century London Stage', *European Romantic Review*, 21, 469–87.

Taylor, George (1980). *Henry Irving at the Lyceum*. Cambridge: Chadwick-Healey.

——(1989). *Players and Performances in the Victorian Theatre*. Manchester: Manchester University Press.

Thomas, Ardel (2012). *Queer Others in Victorian Gothic: Transgressing Monstrosity*. Cardiff: University of Wales Press.

Thomas, Deborah A. (2000). 'Ghost Stories', in *The Oxford Reader's Companion to Dickens*, ed. Paul Schlicke. Oxford: Oxford University Press, pp. 256–7.

Thomas, Keith (1984). *Man and the Natural World: A History of the Modern Sensibility*. Harmondsworth: Penguin.

Thomas, Ronald R. (1999). *Detective Fiction and the Rise of Forensic Science*. Cambridge: Cambridge University Press.

Thomas, Trefor (2000). 'Rereading G. W. Reynolds's *The Mysteries of London*', in *Rereading Victorian Fiction*, ed. Alice Jenkins and Juliet John. Basingstoke: Macmillan, pp. 59–80.

Thompson, W. and A. Wheeler (1994). *Appeal of One-Half the Human Race, Women, Against the Pretentions of the Other Half, Men, To Retain Them in Political, and Thence in Civil and Domestic Slavery* [1825]. Bristol: Thoemmes Press.

Thomson, St Clair (1890). 'The Dangers of Hypnotism', *Westminster Review*, 134, 624–31.

Tosh, J. (2005). *Manliness and Masculinities in Nineteenth-Century Britain: Essays on Gender, Family and Empire*. Harlow: Pearson Education Limited.

Vendler, Helen (2010). *Dickinson: Selected Poems and Commentaries*. Cambridge, MA: Harvard University Press.

Warwick, Alexandra (2007). 'Feeling Gothicky?', *Gothic Studies*, 9/1, 5–15.

——(2007). 'Victorian Gothic', in *The Routledge Companion to Gothic*, ed. Catherine Spooner and Emma McEvoy. London and New York: Routledge, pp. 29–37.

Weeks, Jeffrey (1979). *Coming Out: Homosexual Politics from the Nineteenth Century to the Present*. London: Quartet.

Wells, H. G. (1968). *The War of the Worlds* [1898], in *The Time Machine* and *The War of the Worlds*. New York: Fawcett.

White, Jerry (2006). *London in the Nineteenth Century: 'A Human Awful Wonder of God'*. London: Jonathan Cape.

Wicke, Jennifer (1992). 'Vampiric Typewriting: *Dracula* and its Media', *English Literary History*, 59, 467–93.

Wiener, Martin J. (1990). *Reconstructing the Criminal: Culture, Law, and Policy in England, 1830–1914*. Cambridge: Cambridge University Press.

Wilde, Oscar (1985). *The Picture of Dorian Gray* [1890]. Harmondsworth: Penguin.

Willis, Martin (2006). *Mesmerists, Monsters, and Machines: Science Fiction and the Cultures of Science in the Nineteenth Century*. Kent, OH: Kent State University Press.

Winter, Alison (1998). *Mesmerized: Powers of Mind in Victorian Britain*. Chicago and London: University of Chicago Press.

Wirth, Louis (1938). 'Urbanism as a Way of Life', *The American Journal of Sociology*, 44, 1, 1–24.

Wolfreys, Julian (2000). 'Preface' to *Victorian Gothic: Literary and Cultural Manifestations in the Nineteenth Century*, ed. Ruth Robbins and Julian Wolfreys. Basingstoke: Palgrave, pp. xi–xx.

——(2002). *Victorian Hauntings: Spectrality, Gothic, the Uncanny and Literature*. Basingstoke: Palgrave.

——(2006). 'Victorian Gothic', in *Teaching the Gothic*, ed. Anna Powell and Andrew Smith. Basingstoke: Palgrave, pp. 62–77.

——(2010). 'Towards a Phenomenology of Urban Gothic: The Example of Dickens', in *London Gothic: Place, Space and the Gothic Imagination*, ed. Lawrence Phillips and Anne Witchard. London: Continuum, pp. 9–22.

Wynne, Catherine (2006). 'Arthur Conan Doyle's Domestic Desires: Mesmerism, Mediumship and *Femmes Fatales*', in *Victorian Literary Mesmerism*, ed. Martin Willis and Catherine Wynne. Amsterdam and New York: Rodopi, pp. 223–43.

——(2006). 'Bram Stoker, Genevieve Ward, and the *Lady of the Shroud*: Gothic Weddings and Performing Vampires', *English Literature in Transition, 1880–1920*, 49, 251–72.

Young, Robert M. (1990). *Mind, Brain, and Adaptation in the Nineteenth Century: Cerebral Localization and its Biological Context from Gall to Ferrier*. New York and Oxford: Oxford University Press.

Yzereef, Barry (1992). 'Ghostly Appearances: The Vision Scene in *The Corsican Brothers*', *Theatre Notebook*, 46, 4–14.

Zimmerman, Virginia (2008). *Excavating Victorians*. Albany: State University of New York Press.

Notes on Contributors

Patrick Brantlinger is James Rudy Professor of English (Emeritus) at Indiana University; former editor of *Victorian Studies*; and author of *Rule of Darkness: British Literature and Imperialism* (1988), *Victorian Literature and Postcolonial Studies* (2009) and *Taming Cannibals: Race and the Victorians* (2011).

Carol Margaret Davison is Professor of English Literature at the University of Windsor. She is the author of *Anti-Semitism and British Gothic Literature* (2004) and *History of the Gothic: Gothic Literature, 1764–1824* (2009). She is currently at work on *Gothic Scotland/Scottish Gothic*, a theoretical examination of the Scottish Gothic tradition.

Caroline Franklin is Professor of English at Swansea University and recently edited *The Longman Anthology of Gothic Verse*. She is currently completing a monograph entitled *The Female Romantics: Nineteenth-Century Women Writers and Byronism*.

Michael J. Franklin is Senior Lecturer in English at Swansea University. His most recent books are an edited collection of essays, *Romantic Representations of British India* (2006); a scholarly edition of Phebe Gibbes, *Hartly House, Calcutta* (2007); and *'Orientalist Jones': Sir William Jones, Poet, Lawyer, and Linguist, 1746–1794* (forthcoming).

Nick Freeman is Senior Lecturer in English at Loughborough University. He has published widely on the literature and culture of the fin de siècle and is the author of two books *Conceiving the City: London, Literature and Art 1870–1914* (2007) and *1895: Drama, Disaster and Disgrace in Late Victorian Britain* (2011).

Diane Long Hoeveler is Professor of English at Marquette University. She is author of *Romantic Androgyny* (1990), *Gothic Feminism* (1998) and most recently of *Gothic Riffs: Secularizing the Uncanny in the European Imaginary, 1780–1820* (2010), which was awarded the Allan Lloyd Smith award by the International Gothic Association. She is currently working on a study of the Gothic and the British anti-Catholic campaign, 1780–1829.

Avril Horner is Emeritus Professor of English at Kingston University, London. She has co-authored and co-edited many essays and several books on the Gothic with Sue Zlosnik, including *Daphne du Maurier: Writing, Identity and the Gothic Imagination* (1998), *Gothic and the Comic Turn* (2005) and a scholarly edition of Eaton Stannard Barrett's *The Heroine* (2011). She is also the editor of *European Gothic: A Spirited Exchange, 1760–1960* (2002). Her most recent publication is *Edith Wharton: Sex, Satire and the Older Woman* (2011), co-authored with Janet Beer.

William Hughes is Professor of Gothic Studies at Bath Spa University and the editor of the refereed journal *Gothic Studies*. His publications include *Beyond Dracula* (2000), *Dracula: A Reader's Guide to Essential Criticism* (2008); and the collections *Bram Stoker: History, Psychoanalysis and the Gothic* (1998), *Empire and the Gothic* (2003) and *Queering the Gothic* (2009), all co-edited with Andrew Smith.

Kelly Hurley is Associate Professor of English at the University of Colorado at Boulder. She is the author of *The Gothic Body: Sexuality, Materialism, and Degeneration at the Fin de Siècle*, as well as various articles on Victorian and contemporary Gothic. She is currently completing a monograph on horror film spectatorship.

Jarlath Killeen is a lecturer in Victorian literature at Trinity College Dublin. He is the editor of *Oscar Wilde: Irish Writers in their Time* (2010) and author of *Gothic Ireland* (2005), *The Faiths of Oscar Wilde* (2005), *The Fairy Tales of Oscar Wilde* (2007) and *British Gothic Literature, 1825–1914* (2009).

Victoria Margree is Senior Lecturer in the Humanities at the University of Brighton. Her publications include articles on Richard Marsh and Bessie Head, as well as co-authored articles on race, gender and identity politics. Her research on Gothic fiction continues with a project on Richard Marsh.

Bryony Randall teaches English Literature at the University of Glasgow. Her book, *Modernism, Daily Time and Everyday Life* was published in 2007; other publications include articles on Dorothy Richardson and Beatrice Potter Webb, and New Woman short stories. She is currently working on a monograph provisionally entitled 'The Working Woman Writer 1880–1920'.

Andrew Smith is Professor of English Studies at the University of Glamorgan where he is Head of English and Modern Languages. Published books include *Gothic Radicalism* (2000), *Victorian Demons* (2004), *Gothic Literature* (2007) and *The Ghost Story 1840–1920: A Cultural History* (2010). He is joint president of the International Gothic Association with William Hughes.

Laurence Talairach-Vielmas is Professor of English at the University of Toulouse (UTM), France. She is the author of *Moulding the Female Body in Victorian Fairy Tales and Sensation Novels* (2007) and *Wilkie Collins, Medicine and the Gothic* (2009), and has edited Mary Elizabeth Braddon's *Thou Art the Man* (2008). She has also edited a collection of articles on the popularisation of science in the long nineteenth century, *Science in the Nursery: The Popularisation of Science in Britain and France, 1761–1901* (2011).

Ardel Thomas is the Chair of Lesbian, Gay, Bisexual and Transgender Studies at City College of San Francisco. Ardel has published a book *Queer Others in Victorian Gothic: Transgressing Monstrosity* (2012) and numerous pieces on Victorian Gothic and queer Gothic, as well as essays on global public policy and contemporary LGBT rights. Her areas of research interest include historic approaches to the intersections of race and sexuality from the nineteenth century to today.

Martin Willis is Reader in English at the University of Glamorgan. His work considers the intersections between literature and science, with a focus on genre fictions and especially on nineteenth-century Gothic. His latest book is *Vision, Science and Literature, 1870–1920: Ocular Horizons* (2011).

Index